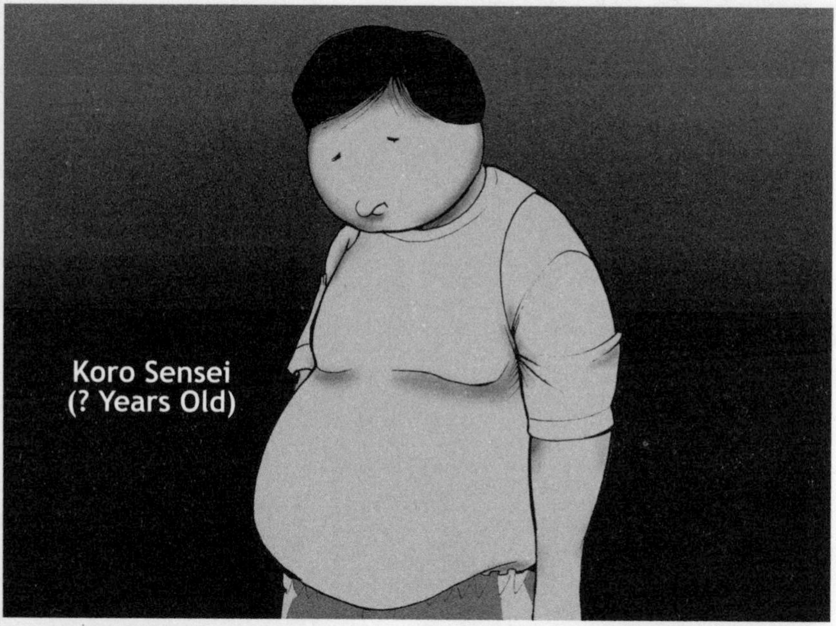
Koro Sensei
(? Years Old)

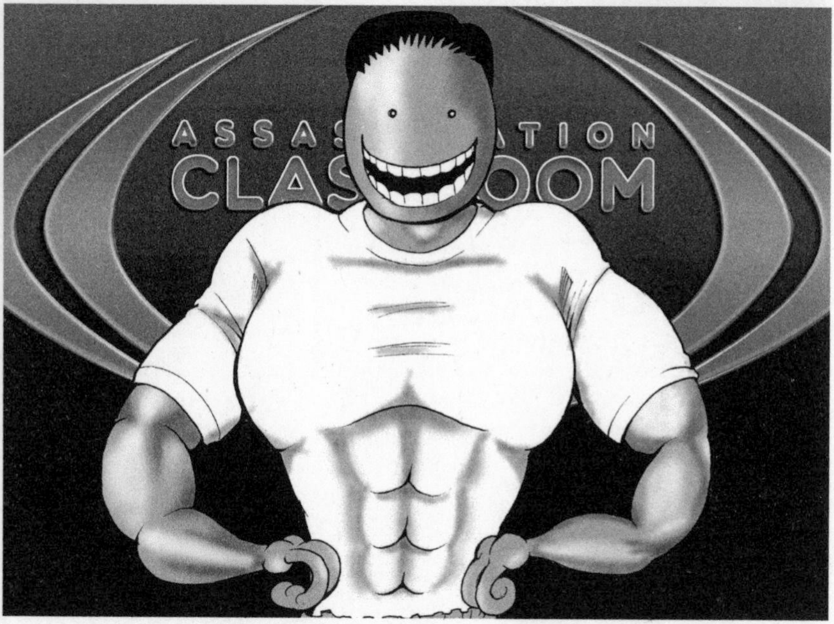

YUSEI MATSUI 13 TIME FOR A LITTLE CAREER COUNSELING

SHONEN JUMP ADVANCED

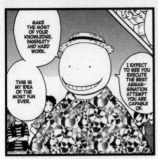

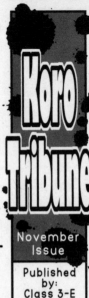

Koro Tribune

November Issue

Published by: Class 3-E Newspaper Staff

Although we have a lot of data on his weaknesses, we are still far from successfully assassinating Koro Sensei...

Story Thus Far

MAKE THE MOST OF YOUR KNOWLEDGE, INGENUITY AND HARD WORK.
I EXPECT TO SEE YOU EXECUTE THE BEST ASSASSINATION ATTEMPT YOU ARE CAPABLE OF.
THIS IS MY IDEA OF THE MOST FUN EVER.

Kunugigaoka Junior High, Class 3-E is led by a monster who has disintegrated the moon and is planning to do the same to the Earth next March.

Even the armies of the world with the latest technology can't kill the super creature Koro Sensei and collect the 30 billion yen (300 million dollar) bounty for a group assassination! So it comes down to his Kunugigaoka Junior High students in 3-E, the so-called "End Class," whom he has promised not to harm. Thanks to Koro Sensei's dedication, his charges are turning into fine students. Likewise, the 3-E students' athleticism and mental concentration are rapidly improving as the Ministry of Defense's Mr. Karasuma molds them into a professional team of assassins. Will the misfit students of 3-E manage to assassinate their target before graduation...?!

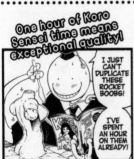

One hour of Koro Sensei time means exceptional quality!

I JUST CAN'T DUPLICATE THESE ROCKET BOOBS!
I'VE SPENT AN HOUR ON THEM ALREADY!

Koro Sensei

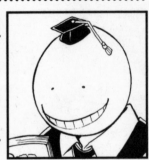

A mysterious, man-made, octopus-like creature whose name is a play on the words "koro senai," which means "can't kill." He is capable of flying at Mach 20 and his versatile tentacles protect him from attacks and aid him in everyday activities. Nobody knows who created him or why he wants to teach Class 3-E, but he has proven to be an extremely capable instructor.

Kaede Kayano

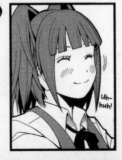

Class E student. She's the one who named Koro Sensei. She sits at the desk next to Nagisa, and they seem to get along well.

Uh-huh!

Nagisa Shiota

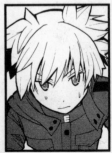

Class E student. Skilled at information gathering, he has been taking notes on Koro Sensei's weaknesses. He has a hidden talent for assassinations and even the assassin broker Lovro sees his potential.

Hinata Okano

pick up!

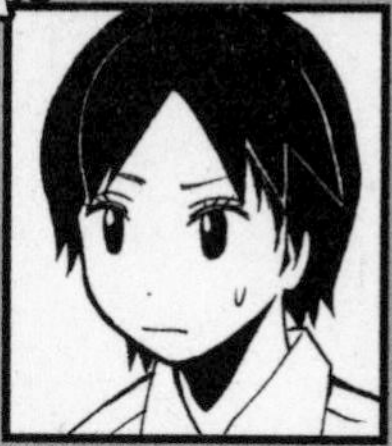

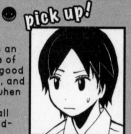

She's very flexible, has an acute sense of smell, very good night vision, and scratches when she's angry. Let's just call her...er..."wild-natured."

Karma Akabane

Class E student. A quick thinker skilled at surprise attacks who has succeeded in injuring Koro Sensei a few times. His failure in the final exam of the first semester has forced him to grow up and take things a bit more seriously.

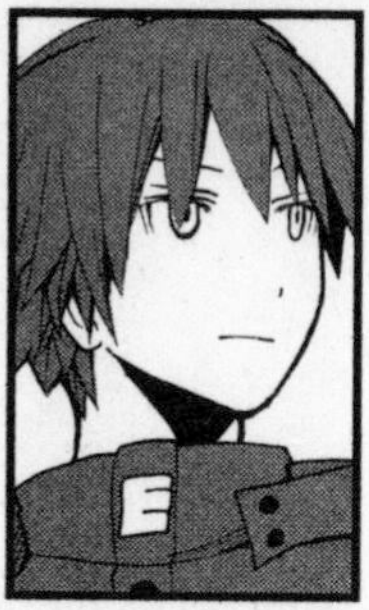

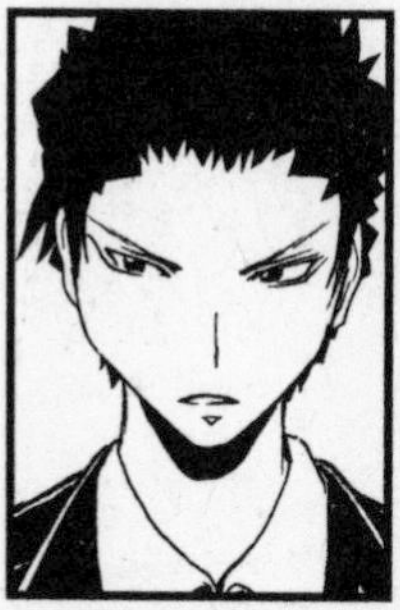

Tadaomi Karasuma

Member of the Ministry of Defense and the Class E students' P.E. teacher. Though serious about his duties, he is successfully building good relationships with his students.

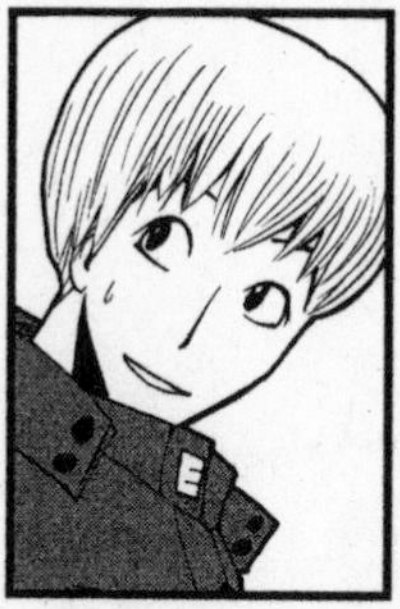

Koki Mimura

Class E student. A brilliant graphic designer and videographer who hopes to work in the TV industry someday. He already has clients, such as Okajima.

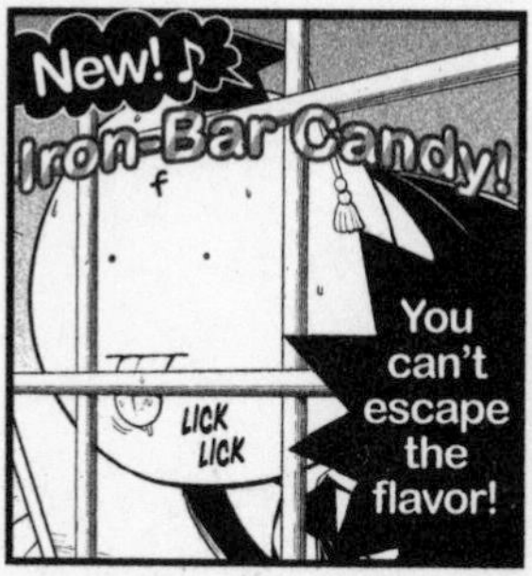
New! ♪
Iron-Bar Candy!
LICK LICK
You can't escape the flavor!

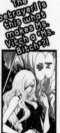

The betrayer! Is this what makes Ms. Vitch a "Ms. Bitch"?!

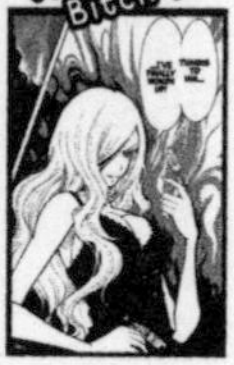

Irina Jelavich

A sexy assassin hired as an English teacher. She's known for using her "womanly charms" to get close to a target. She often flirts with Karasuma, but hasn't made any progress yet.

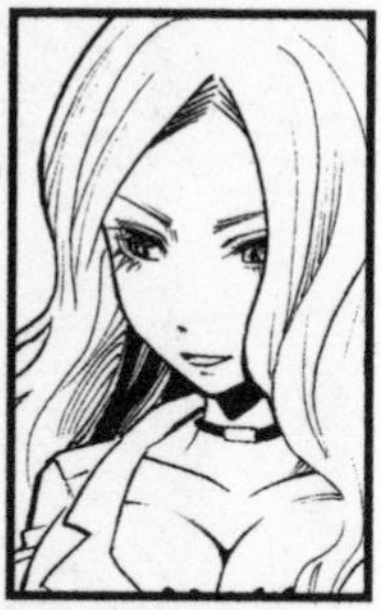

The Climax of the Grim Reaper Story Arc

Mr. Karasuma fights for the lives of his students and himself in a deadly battle against the Grim Reaper. Trapped in a cage, the students place bets on which of them will win. The odds are 6:4 on Mr. Karasuma...

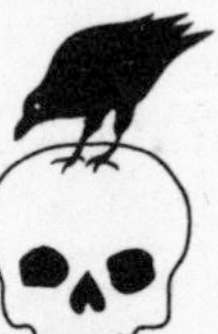

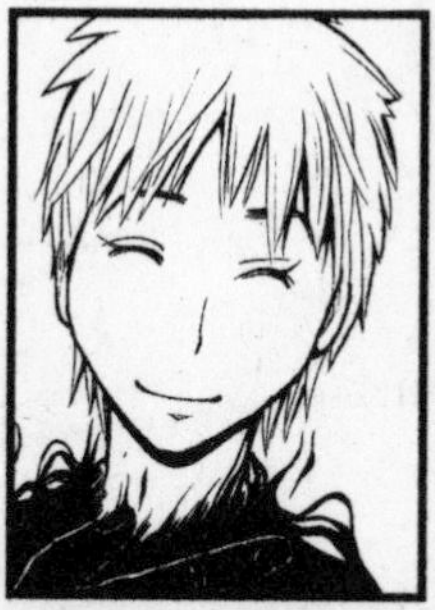

The Grim Reaper

The greatest assassin in the world. He attacked several skilled assassins to prepare himself to take on Koro Sensei, and now he has kidnapped Class E.

ASSASSINATION

CLASSROOM 13 CONTENTS

(Question 1): Write the pronunciation of the following kanji on the line next to it.

① 命を脅かされる ② ビッチ先生の美貌 ③ 緻

④ 任務の遂行 ⑤ 殺せんせーの煩悩

(Question 2): Write the correct kanji based on the katakana.

① 身のタケに合った暗殺 ② ヤクドウする触手

③ 総理府からのシモン ④ 暗殺者をシリゾける

(Question 3): One of the kanji in the following four-character idioms is wrong. Correct the four-character idiom.

① 異句同音 ② 困果応報 ③ 意心伝

④ 短刀直入 ⑤ 主客転倒

(Question 4): Read the following paragraph and answer the questions below.

今は昔、殺せんせへ、と言ひけるⓐ、越前

いみじく*不幸なりける生徒の、夜昼まめ*な

冬なれど超体育着をなん着たりける。

雪のいみじく降る日、この生徒、浄めす*

物*のつきたるやうに震ふⓑを見て、

守、「歌詠め。をかしう降る雪かな」と

この生徒、「何を題にて仕るべきぞ」、

「裸なる由を詠め」と言ふに、ほどもな

はだかなる我が身にかかる白雪は①

(ANSWER SHEET)

Grade	3	Class	E	Name	CONTENTS	Score	

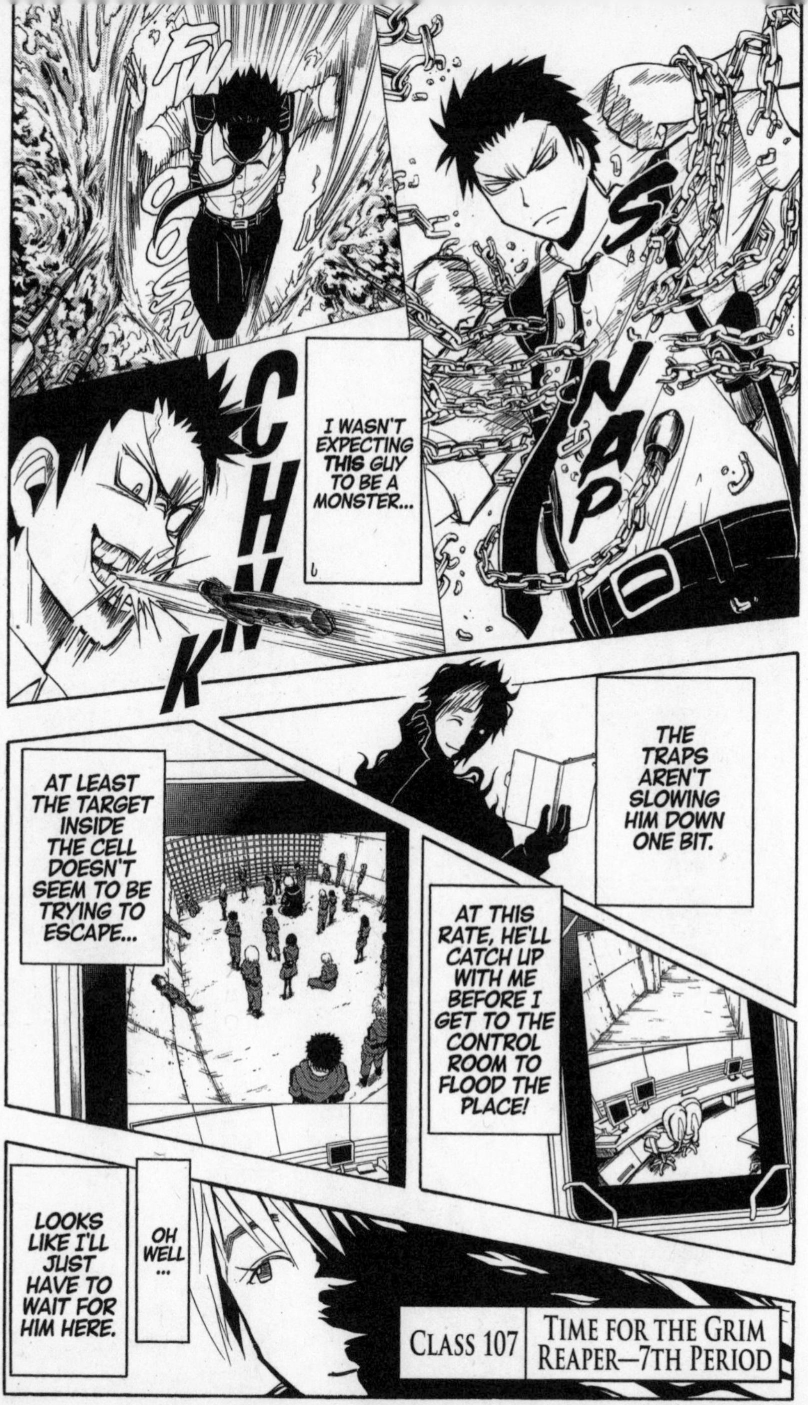
SNAP
FWOOSH
I WASN'T EXPECTING THIS GUY TO BE A MONSTER...
CHNK
THE TRAPS AREN'T SLOWING HIM DOWN ONE BIT.
AT THIS RATE, HE'LL CATCH UP WITH ME BEFORE I GET TO THE CONTROL ROOM TO FLOOD THE PLACE!
AT LEAST THE TARGET INSIDE THE CELL DOESN'T SEEM TO BE TRYING TO ESCAPE...
OH WELL...
LOOKS LIKE I'LL JUST HAVE TO WAIT FOR HIM HERE.
CLASS 107
TIME FOR THE GRIM REAPER—7TH PERIOD

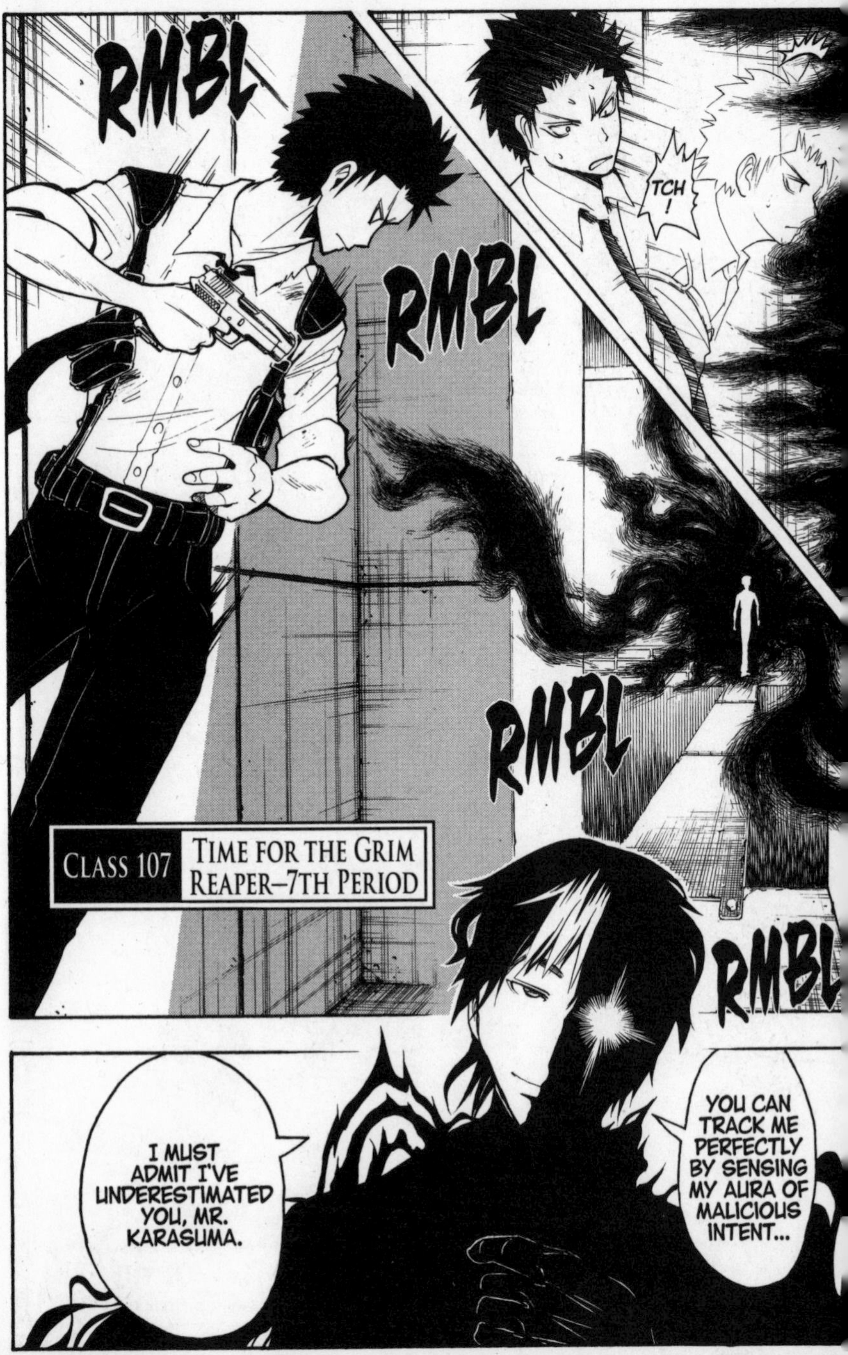
TCH!
RMBL
RMBL
RMBL
RMBL
CLASS 107 TIME FOR THE GRIM REAPER–7TH PERIOD
RMBL
YOU CAN TRACK ME PERFECTLY BY SENSING MY AURA OF MALICIOUS INTENT...
I MUST ADMIT I'VE UNDERESTIMATED YOU, MR. KARASUMA.

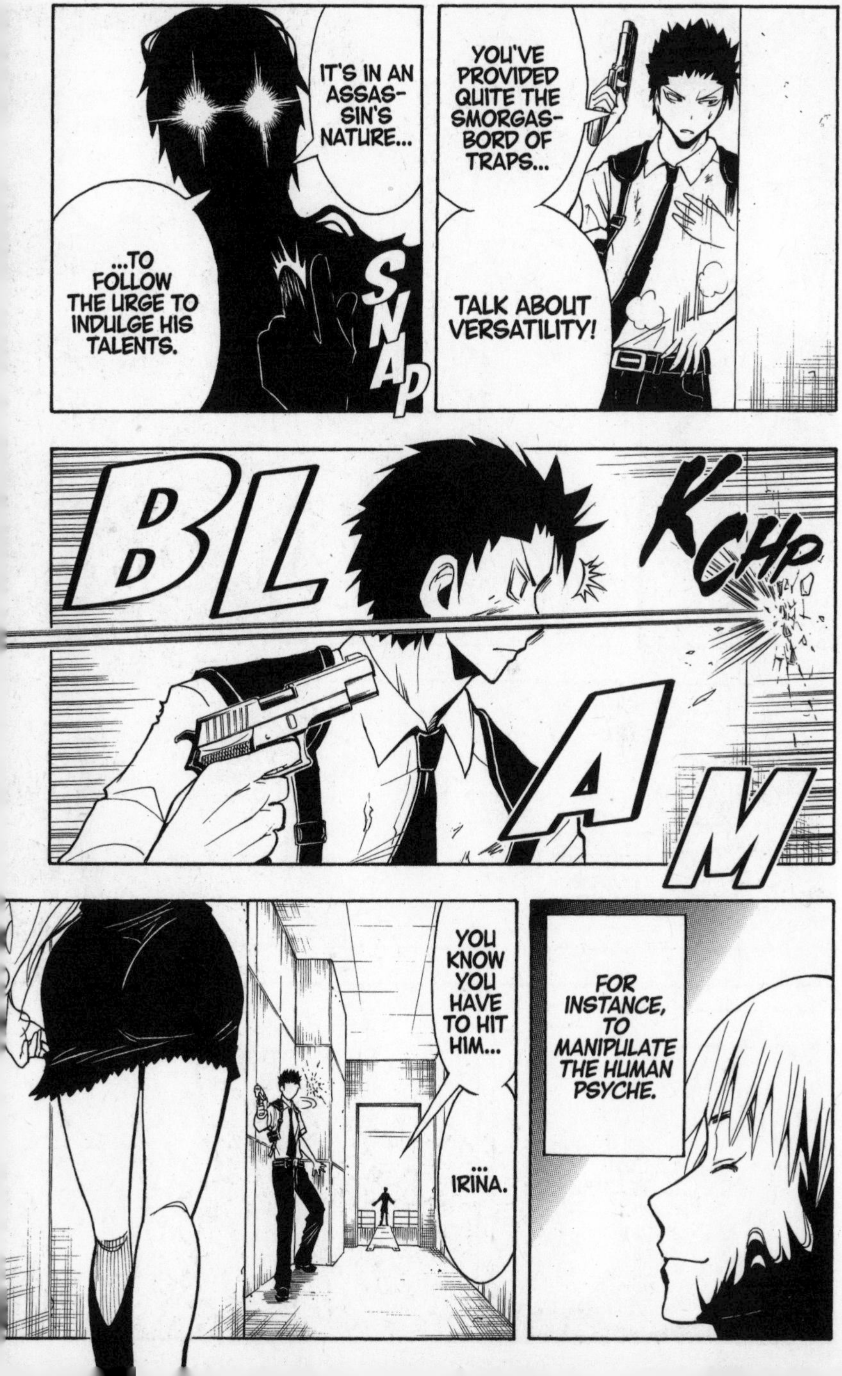
YOU'VE PROVIDED QUITE THE SMORGAS-BORD OF TRAPS...
TALK ABOUT VERSATILITY!
IT'S IN AN ASSAS-SIN'S NATURE...
...TO FOLLOW THE URGE TO INDULGE HIS TALENTS.
SNAP
BLAM
KCHP
FOR INSTANCE, TO MANIPULATE THE HUMAN PSYCHE.
YOU KNOW YOU HAVE TO HIT HIM...
... IRIÑA.

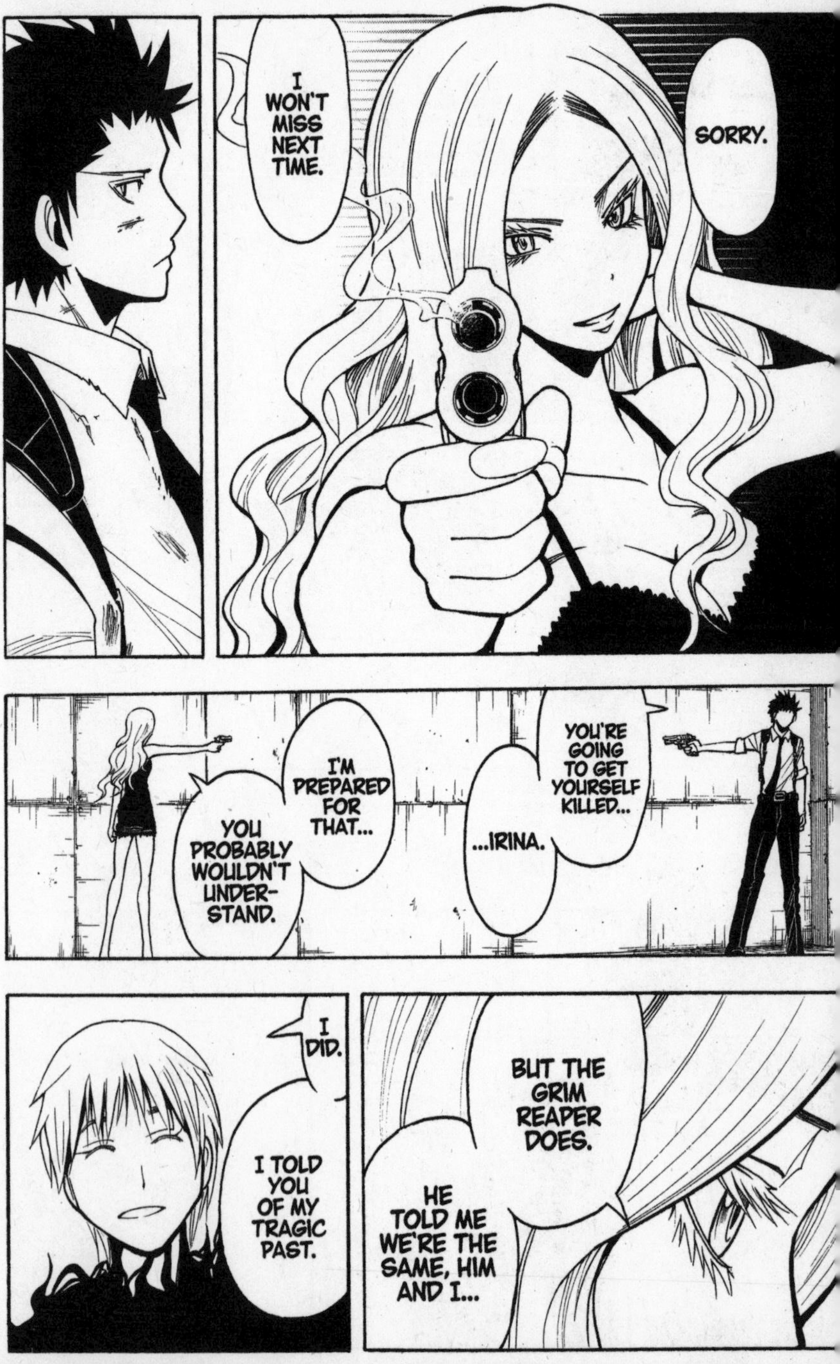
SORRY.
I WON'T MISS NEXT TIME.
YOU'RE GOING TO GET YOURSELF KILLED...
...IRINA.
I'M PREPARED FOR THAT...
YOU PROBABLY WOULDN'T UNDER-STAND.
BUT THE GRIM REAPER DOES.
HE TOLD ME WE'RE THE SAME, HIM AND I...
I DID.
I TOLD YOU OF MY TRAGIC PAST.

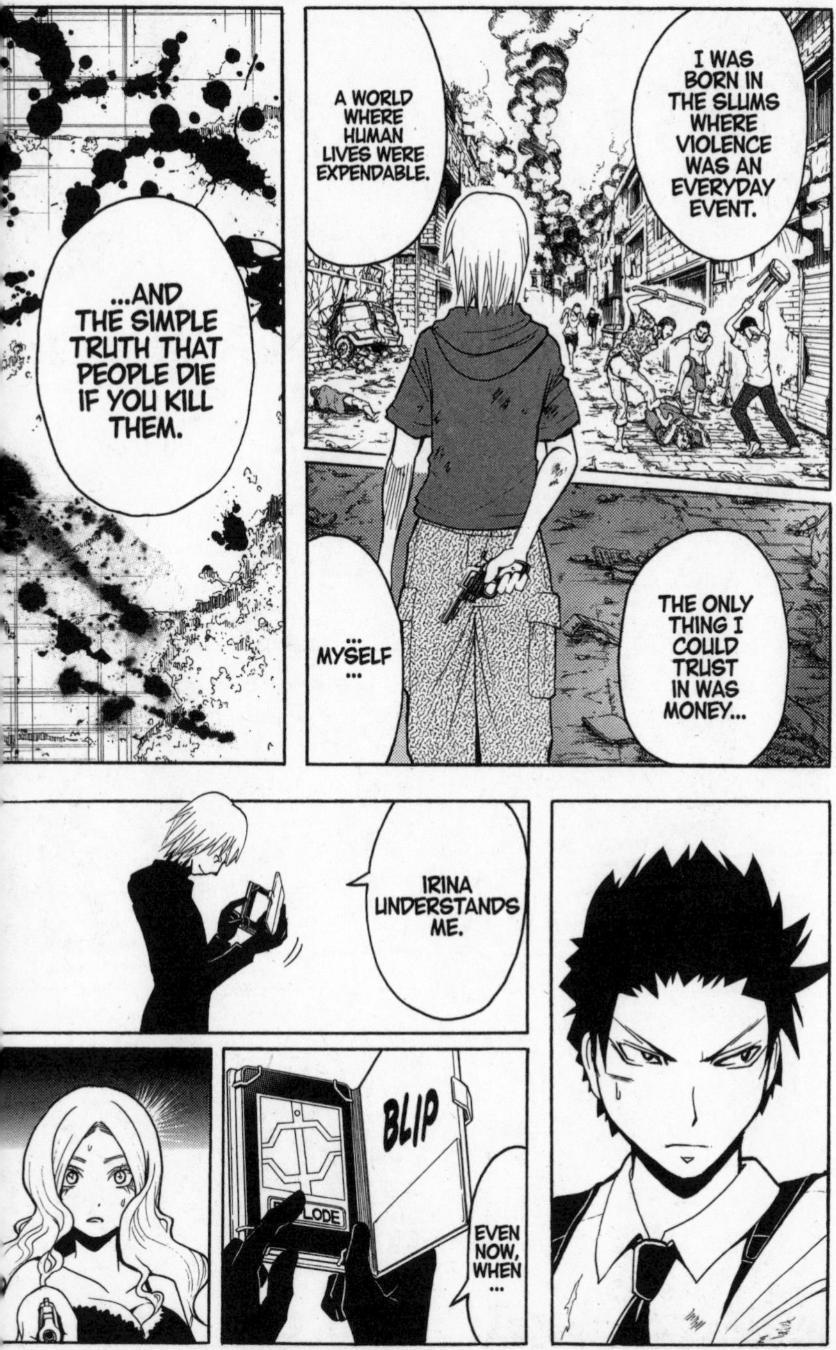
I WAS BORN IN THE SLUMS WHERE VIOLENCE WAS AN EVERYDAY EVENT.
A WORLD WHERE HUMAN LIVES WERE EXPENDABLE.
THE ONLY THING I COULD TRUST IN WAS MONEY...
...MYSELF...
...AND THE SIMPLE TRUTH THAT PEOPLE DIE IF YOU KILL THEM.
IRINA UNDERSTANDS ME.
BLIP
EVEN NOW, WHEN...

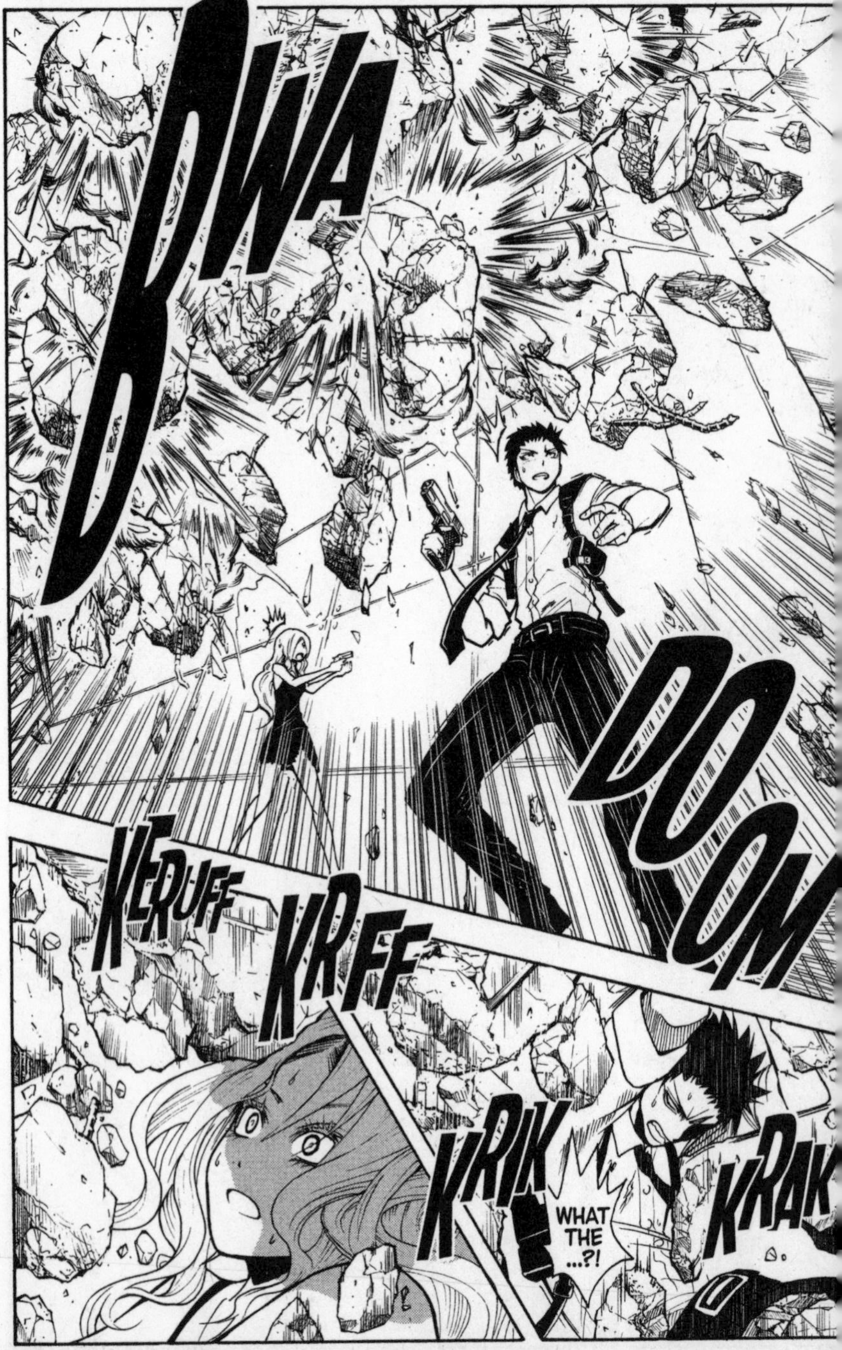
DOOM
BWA
KRAK
WHAT THE ...?!
KRIK
KRFF
KERUFF

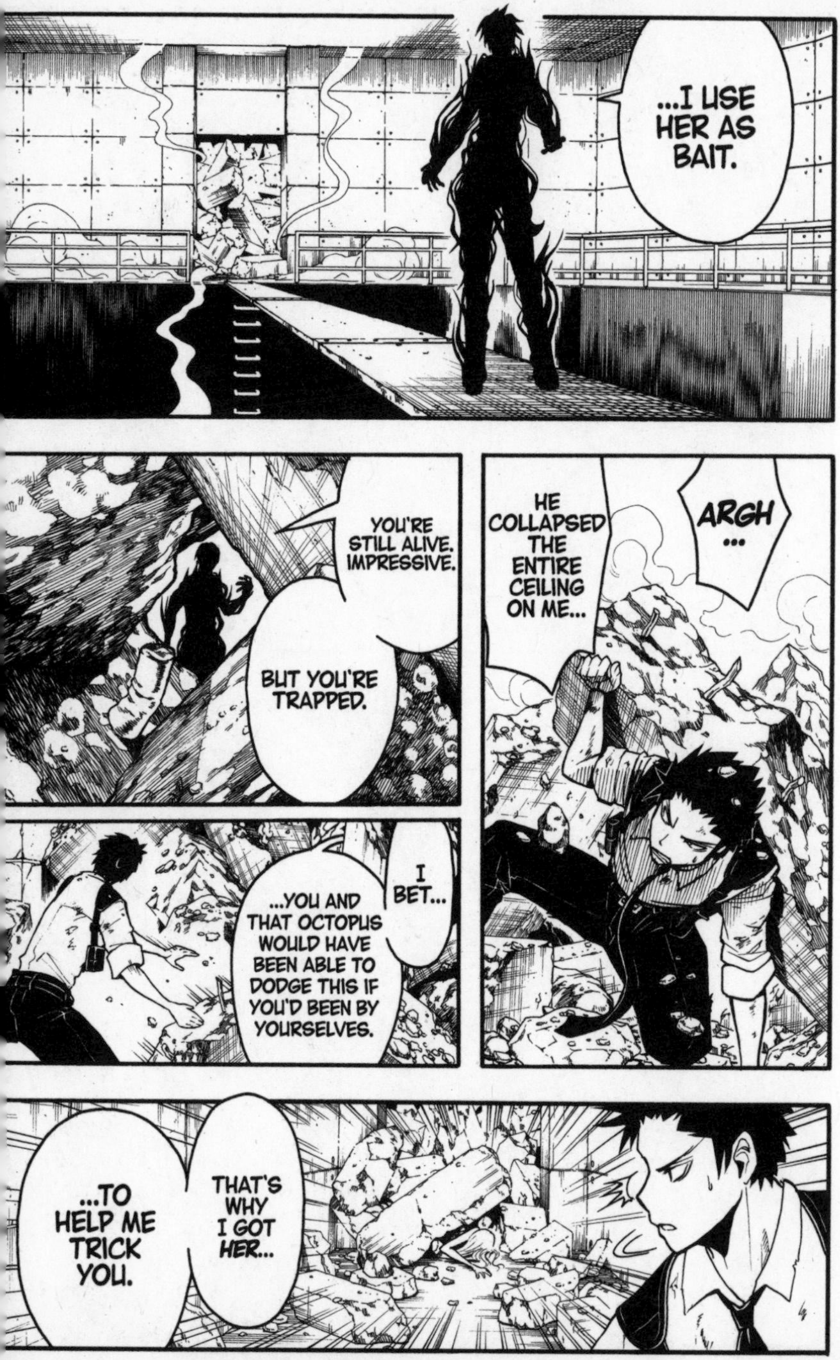
...I USE HER AS BAIT.
ARGH...
HE COLLAPSED THE ENTIRE CEILING ON ME...
YOU'RE STILL ALIVE. IMPRESSIVE.
BUT YOU'RE TRAPPED.
I BET...
...YOU AND THAT OCTOPUS WOULD HAVE BEEN ABLE TO DODGE THIS IF YOU'D BEEN BY YOURSELVES.
THAT'S WHY I GOT HER...
...TO HELP ME TRICK YOU.

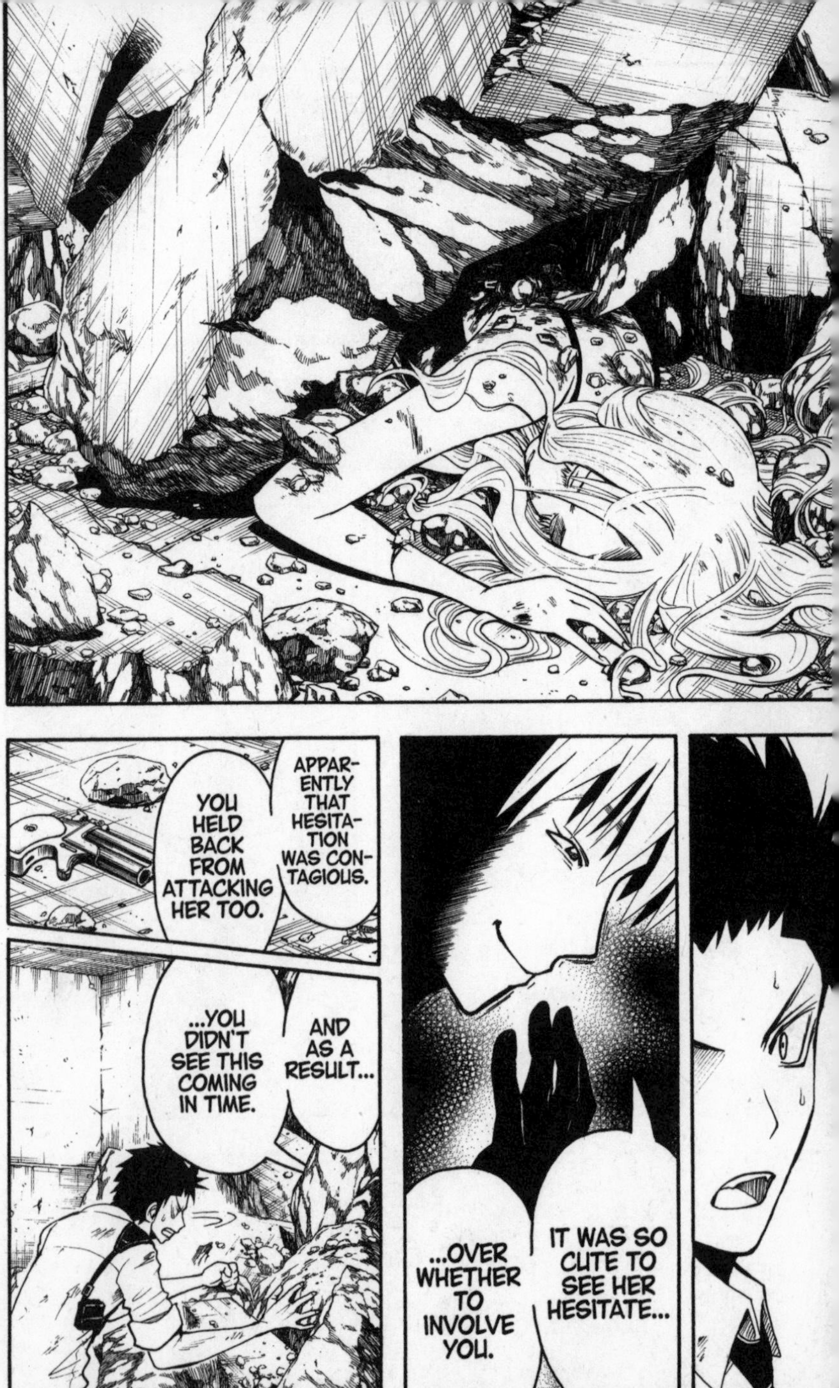
IT WAS SO CUTE TO SEE HER HESITATE...
...OVER WHETHER TO INVOLVE YOU.
APPARENTLY THAT HESITATION WAS CONTAGIOUS.
YOU HELD BACK FROM ATTACKING HER TOO.
AND AS A RESULT...
...YOU DIDN'T SEE THIS COMING IN TIME.

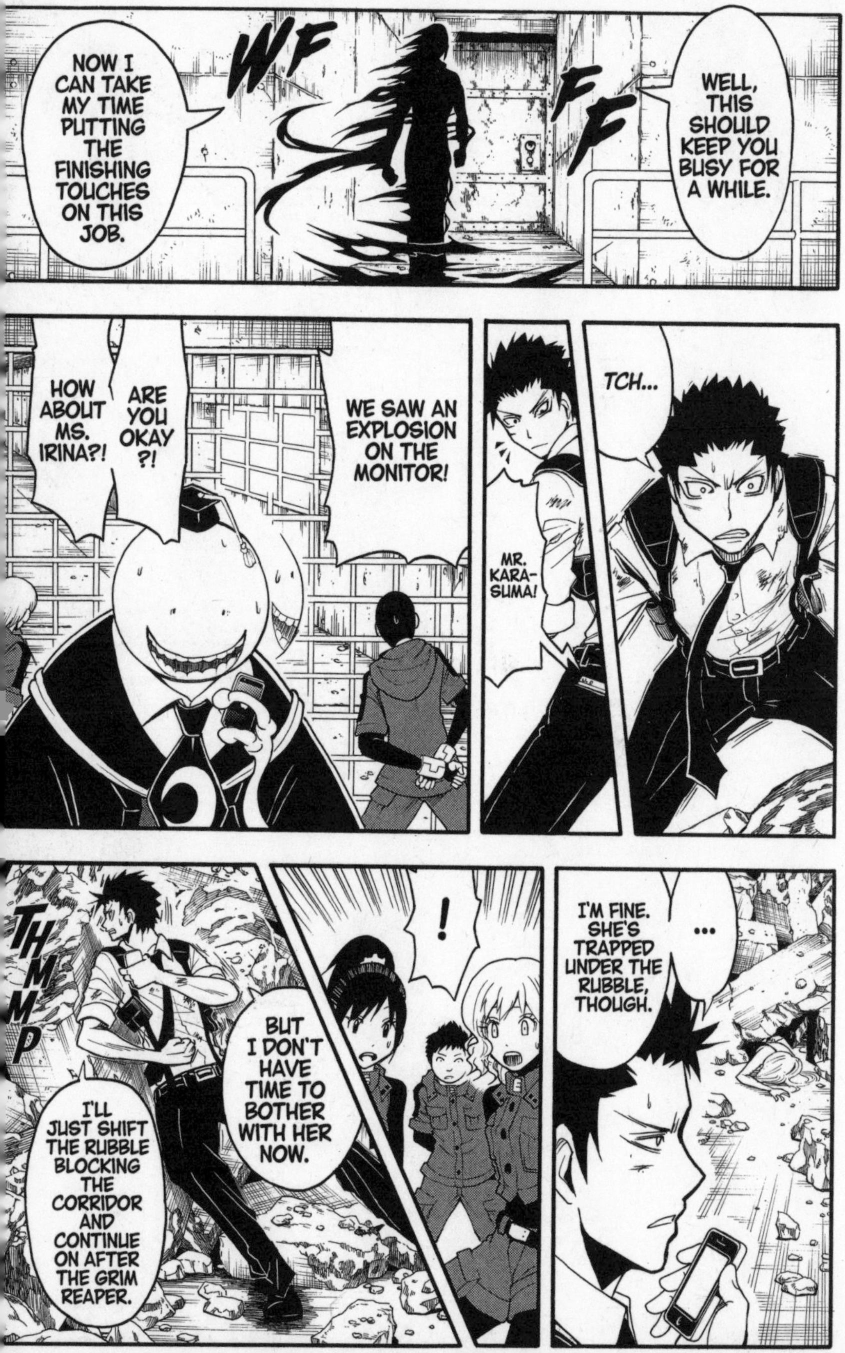
WELL, THIS SHOULD KEEP YOU BUSY FOR A WHILE.
WFFF
NOW I CAN TAKE MY TIME PUTTING THE FINISHING TOUCHES ON THIS JOB.
TCH...
MR. KARA-SUMA!
WE SAW AN EXPLOSION ON THE MONITOR!
ARE YOU OKAY ?!
HOW ABOUT MS. IRINA?!
...
I'M FINE. SHE'S TRAPPED UNDER THE RUBBLE, THOUGH.
!
BUT I DON'T HAVE TIME TO BOTHER WITH HER NOW.
I'LL JUST SHIFT THE RUBBLE BLOCKING THE CORRIDOR AND CONTINUE ON AFTER THE GRIM REAPER.
THMMP

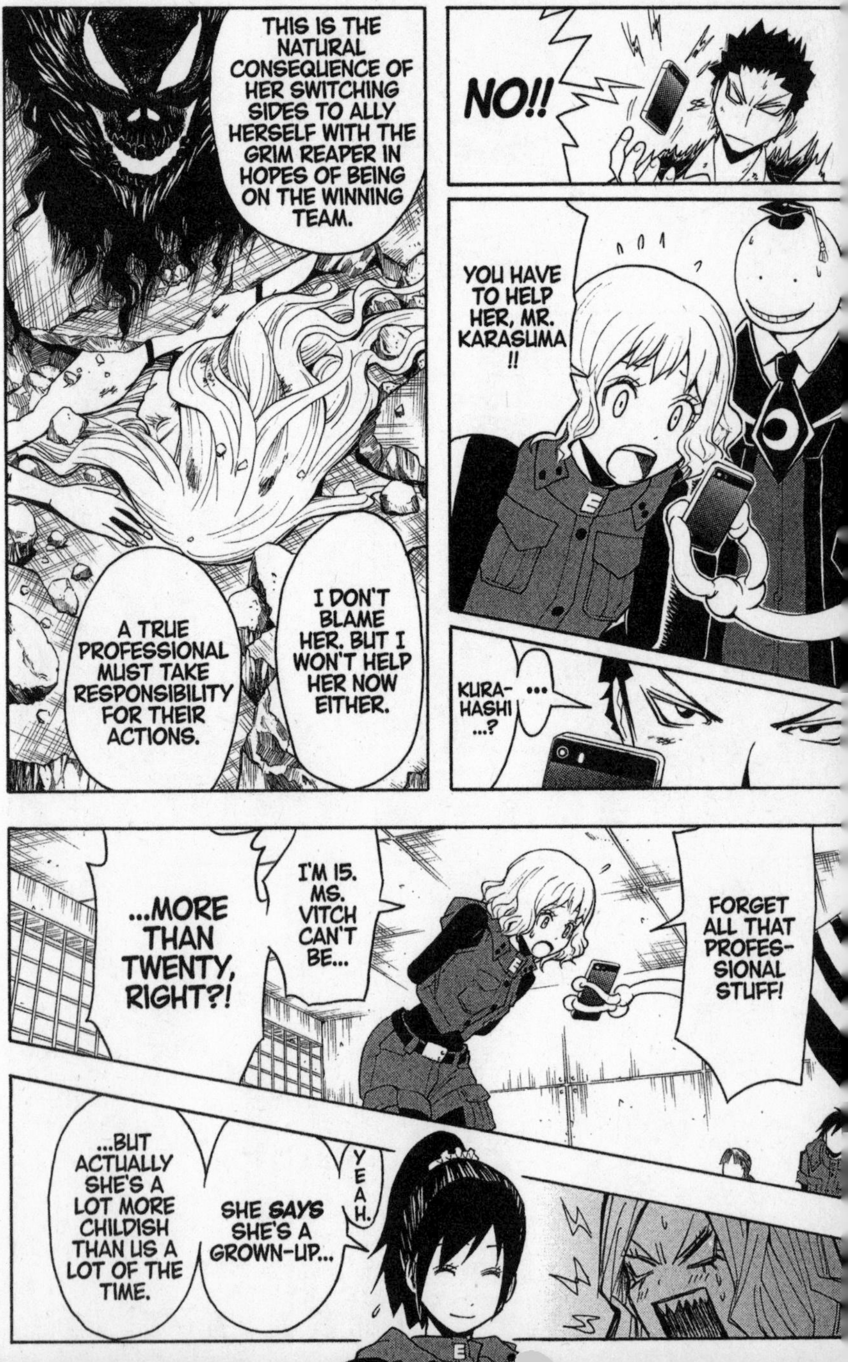
NO!!
YOU HAVE TO HELP HER, MR. KARASUMA !!
...
KURA-HASHI ...?
THIS IS THE NATURAL CONSEQUENCE OF HER SWITCHING SIDES TO ALLY HERSELF WITH THE GRIM REAPER IN HOPES OF BEING ON THE WINNING TEAM.
I DON'T BLAME HER. BUT I WON'T HELP HER NOW EITHER.
A TRUE PROFESSIONAL MUST TAKE RESPONSIBILITY FOR THEIR ACTIONS.
FORGET ALL THAT PROFES-SIONAL STUFF!
I'M 15. MS. VITCH CAN'T BE...
...MORE THAN TWENTY, RIGHT?!
YEAH.
SHE SAYS SHE'S A GROWN-UP...
...BUT ACTUALLY SHE'S A LOT MORE CHILDISH THAN US A LOT OF THE TIME.

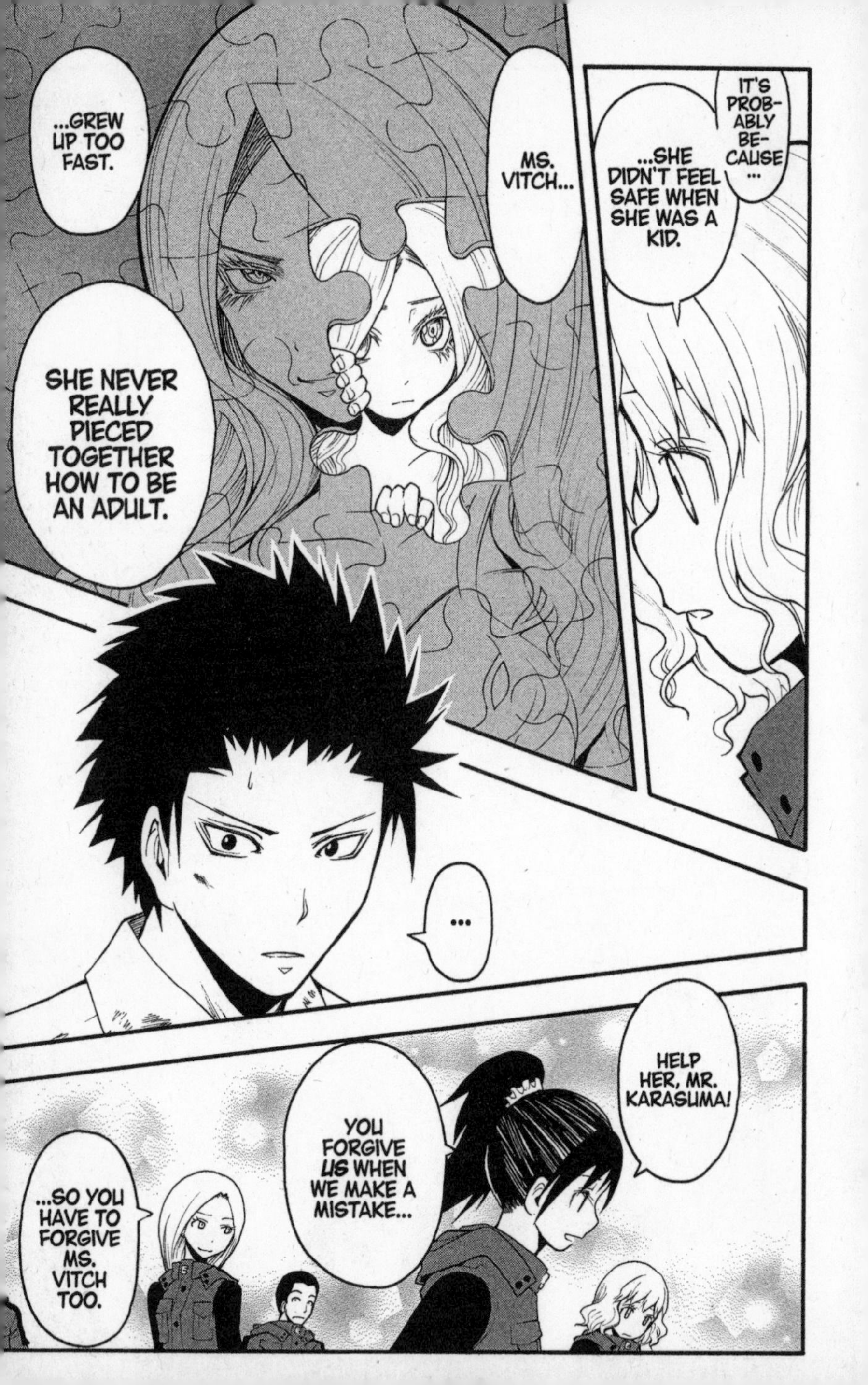
IT'S PROBABLY BECAUSE...
...SHE DIDN'T FEEL SAFE WHEN SHE WAS A KID.
MS. VITCH...
...GREW UP TOO FAST.
SHE NEVER REALLY PIECED TOGETHER HOW TO BE AN ADULT.
...
HELP HER, MR. KARASUMA!
YOU FORGIVE *US* WHEN WE MAKE A MISTAKE...
...SO YOU HAVE TO FORGIVE MS. VITCH TOO.

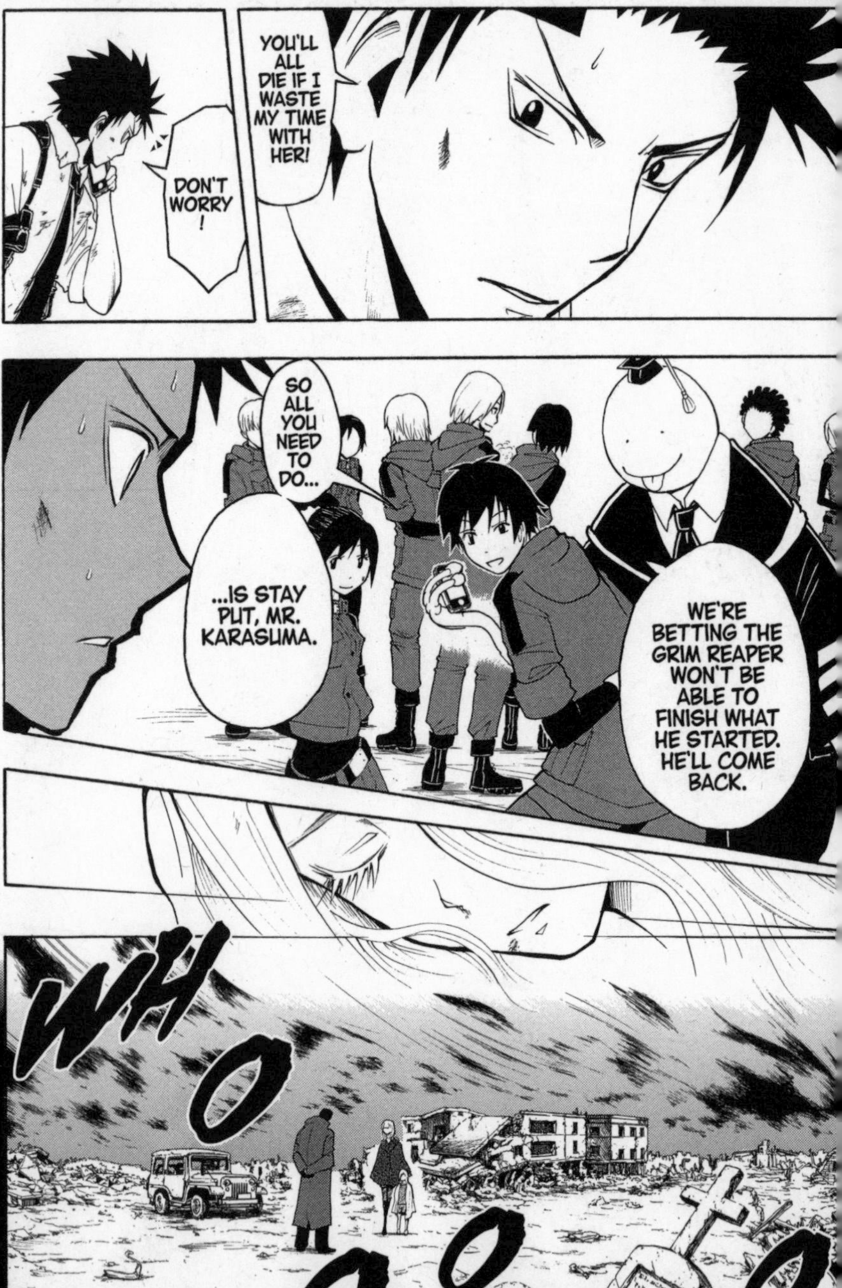
YOU'LL ALL DIE IF I WASTE MY TIME WITH HER!
DON'T WORRY!
WE'RE BETTING THE GRIM REAPER WON'T BE ABLE TO FINISH WHAT HE STARTED. HE'LL COME BACK.
SO ALL YOU NEED TO DO...
...IS STAY PUT, MR. KARASUMA.
WHOOOOO

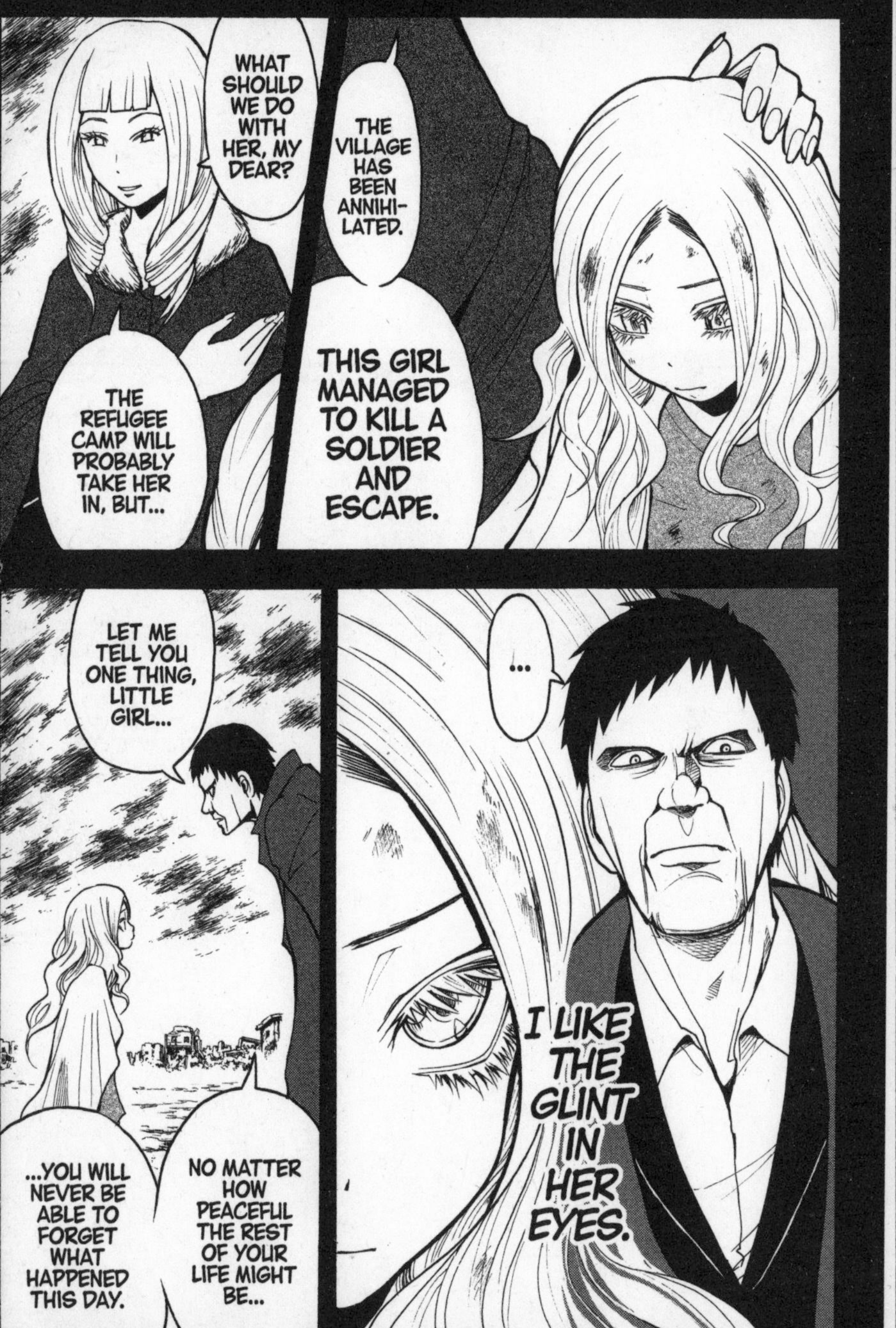
THE VILLAGE HAS BEEN ANNIHILATED.
THIS GIRL MANAGED TO KILL A SOLDIER AND ESCAPE.
WHAT SHOULD WE DO WITH HER, MY DEAR?
THE REFUGEE CAMP WILL PROBABLY TAKE HER IN, BUT...
...
I LIKE THE GLINT IN HER EYES.
LET ME TELL YOU ONE THING, LITTLE GIRL...
NO MATTER HOW PEACEFUL THE REST OF YOUR LIFE MIGHT BE...
...YOU WILL NEVER BE ABLE TO FORGET WHAT HAPPENED THIS DAY.

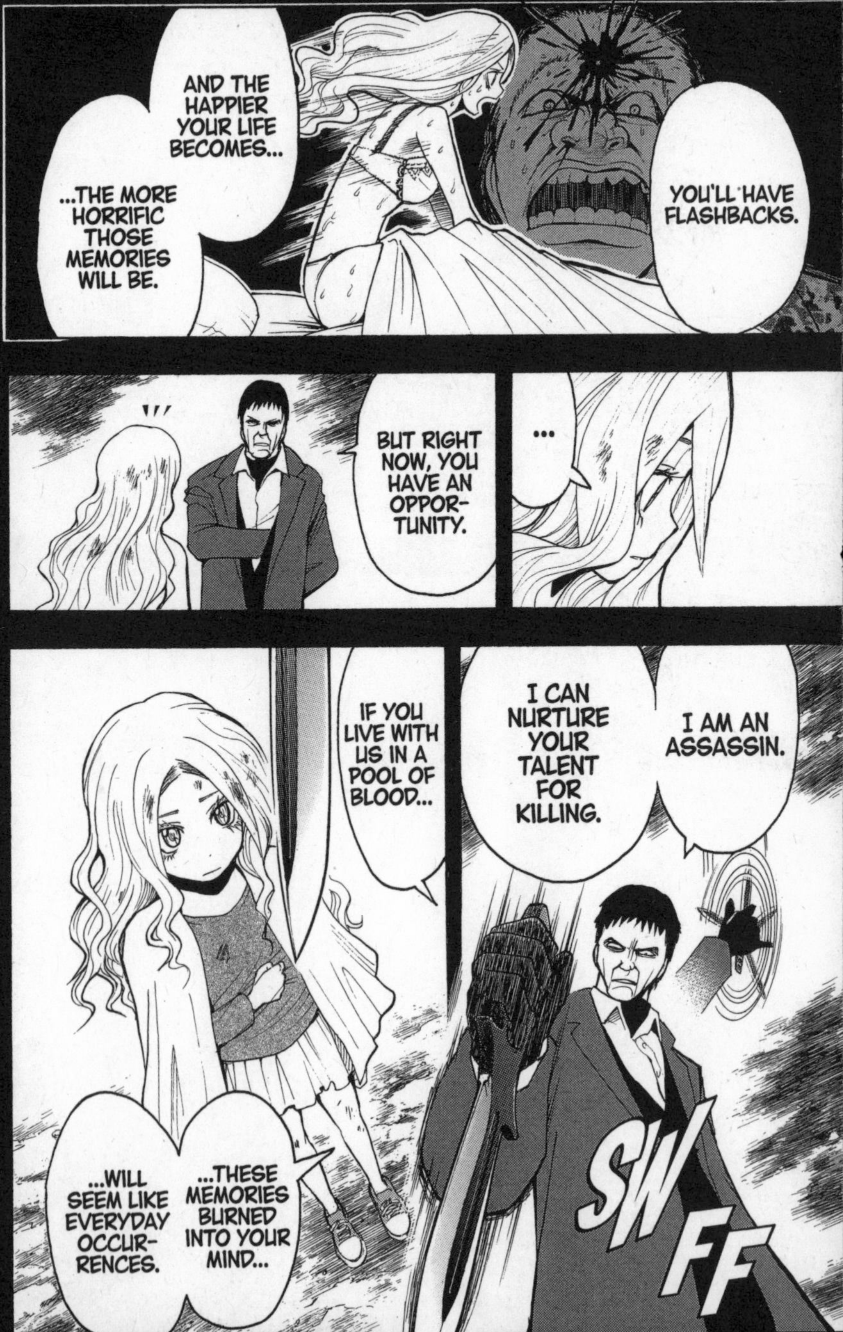
YOU'LL HAVE FLASHBACKS.
AND THE HAPPIER YOUR LIFE BECOMES...
...THE MORE HORRIFIC THOSE MEMORIES WILL BE.
...
BUT RIGHT NOW, YOU HAVE AN OPPOR-TUNITY.
I AM AN ASSASSIN.
I CAN NURTURE YOUR TALENT FOR KILLING.
IF YOU LIVE WITH US IN A POOL OF BLOOD...
...THESE MEMORIES BURNED INTO YOUR MIND...
...WILL SEEM LIKE EVERYDAY OCCUR-RENCES.
SWFF

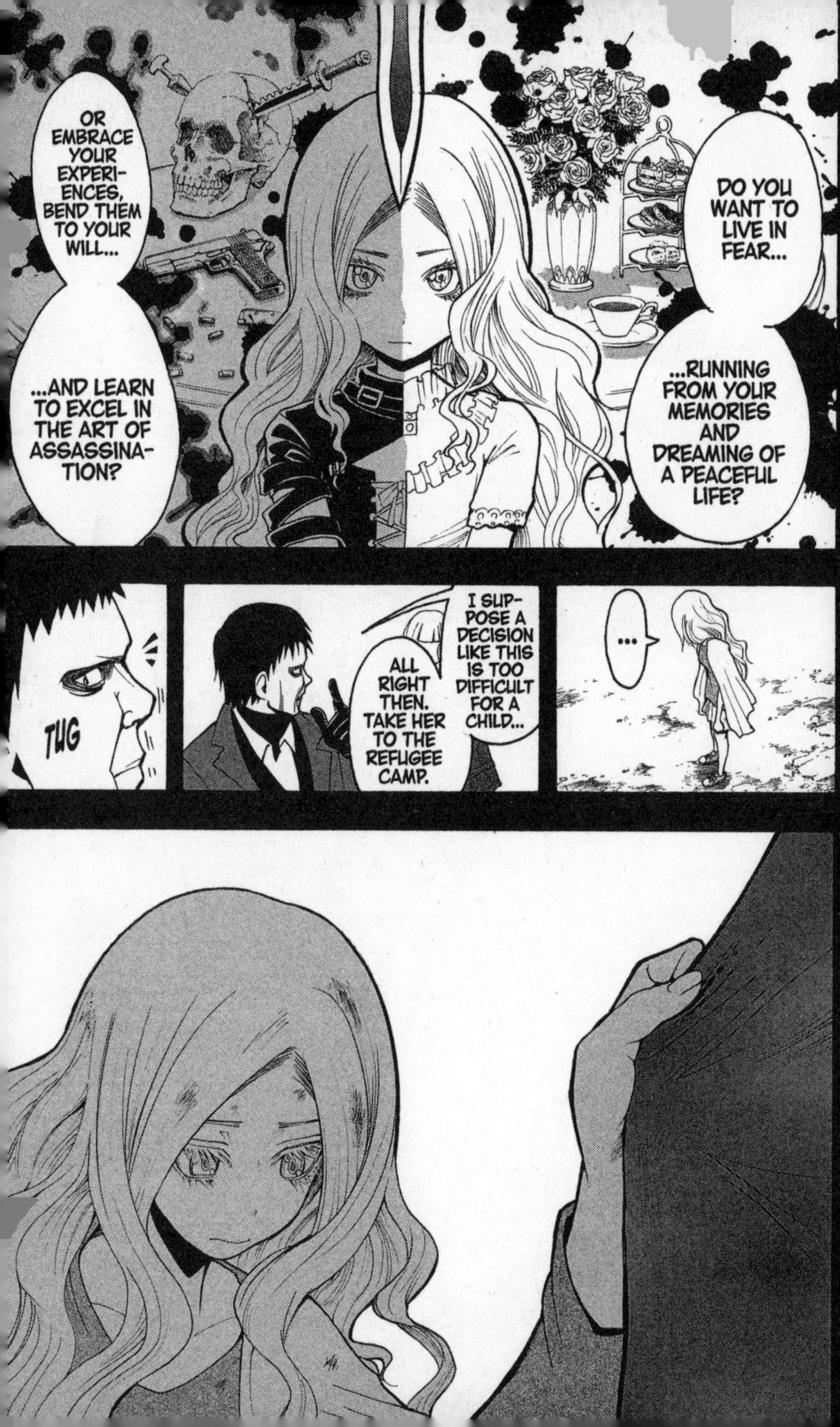
DO YOU WANT TO LIVE IN FEAR...
...RUNNING FROM YOUR MEMORIES AND DREAMING OF A PEACEFUL LIFE?
OR EMBRACE YOUR EXPERIENCES, BEND THEM TO YOUR WILL...
...AND LEARN TO EXCEL IN THE ART OF ASSASSINATION?
...
I SUPPOSE A DECISION LIKE THIS IS TOO DIFFICULT FOR A CHILD...
ALL RIGHT THEN. TAKE HER TO THE REFUGEE CAMP.
TUG

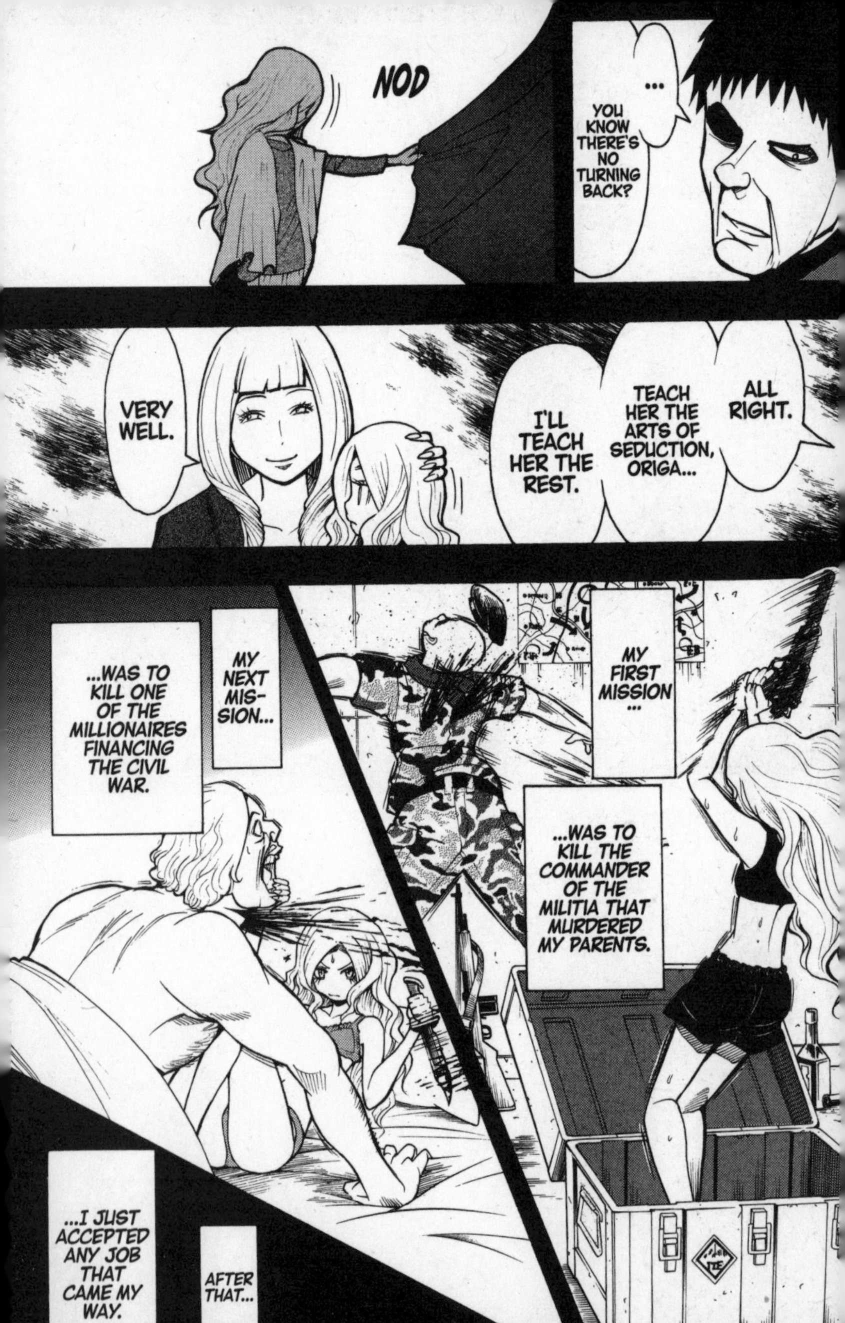
...
YOU KNOW THERE'S NO TURNING BACK?
NOD
ALL RIGHT.
TEACH HER THE ARTS OF SEDUCTION, ORIGA...
I'LL TEACH HER THE REST.
VERY WELL.
MY FIRST MISSION...
...WAS TO KILL THE COMMANDER OF THE MILITIA THAT MURDERED MY PARENTS.
MY NEXT MIS-SION...
...WAS TO KILL ONE OF THE MILLIONAIRES FINANCING THE CIVIL WAR.
AFTER THAT...
...I JUST ACCEPTED ANY JOB THAT CAME MY WAY.

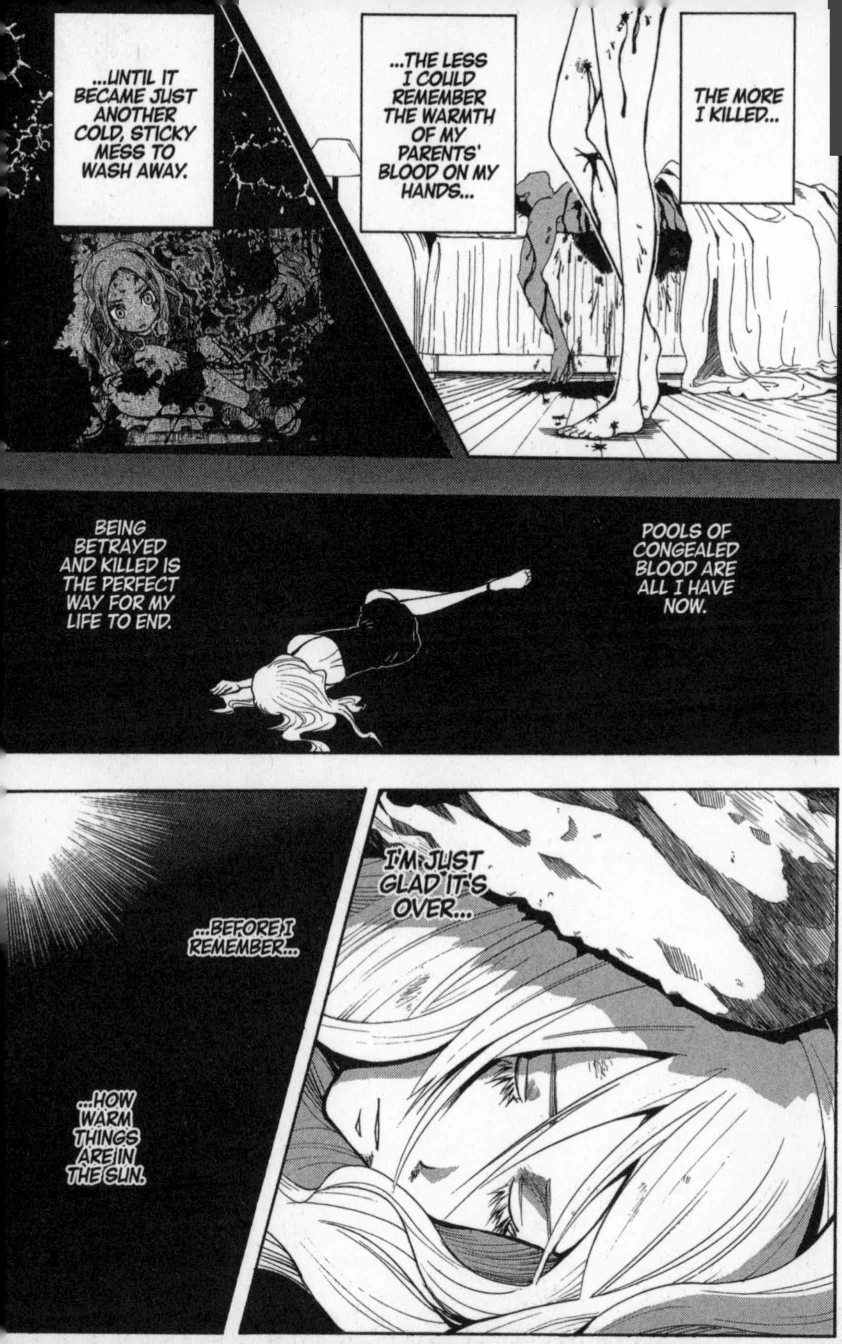
THE MORE I KILLED...
...THE LESS I COULD REMEMBER THE WARMTH OF MY PARENTS' BLOOD ON MY HANDS...
...UNTIL IT BECAME JUST ANOTHER COLD, STICKY MESS TO WASH AWAY.
POOLS OF CONGEALED BLOOD ARE ALL I HAVE NOW.
BEING BETRAYED AND KILLED IS THE PERFECT WAY FOR MY LIFE TO END.
I'M JUST GLAD IT'S OVER...
...BEFORE I REMEMBER...
...HOW WARM THINGS ARE IN THE SUN.

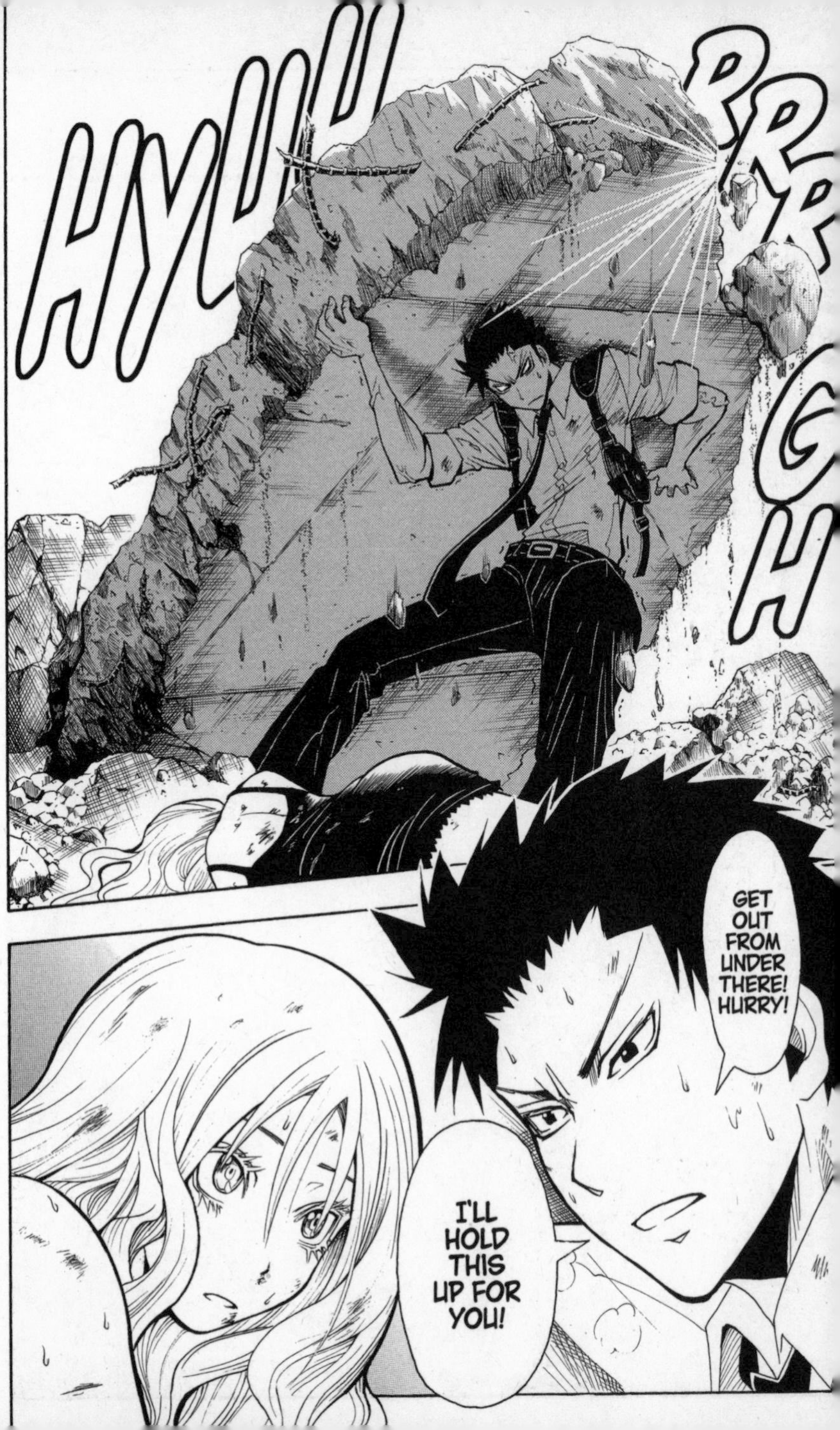
PRRGH
HYUUU
GET OUT FROM UNDER THERE! HURRY!
I'LL HOLD THIS UP FOR YOU!

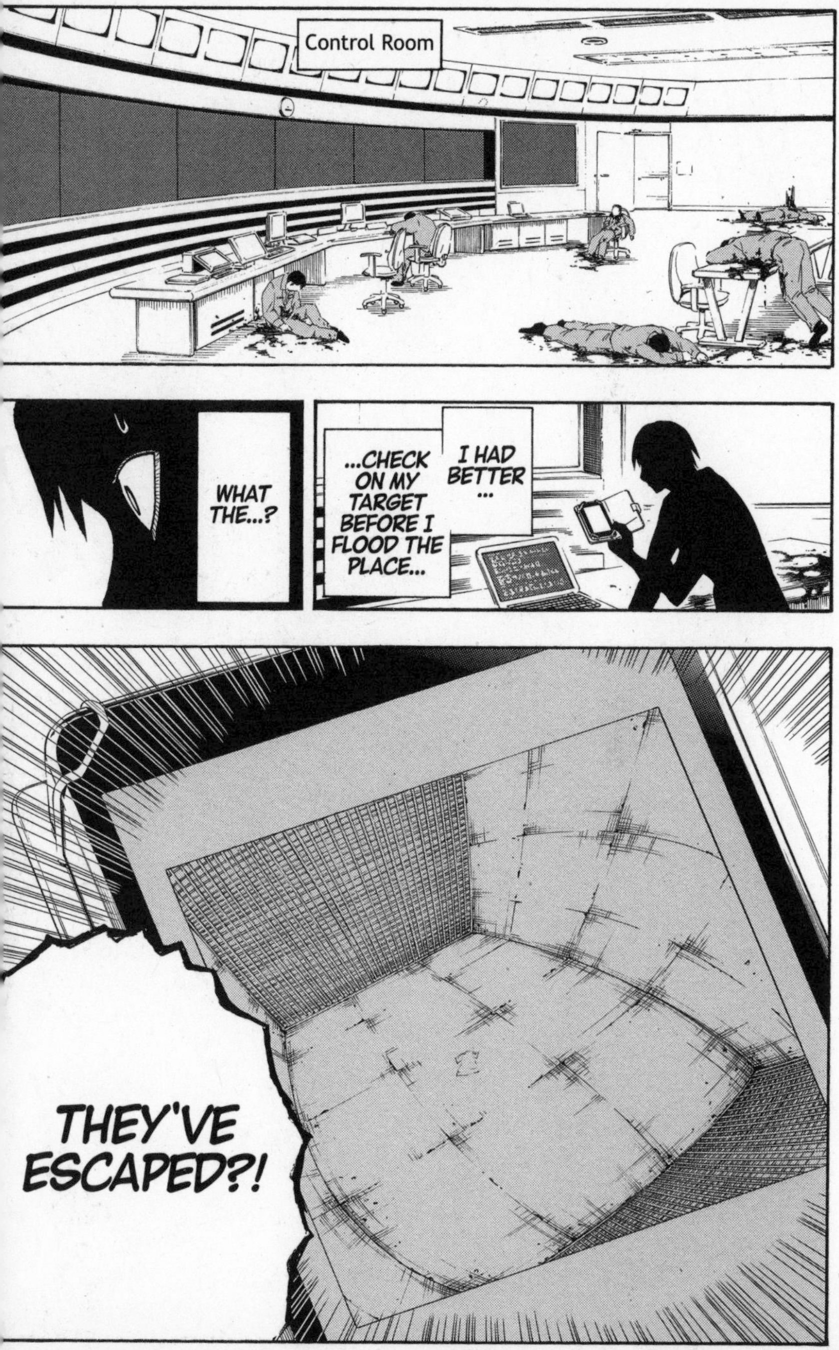
Control Room
I HAD BETTER...
...CHECK ON MY TARGET BEFORE I FLOOD THE PLACE...
WHAT THE...?
THEY'VE ESCAPED?!

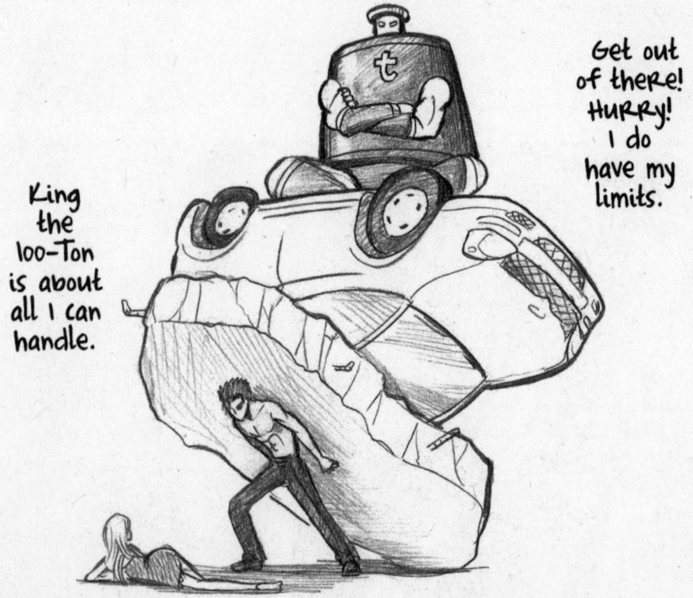
Get out of there! HURRY! I do have my limits.
King the 100-Ton is about all I can handle.

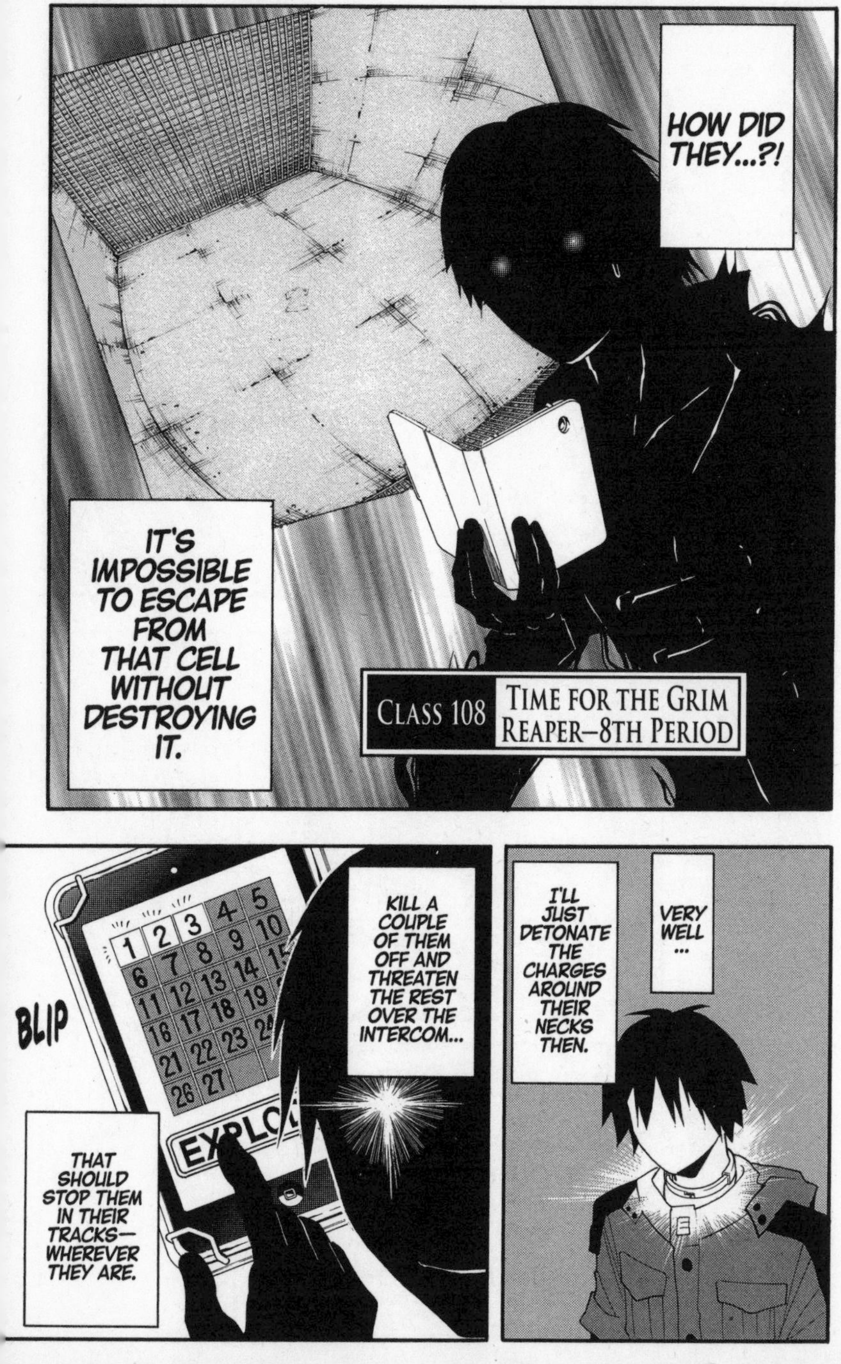
HOW DID THEY...?!
IT'S IMPOSSIBLE TO ESCAPE FROM THAT CELL WITHOUT DESTROYING IT.
CLASS 108 TIME FOR THE GRIM REAPER—8TH PERIOD
VERY WELL...
I'LL JUST DETONATE THE CHARGES AROUND THEIR NECKS THEN.
KILL A COUPLE OF THEM OFF AND THREATEN THE REST OVER THE INTERCOM...
BLIP
THAT SHOULD STOP THEM IN THEIR TRACKS—WHEREVER THEY ARE.

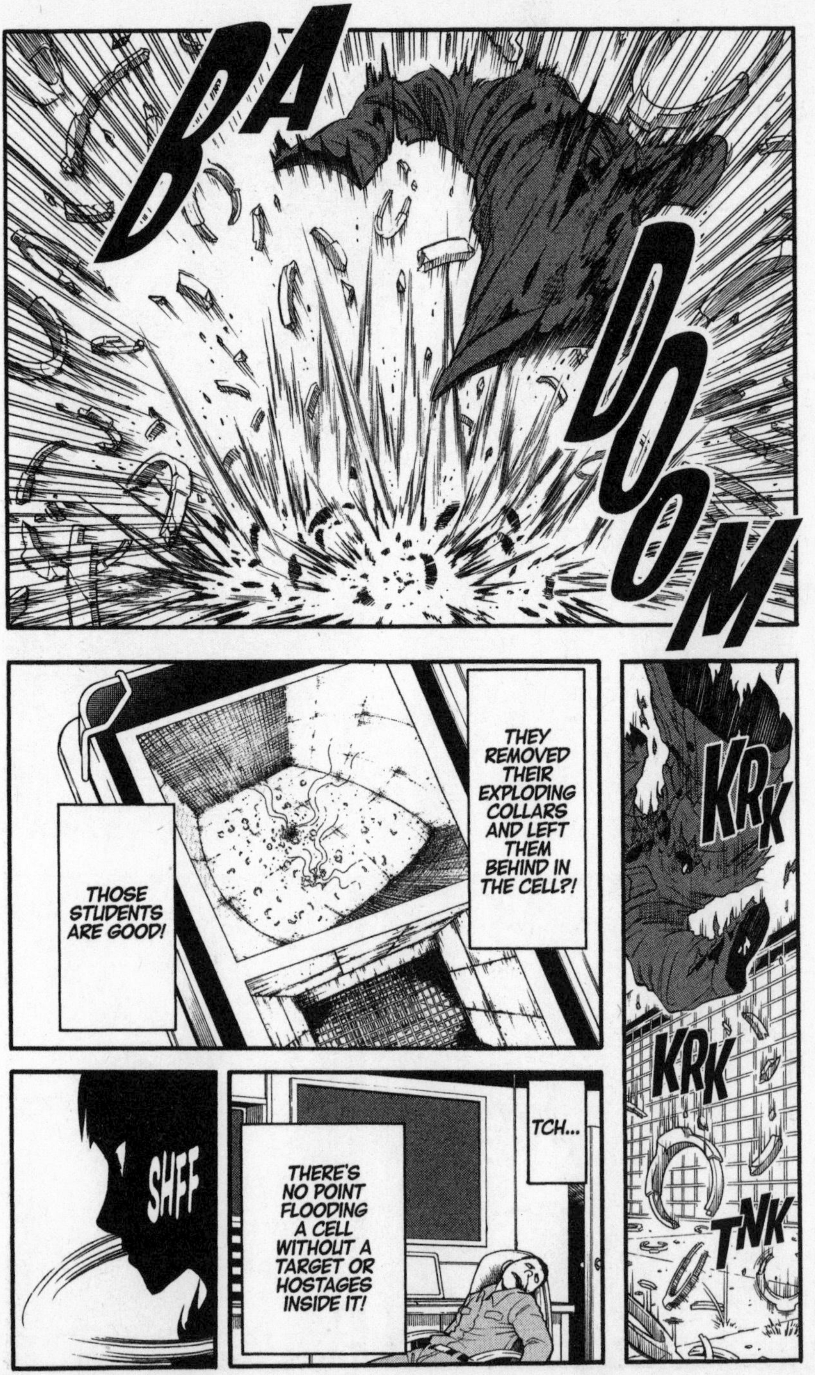
BA
DOOM
KRK
KRK
TNK
THEY REMOVED THEIR EXPLODING COLLARS AND LEFT THEM BEHIND IN THE CELL?!
THOSE STUDENTS ARE GOOD!
TCH...
THERE'S NO POINT FLOODING A CELL WITHOUT A TARGET OR HOSTAGES INSIDE IT!
SHFF

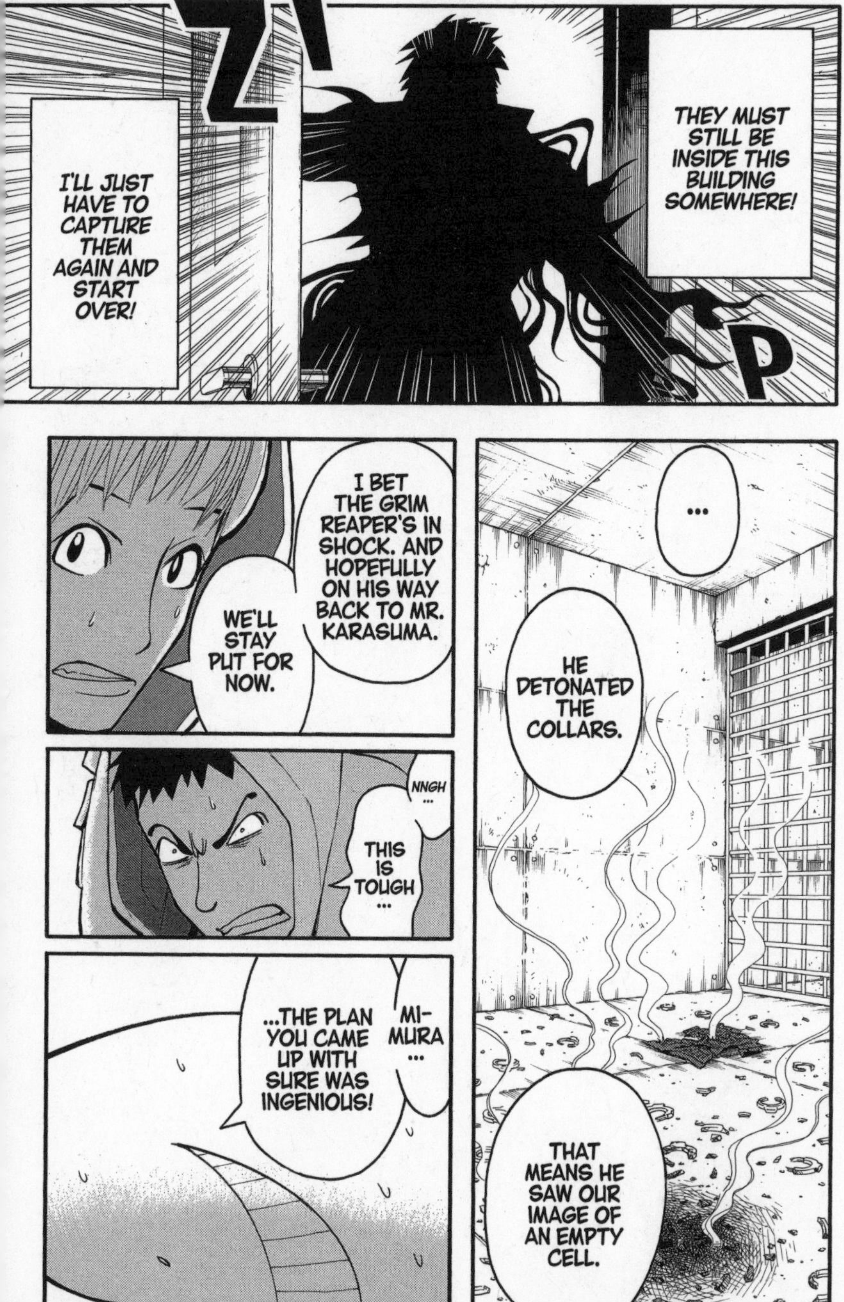
THEY MUST STILL BE INSIDE THIS BUILDING SOMEWHERE!
ZIP
I'LL JUST HAVE TO CAPTURE THEM AGAIN AND START OVER!
...
HE DETONATED THE COLLARS.
THAT MEANS HE SAW OUR IMAGE OF AN EMPTY CELL.
I BET THE GRIM REAPER'S IN SHOCK. AND HOPEFULLY ON HIS WAY BACK TO MR. KARASUMA.
WE'LL STAY PUT FOR NOW.
NNGH...
THIS IS TOUGH...
MI-MURA...
...THE PLAN YOU CAME UP WITH SURE WAS INGENIOUS!

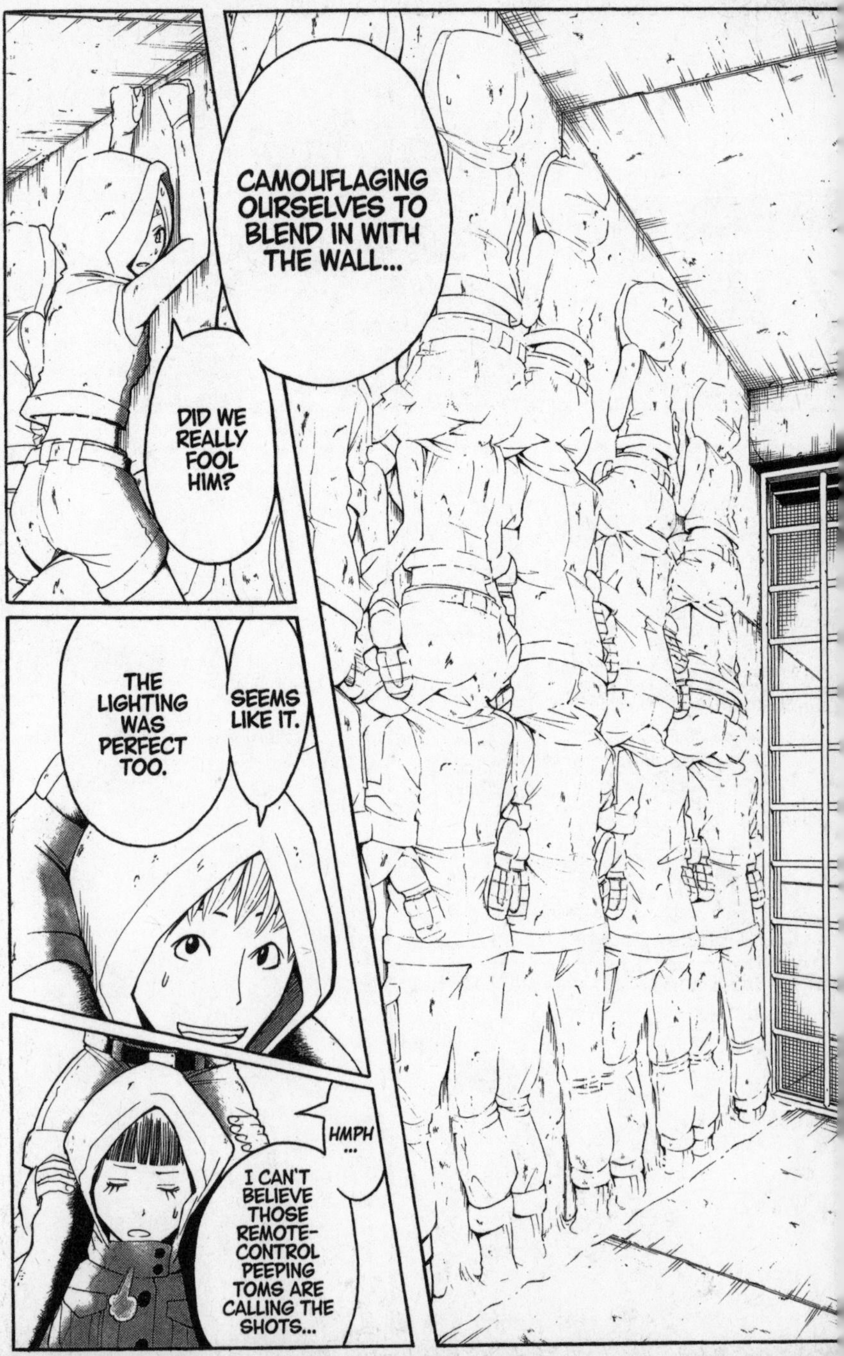
CAMOUFLAGING OURSELVES TO BLEND IN WITH THE WALL...
DID WE REALLY FOOL HIM?
SEEMS LIKE IT.
THE LIGHTING WAS PERFECT TOO.
HMPH...
I CAN'T BELIEVE THOSE REMOTE-CONTROL PEEPING TOMS ARE CALLING THE SHOTS...

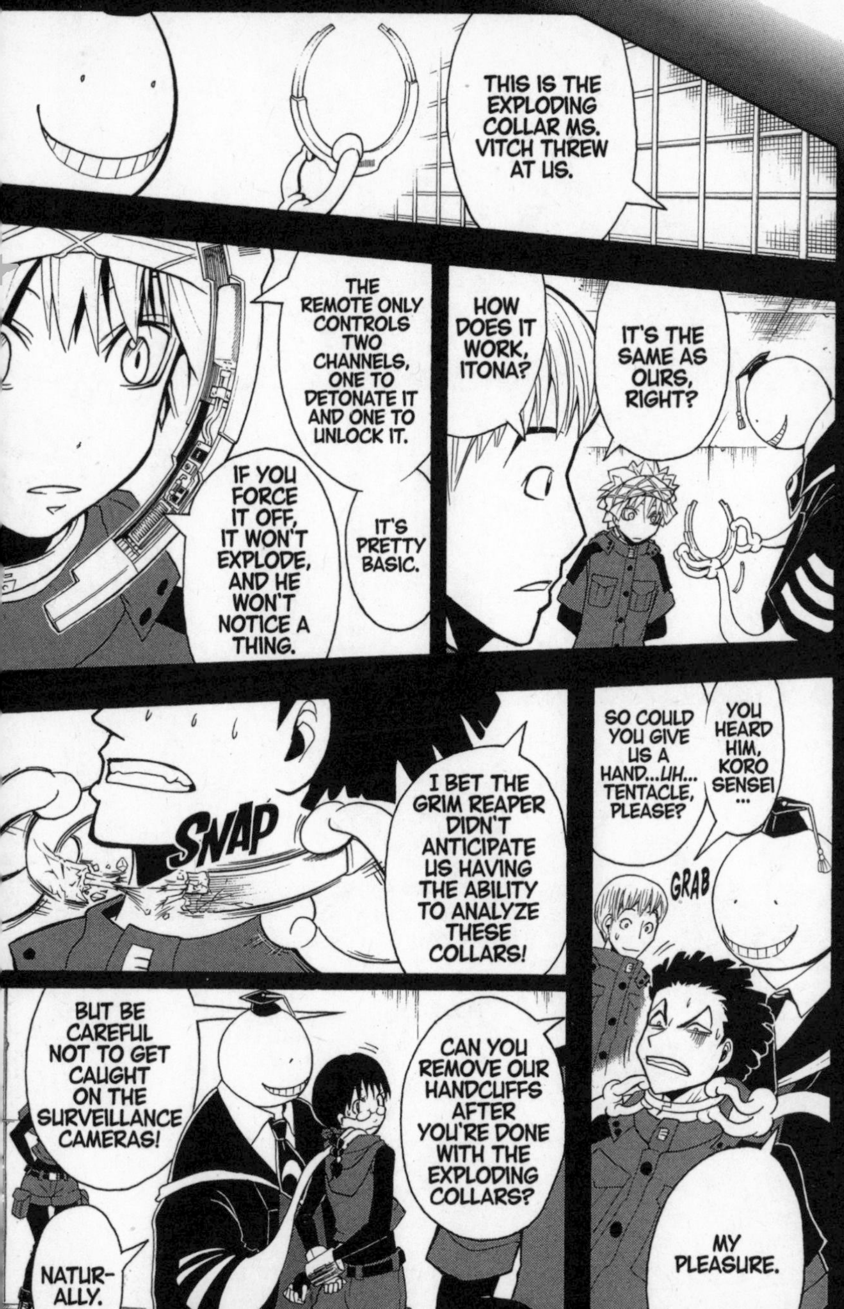
THIS IS THE EXPLODING COLLAR MS. VITCH THREW AT US.
IT'S THE SAME AS OURS, RIGHT?
HOW DOES IT WORK, ITONA?
THE REMOTE ONLY CONTROLS TWO CHANNELS, ONE TO DETONATE IT AND ONE TO UNLOCK IT.
IT'S PRETTY BASIC.
IF YOU FORCE IT OFF, IT WON'T EXPLODE, AND HE WON'T NOTICE A THING.
YOU HEARD HIM, KORO SENSEI...
SO COULD YOU GIVE US A HAND...UH... TENTACLE, PLEASE?
GRAB
MY PLEASURE.
SNAP
I BET THE GRIM REAPER DIDN'T ANTICIPATE US HAVING THE ABILITY TO ANALYZE THESE COLLARS!
CAN YOU REMOVE OUR HANDCUFFS AFTER YOU'RE DONE WITH THE EXPLODING COLLARS?
BUT BE CAREFUL NOT TO GET CAUGHT ON THE SURVEILLANCE CAMERAS!
NATUR-ALLY.

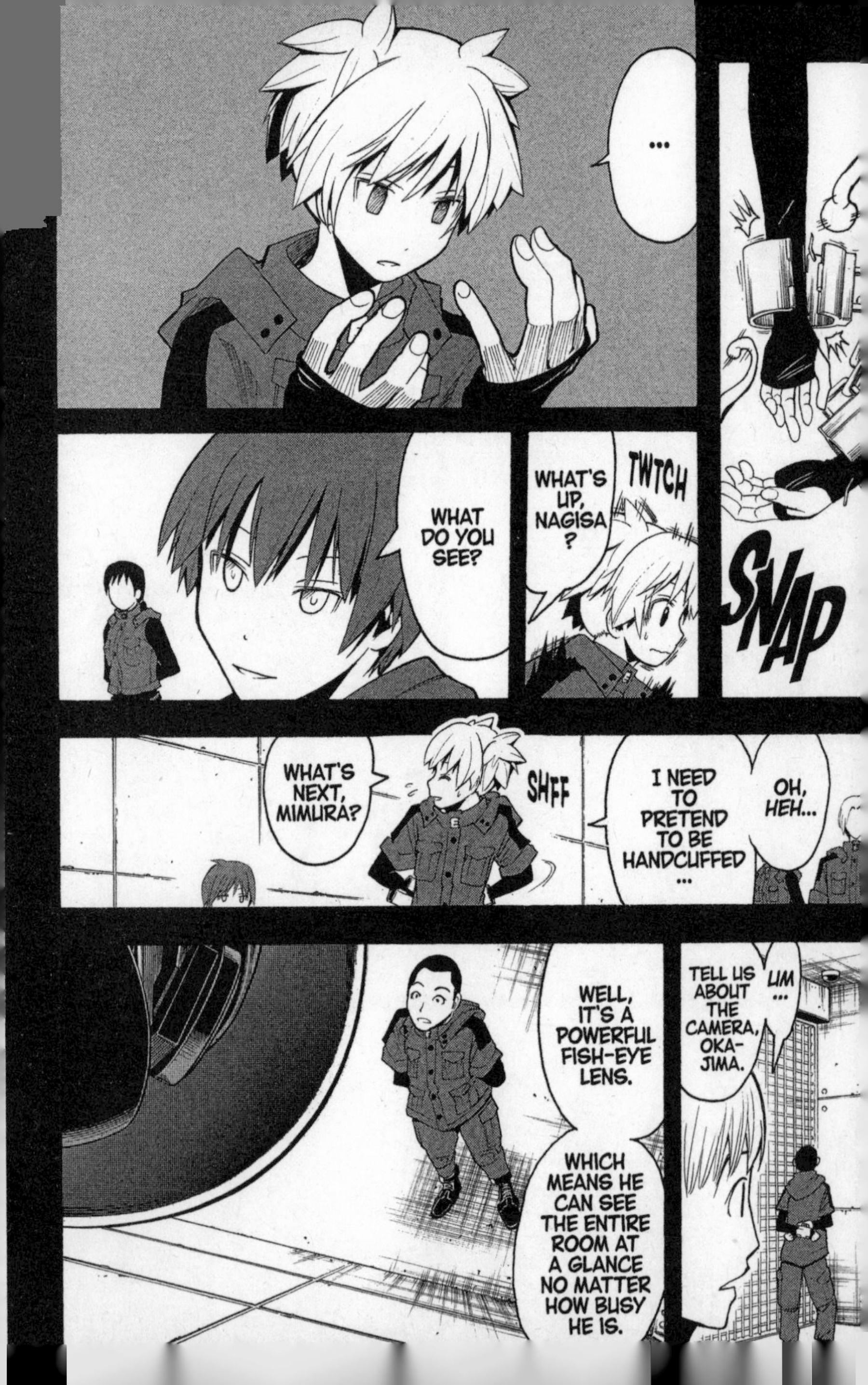
SNAP
...
TWTCH
WHAT'S UP, NAGISA?
WHAT DO YOU SEE?
OH, HEH...
I NEED TO PRETEND TO BE HANDCUFFED ...
SHFF
WHAT'S NEXT, MIMURA?
UM ...
TELL US ABOUT THE CAMERA, OKAJIMA.
WELL, IT'S A POWERFUL FISH-EYE LENS.
WHICH MEANS HE CAN SEE THE ENTIRE ROOM AT A GLANCE NO MATTER HOW BUSY HE IS.

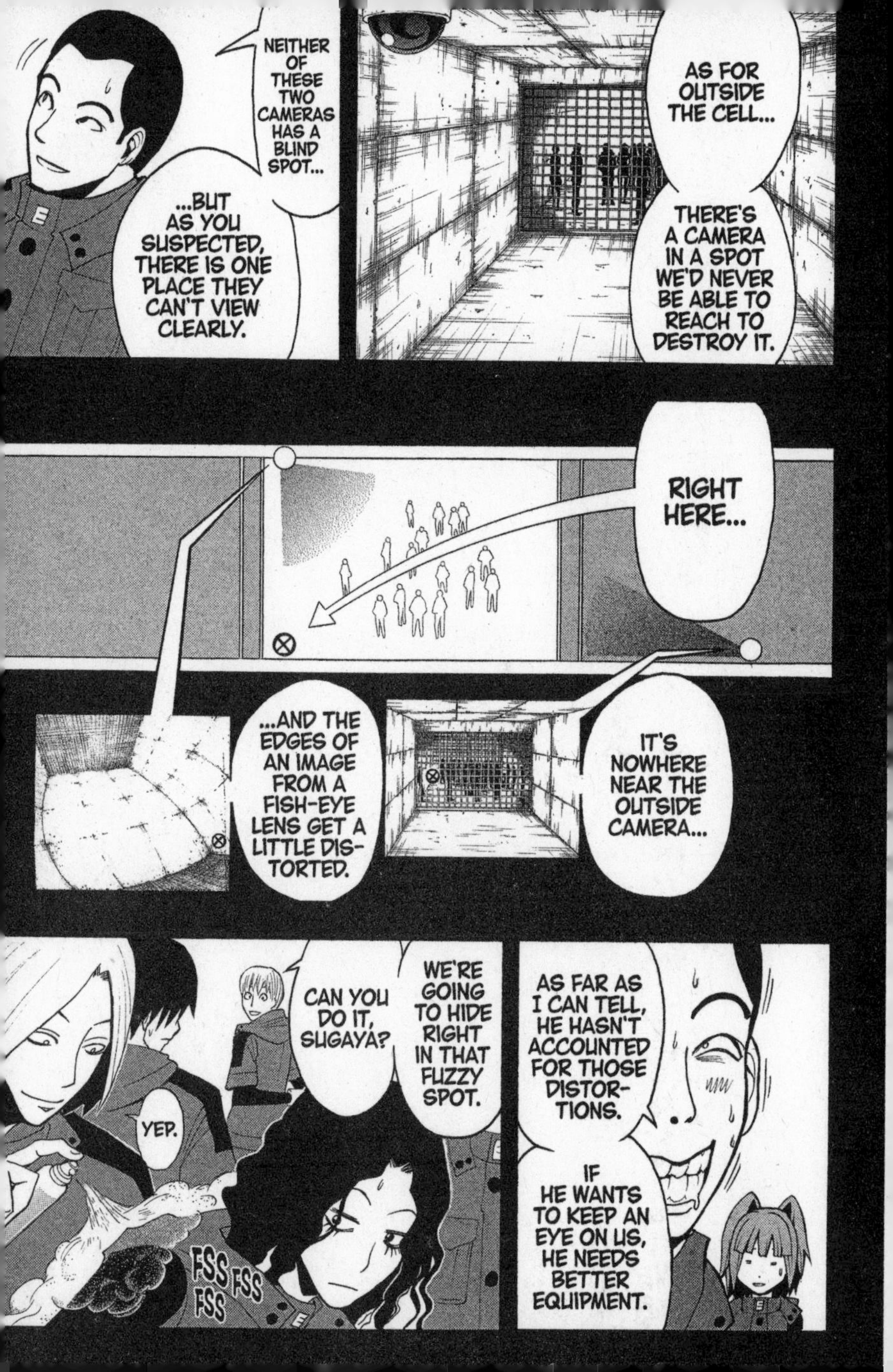
AS FOR OUTSIDE THE CELL...
THERE'S A CAMERA IN A SPOT WE'D NEVER BE ABLE TO REACH TO DESTROY IT.
NEITHER OF THESE TWO CAMERAS HAS A BLIND SPOT...
...BUT AS YOU SUSPECTED, THERE IS ONE PLACE THEY CAN'T VIEW CLEARLY.
RIGHT HERE...
IT'S NOWHERE NEAR THE OUTSIDE CAMERA...
...AND THE EDGES OF AN IMAGE FROM A FISH-EYE LENS GET A LITTLE DISTORTED.
AS FAR AS I CAN TELL, HE HASN'T ACCOUNTED FOR THOSE DISTORTIONS.
IF HE WANTS TO KEEP AN EYE ON US, HE NEEDS BETTER EQUIPMENT.
WE'RE GOING TO HIDE RIGHT IN THAT FUZZY SPOT.
CAN YOU DO IT, SUGAYA?
YEP.
FSS FSS FSS

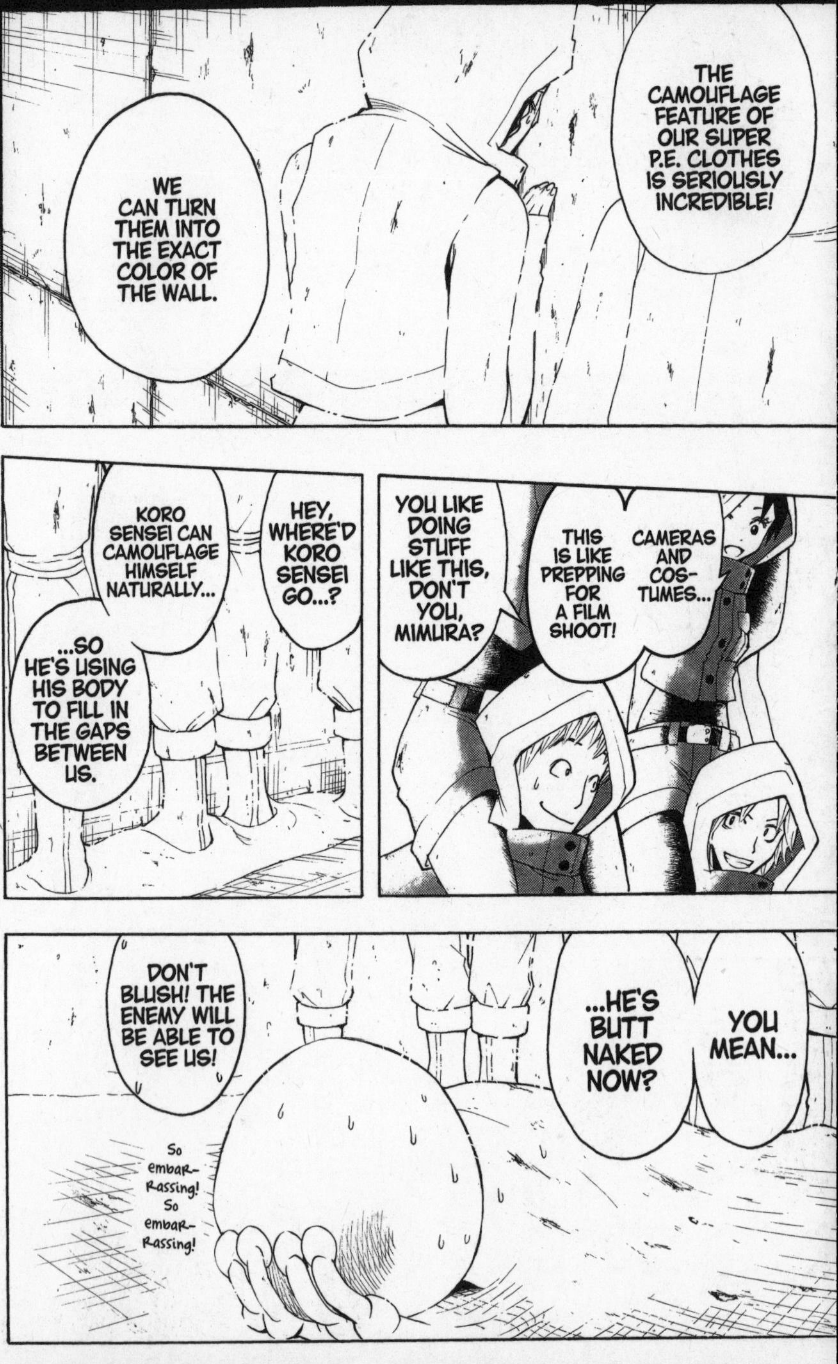
THE CAMOUFLAGE FEATURE OF OUR SUPER P.E. CLOTHES IS SERIOUSLY INCREDIBLE!
WE CAN TURN THEM INTO THE EXACT COLOR OF THE WALL.
CAMERAS AND COS-TUMES...
THIS IS LIKE PREPPING FOR A FILM SHOOT!
YOU LIKE DOING STUFF LIKE THIS, DON'T YOU, MIMURA?
HEY, WHERE'D KORO SENSEI GO...?
KORO SENSEI CAN CAMOUFLAGE HIMSELF NATURALLY...
...SO HE'S USING HIS BODY TO FILL IN THE GAPS BETWEEN US.
YOU MEAN...
...HE'S BUTT NAKED NOW?
DON'T BLUSH! THE ENEMY WILL BE ABLE TO SEE US!
So embar-rassing! So embar-rassing!

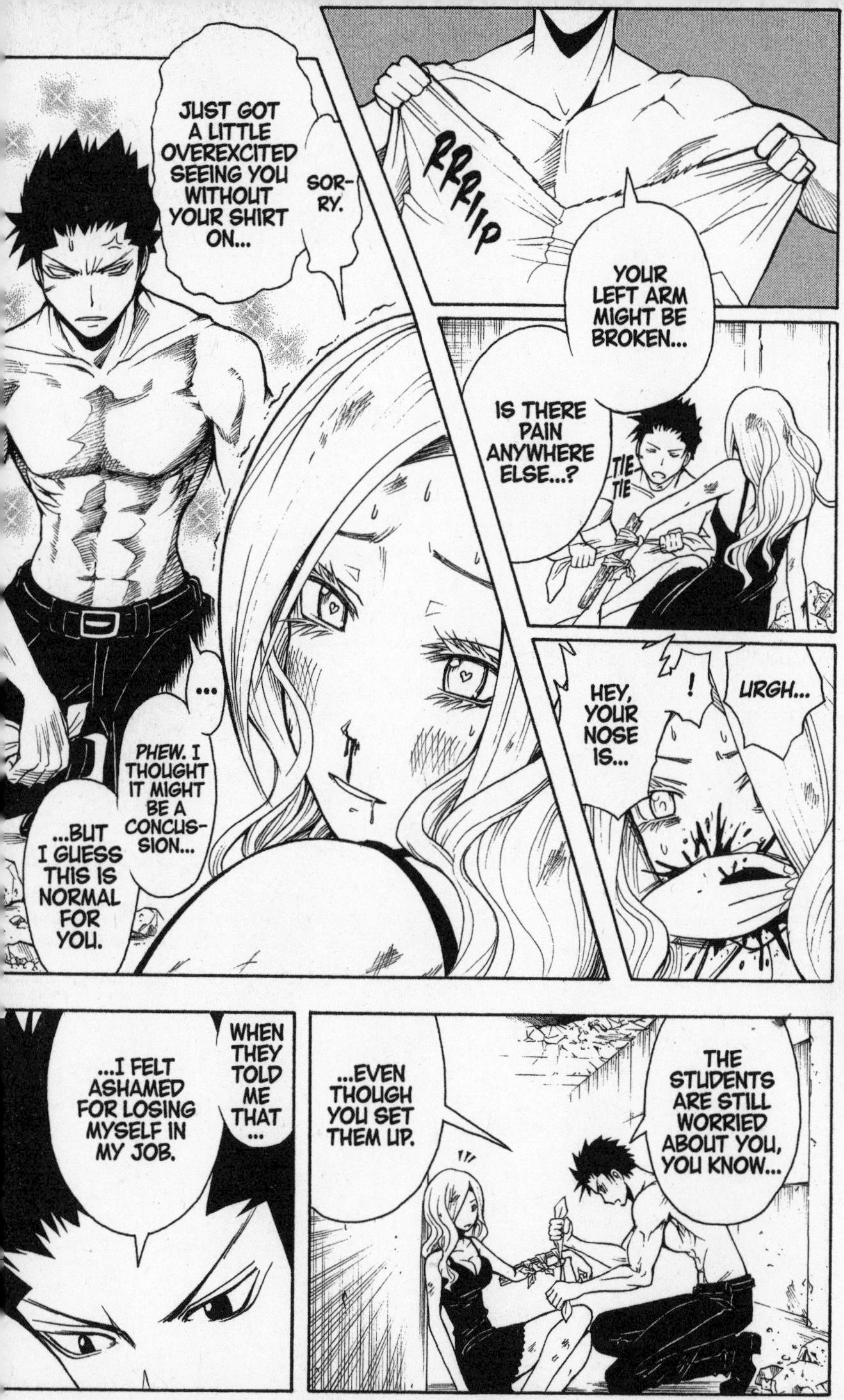
RRRIIP
YOUR LEFT ARM MIGHT BE BROKEN...
IS THERE PAIN ANYWHERE ELSE...?
TIE TIE
HEY, YOUR NOSE IS...
!
URGH...
...
PHEW. I THOUGHT IT MIGHT BE A CONCUSSION...
...BUT I GUESS THIS IS NORMAL FOR YOU.
JUST GOT A LITTLE OVEREXCITED SEEING YOU WITHOUT YOUR SHIRT ON...
SOR-RY.
THE STUDENTS ARE STILL WORRIED ABOUT YOU, YOU KNOW...
...EVEN THOUGH YOU SET THEM UP.
WHEN THEY TOLD ME THAT...
...I FELT ASHAMED FOR LOSING MYSELF IN MY JOB.

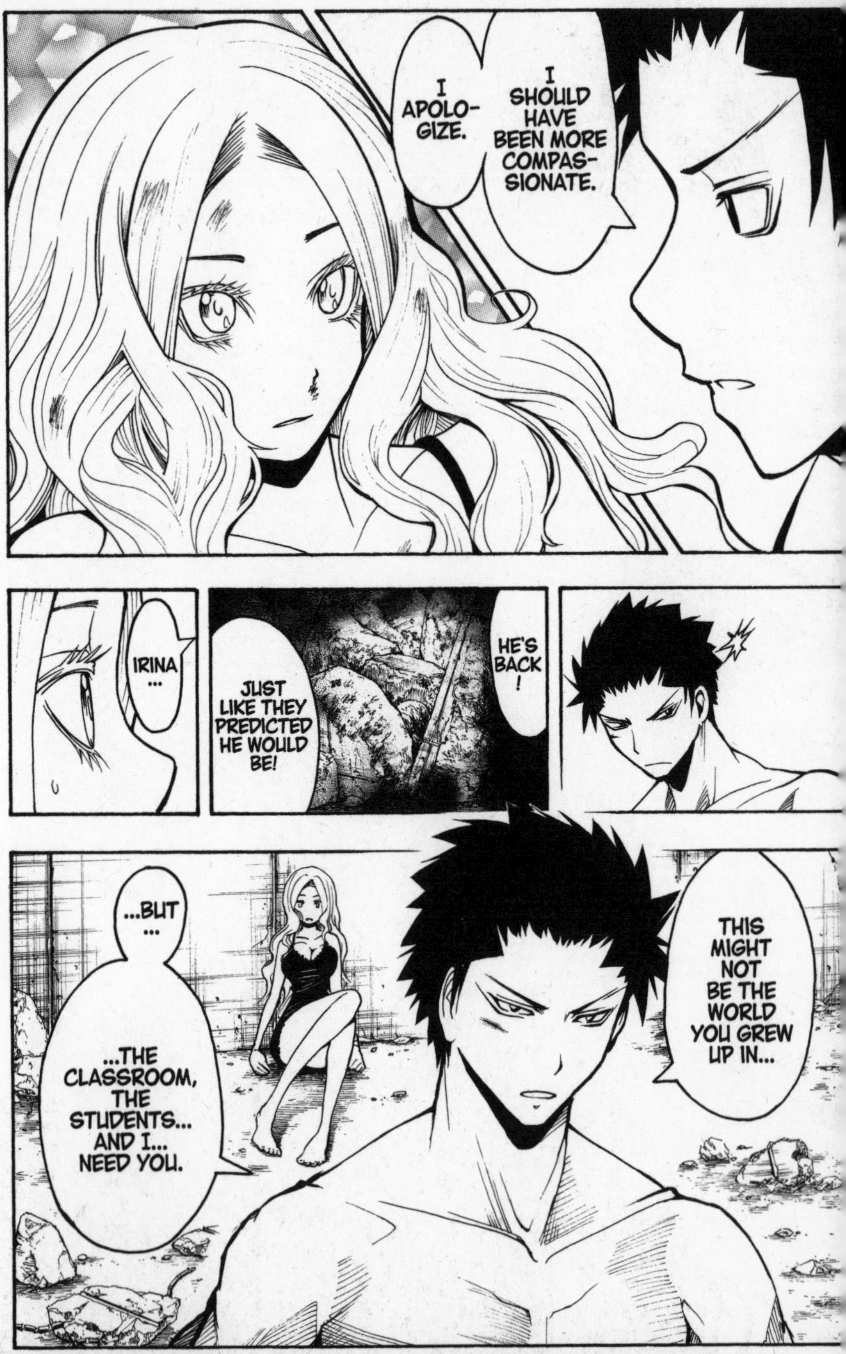
I SHOULD HAVE BEEN MORE COMPASSIONATE.
I APOLOGIZE.
HE'S BACK!
JUST LIKE THEY PREDICTED HE WOULD BE!
IRINA...
THIS MIGHT NOT BE THE WORLD YOU GREW UP IN...
...BUT...
...THE CLASSROOM, THE STUDENTS... AND I... NEED YOU.

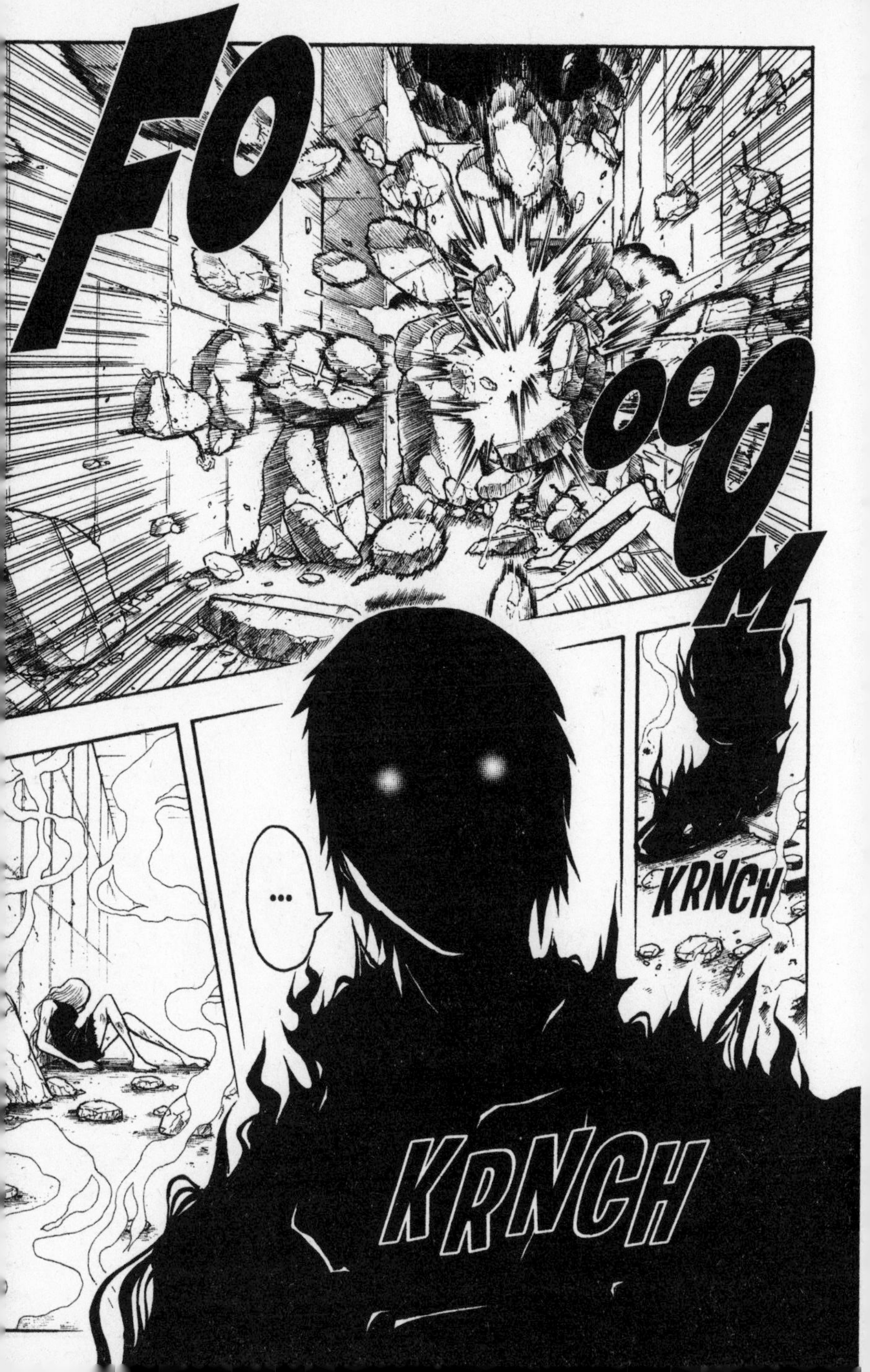
FOOOOM
KRNCH
...
KRNCH

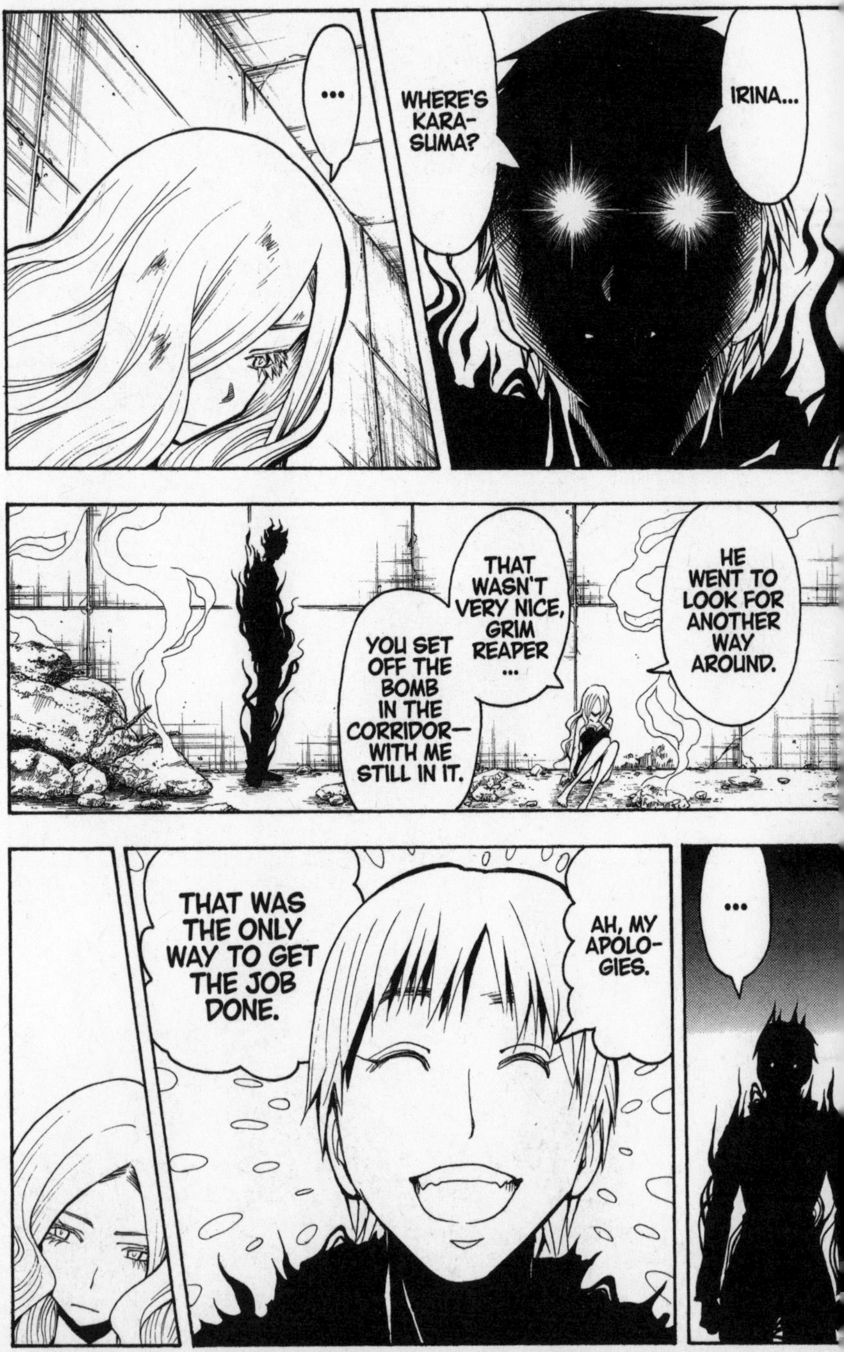
IRINA...
WHERE'S KARA-SUMA?
...
HE WENT TO LOOK FOR ANOTHER WAY AROUND.
THAT WASN'T VERY NICE, GRIM REAPER...
YOU SET OFF THE BOMB IN THE CORRIDOR—WITH ME STILL IN IT.
...
AH, MY APOLO-GIES.
THAT WAS THE ONLY WAY TO GET THE JOB DONE.

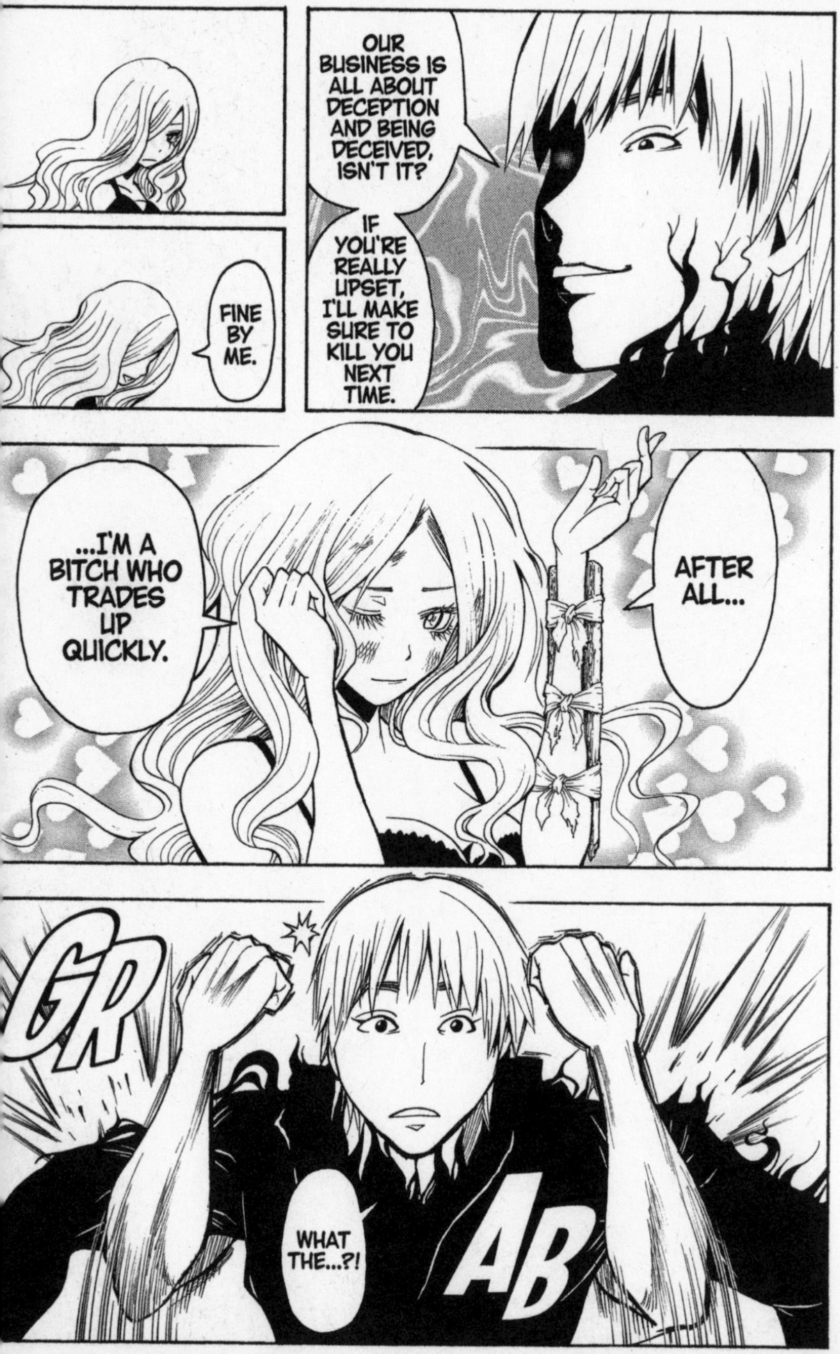
OUR BUSINESS IS ALL ABOUT DECEPTION AND BEING DECEIVED, ISN'T IT?
IF YOU'RE REALLY UPSET, I'LL MAKE SURE TO KILL YOU NEXT TIME.
FINE BY ME.
AFTER ALL...
...I'M A BITCH WHO TRADES UP QUICKLY.
GR
AB
WHAT THE...?!

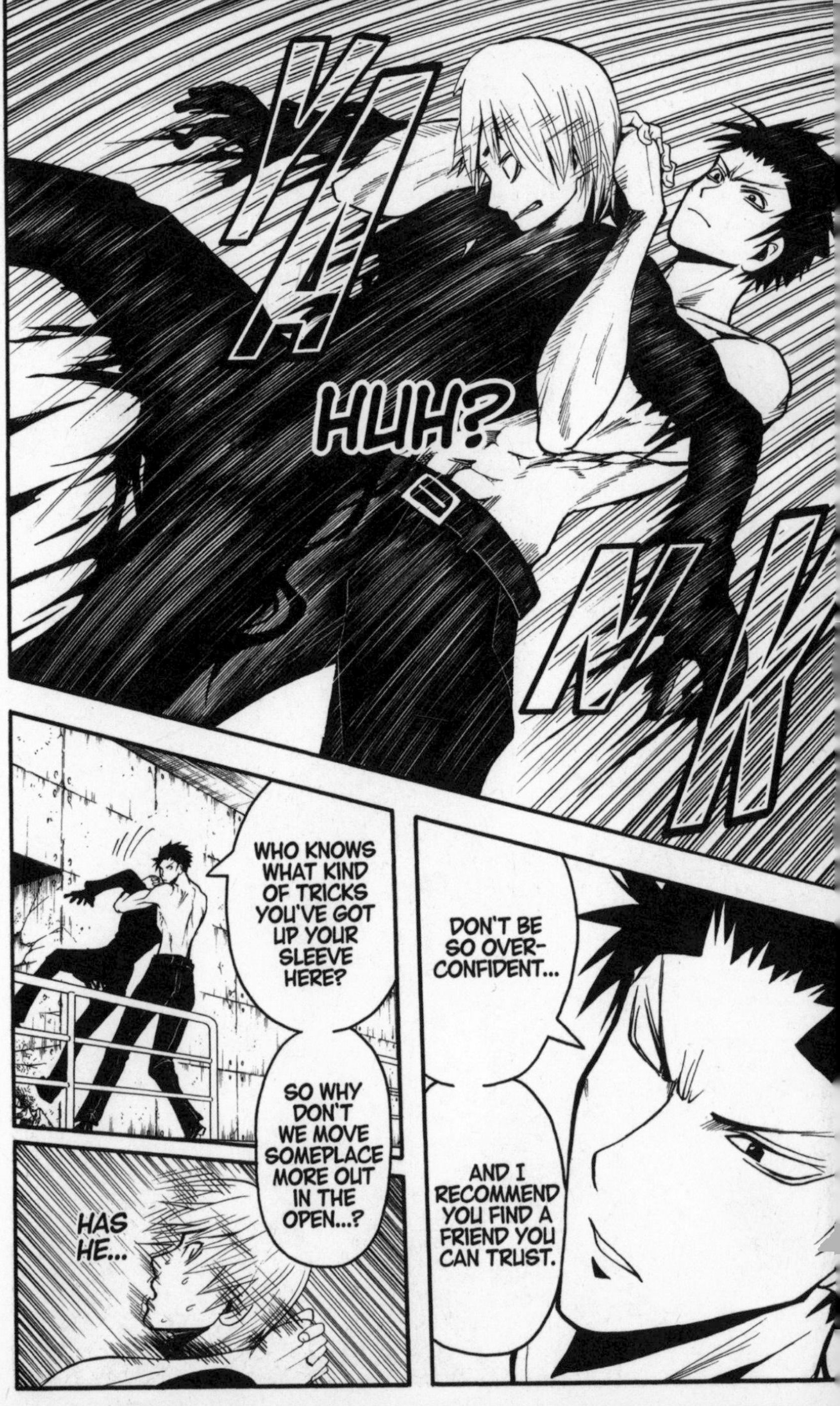
HUH?
DON'T BE SO OVER-CONFIDENT...
AND I RECOMMEND YOU FIND A FRIEND YOU CAN TRUST.
WHO KNOWS WHAT KIND OF TRICKS YOU'VE GOT UP YOUR SLEEVE HERE?
SO WHY DON'T WE MOVE SOMEPLACE MORE OUT IN THE OPEN...?
HAS HE...

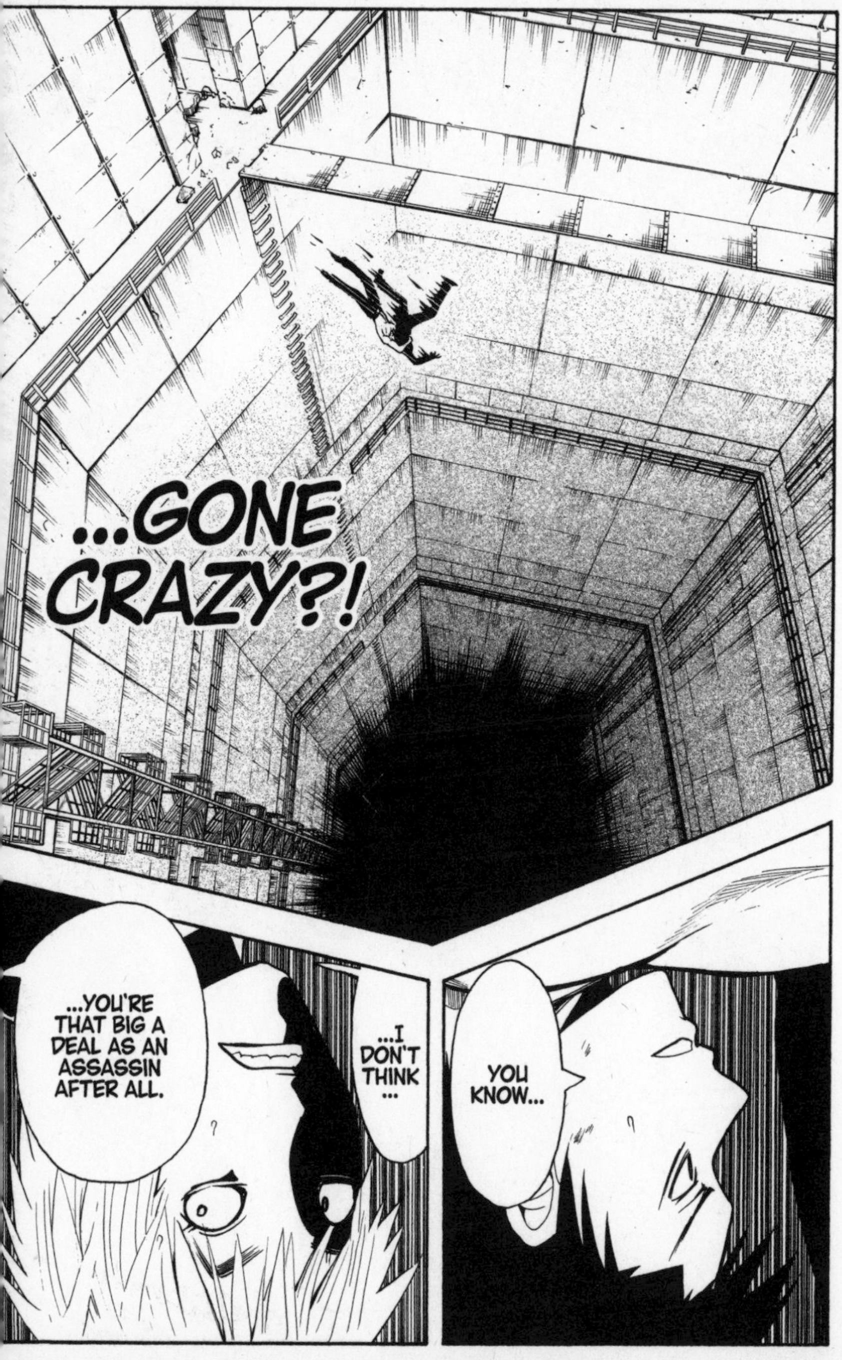
...GONE CRAZY?!
YOU KNOW...
...I DON'T THINK...
...YOU'RE THAT BIG A DEAL AS AN ASSASSIN AFTER ALL.

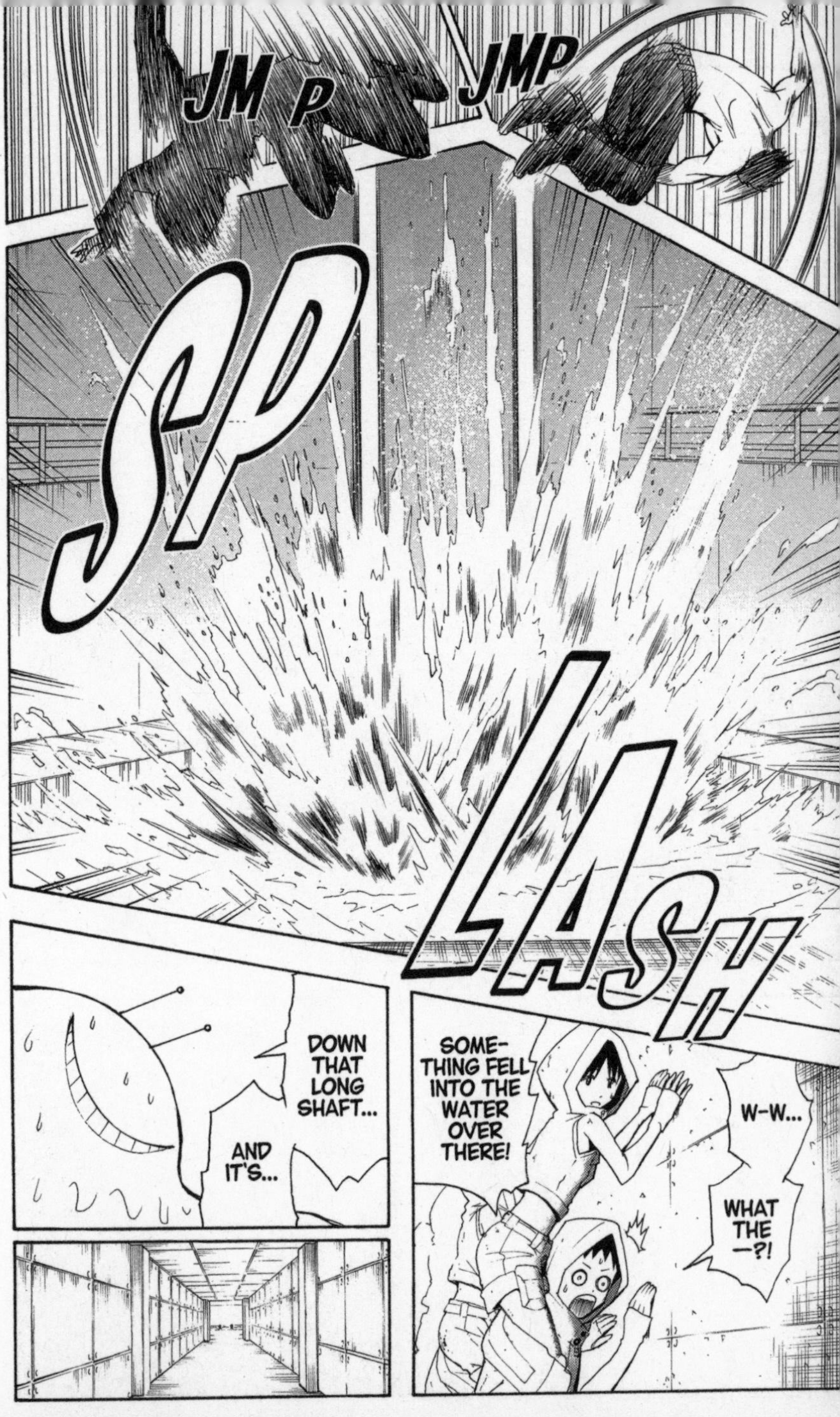
JMP
JM P
SPLASH
W-W...
WHAT THE—?!
SOMETHING FELL INTO THE WATER OVER THERE!
DOWN THAT LONG SHAFT...
AND IT'S...

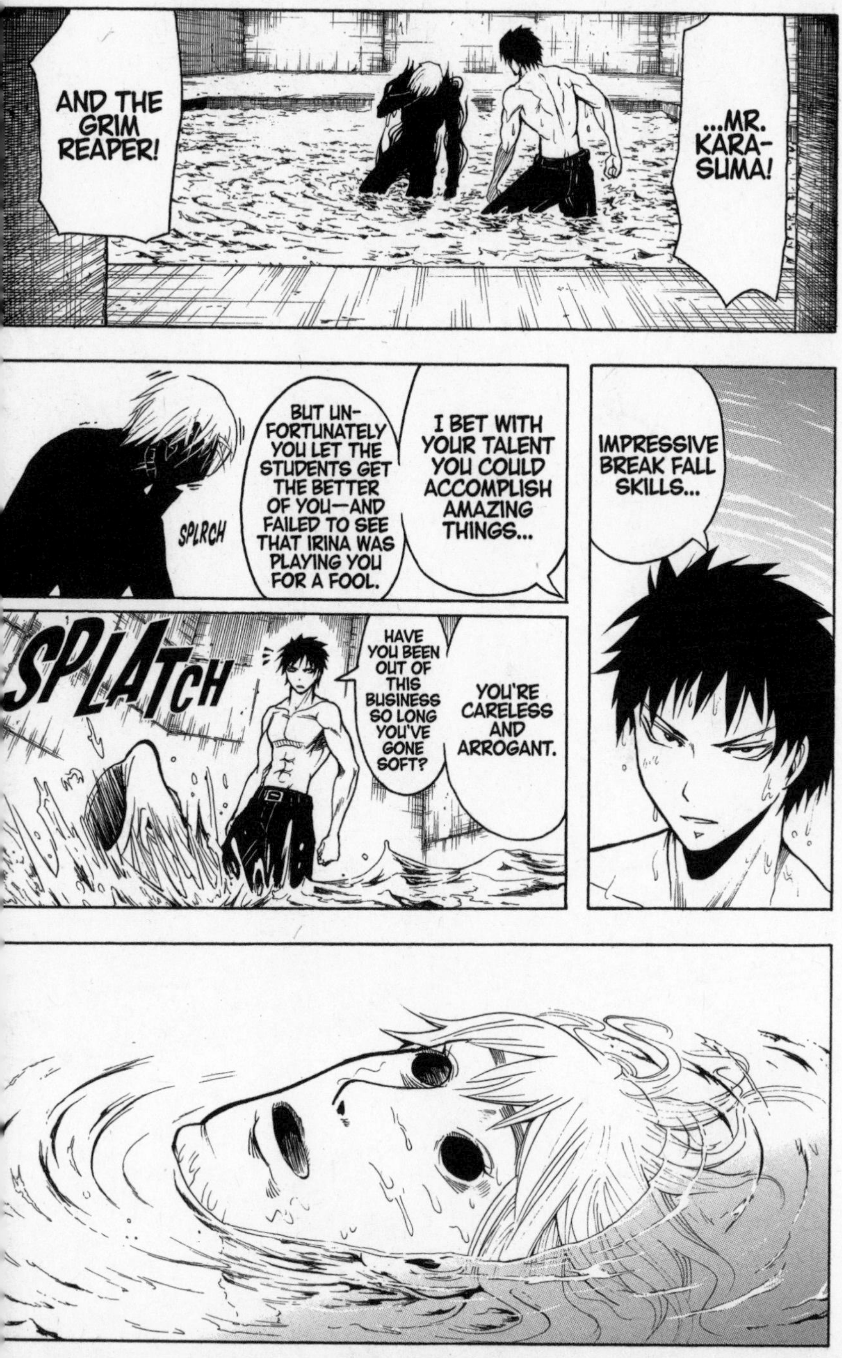
...MR. KARA-SUMA!
AND THE GRIM REAPER!
IMPRESSIVE BREAK FALL SKILLS...
I BET WITH YOUR TALENT YOU COULD ACCOMPLISH AMAZING THINGS...
BUT UN-FORTUNATELY YOU LET THE STUDENTS GET THE BETTER OF YOU—AND FAILED TO SEE THAT IRINA WAS PLAYING YOU FOR A FOOL.
SPLRCH
YOU'RE CARELESS AND ARROGANT.
HAVE YOU BEEN OUT OF THIS BUSINESS SO LONG YOU'VE GONE SOFT?
SPLATCH

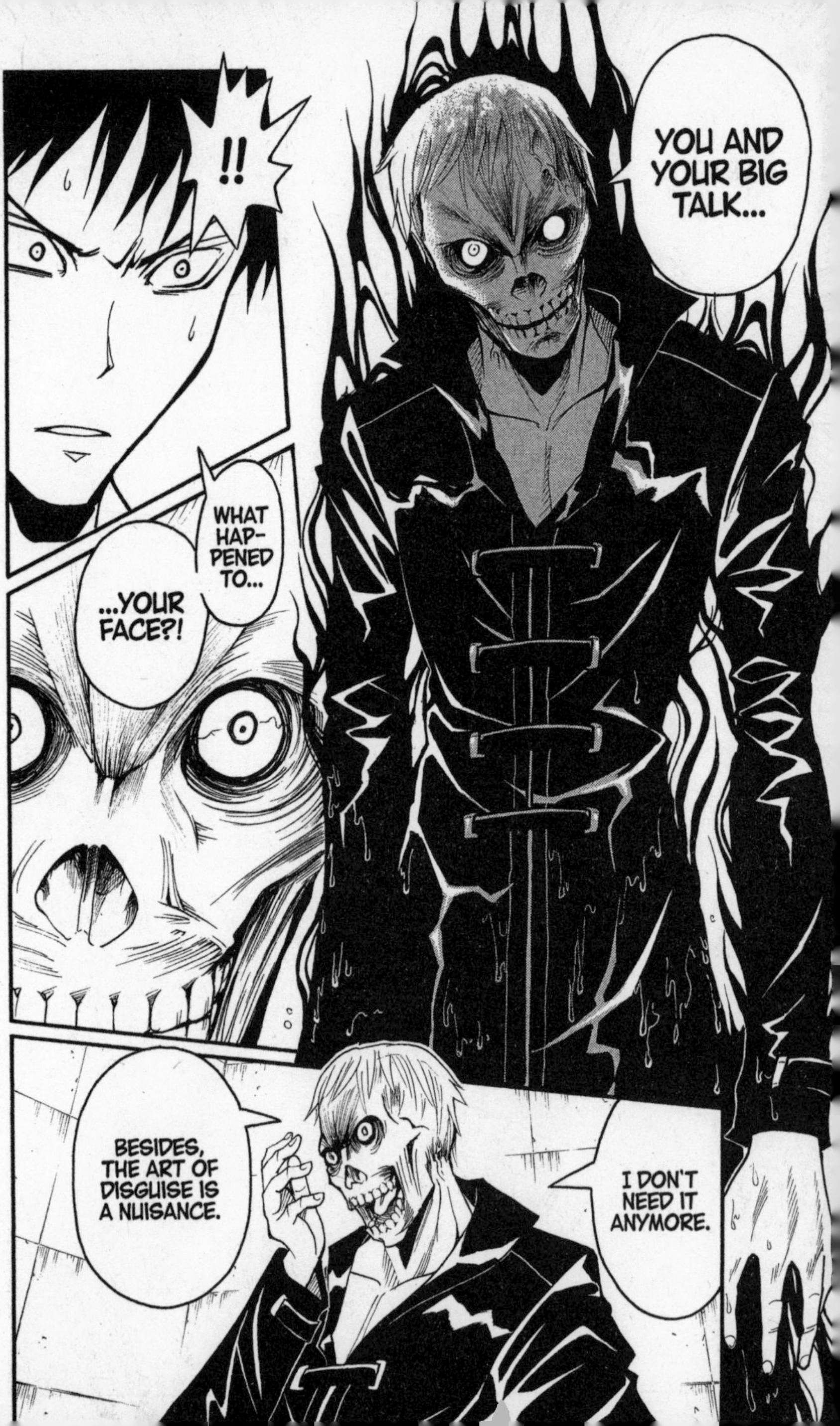
YOU AND YOUR BIG TALK...
!!
WHAT HAP-PENED TO...
...YOUR FACE?!
I DON'T NEED IT ANYMORE.
BESIDES, THE ART OF DISGUISE IS A NUISANCE.

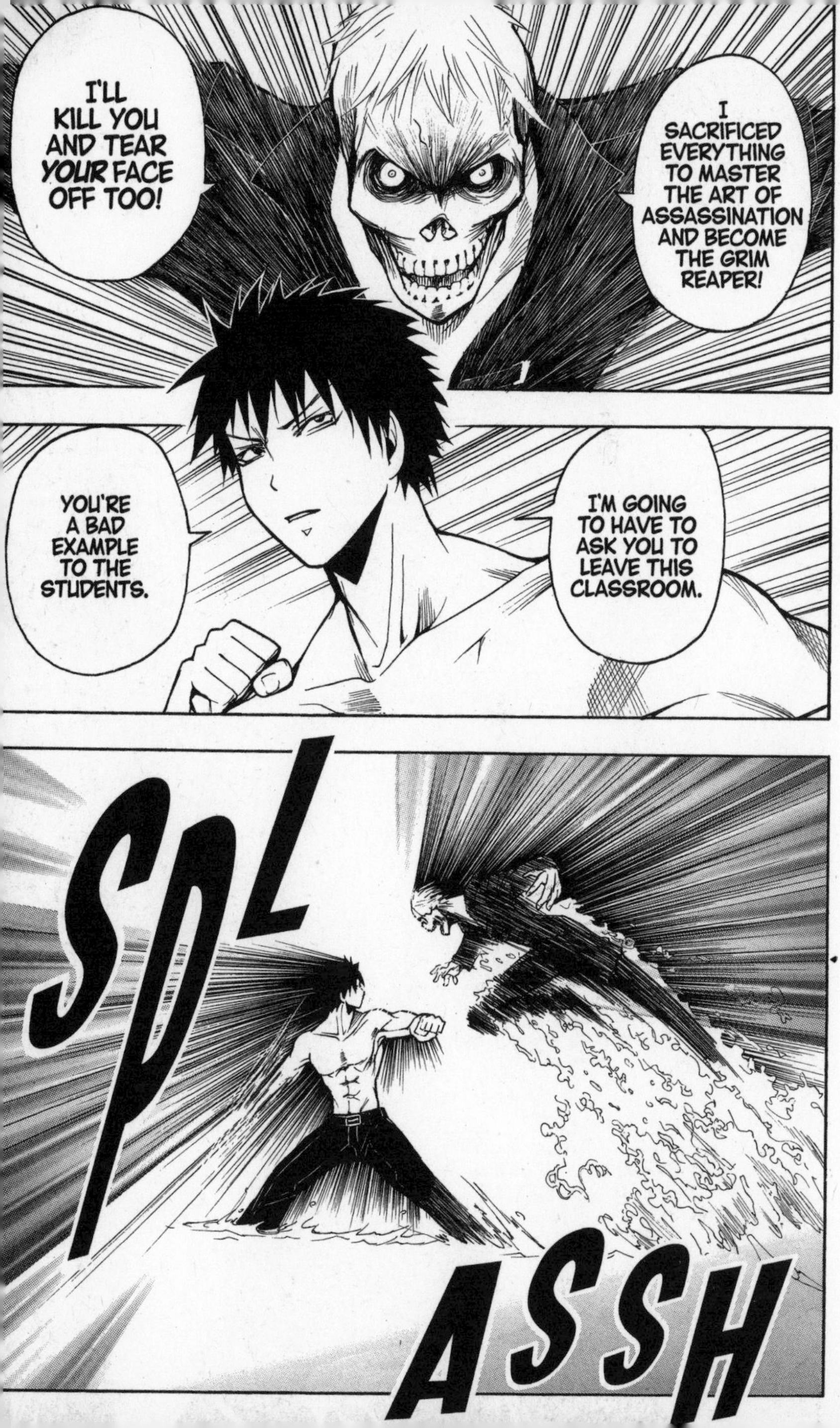
I SACRIFICED EVERYTHING TO MASTER THE ART OF ASSASSINATION AND BECOME THE GRIM REAPER!
I'LL KILL YOU AND TEAR *YOUR* FACE OFF TOO!
I'M GOING TO HAVE TO ASK YOU TO LEAVE THIS CLASSROOM.
YOU'RE A BAD EXAMPLE TO THE STUDENTS.
SPLASSH

E-12 SOSUKE SUGAYA

🙂 BIRTHDAY: OCTOBER 25

🙂 HEIGHT: 5' 10"

🙂 WEIGHT: 130 LBS.

🙂 FAVORITE SUBJECT: ART

🙂 LEAST FAVORITE SUBJECT: ALL SCIENCE SUBJECTS

🙂 HOBBY/SKILLS: GRAFFITI

🙂 FUTURE GOAL: ARTIST

🙂 HIS BIGGEST MOST RECENT TAG: SNEAKING INTO THE
   AUDIOVISUAL ROOM OF THE MAIN SCHOOL BUILDING
   AND TURNING IT INTO A KARAOKE LOUNGE WITH
   LASSEN-STYLE ARTWORK EXECUTED IN LUMINOUS PAINT

Class 109 Time for the Grim Reaper—9th Period

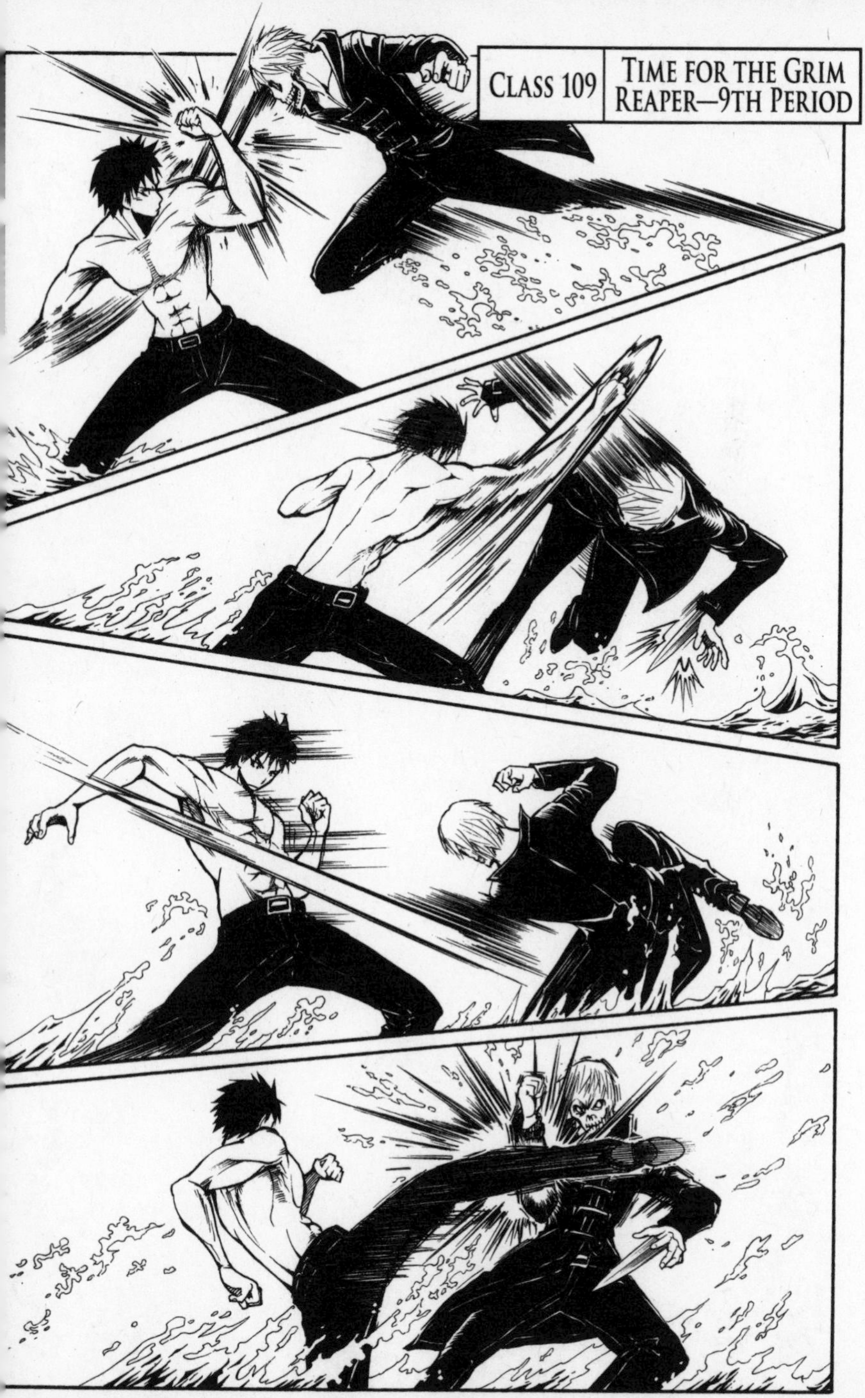

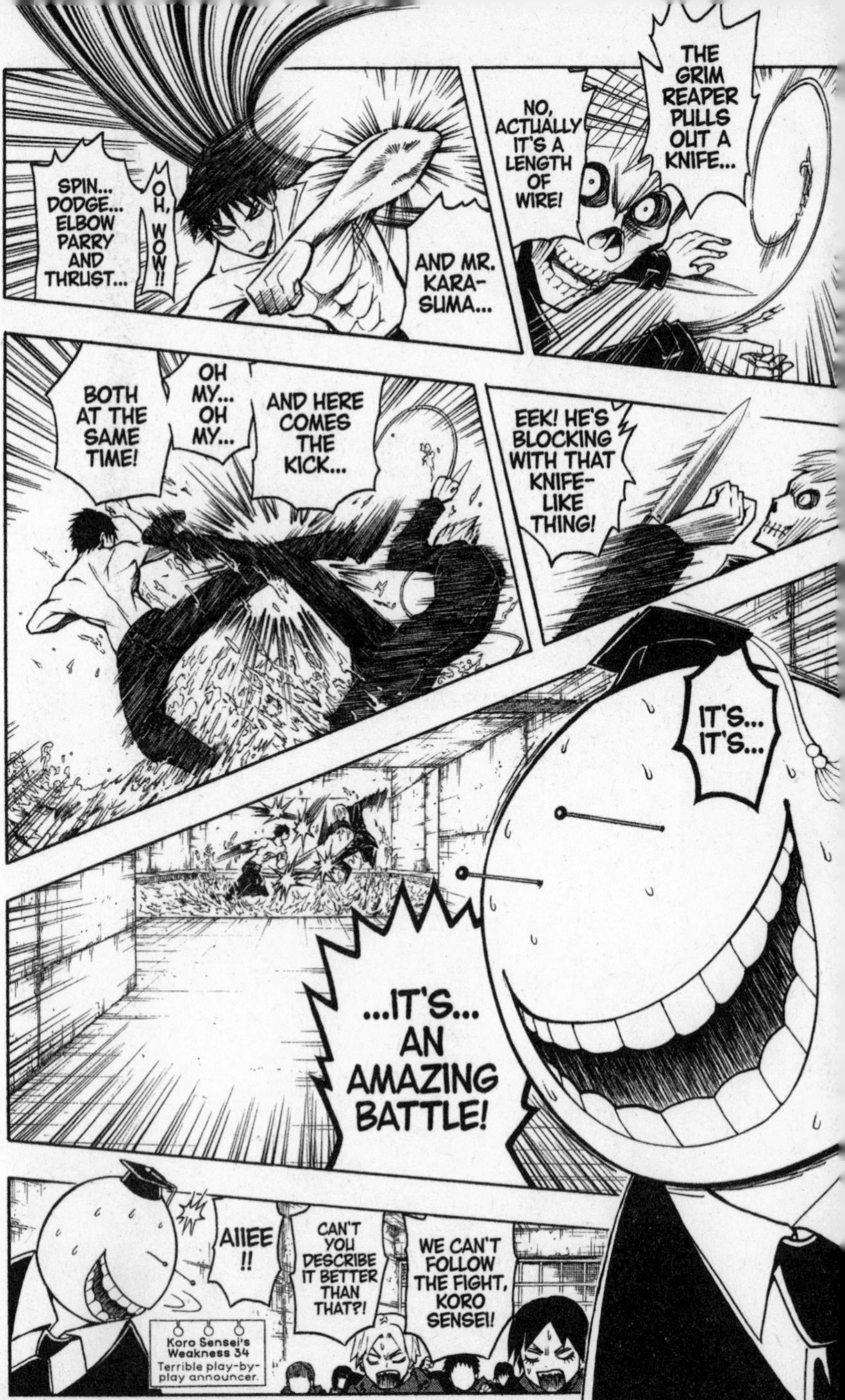
THE GRIM REAPER PULLS OUT A KNIFE...
NO, ACTUALLY IT'S A LENGTH OF WIRE!
AND MR. KARASUMA...
OH, WOW!!
SPIN... DODGE... ELBOW PARRY AND THRUST...
EEK! HE'S BLOCKING WITH THAT KNIFE-LIKE THING!
AND HERE COMES THE KICK...
OH MY... OH MY...
BOTH AT THE SAME TIME!
IT'S... IT'S...
...IT'S... AN AMAZING BATTLE!
WE CAN'T FOLLOW THE FIGHT, KORO SENSEI!
CAN'T YOU DESCRIBE IT BETTER THAN THAT?!
AIIEE!!
Koro Sensei's Weakness 34
Terrible play-by-play announcer.

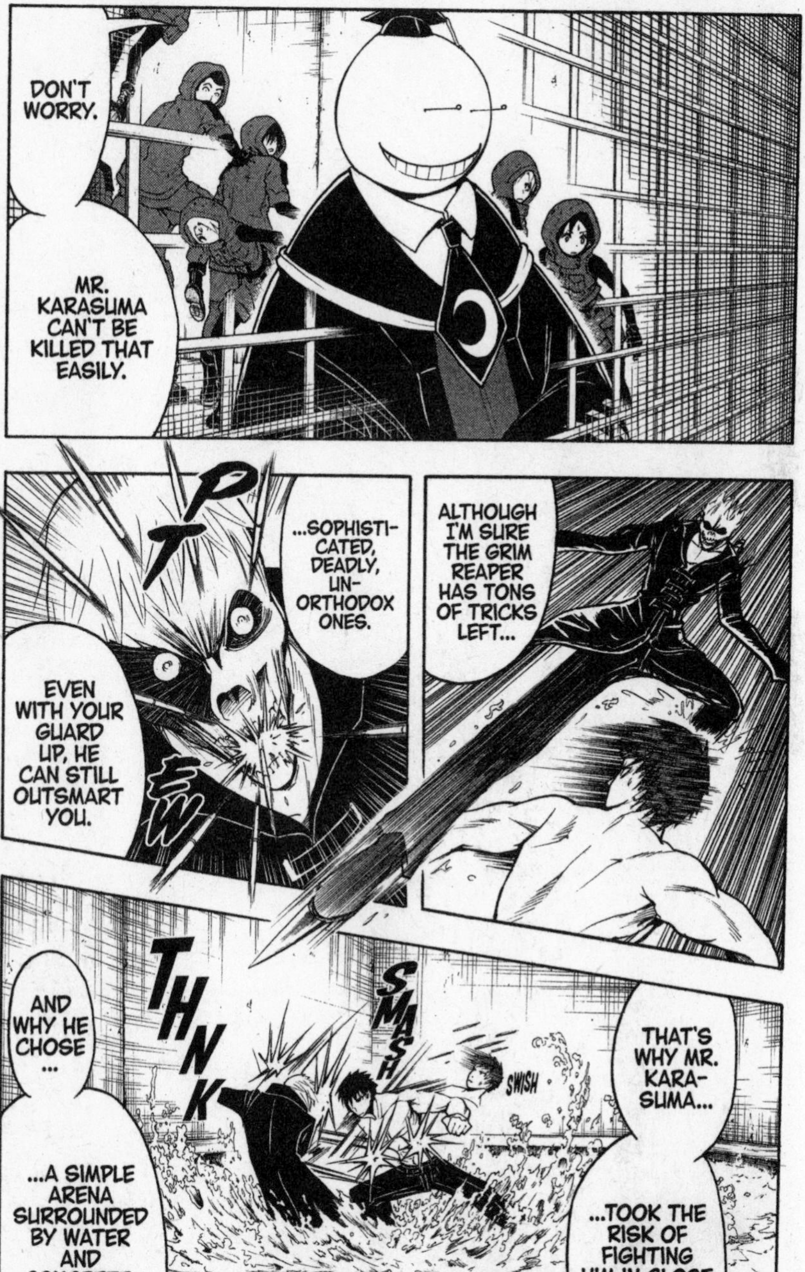
DON'T WORRY.
MR. KARASUMA CAN'T BE KILLED THAT EASILY.
ALTHOUGH I'M SURE THE GRIM REAPER HAS TONS OF TRICKS LEFT...
...SOPHISTI-CATED, DEADLY, UN-ORTHODOX ONES.
PT
EVEN WITH YOUR GUARD UP, HE CAN STILL OUTSMART YOU.
THAT'S WHY MR. KARA-SUMA...
...TOOK THE RISK OF FIGHTING HIM IN CLOSE COMBAT.
SWISH
SMASH
THNK
AND WHY HE CHOSE...
...A SIMPLE ARENA SURROUNDED BY WATER AND CONCRETE.

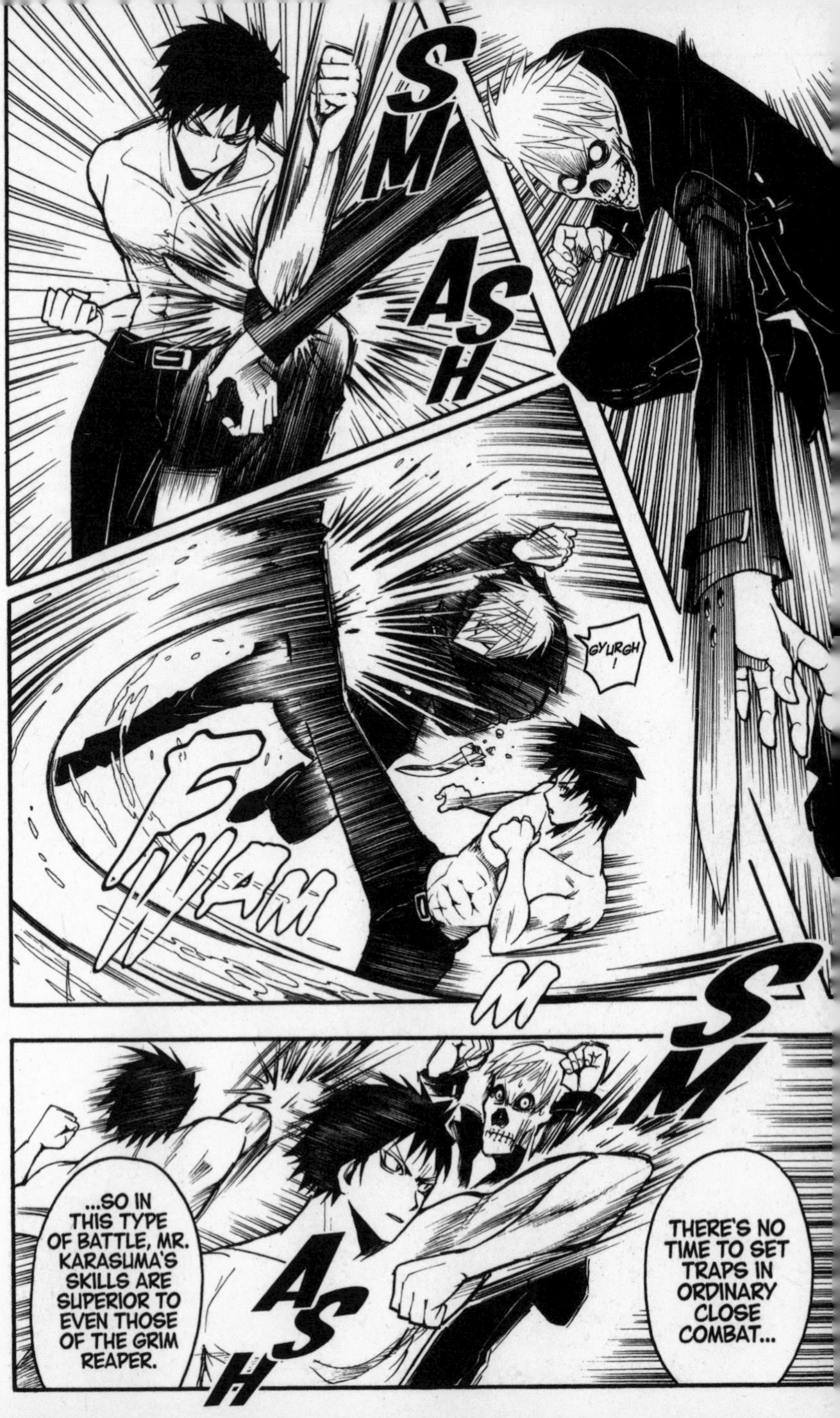
SMASH
GYURGH!
WHAM
SMASH
THERE'S NO TIME TO SET TRAPS IN ORDINARY CLOSE COMBAT...
...SO IN THIS TYPE OF BATTLE, MR. KARASUMA'S SKILLS ARE SUPERIOR TO EVEN THOSE OF THE GRIM REAPER.

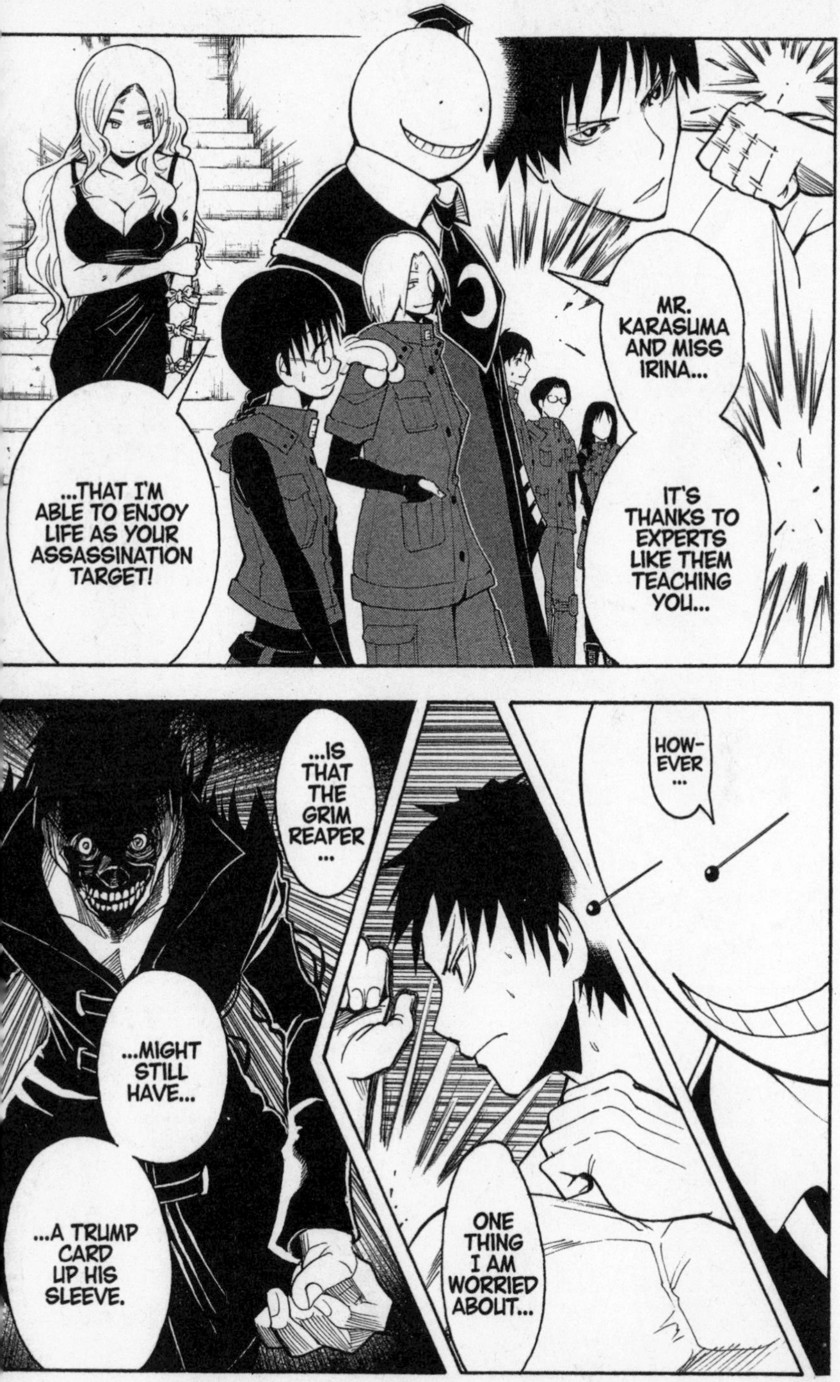
MR. KARASUMA AND MISS IRINA...
IT'S THANKS TO EXPERTS LIKE THEM TEACHING YOU...
...THAT I'M ABLE TO ENJOY LIFE AS YOUR ASSASSINATION TARGET!
HOW-EVER...
ONE THING I AM WORRIED ABOUT...
...IS THAT THE GRIM REAPER...
...MIGHT STILL HAVE...
...A TRUMP CARD UP HIS SLEEVE.

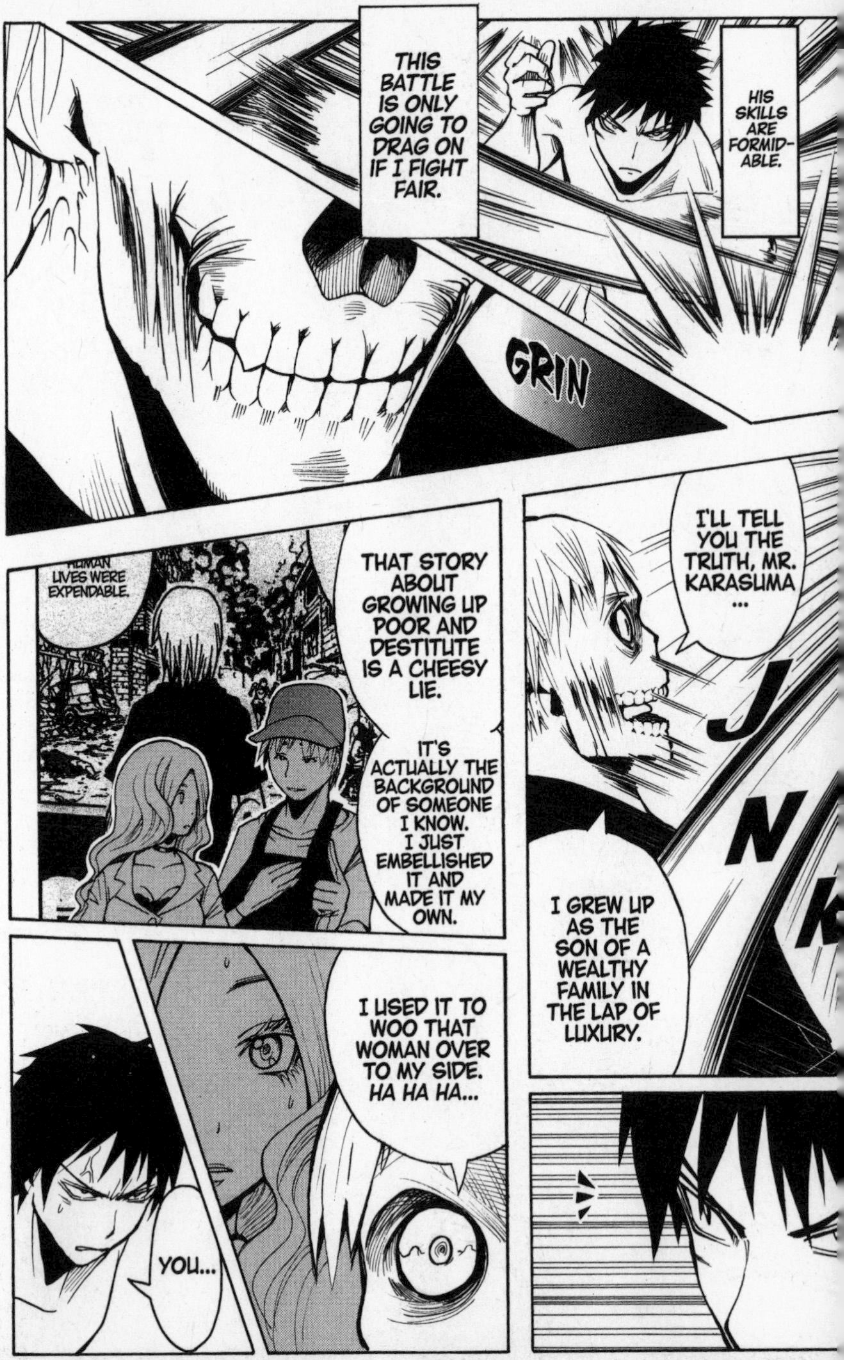
HIS SKILLS ARE FORMID-ABLE.
THIS BATTLE IS ONLY GOING TO DRAG ON IF I FIGHT FAIR.
GRIN
I'LL TELL YOU THE TRUTH, MR. KARASUMA...
I GREW UP AS THE SON OF A WEALTHY FAMILY IN THE LAP OF LUXURY.
THAT STORY ABOUT GROWING UP POOR AND DESTITUTE IS A CHEESY LIE.
IT'S ACTUALLY THE BACKGROUND OF SOMEONE I KNOW. I JUST EMBELLISHED IT AND MADE IT MY OWN.
LIVES WERE EXPENDABLE.
I USED IT TO WOO THAT WOMAN OVER TO MY SIDE. HA HA HA...
YOU...

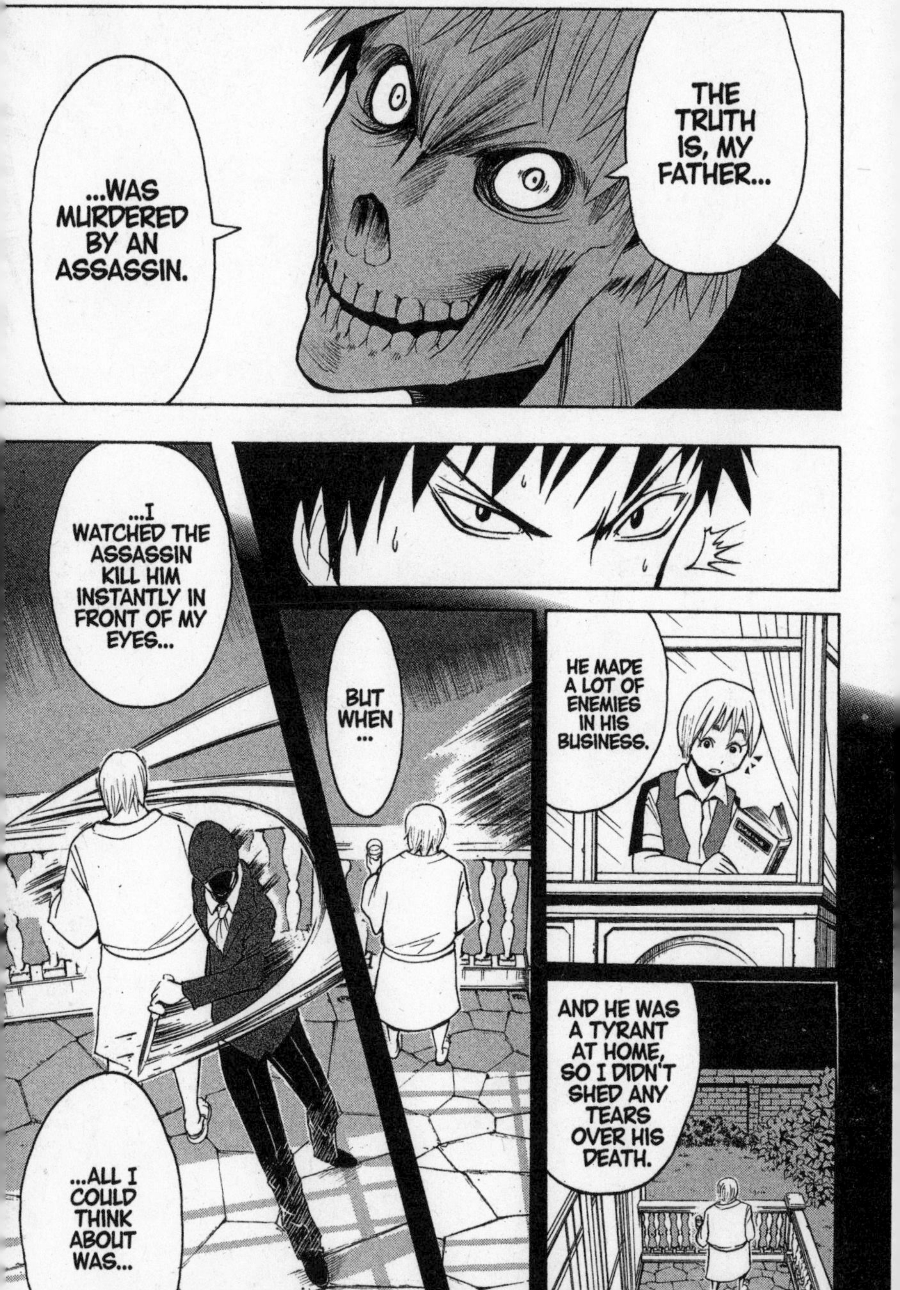
THE TRUTH IS, MY FATHER...
...WAS MURDERED BY AN ASSASSIN.
HE MADE A LOT OF ENEMIES IN HIS BUSINESS.
AND HE WAS A TYRANT AT HOME, SO I DIDN'T SHED ANY TEARS OVER HIS DEATH.
BUT WHEN...
...I WATCHED THE ASSASSIN KILL HIM INSTANTLY IN FRONT OF MY EYES...
...ALL I COULD THINK ABOUT WAS...

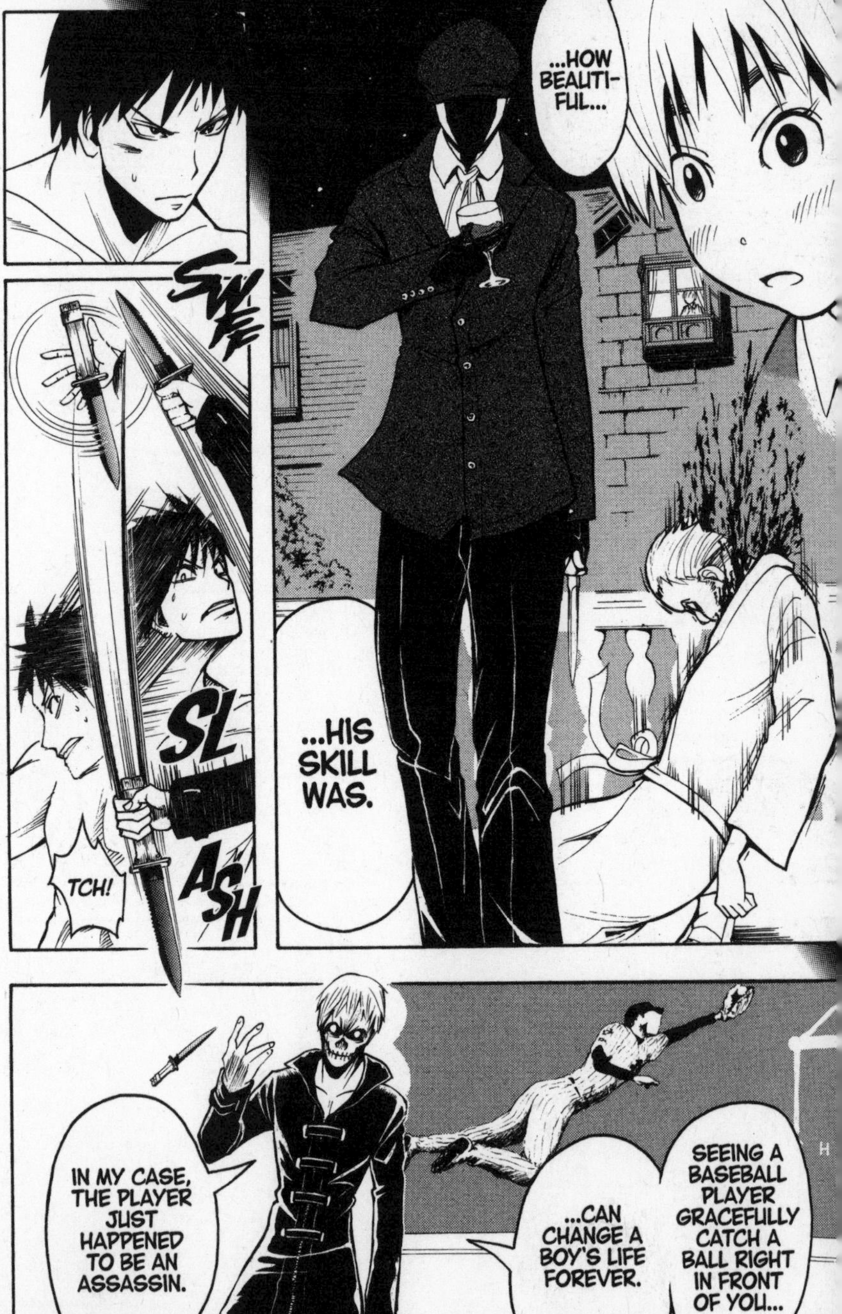
...HOW BEAUTIFUL...
...HIS SKILL WAS.
SWEE
SLASH
TCH!
SEEING A BASEBALL PLAYER GRACEFULLY CATCH A BALL RIGHT IN FRONT OF YOU...
...CAN CHANGE A BOY'S LIFE FOREVER.
IN MY CASE, THE PLAYER JUST HAPPENED TO BE AN ASSASSIN.

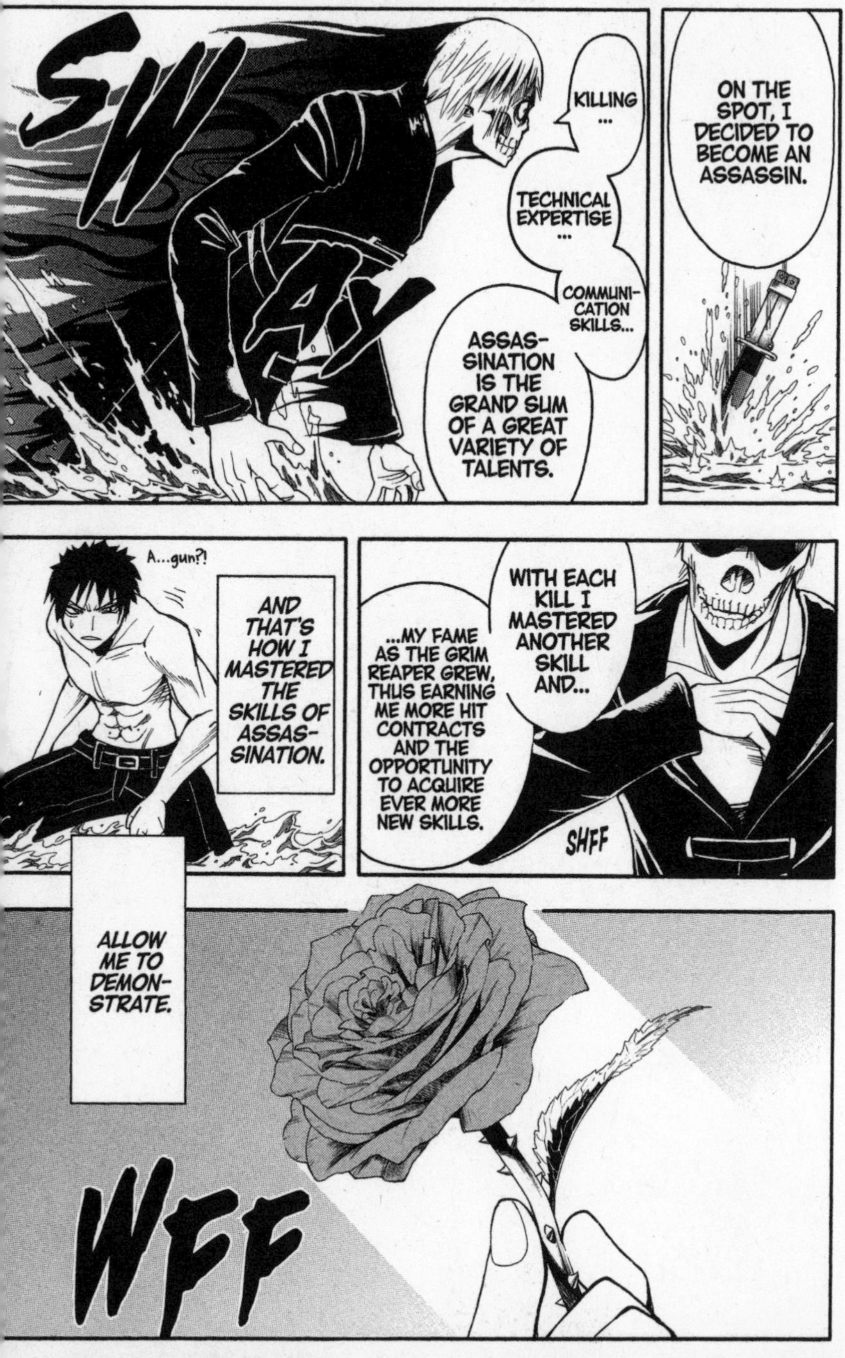
ON THE SPOT, I DECIDED TO BECOME AN ASSASSIN.
KILLING...
TECHNICAL EXPERTISE...
COMMUNICATION SKILLS...
ASSASSINATION IS THE GRAND SUM OF A GREAT VARIETY OF TALENTS.
SWAY
WITH EACH KILL I MASTERED ANOTHER SKILL AND...
...MY FAME AS THE GRIM REAPER GREW, THUS EARNING ME MORE HIT CONTRACTS AND THE OPPORTUNITY TO ACQUIRE EVER MORE NEW SKILLS.
SHFF
A...gun?!
AND THAT'S HOW I MASTERED THE SKILLS OF ASSASSINATION.
ALLOW ME TO DEMONSTRATE.
WFF

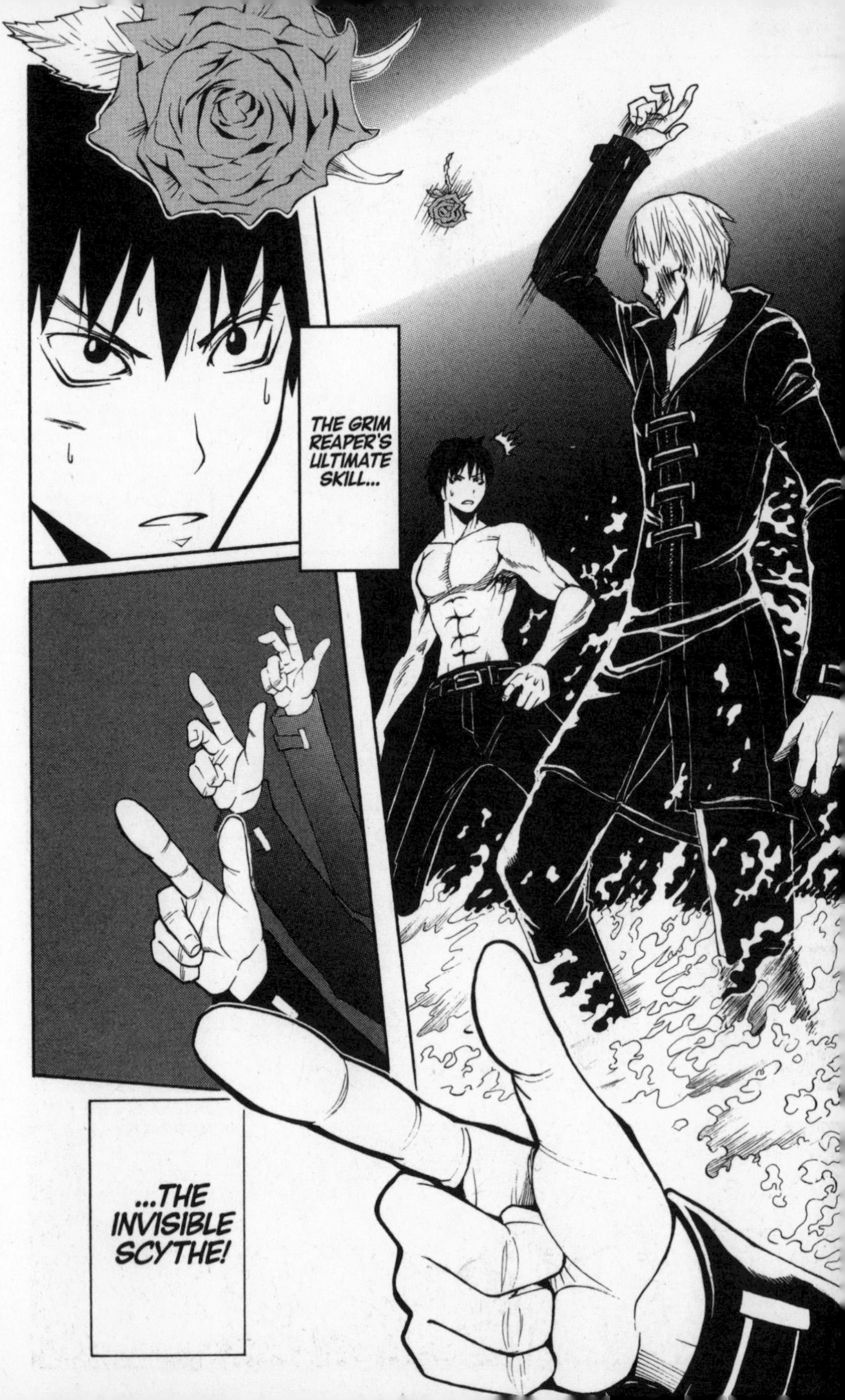
THE GRIM REAPER'S ULTIMATE SKILL...
...THE INVISIBLE SCYTHE!

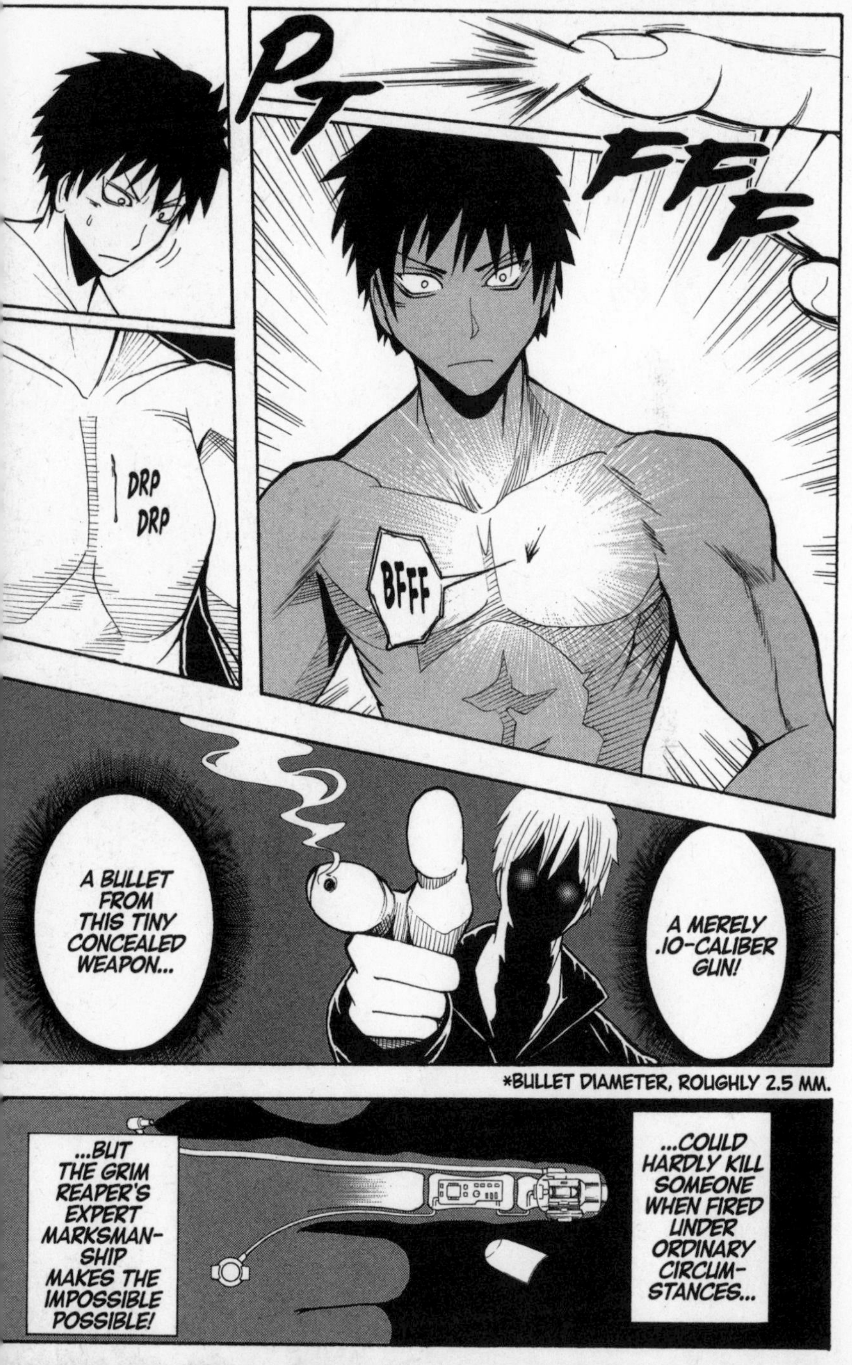
PTFFF
BFFF
DRP DRP
A MERELY .10-CALIBER GUN!
A BULLET FROM THIS TINY CONCEALED WEAPON...
*BULLET DIAMETER, ROUGHLY 2.5 MM.
...COULD HARDLY KILL SOMEONE WHEN FIRED UNDER ORDINARY CIRCUM-STANCES...
...BUT THE GRIM REAPER'S EXPERT MARKSMAN-SHIP MAKES THE IMPOSSIBLE POSSIBLE!

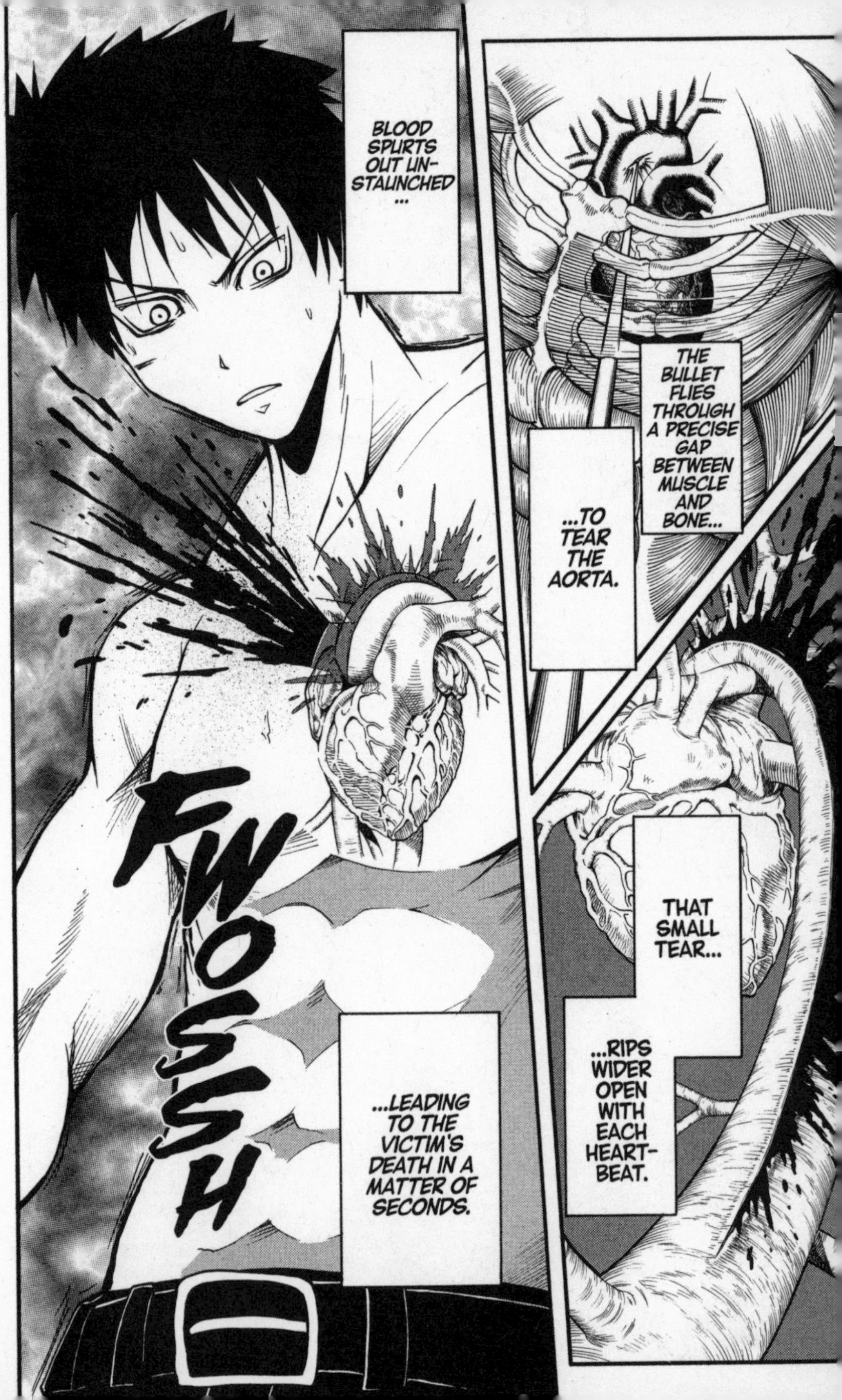
THE BULLET FLIES THROUGH A PRECISE GAP BETWEEN MUSCLE AND BONE...
...TO TEAR THE AORTA.
THAT SMALL TEAR...
...RIPS WIDER OPEN WITH EACH HEART-BEAT.
BLOOD SPURTS OUT UN-STAUNCHED...
FWOSSH
...LEADING TO THE VICTIM'S DEATH IN A MATTER OF SECONDS.

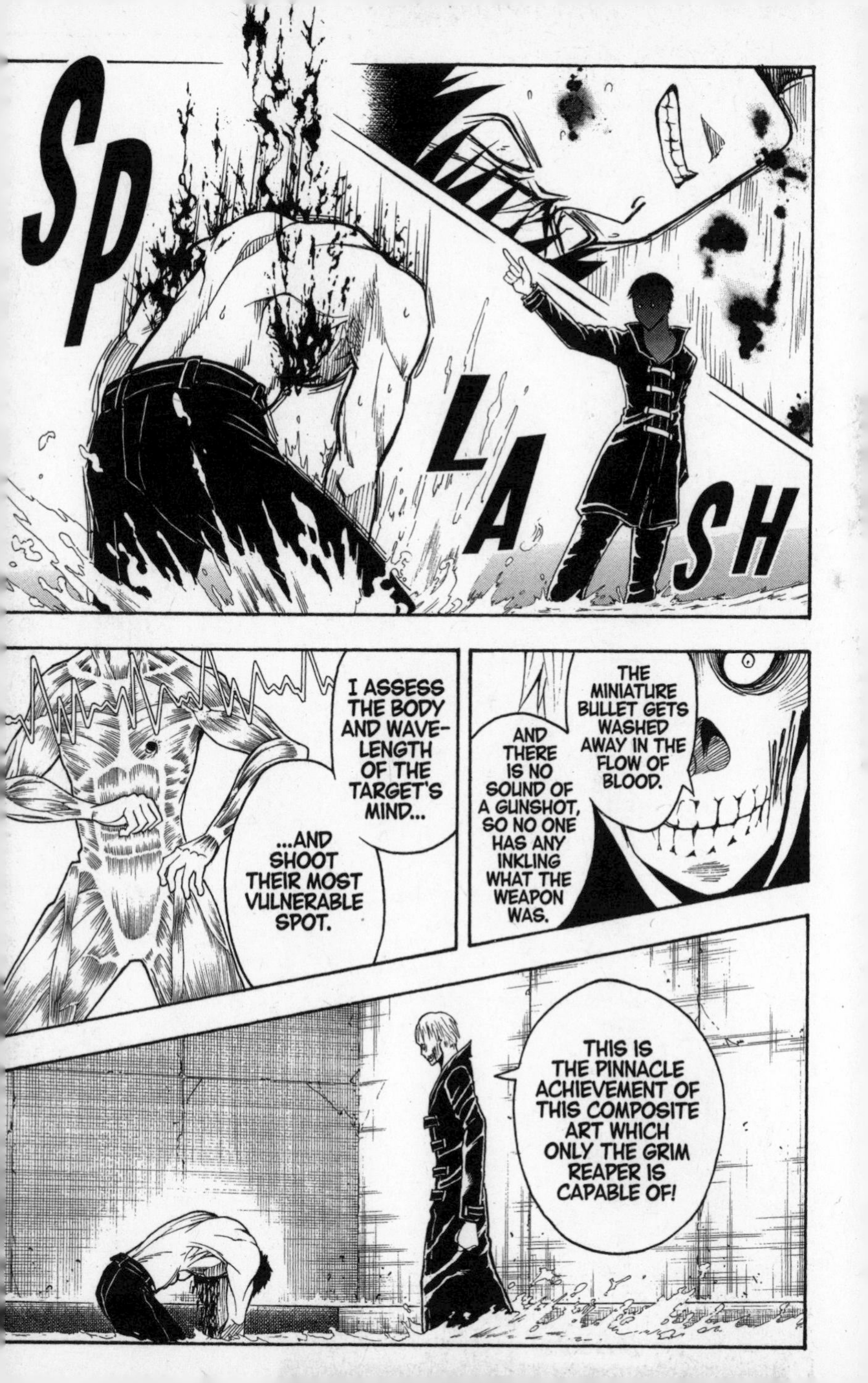
SPLASH
THE MINIATURE BULLET GETS WASHED AWAY IN THE FLOW OF BLOOD.
AND THERE IS NO SOUND OF A GUNSHOT, SO NO ONE HAS ANY INKLING WHAT THE WEAPON WAS.
I ASSESS THE BODY AND WAVE-LENGTH OF THE TARGET'S MIND...
...AND SHOOT THEIR MOST VULNERABLE SPOT.
THIS IS THE PINNACLE ACHIEVEMENT OF THIS COMPOSITE ART WHICH ONLY THE GRIM REAPER IS CAPABLE OF!

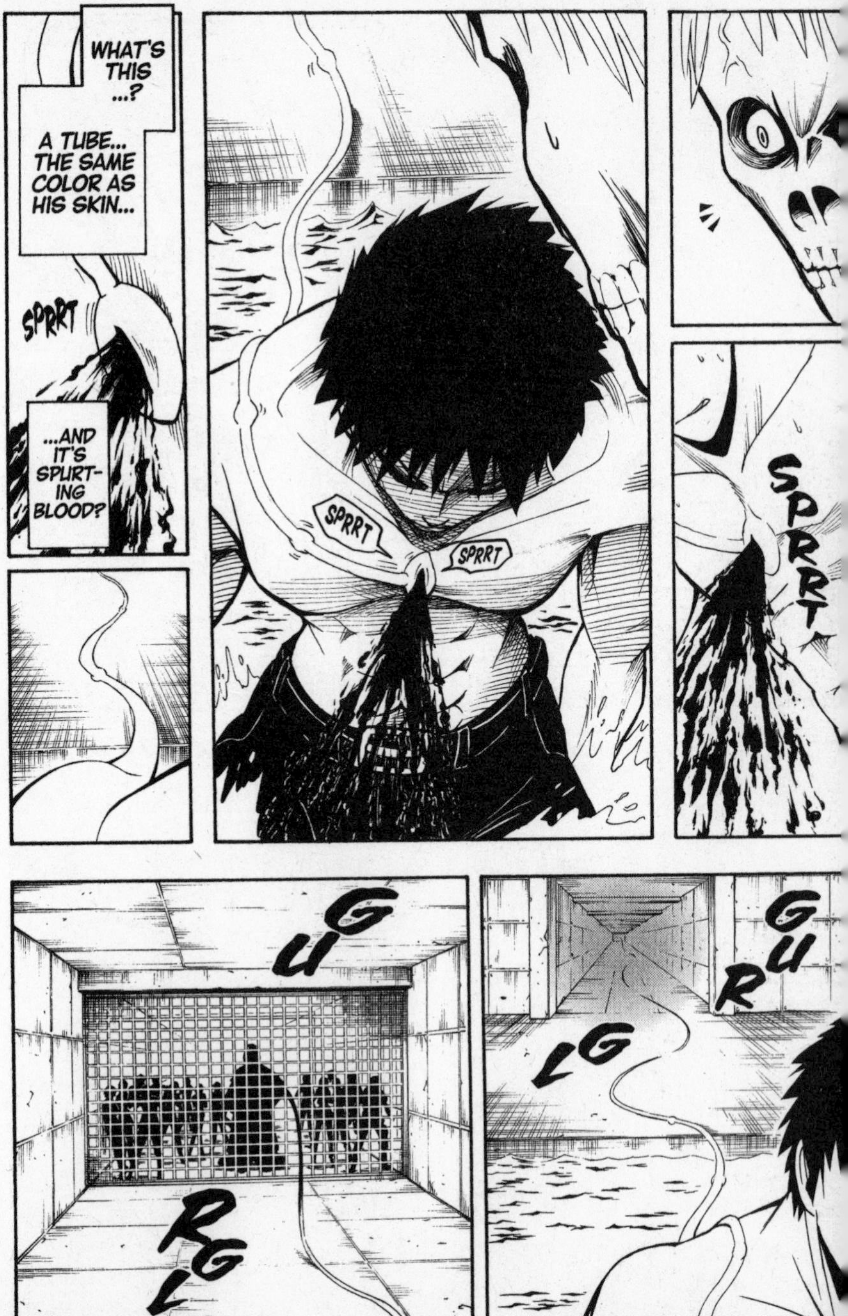
SPRRT
SPRRT
SPRRT
WHAT'S THIS ...?
A TUBE... THE SAME COLOR AS HIS SKIN...
SPRRT
...AND IT'S SPURT-ING BLOOD?
GUR
LG
GU
RGL

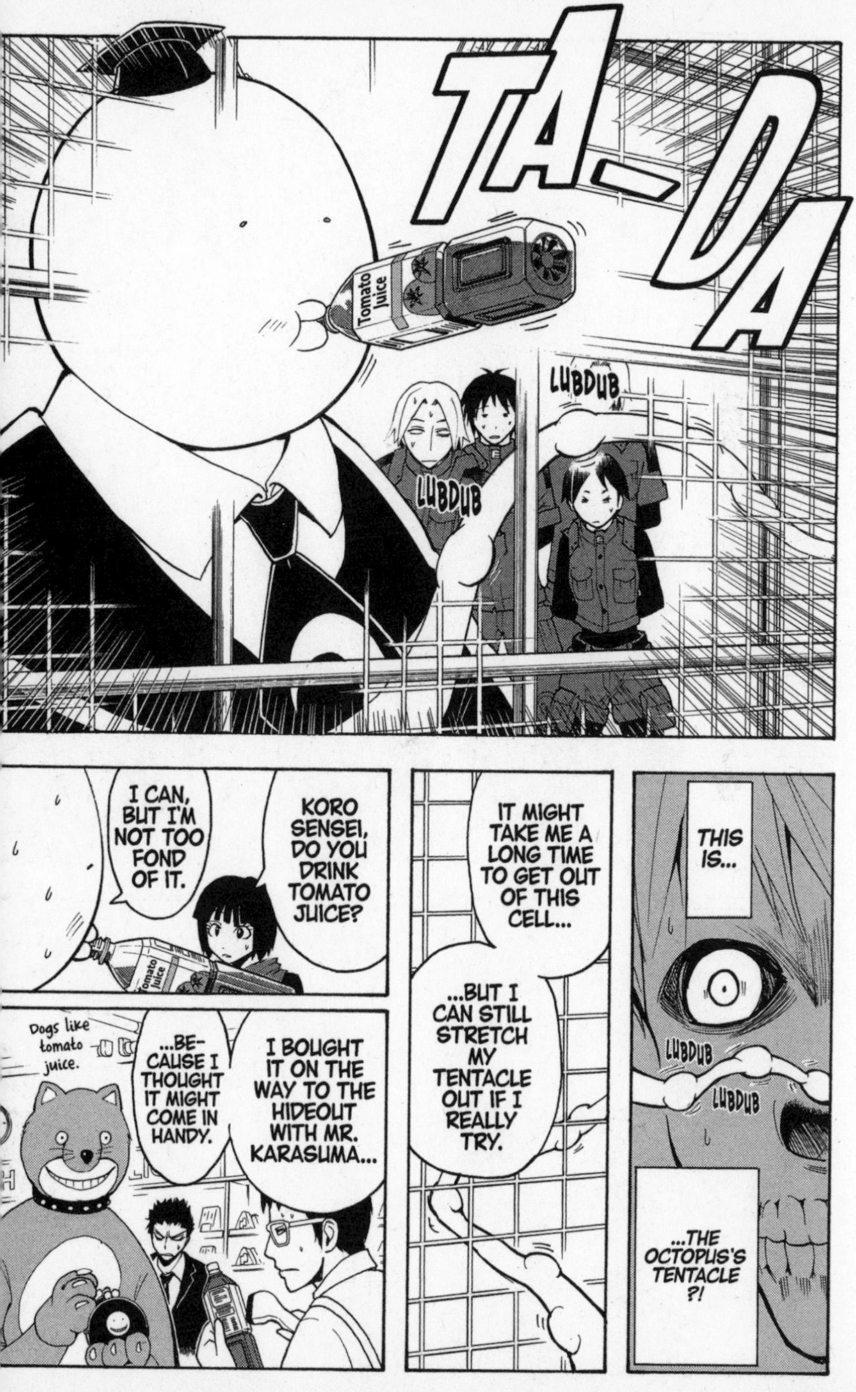
TA-DA
Tomato Juice
LUBDUB
LUBDUB
THIS IS...
LUBDUB
LUBDUB
...THE OCTOPUS'S TENTACLE ?!
IT MIGHT TAKE ME A LONG TIME TO GET OUT OF THIS CELL...
...BUT I CAN STILL STRETCH MY TENTACLE OUT IF I REALLY TRY.
KORO SENSEI, DO YOU DRINK TOMATO JUICE?
I CAN, BUT I'M NOT TOO FOND OF IT.
Tomato Juice
I BOUGHT IT ON THE WAY TO THE HIDEOUT WITH MR. KARASUMA...
...BE-CAUSE I THOUGHT IT MIGHT COME IN HANDY.
Dogs like tomato juice.

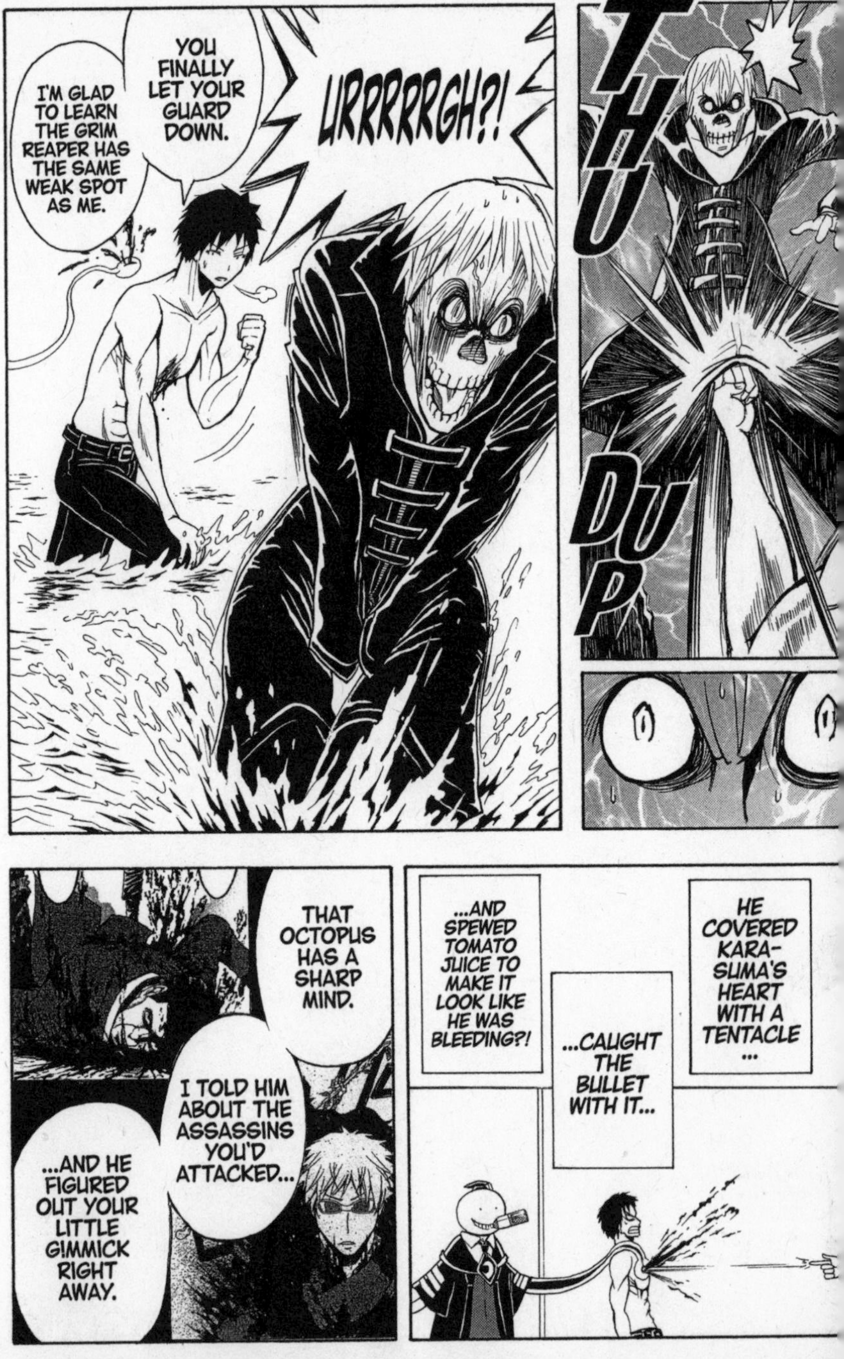
THUDUP
URRRRRGH?!
YOU FINALLY LET YOUR GUARD DOWN.
I'M GLAD TO LEARN THE GRIM REAPER HAS THE SAME WEAK SPOT AS ME.
HE COVERED KARASUMA'S HEART WITH A TENTACLE...
...CAUGHT THE BULLET WITH IT...
...AND SPEWED TOMATO JUICE TO MAKE IT LOOK LIKE HE WAS BLEEDING?!
THAT OCTOPUS HAS A SHARP MIND.
I TOLD HIM ABOUT THE ASSASSINS YOU'D ATTACKED...
...AND HE FIGURED OUT YOUR LITTLE GIMMICK RIGHT AWAY.

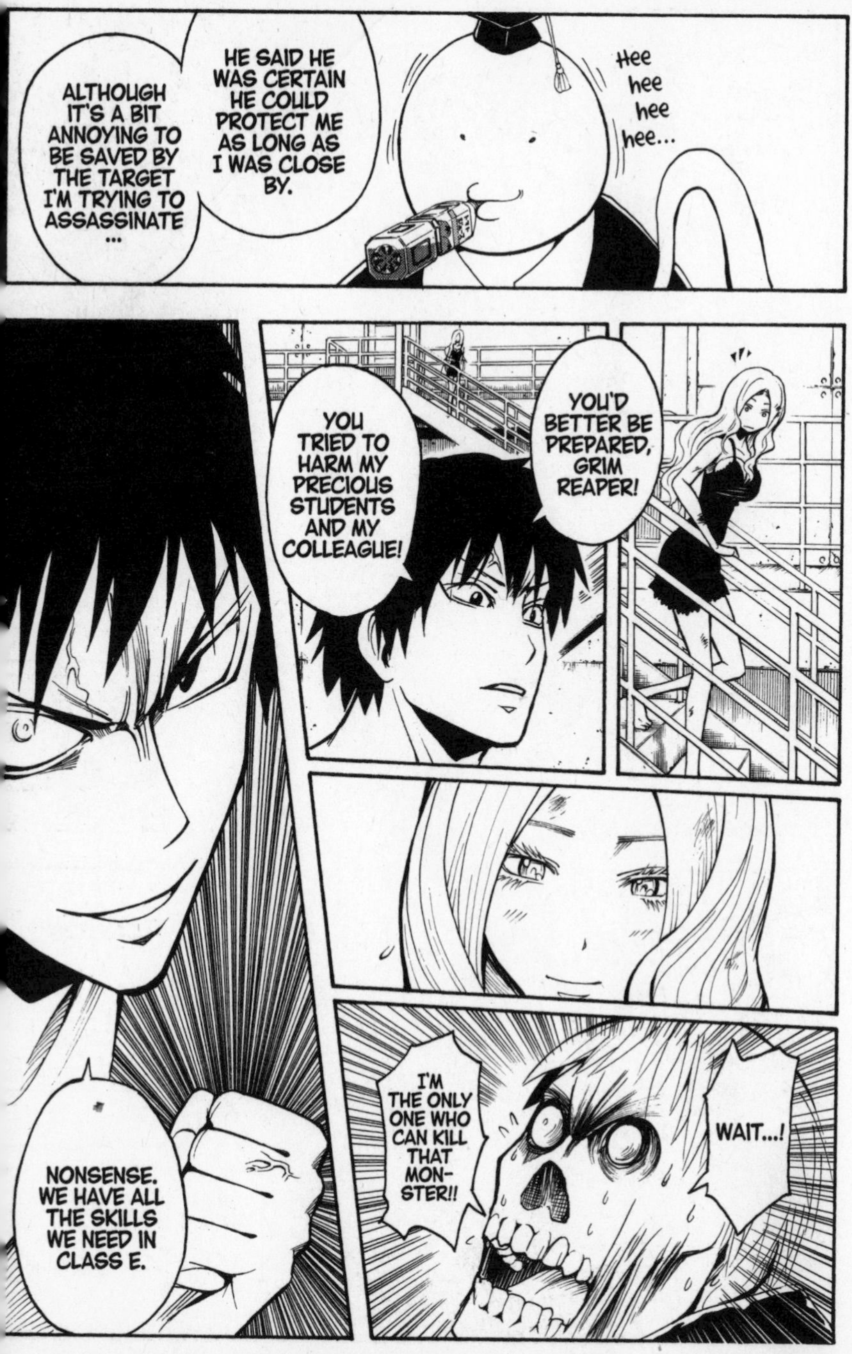
Hee hee hee hee...
HE SAID HE WAS CERTAIN HE COULD PROTECT ME AS LONG AS I WAS CLOSE BY.
ALTHOUGH IT'S A BIT ANNOYING TO BE SAVED BY THE TARGET I'M TRYING TO ASSASSINATE...
YOU'D BETTER BE PREPARED, GRIM REAPER!
YOU TRIED TO HARM MY PRECIOUS STUDENTS AND MY COLLEAGUE!
WAIT...!
I'M THE ONLY ONE WHO CAN KILL THAT MON-STER!!
NONSENSE. WE HAVE ALL THE SKILLS WE NEED IN CLASS E.

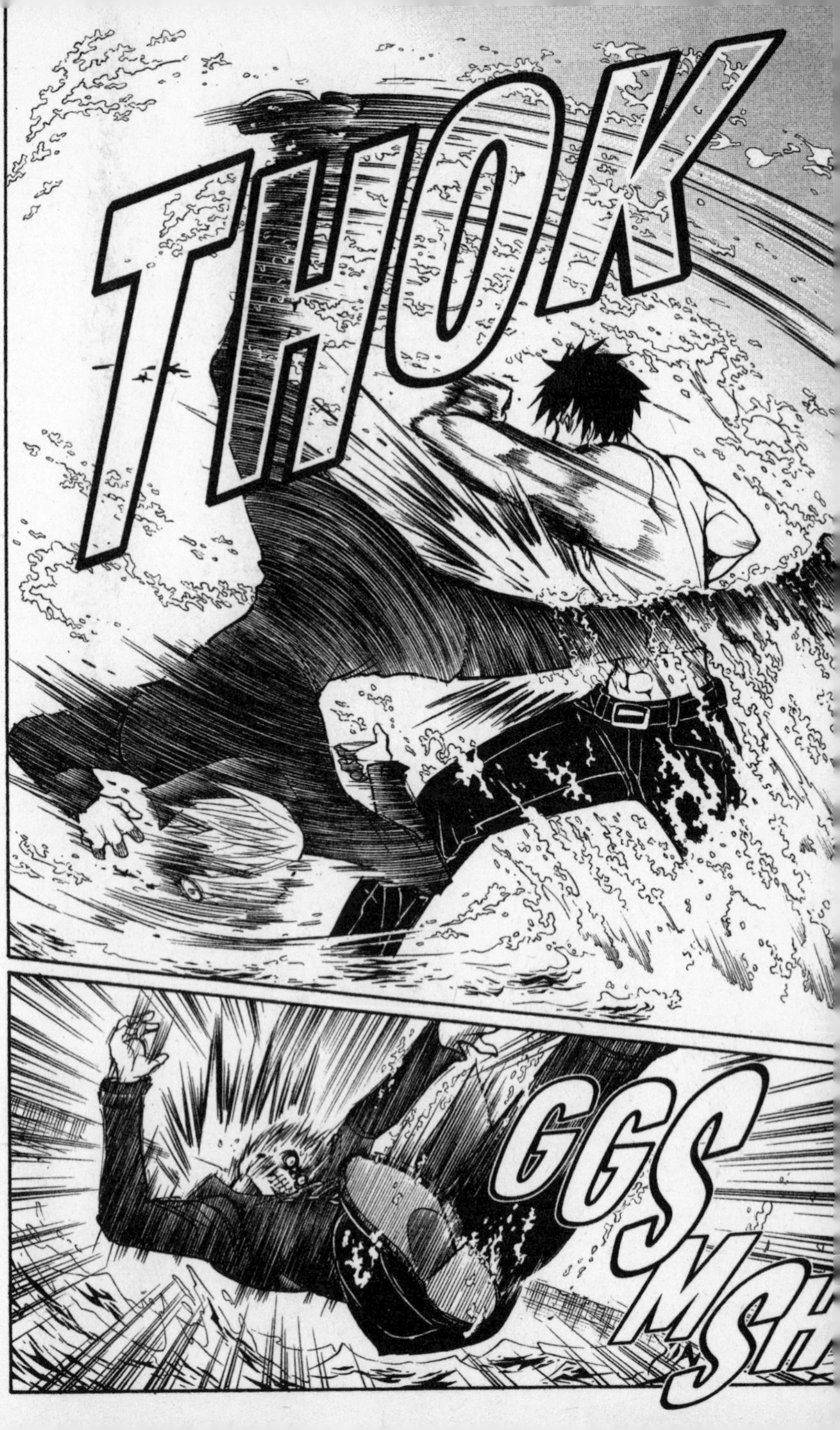
THOK
GGSMSH

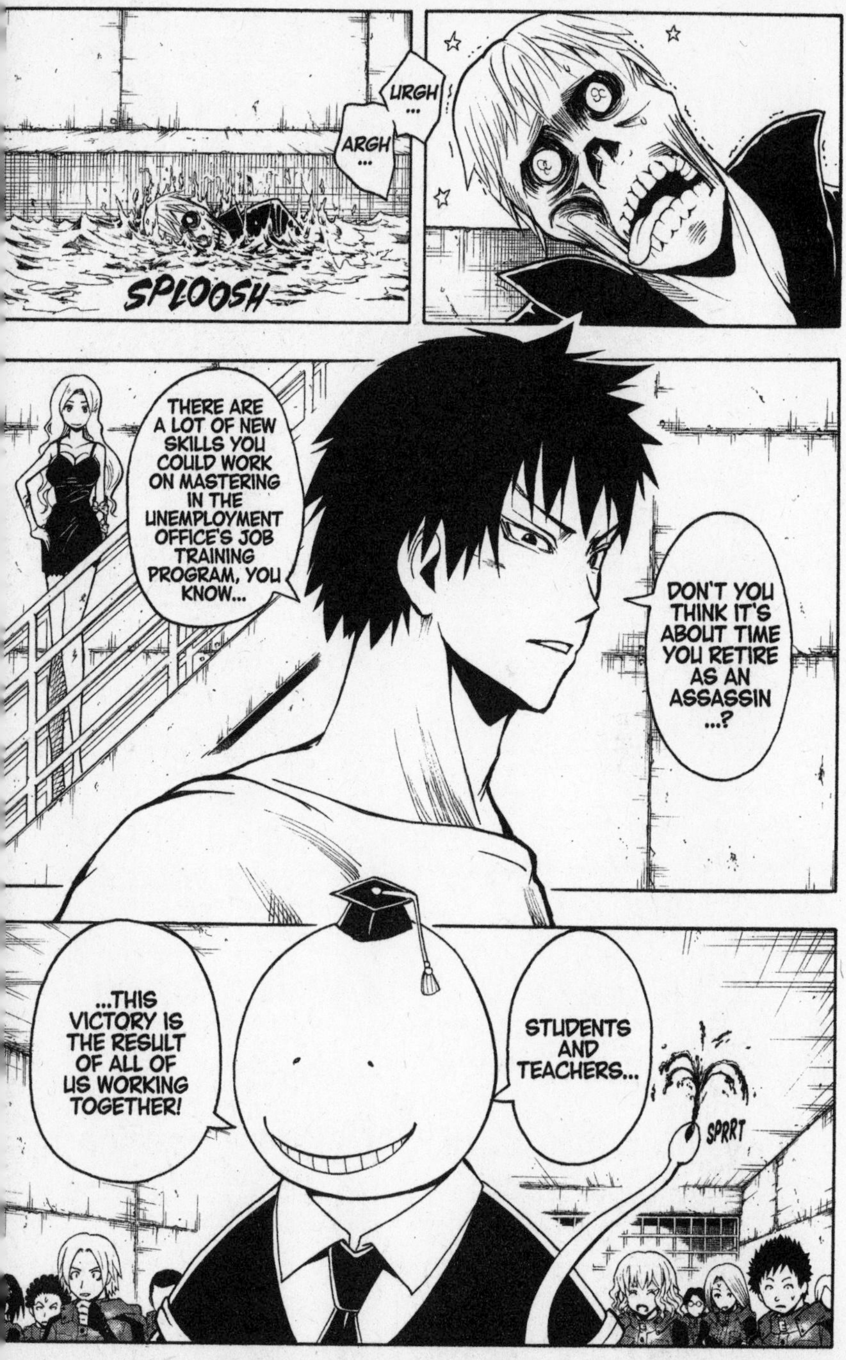
URGH...
ARGH...
SPLOOSH
DON'T YOU THINK IT'S ABOUT TIME YOU RETIRE AS AN ASSASSIN...?
THERE ARE A LOT OF NEW SKILLS YOU COULD WORK ON MASTERING IN THE UNEMPLOYMENT OFFICE'S JOB TRAINING PROGRAM, YOU KNOW...
SPRRT
STUDENTS AND TEACHERS...
...THIS VICTORY IS THE RESULT OF ALL OF US WORKING TOGETHER!

Class 3-E Best 5

Science & Technology/Home Economics

Science & Technology/Home Economics ranking of Class E students as determined (solely) by Koro Sensei

Science & Technology

1 Itona Horibe

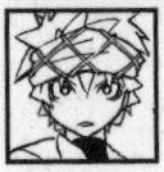

His electronic engineering skills are top-notch. The rapid-fire Booby Trap Robot he invented shoots boobs.

2 Taisei Yoshida

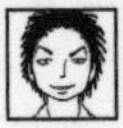

Large machinery is his specialty. I recorded Mach 1.5 on the iron tricycle he built.

3 Taiga Okajima

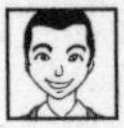

He has exceptional high-tech skills from fiddling with all kinds of delicate photography equipment with his agile fingers.

4 Rio Nakamura

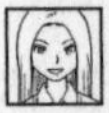

She is very intelligent and able to disassemble a radio in a flash. It's a pity she considers reassembling it boring.

5 Hiroto Maehara

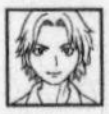

He has a taste for setting up and modifying guns, but ironically, Maehara actually excels at wielding a knife.

Home Economics

1 Sumire Hara

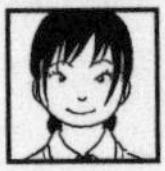

First place by a landslide in all aspects. The beanie she knitted for me using anti-me yarn was so comfortable I almost died!

2 Takuya Muramatsu

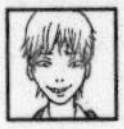

His cooking skills are pretty much equivalent to Hara's. He'll become a fine househusband once he learns how to sew and do other forms of housework.

3 Toka Yada

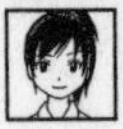

She's growing up and her home economic skills have improved greatly over the past year. She's going to be very popular someday...

4 Rinka Hayami

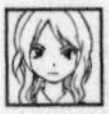

She has nimble, flexible fingertips. Seeing her casually patch and iron someone's clothes is amazing. She truly is the Hot-and-Cold Sniper.

5 Kirara Hazama

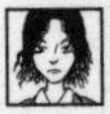

She has developed a growing interest in Home Economics since the end of the first semester. She's the spitting image of a witch if you see her stirring a stew with an evil smirk on her face.

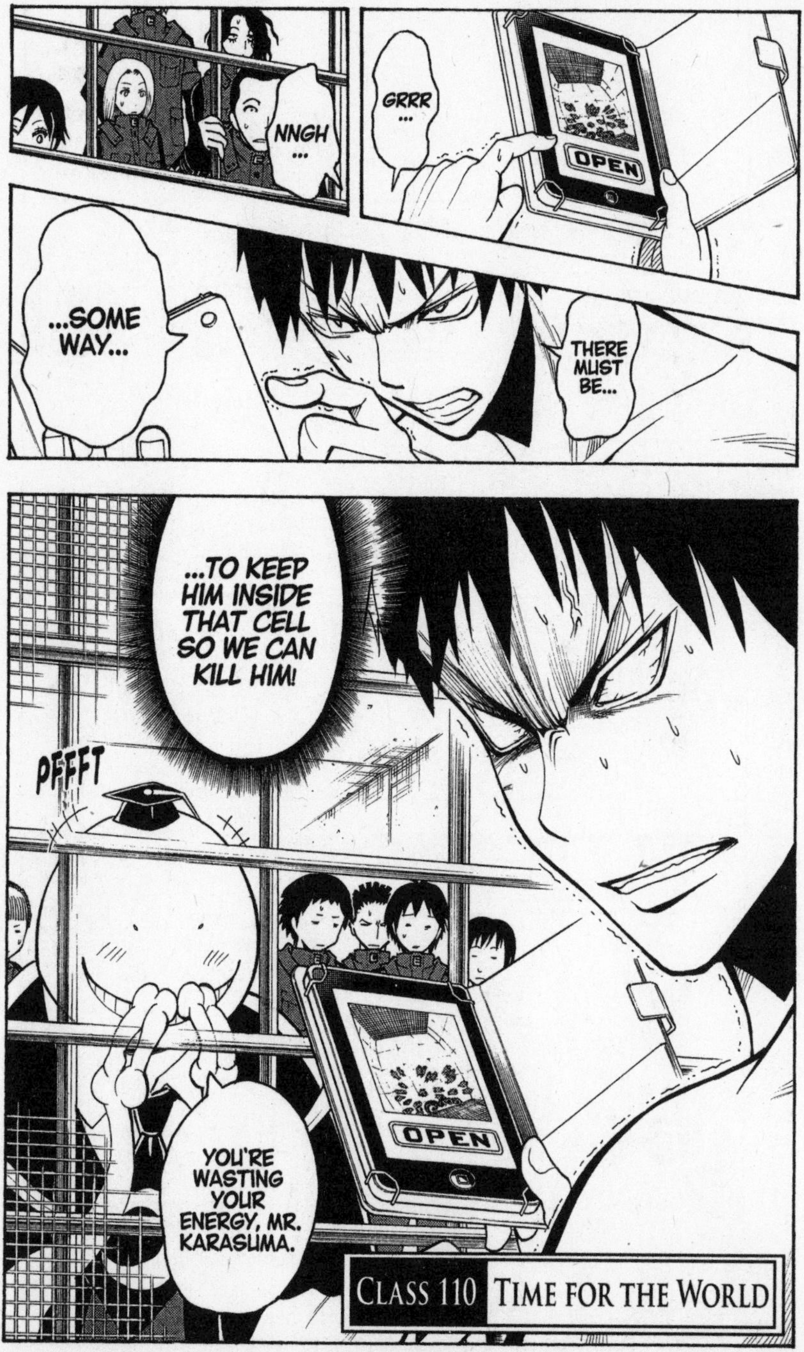
GRRR...
NNGH...
THERE MUST BE...
...SOME WAY...
...TO KEEP HIM INSIDE THAT CELL SO WE CAN KILL HIM!
PFFFT
YOU'RE WASTING YOUR ENERGY, MR. KARASUMA.

CLASS 110 TIME FOR THE WORLD

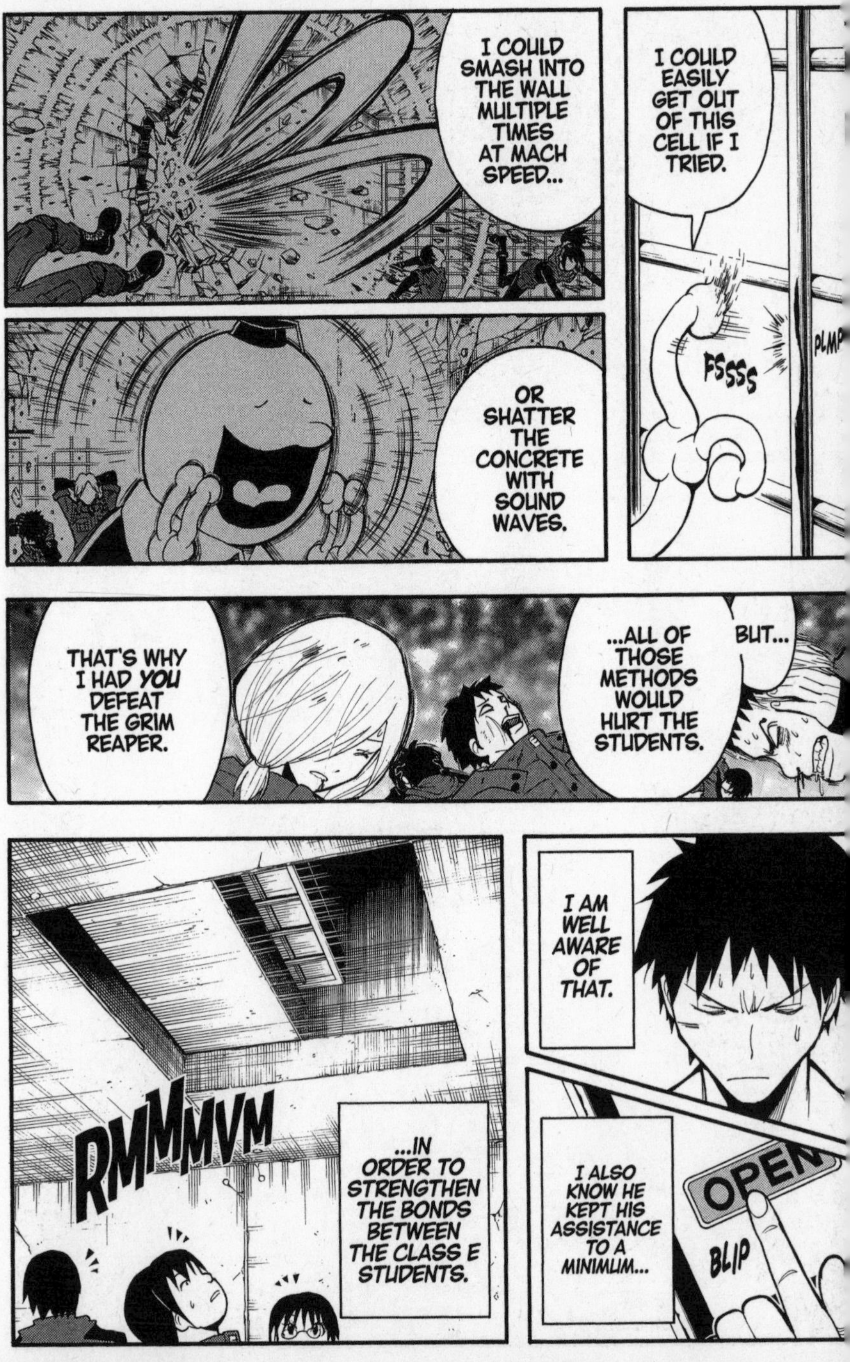
I COULD EASILY GET OUT OF THIS CELL IF I TRIED.
FSSSS
PLMP
I COULD SMASH INTO THE WALL MULTIPLE TIMES AT MACH SPEED...
OR SHATTER THE CONCRETE WITH SOUND WAVES.
BUT...
...ALL OF THOSE METHODS WOULD HURT THE STUDENTS.
THAT'S WHY I HAD *YOU* DEFEAT THE GRIM REAPER.
I AM WELL AWARE OF THAT.
I ALSO KNOW HE KEPT HIS ASSISTANCE TO A MINIMUM...
OPEN
BLIP
...IN ORDER TO STRENGTHEN THE BONDS BETWEEN THE CLASS E STUDENTS.
RMMMVM

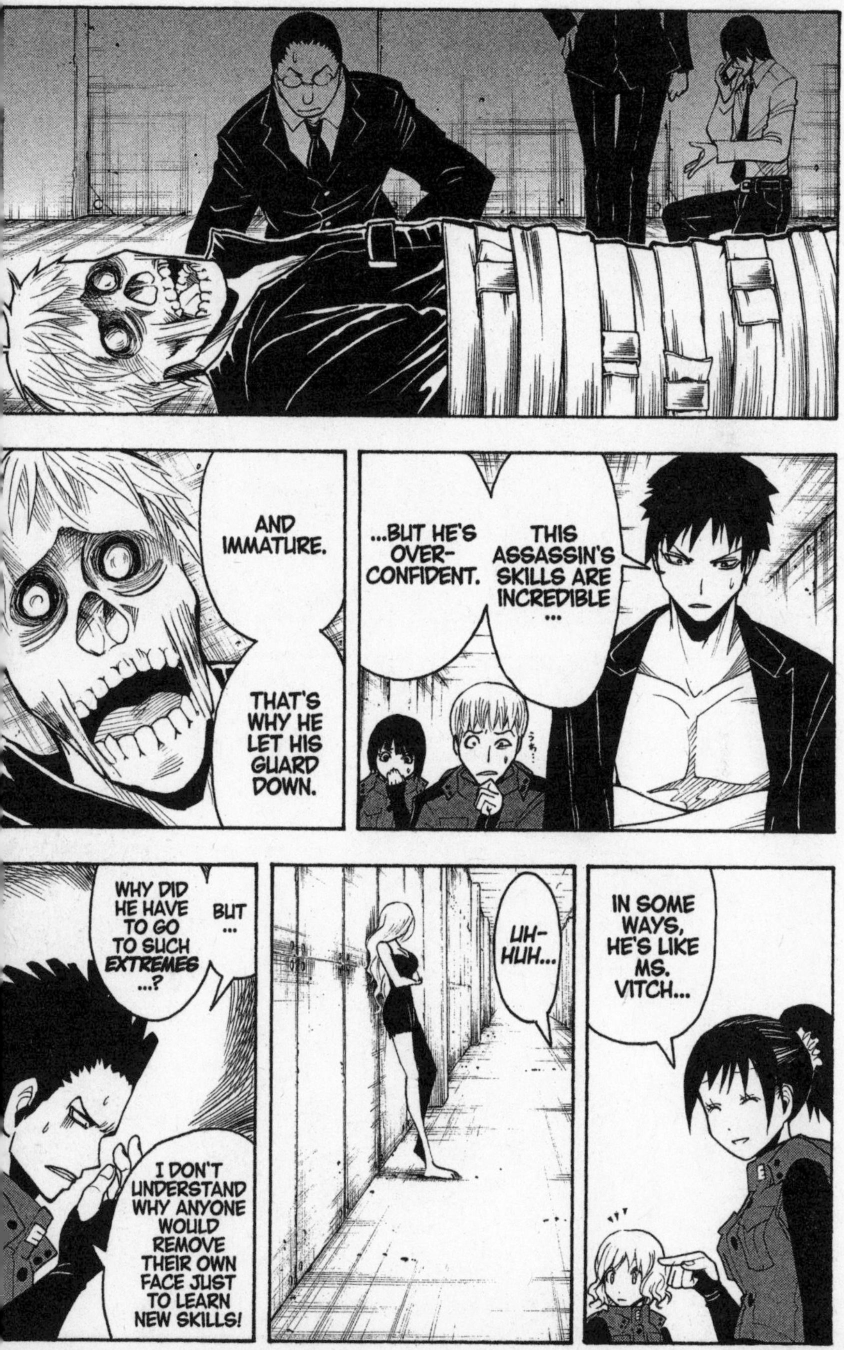
THIS ASSASSIN'S SKILLS ARE INCREDIBLE...
...BUT HE'S OVER-CONFIDENT.
AND IMMATURE.
THAT'S WHY HE LET HIS GUARD DOWN.
IN SOME WAYS, HE'S LIKE MS. VITCH...
UH-HUH...
BUT...
WHY DID HE HAVE TO GO TO SUCH EXTREMES...?
I DON'T UNDERSTAND WHY ANYONE WOULD REMOVE THEIR OWN FACE JUST TO LEARN NEW SKILLS!

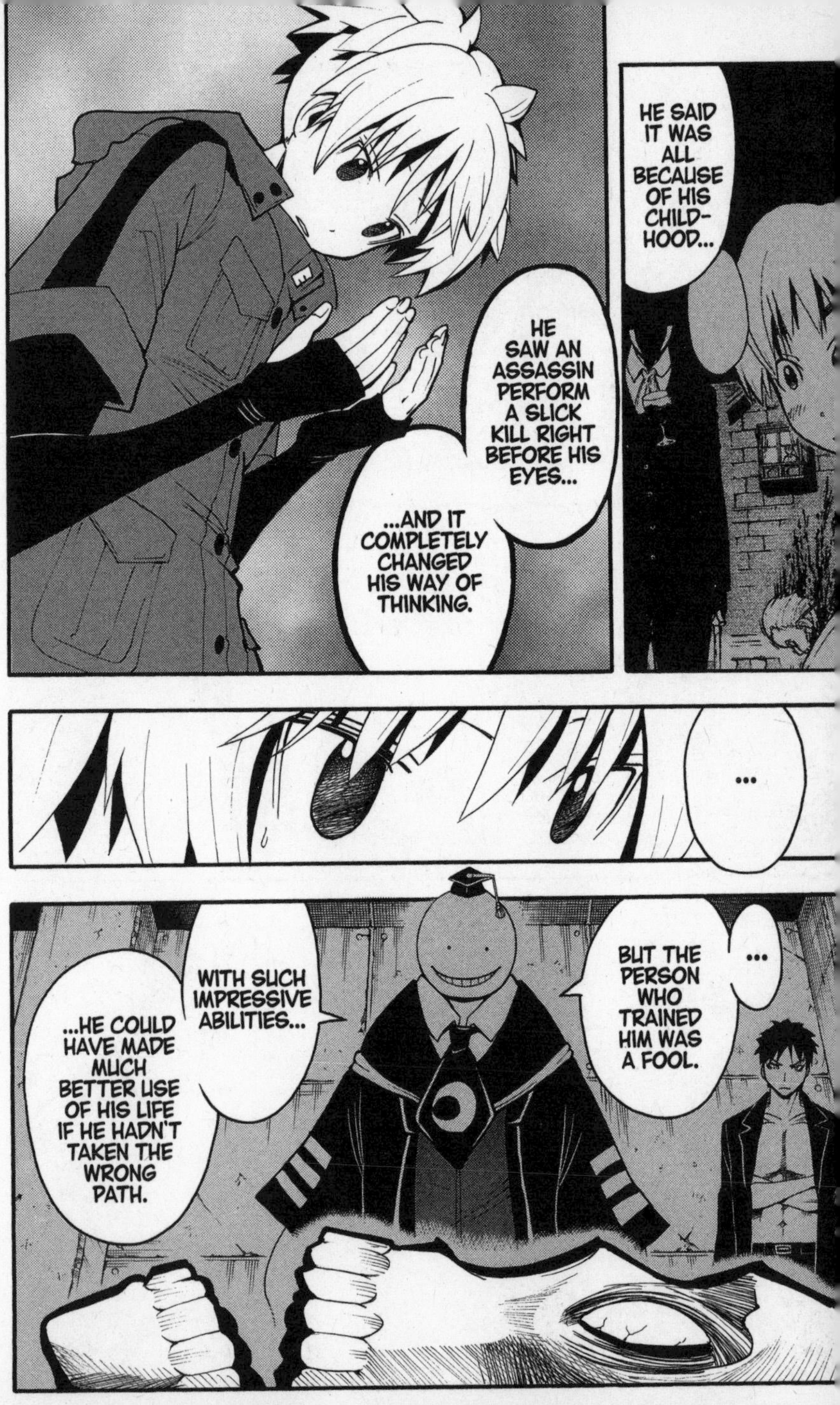
HE SAID IT WAS ALL BECAUSE OF HIS CHILD-HOOD...
HE SAW AN ASSASSIN PERFORM A SLICK KILL RIGHT BEFORE HIS EYES...
...AND IT COMPLETELY CHANGED HIS WAY OF THINKING.
...
...
BUT THE PERSON WHO TRAINED HIM WAS A FOOL.
WITH SUCH IMPRESSIVE ABILITIES...
...HE COULD HAVE MADE MUCH BETTER USE OF HIS LIFE IF HE HADN'T TAKEN THE WRONG PATH.

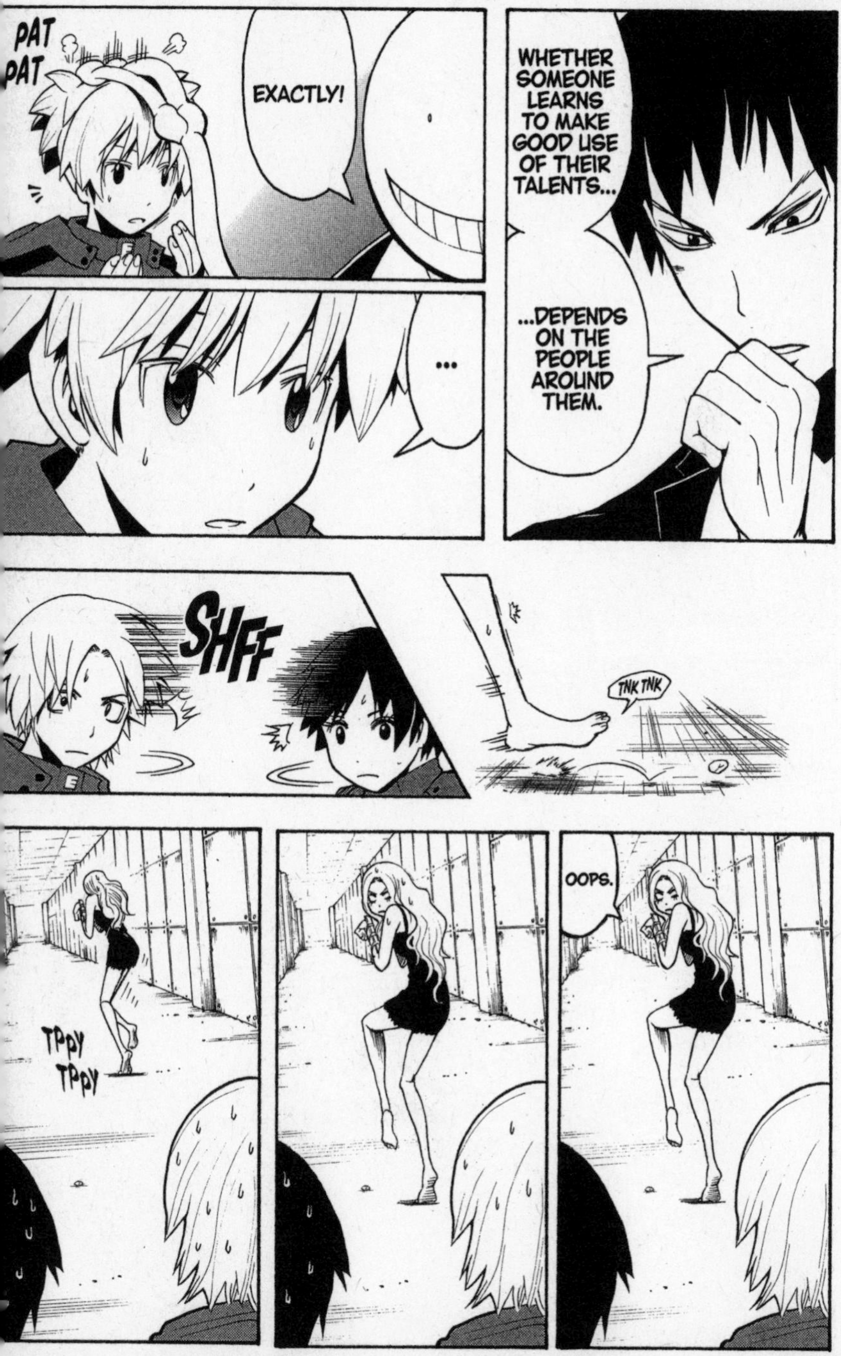
WHETHER SOMEONE LEARNS TO MAKE GOOD USE OF THEIR TALENTS...
...DEPENDS ON THE PEOPLE AROUND THEM.
EXACTLY!
PAT PAT
...
TNK TNK
SHFF
OOPS.
TPPY TPPY

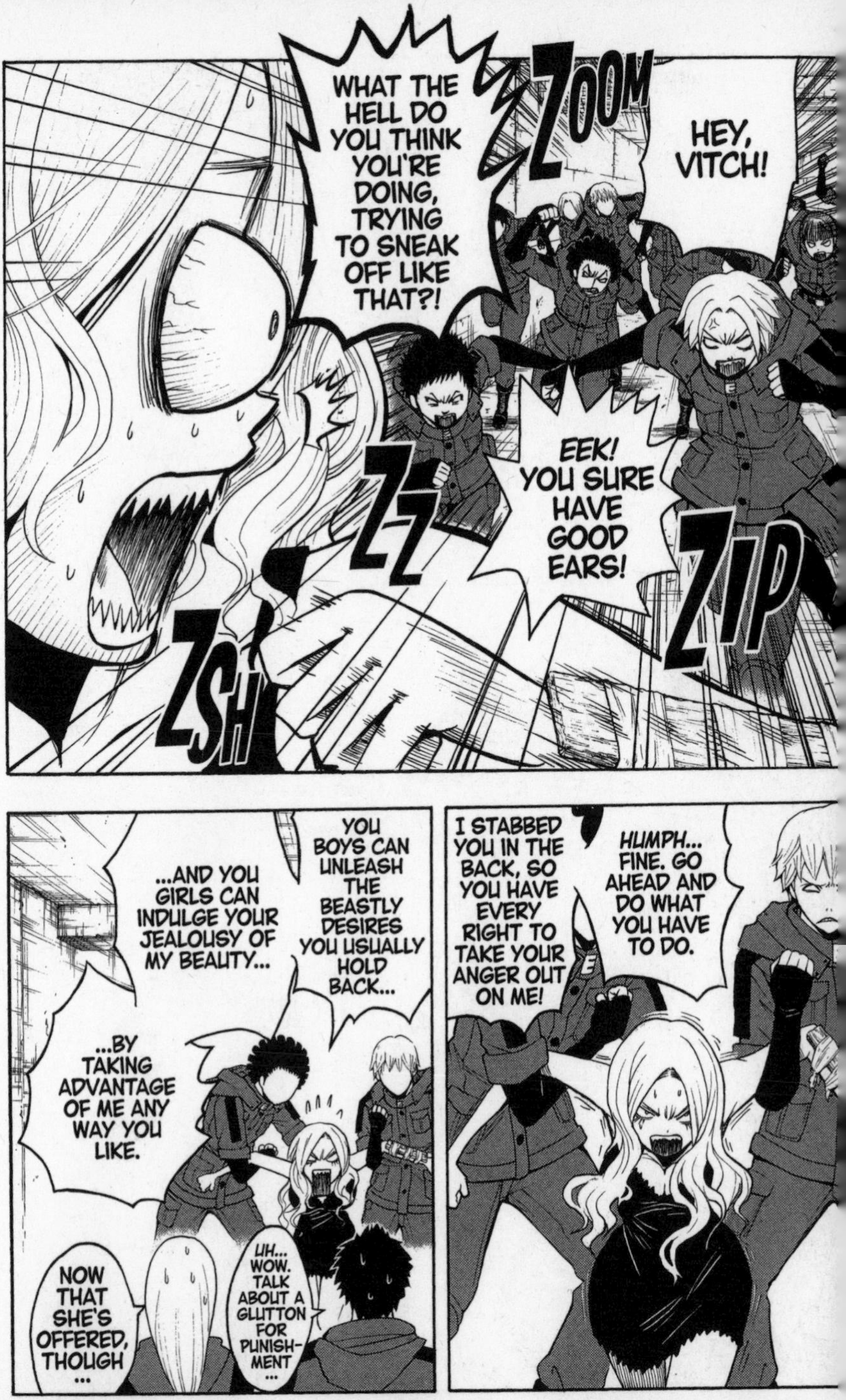
HEY, VITCH!
ZOOM
WHAT THE HELL DO YOU THINK YOU'RE DOING, TRYING TO SNEAK OFF LIKE THAT?!
ZIP
EEK! YOU SURE HAVE GOOD EARS!
ZZ
ZSH
HUMPH... FINE. GO AHEAD AND DO WHAT YOU HAVE TO DO.
I STABBED YOU IN THE BACK, SO YOU HAVE EVERY RIGHT TO TAKE YOUR ANGER OUT ON ME!
YOU BOYS CAN UNLEASH THE BEASTLY DESIRES YOU USUALLY HOLD BACK...
...AND YOU GIRLS CAN INDULGE YOUR JEALOUSY OF MY BEAUTY...
...BY TAKING ADVANTAGE OF ME ANY WAY YOU LIKE.
UH... WOW. TALK ABOUT A GLUTTON FOR PUNISH-MENT...
NOW THAT SHE'S OFFERED, THOUGH...

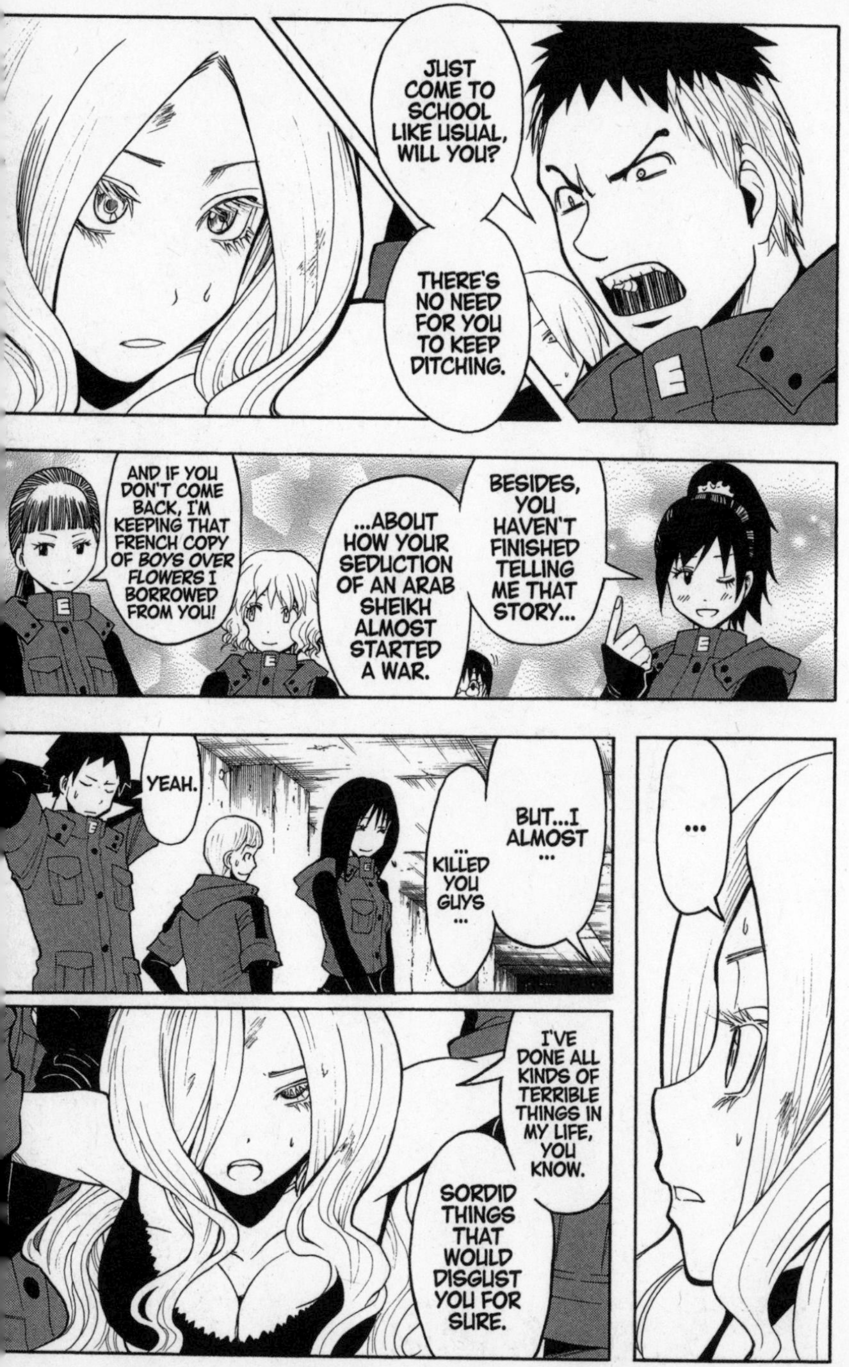
JUST COME TO SCHOOL LIKE USUAL, WILL YOU?
THERE'S NO NEED FOR YOU TO KEEP DITCHING.
BESIDES, YOU HAVEN'T FINISHED TELLING ME THAT STORY...
...ABOUT HOW YOUR SEDUCTION OF AN ARAB SHEIKH ALMOST STARTED A WAR.
AND IF YOU DON'T COME BACK, I'M KEEPING THAT FRENCH COPY OF BOYS OVER FLOWERS I BORROWED FROM YOU!
...
BUT...I ALMOST ...
... KILLED YOU GUYS ...
YEAH.
I'VE DONE ALL KINDS OF TERRIBLE THINGS IN MY LIFE, YOU KNOW.
SORDID THINGS THAT WOULD DISGUST YOU FOR SURE.

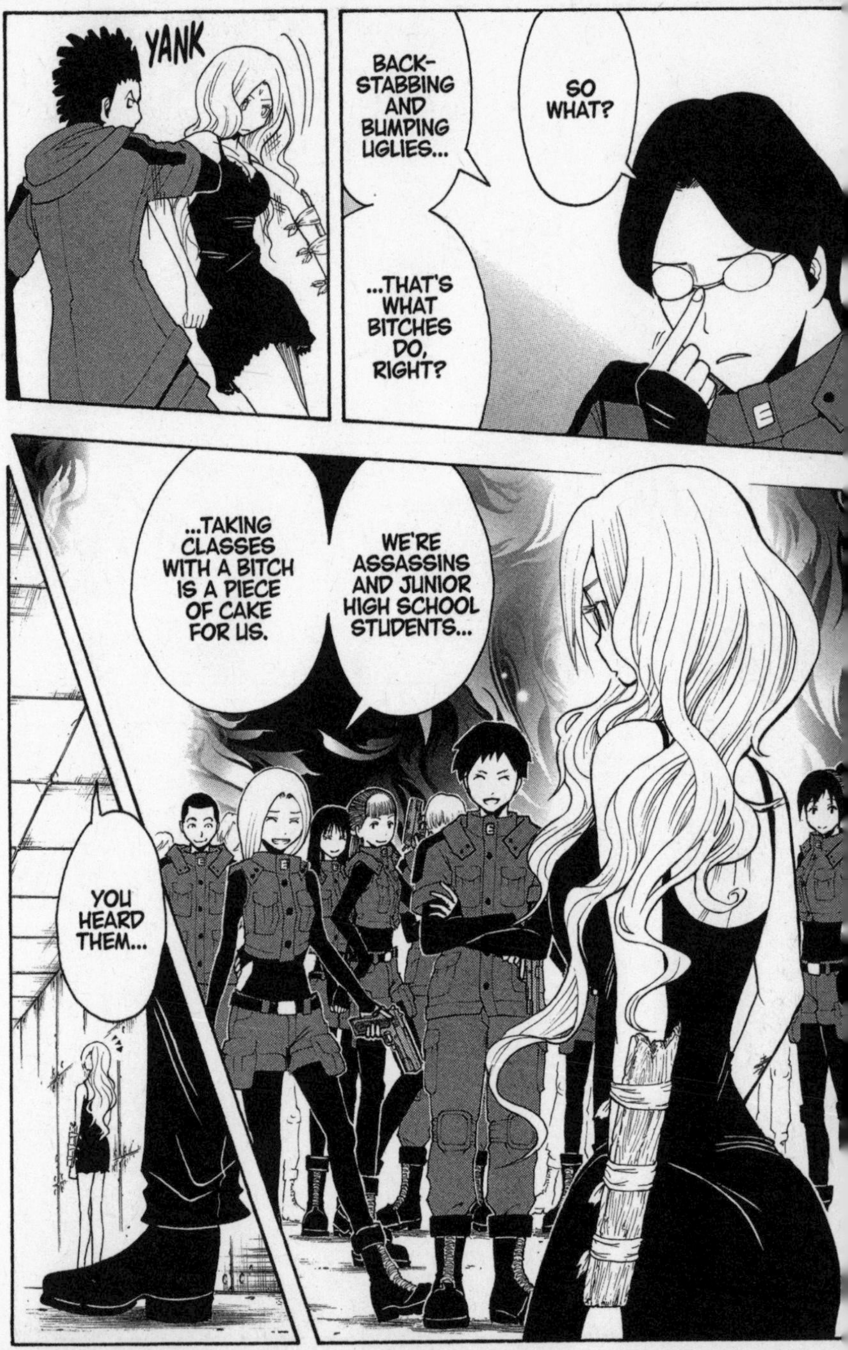
SO WHAT?
BACK-STABBING AND BUMPING UGLIES...
...THAT'S WHAT BITCHES DO, RIGHT?
YANK
WE'RE ASSASSINS AND JUNIOR HIGH SCHOOL STUDENTS...
...TAKING CLASSES WITH A BITCH IS A PIECE OF CAKE FOR US.
YOU HEARD THEM...

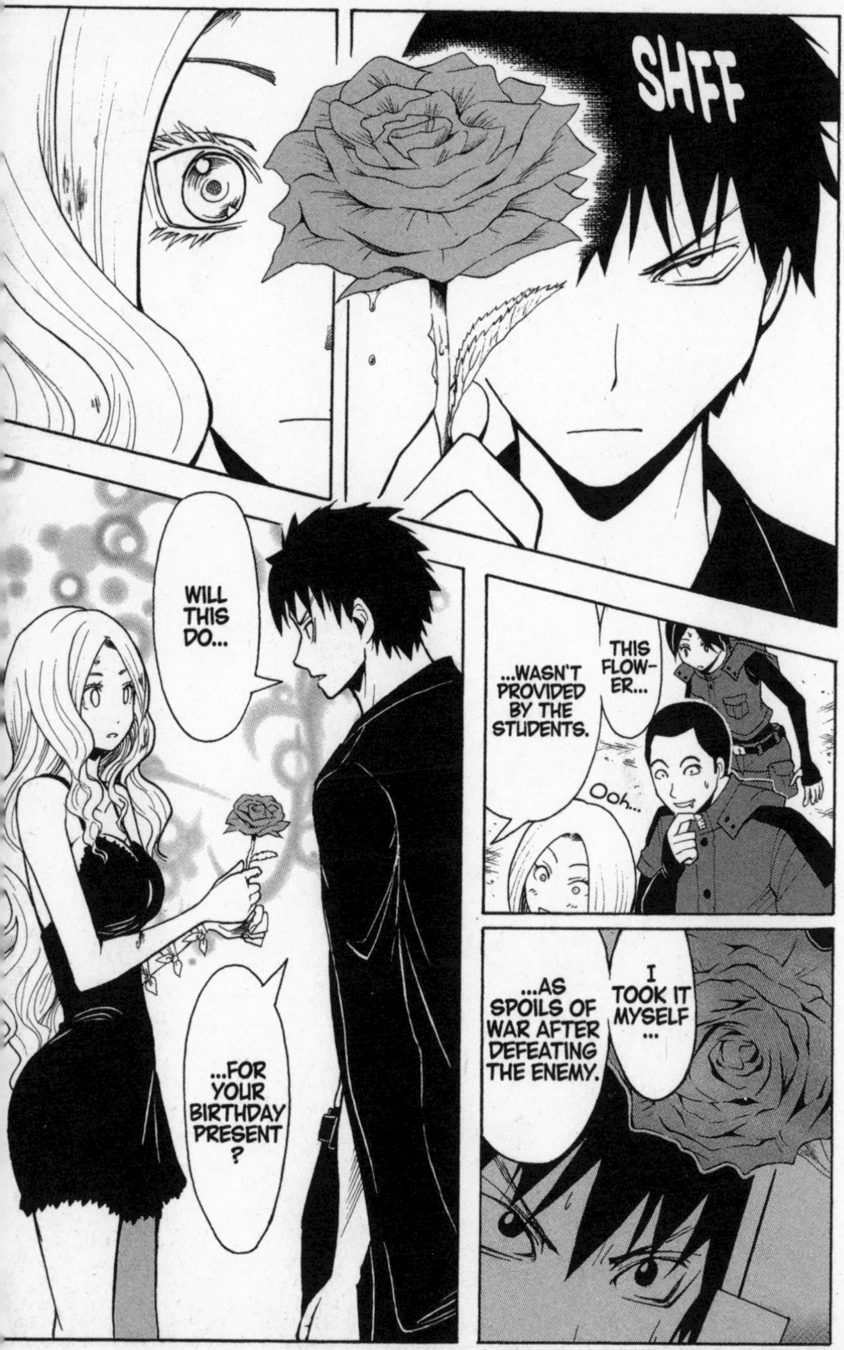
SHFF
THIS FLOWER...
...WASN'T PROVIDED BY THE STUDENTS.
Ooh...
I TOOK IT MYSELF...
...AS SPOILS OF WAR AFTER DEFEATING THE ENEMY.
WILL THIS DO...
...FOR YOUR BIRTHDAY PRESENT?

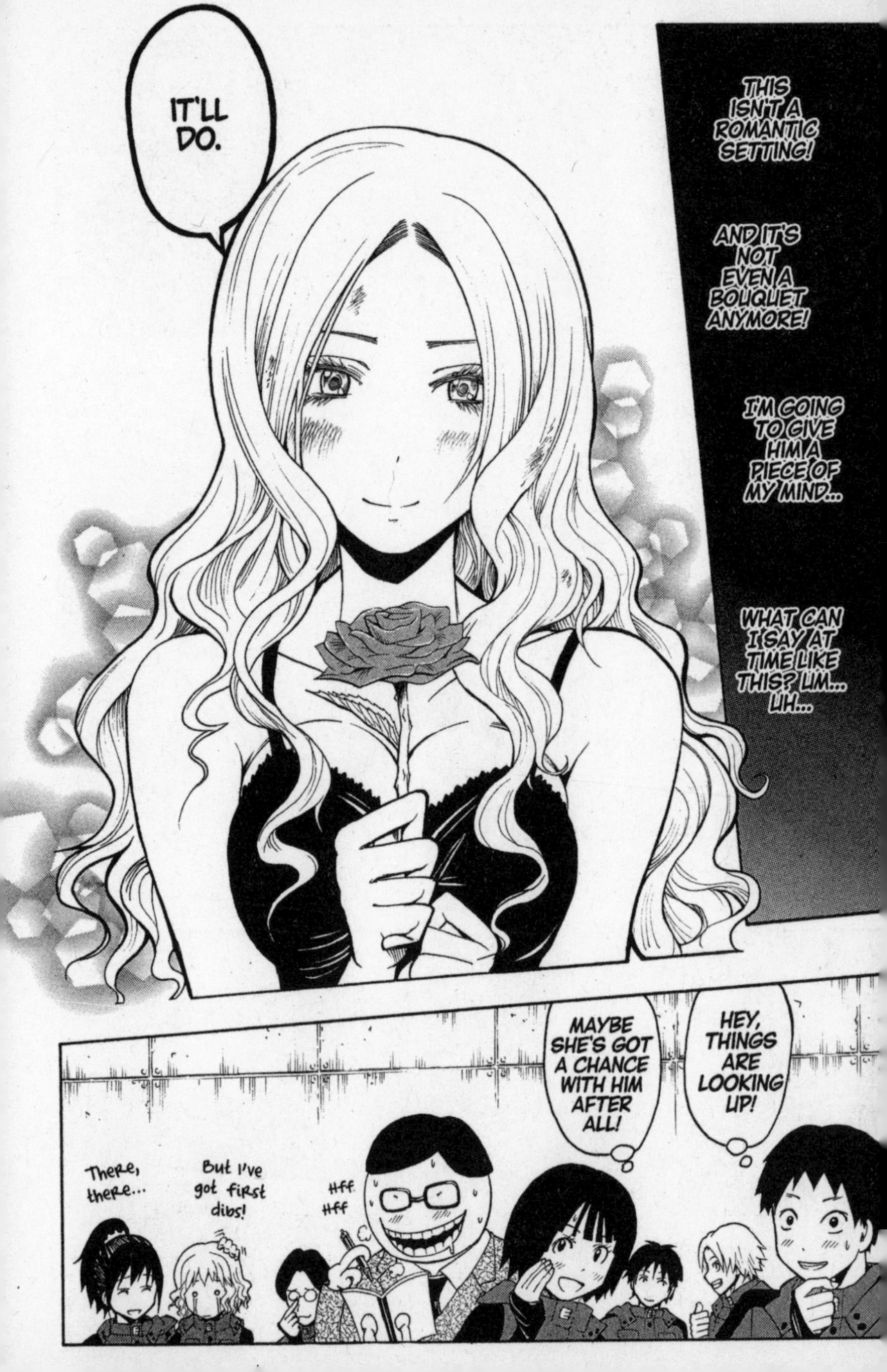
THIS ISN'T A ROMANTIC SETTING!
AND IT'S NOT EVEN A BOUQUET ANYMORE!
I'M GOING TO GIVE HIM A PIECE OF MY MIND...
WHAT CAN I SAY AT TIME LIKE THIS? UM... UH...
IT'LL DO.
HEY, THINGS ARE LOOKING UP!
MAYBE SHE'S GOT A CHANCE WITH HIM AFTER ALL!
Hff Hff
But I've got first dibs!
There, there...

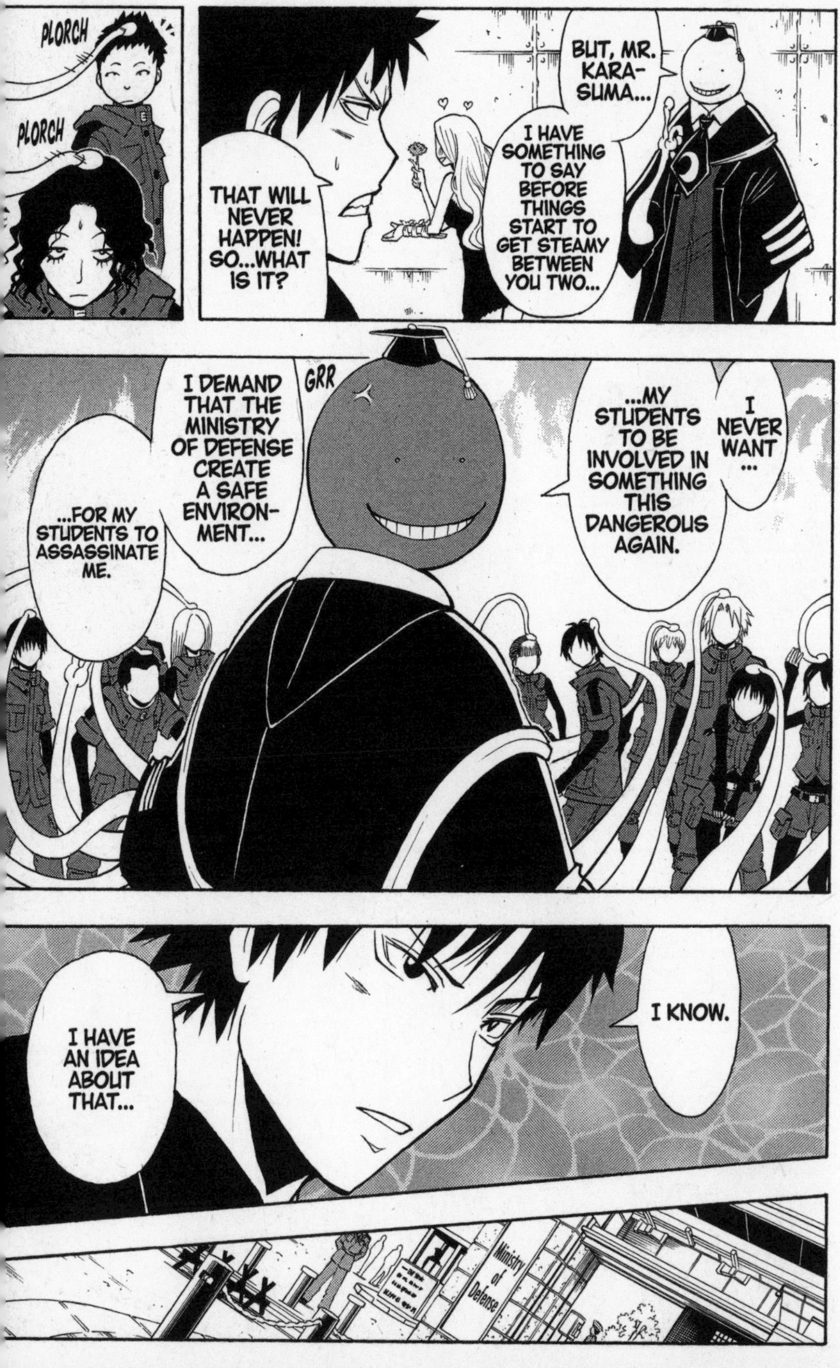
BUT, MR. KARA-SUMA...
I HAVE SOMETHING TO SAY BEFORE THINGS START TO GET STEAMY BETWEEN YOU TWO...
THAT WILL NEVER HAPPEN! SO...WHAT IS IT?
PLORCH
PLORCH
I NEVER WANT...
...MY STUDENTS TO BE INVOLVED IN SOMETHING THIS DANGEROUS AGAIN.
GRR
I DEMAND THAT THE MINISTRY OF DEFENSE CREATE A SAFE ENVIRONMENT...
...FOR MY STUDENTS TO ASSASSINATE ME.
I KNOW.
I HAVE AN IDEA ABOUT THAT...
Ministry of Defense

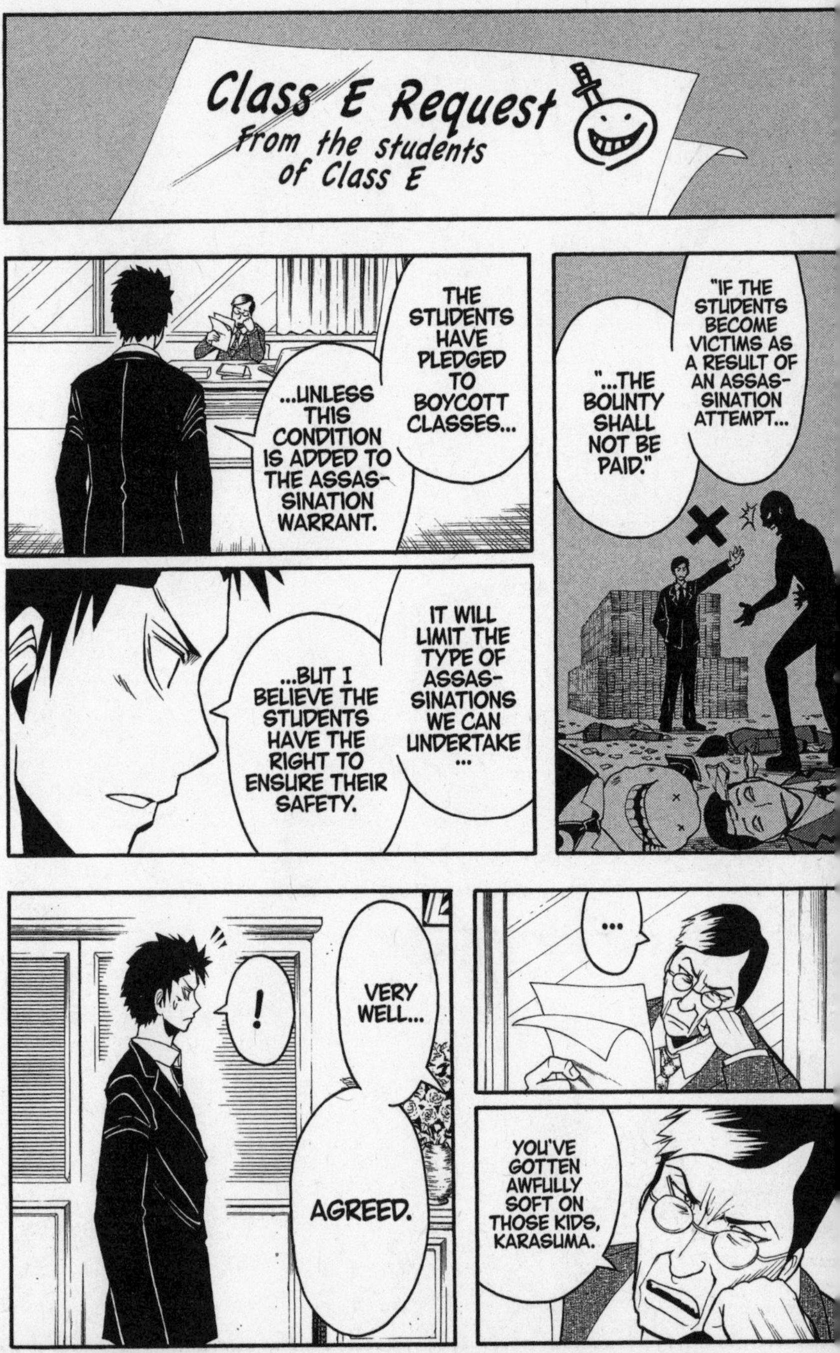
Class E Request
From the students of Class E
"IF THE STUDENTS BECOME VICTIMS AS A RESULT OF AN ASSASSINATION ATTEMPT...
"...THE BOUNTY SHALL NOT BE PAID."
THE STUDENTS HAVE PLEDGED TO BOYCOTT CLASSES...
...UNLESS THIS CONDITION IS ADDED TO THE ASSASSINATION WARRANT.
IT WILL LIMIT THE TYPE OF ASSASSINATIONS WE CAN UNDERTAKE...
...BUT I BELIEVE THE STUDENTS HAVE THE RIGHT TO ENSURE THEIR SAFETY.
...
YOU'VE GOTTEN AWFULLY SOFT ON THOSE KIDS, KARASUMA.
VERY WELL...
!
AGREED.

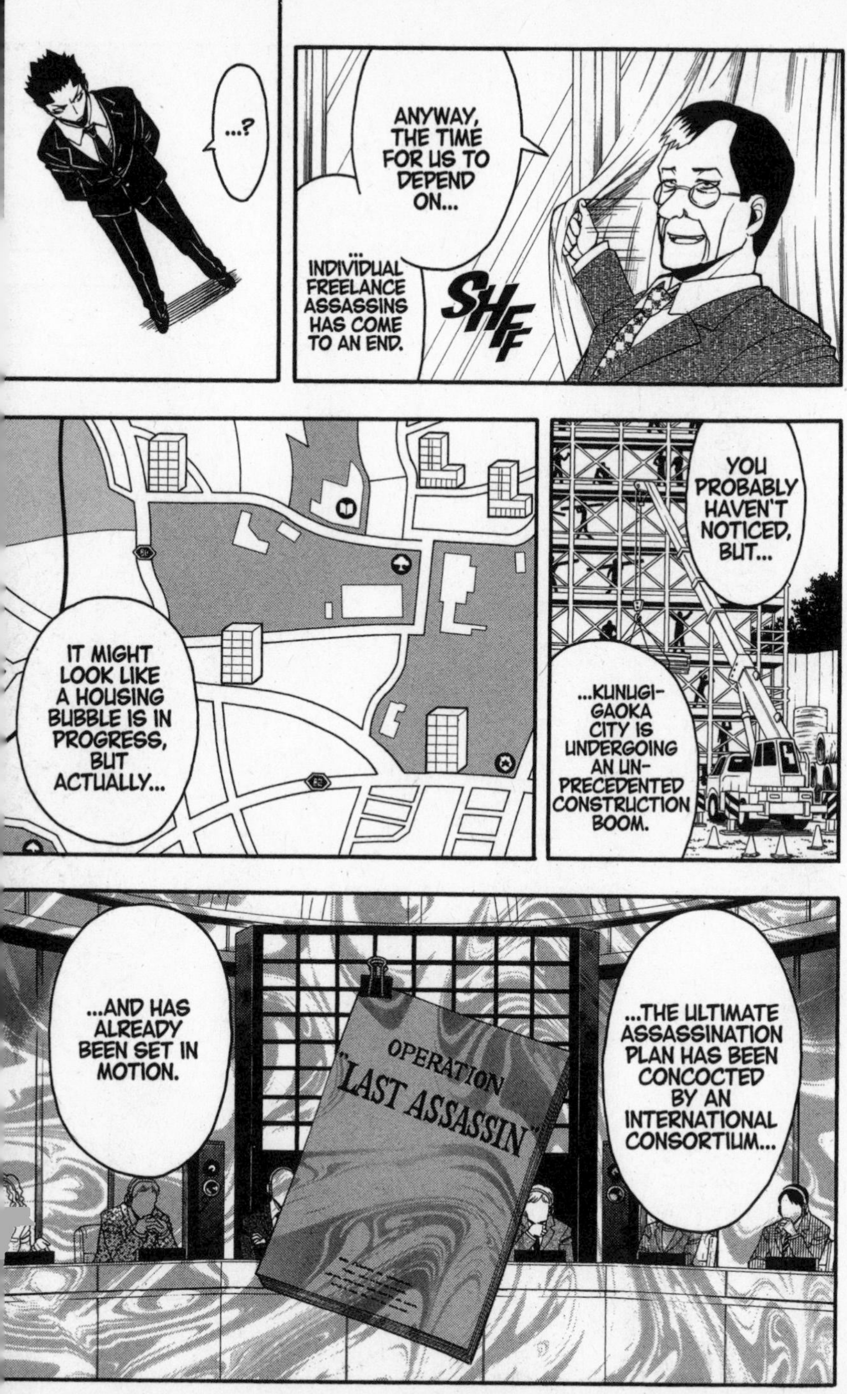
ANYWAY, THE TIME FOR US TO DEPEND ON...
...INDIVIDUAL FREELANCE ASSASSINS HAS COME TO AN END.
SHFF
...?
YOU PROBABLY HAVEN'T NOTICED, BUT...
...KUNUGI-GAOKA CITY IS UNDERGOING AN UN-PRECEDENTED CONSTRUCTION BOOM.
IT MIGHT LOOK LIKE A HOUSING BUBBLE IS IN PROGRESS, BUT ACTUALLY...
...THE ULTIMATE ASSASSINATION PLAN HAS BEEN CONCOCTED BY AN INTERNATIONAL CONSORTIUM...
OPERATION "LAST ASSASSIN"
...AND HAS ALREADY BEEN SET IN MOTION.

I EVALUATED IT, AND I MUST SAY, THE TECHNOLOGY IS EXTRAORDINARY.

NO ASSASSIN COULD POSSIBLY MATCH IT.

I FINALLY FOUND YOU...

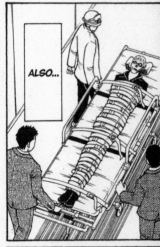

ALSO...

TNK

I HEAR THAT SHIRO HAS PREPARED HIS OWN ULTIMATE WEAPON.

AND I KNOW...

...WHO YOU ARE.

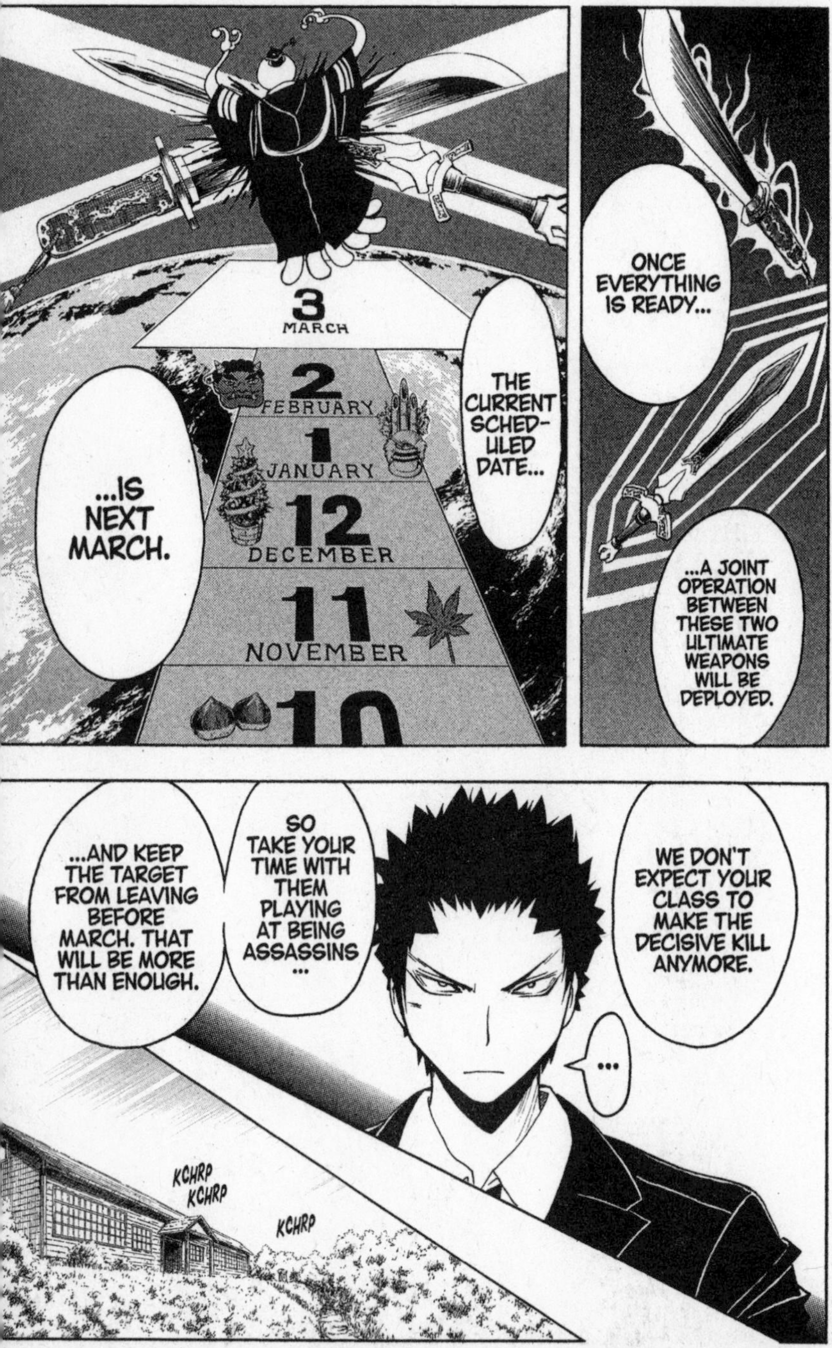
ONCE EVERYTHING IS READY...
...A JOINT OPERATION BETWEEN THESE TWO ULTIMATE WEAPONS WILL BE DEPLOYED.
THE CURRENT SCHED-ULED DATE...
...IS NEXT MARCH.
3 MARCH
2 FEBRUARY
1 JANUARY
12 DECEMBER
11 NOVEMBER
10
WE DON'T EXPECT YOUR CLASS TO MAKE THE DECISIVE KILL ANYMORE.
...
SO TAKE YOUR TIME WITH THEM PLAYING AT BEING ASSASSINS ...
...AND KEEP THE TARGET FROM LEAVING BEFORE MARCH. THAT WILL BE MORE THAN ENOUGH.
KCHRP KCHRP
KCHRP

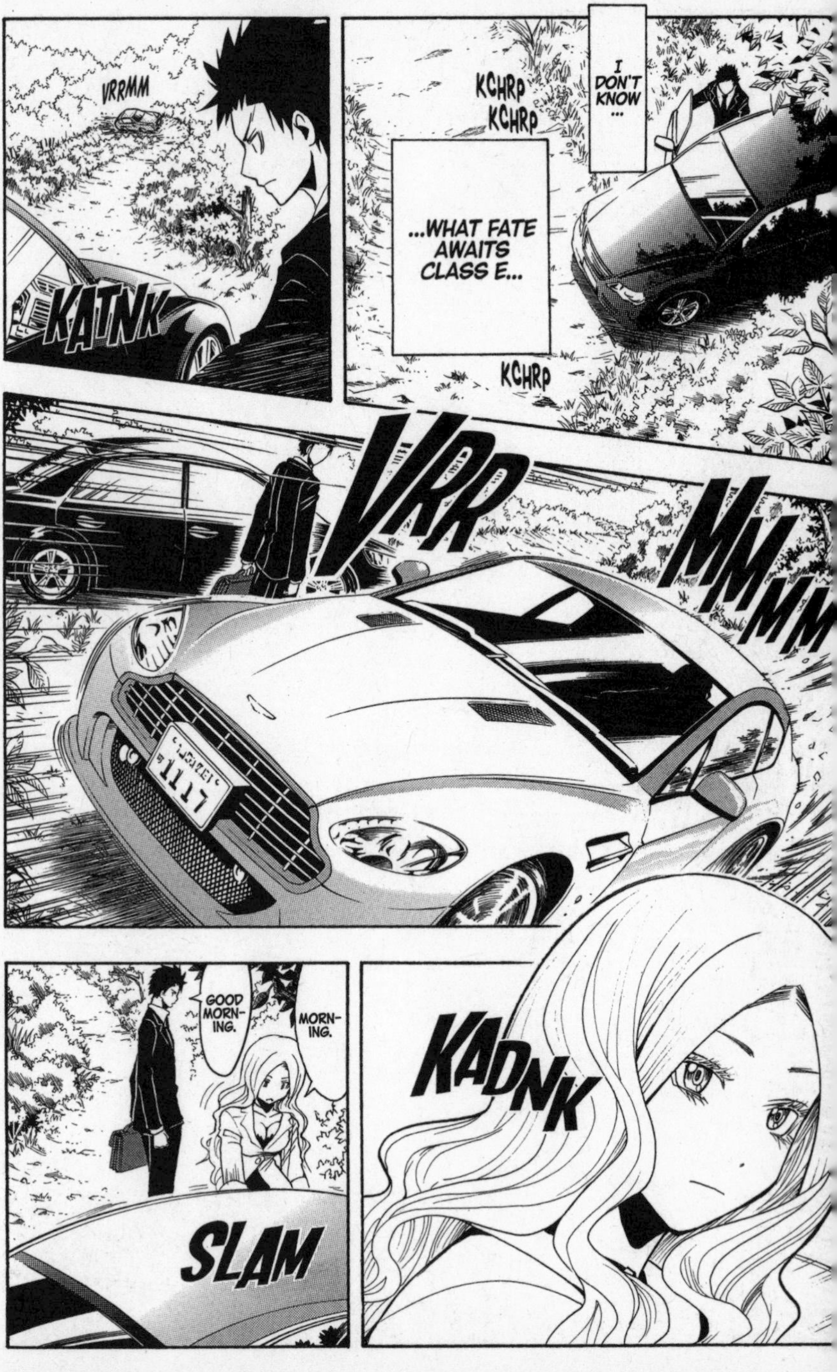
I DON'T KNOW...
...WHAT FATE AWAITS CLASS E...
KCHRP KCHRP
KCHRP
VRRMM
KATNK
VRR
MMMM
KADNK
GOOD MORNING.
MORNING.
SLAM

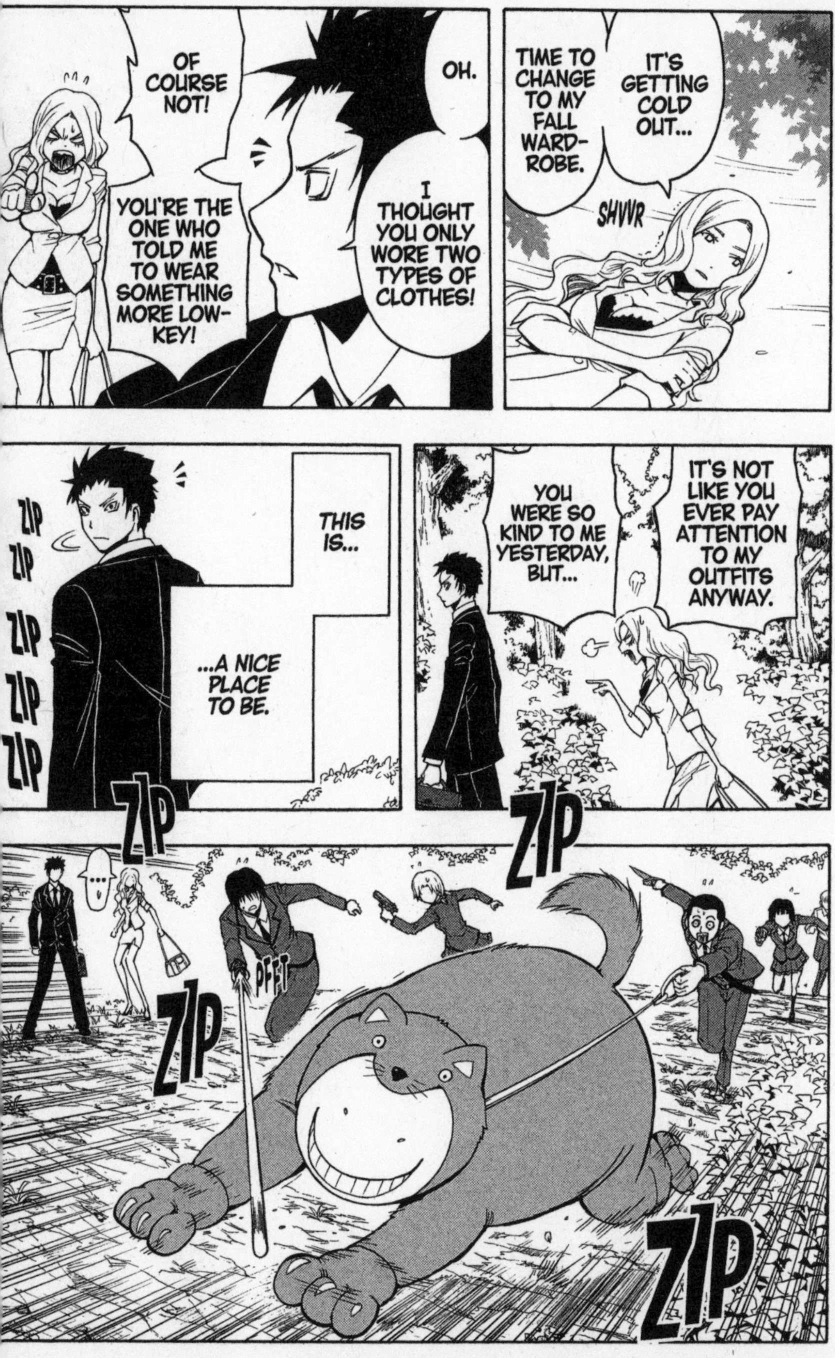
IT'S GETTING COLD OUT...
TIME TO CHANGE TO MY FALL WARD-ROBE.
SHVVR
OH.
I THOUGHT YOU ONLY WORE TWO TYPES OF CLOTHES!
OF COURSE NOT!
YOU'RE THE ONE WHO TOLD ME TO WEAR SOMETHING MORE LOW-KEY!
IT'S NOT LIKE YOU EVER PAY ATTENTION TO MY OUTFITS ANYWAY.
YOU WERE SO KIND TO ME YESTERDAY, BUT...
THIS IS...
...A NICE PLACE TO BE.
ZIP
ZIP
ZIP
ZIP
ZIP
ZIP
ZIP
...
PFFT
ZIP
ZIP

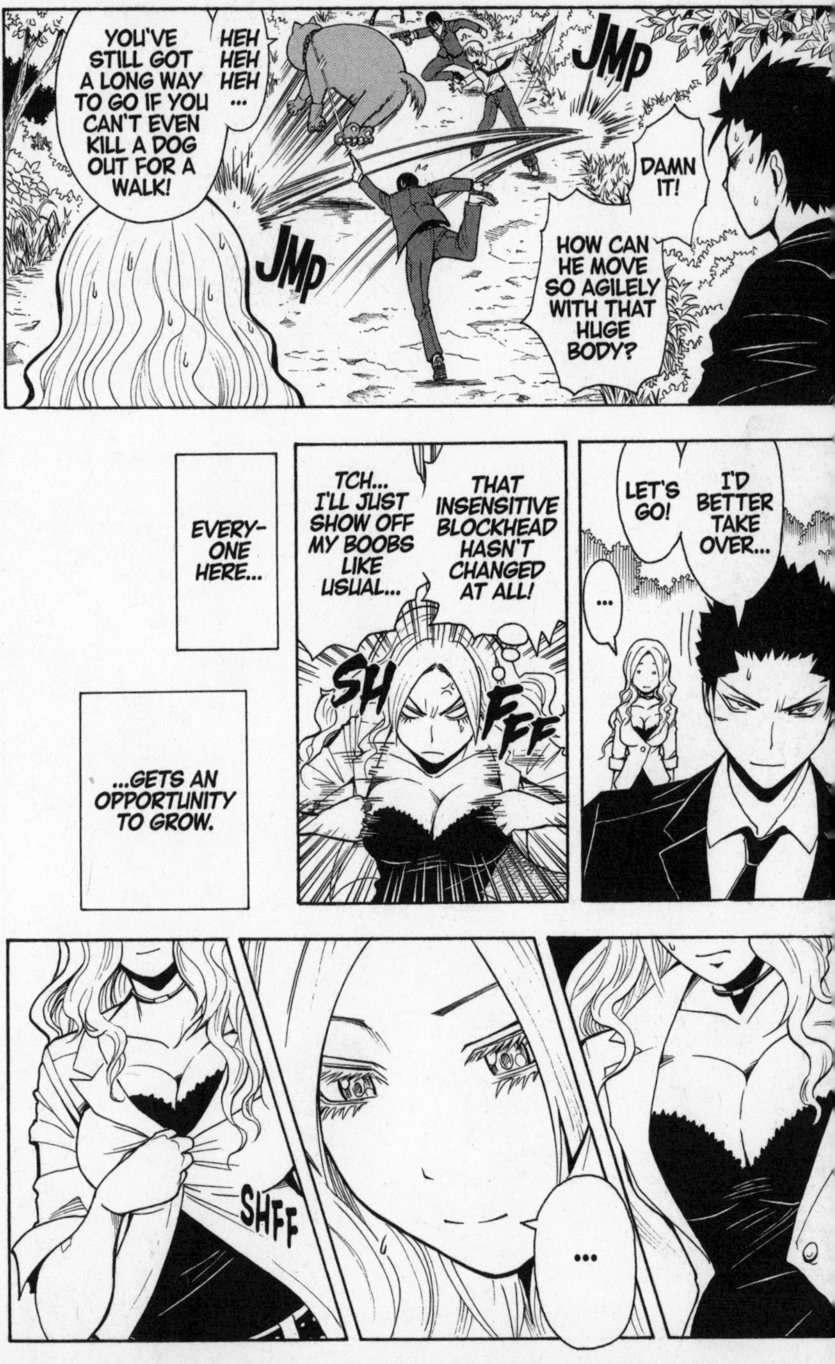
DAMN IT!
HOW CAN HE MOVE SO AGILELY WITH THAT HUGE BODY?
JMP
JMP
HEH HEH HEH...
YOU'VE STILL GOT A LONG WAY TO GO IF YOU CAN'T EVEN KILL A DOG OUT FOR A WALK!
I'D BETTER TAKE OVER...
LET'S GO!
...
THAT INSENSITIVE BLOCKHEAD HASN'T CHANGED AT ALL!
TCH... I'LL JUST SHOW OFF MY BOOBS LIKE USUAL...
SHFFF
EVERYONE HERE...
...GETS AN OPPORTUNITY TO GROW.
...
SHFF

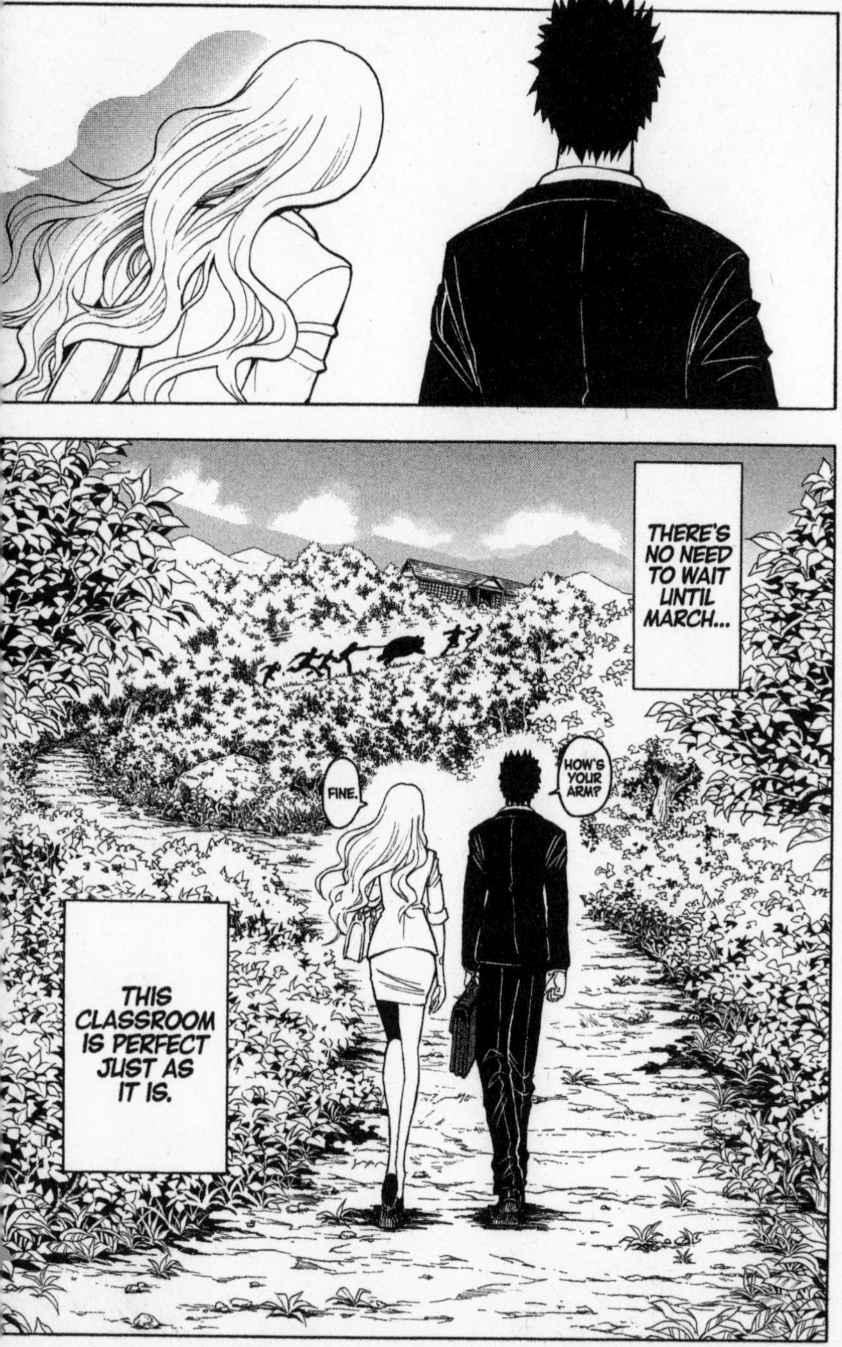
THERE'S NO NEED TO WAIT UNTIL MARCH...
HOW'S YOUR ARM?
FINE.
THIS CLASSROOM IS PERFECT JUST AS IT IS.

Sample Correct Answer

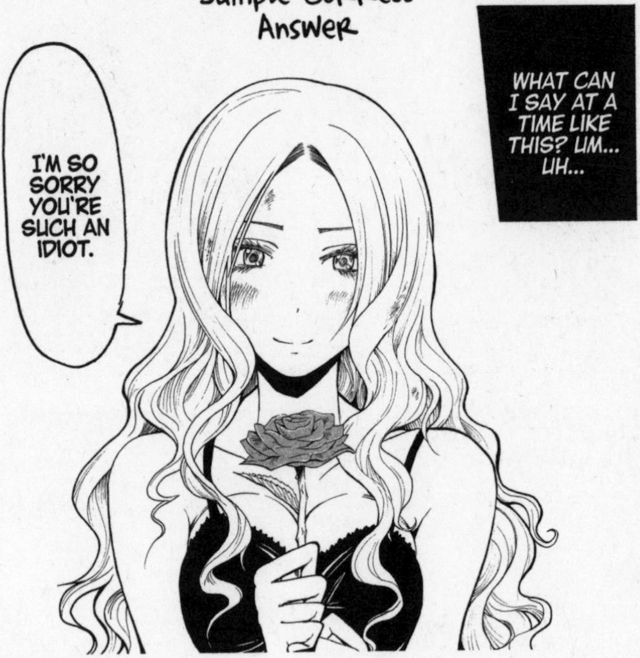
WHAT CAN I SAY AT A TIME LIKE THIS? UM... UH...
I'M SO SORRY YOU'RE SUCH AN IDIOT.

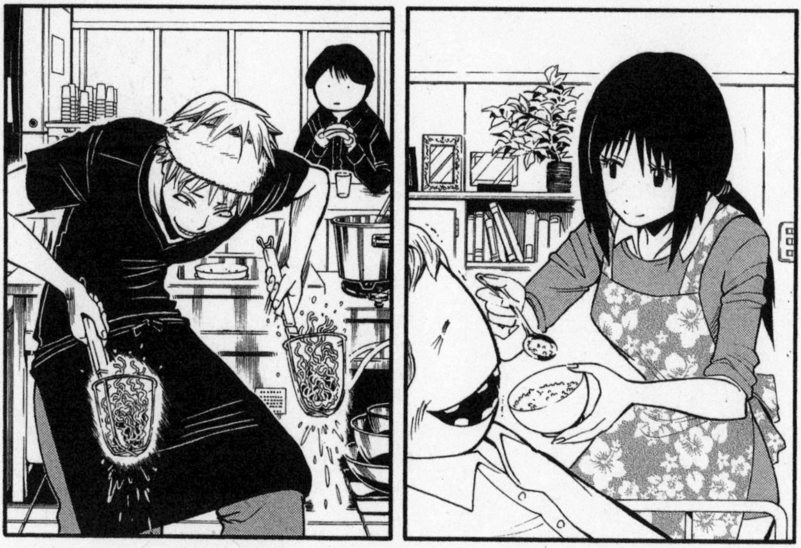

CLASS 111 TIME FOR A LITTLE CAREER COUNSELING

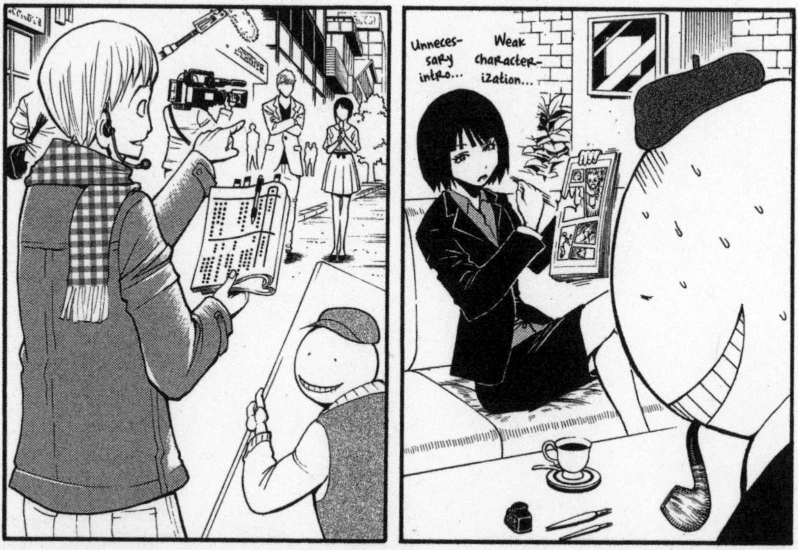
Weak characterization...
Unnecessary intro...

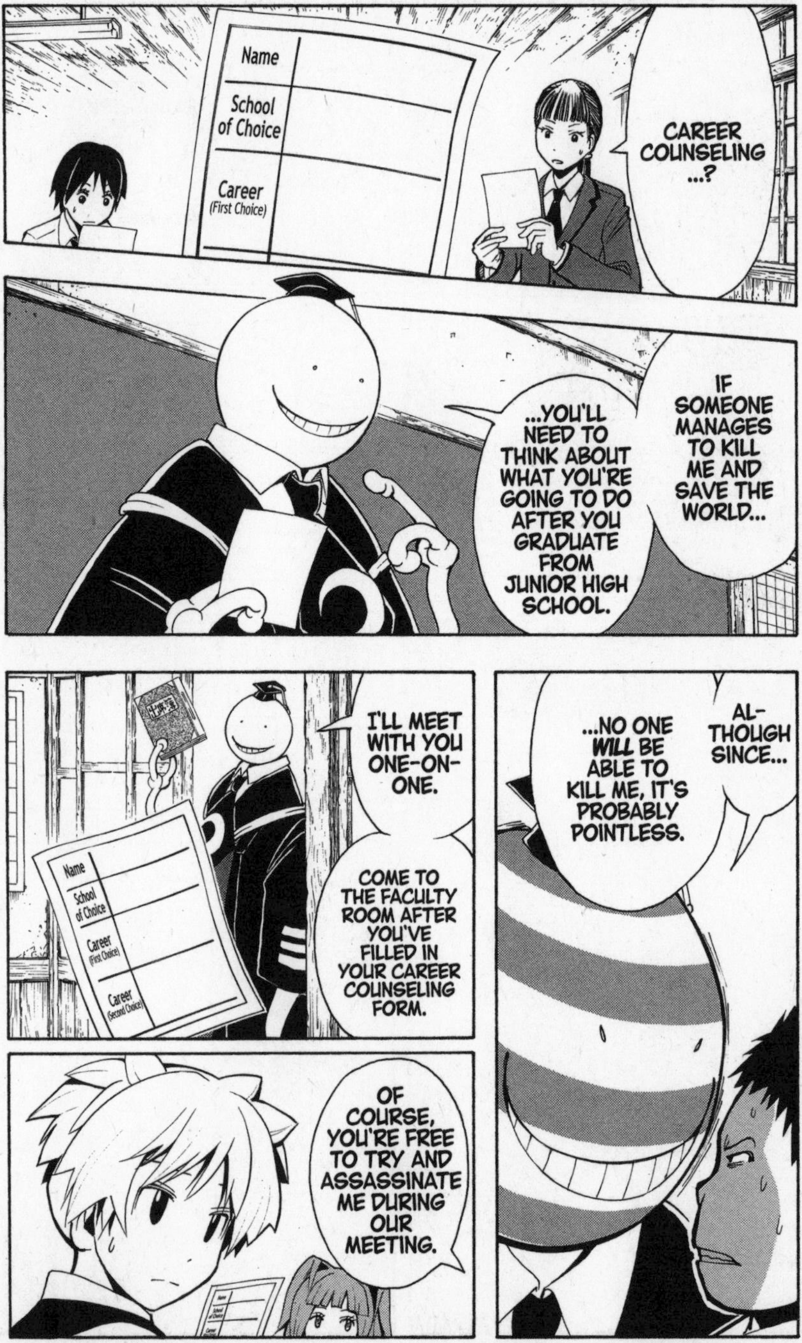

Name
School of Choice
Career (First Choice)
CAREER COUNSELING ...?
IF SOMEONE MANAGES TO KILL ME AND SAVE THE WORLD...
...YOU'LL NEED TO THINK ABOUT WHAT YOU'RE GOING TO DO AFTER YOU GRADUATE FROM JUNIOR HIGH SCHOOL.
AL-THOUGH SINCE...
...NO ONE *WILL* BE ABLE TO KILL ME, IT'S PROBABLY POINTLESS.
I'LL MEET WITH YOU ONE-ON-ONE.
COME TO THE FACULTY ROOM AFTER YOU'VE FILLED IN YOUR CAREER COUNSELING FORM.
Name
School of Choice
Career (First Choice)
Career (Second Choice)
OF COURSE, YOU'RE FREE TO TRY AND ASSASSINATE ME DURING OUR MEETING.

IS HE JUST BEING NICE? OR UNDERESTIMATING US?

WHY SHOULD WE ASK A MONSTER WHO'S OUT TO DESTROY THE WORLD FOR ADVICE ABOUT OUR FUTURE?

CAREER COUNSELING, HUH?

MY CAREER...

Name	Nagisa Shiota
School of Choice	All Girls High School
Career (First Choice)	Nurse
...er (...Choice)	Maid

I...

Faculty Room

WHY DO YOU WANT ME TO TRANSITION, KARMA?!

HEY, NAGISA...

LET'S GO ON AN OVERSEAS TRIP AFTER WE GRADUATE—TO THAILAND OR MOROCCO!

A journey of rebirth!

Thailand

Morocco A Trip A Chang...

A journey of rebirth!

...MACHO JOBS JUST AREN'T FOR YOU.

C'MON, NAGISA...

SERIOUSLY?

NAKAMURA...

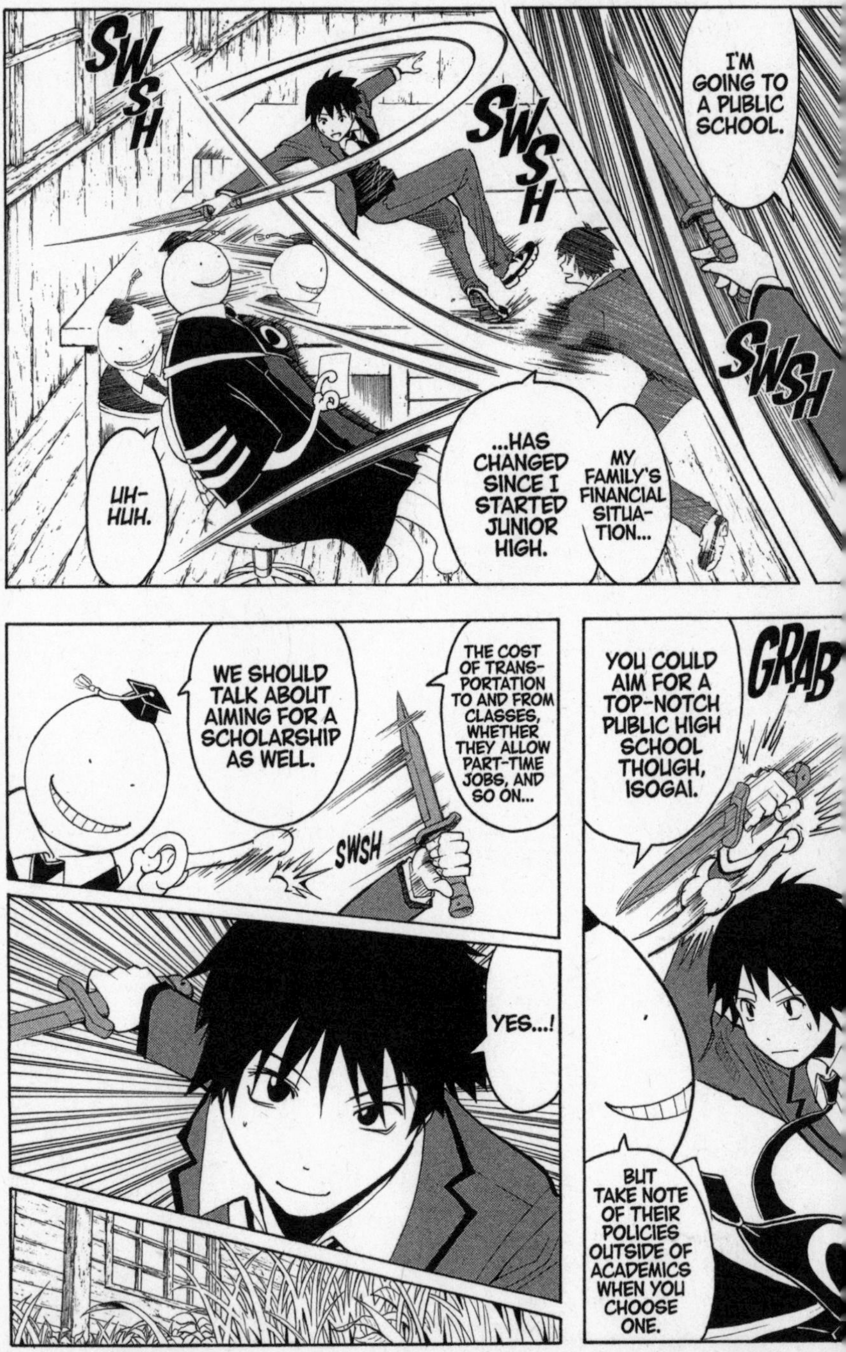
I'M GOING TO A PUBLIC SCHOOL.
SWSH
MY FAMILY'S FINANCIAL SITUATION...
...HAS CHANGED SINCE I STARTED JUNIOR HIGH.
SWSH
SWSH
UH-HUH.
GRAB
YOU COULD AIM FOR A TOP-NOTCH PUBLIC HIGH SCHOOL THOUGH, ISOGAI.
BUT TAKE NOTE OF THEIR POLICIES OUTSIDE OF ACADEMICS WHEN YOU CHOOSE ONE.
THE COST OF TRANSPORTATION TO AND FROM CLASSES, WHETHER THEY ALLOW PART-TIME JOBS, AND SO ON...
WE SHOULD TALK ABOUT AIMING FOR A SCHOLARSHIP AS WELL.
SWSH
YES...!

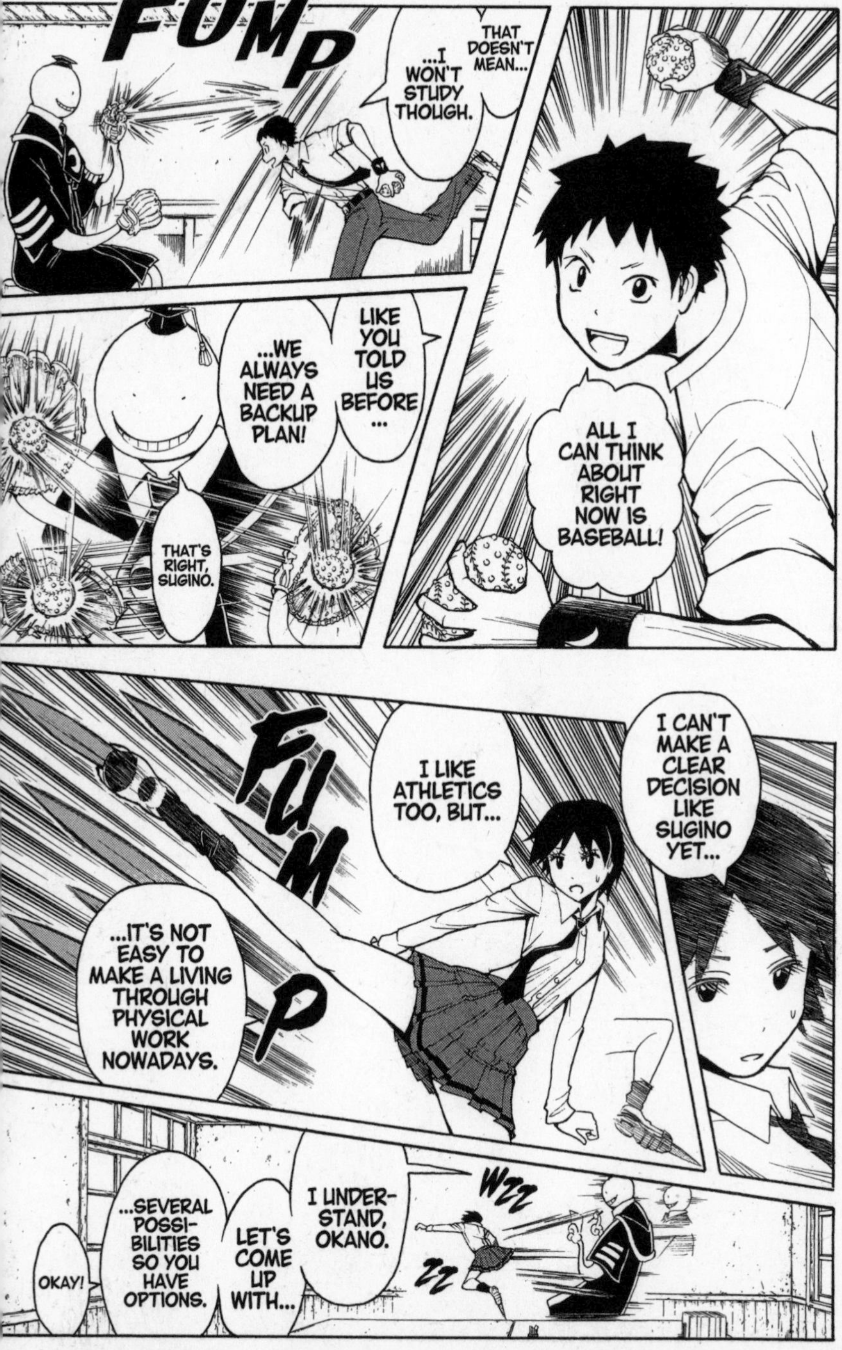
ALL I CAN THINK ABOUT RIGHT NOW IS BASEBALL!
FUMP
THAT DOESN'T MEAN...
...I WON'T STUDY THOUGH.
LIKE YOU TOLD US BEFORE...
...WE ALWAYS NEED A BACKUP PLAN!
THAT'S RIGHT, SUGINO.
I CAN'T MAKE A CLEAR DECISION LIKE SUGINO YET...
I LIKE ATHLETICS TOO, BUT...
FUMP
...IT'S NOT EASY TO MAKE A LIVING THROUGH PHYSICAL WORK NOWADAYS.
I UNDER-STAND, OKANO.
LET'S COME UP WITH...
...SEVERAL POSSI-BILITIES SO YOU HAVE OPTIONS.
OKAY!
WZZ
ZZ

WHAT ABOUT YOU, KAYANO?

HMM... I HAVEN'T DECIDED YET.

I BET A LOT OF US HAVEN'T.

Name	Hiroto Maehara
School of Choice	A high school that's popular with girls
Career (First Choice)	Corporate Boy-Toy
Career (Second Choice)	Sugar Baby

Hmm...

I'LL TELL HIM I'M STILL INTERESTED IN CHEMISTRY RESEARCH.

AND, HOPEFULLY, I'LL MANAGE TO TRICK HIM INTO DRINKING THIS POISONED SODA TOO.

...AFTER WE FINISH WHAT WE SET OUT TO DO IN THIS CLASS.

AND SOME OF US...

...MIGHT ONLY FIND THE ANSWER...

...

I BET THOSE TWO WILL END UP USING THEIR SMARTS AND EDUCATION FOR NEFARIOUS PURPOSES...

THEY'RE A SIMILAR SPECIES—THEY SHOULD GO WELL TOGETHER!

BLEND IN SOME MANTIS EGGS TOO!

LET'S ADD SOME POWDERED COCKROACH EGGS TO THAT!

GRND GRND

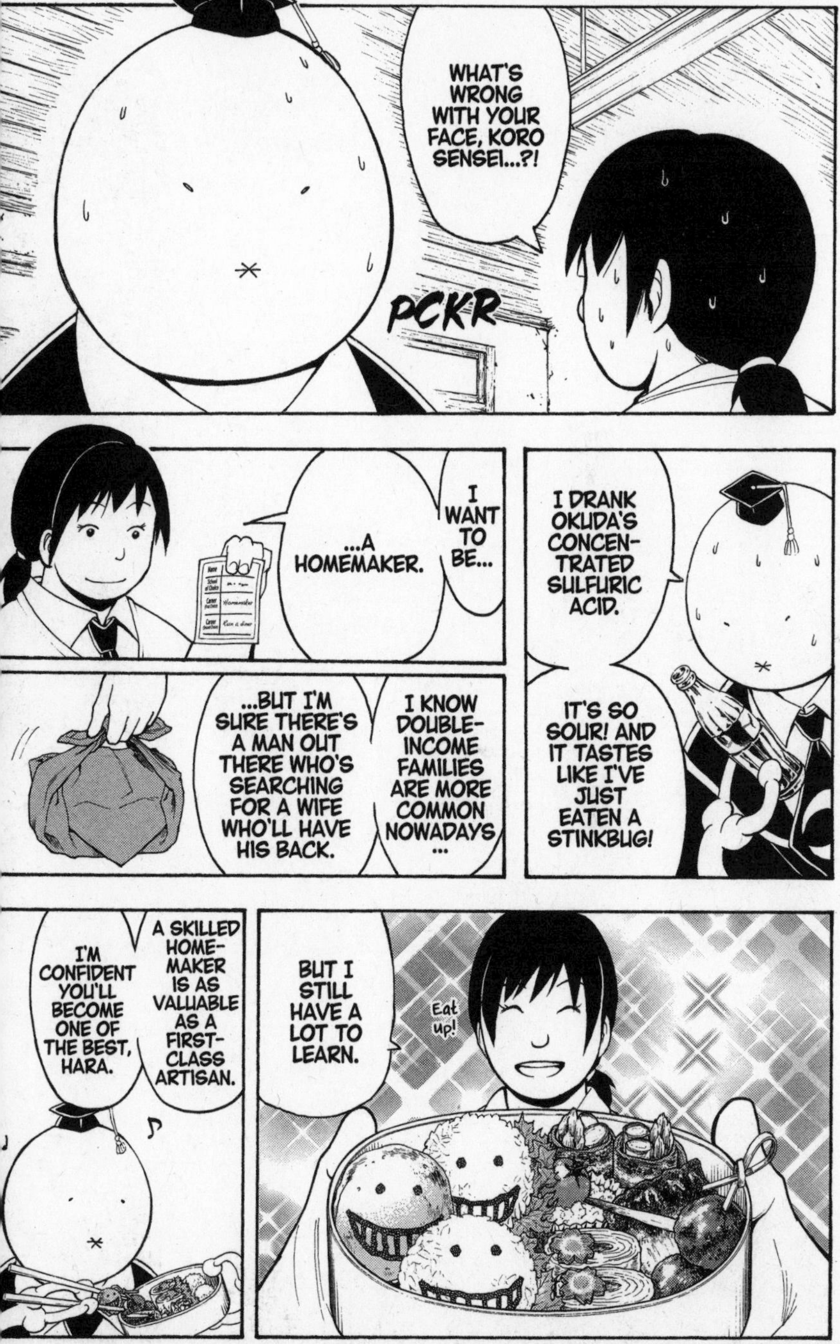
WHAT'S WRONG WITH YOUR FACE, KORO SENSEI...?!
PCKR
I DRANK OKUDA'S CONCEN-TRATED SULFURIC ACID.
IT'S SO SOUR! AND IT TASTES LIKE I'VE JUST EATEN A STINKBUG!
I WANT TO BE...
...A HOMEMAKER.
I KNOW DOUBLE-INCOME FAMILIES ARE MORE COMMON NOWADAYS...
...BUT I'M SURE THERE'S A MAN OUT THERE WHO'S SEARCHING FOR A WIFE WHO'LL HAVE HIS BACK.
BUT I STILL HAVE A LOT TO LEARN.
Eat up!
A SKILLED HOME-MAKER IS AS VALUABLE AS A FIRST-CLASS ARTISAN.
I'M CONFIDENT YOU'LL BECOME ONE OF THE BEST, HARA.

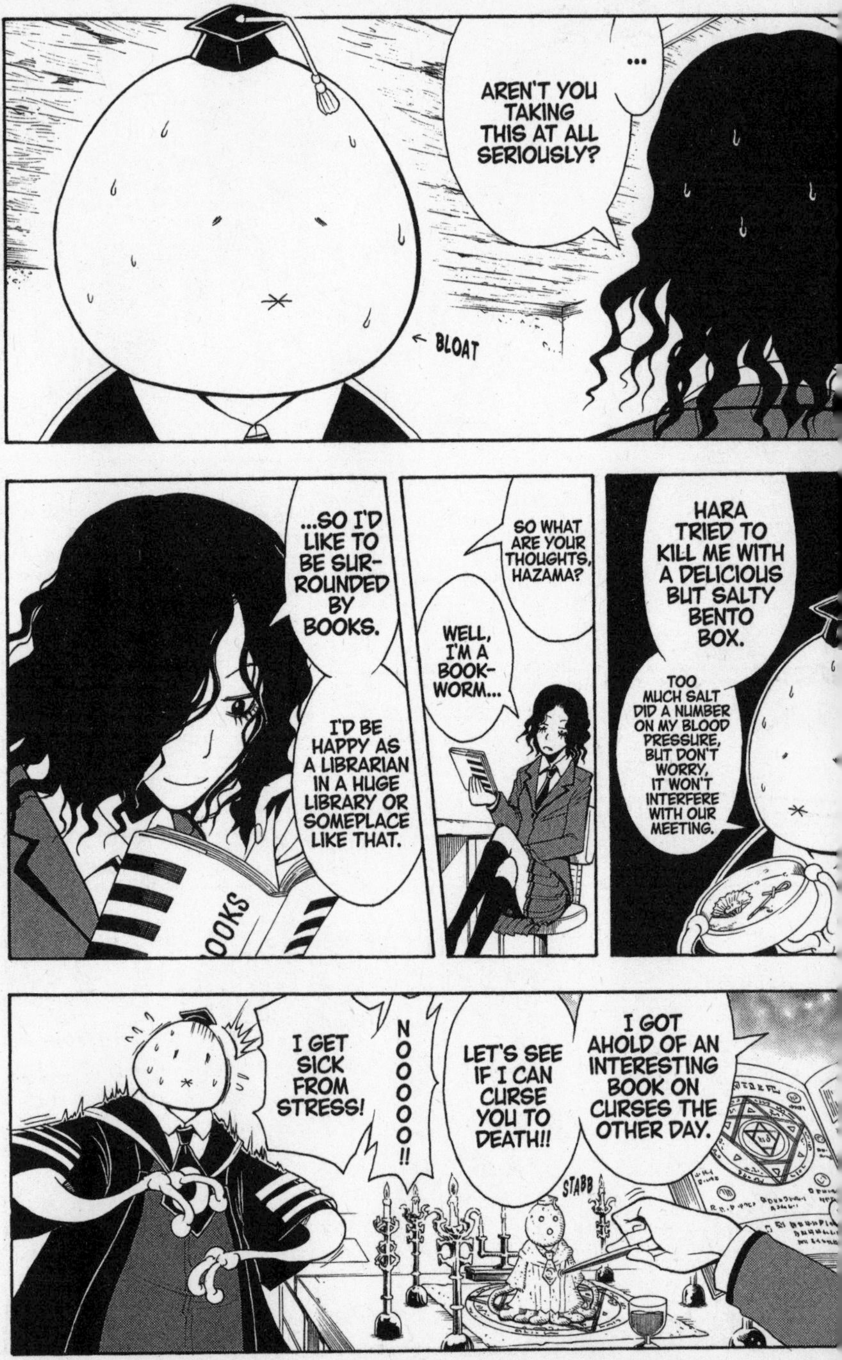
...
AREN'T YOU TAKING THIS AT ALL SERIOUSLY?
BLOAT
HARA TRIED TO KILL ME WITH A DELICIOUS BUT SALTY BENTO BOX.
TOO MUCH SALT DID A NUMBER ON MY BLOOD PRESSURE, BUT DON'T WORRY, IT WON'T INTERFERE WITH OUR MEETING.
SO WHAT ARE YOUR THOUGHTS, HAZAMA?
WELL, I'M A BOOK-WORM...
...SO I'D LIKE TO BE SUR-ROUNDED BY BOOKS.
I'D BE HAPPY AS A LIBRARIAN IN A HUGE LIBRARY OR SOMEPLACE LIKE THAT.
BOOKS
I GOT AHOLD OF AN INTERESTING BOOK ON CURSES THE OTHER DAY.
LET'S SEE IF I CAN CURSE YOU TO DEATH!!
STABB
NOOOOOO!!
I GET SICK FROM STRESS!

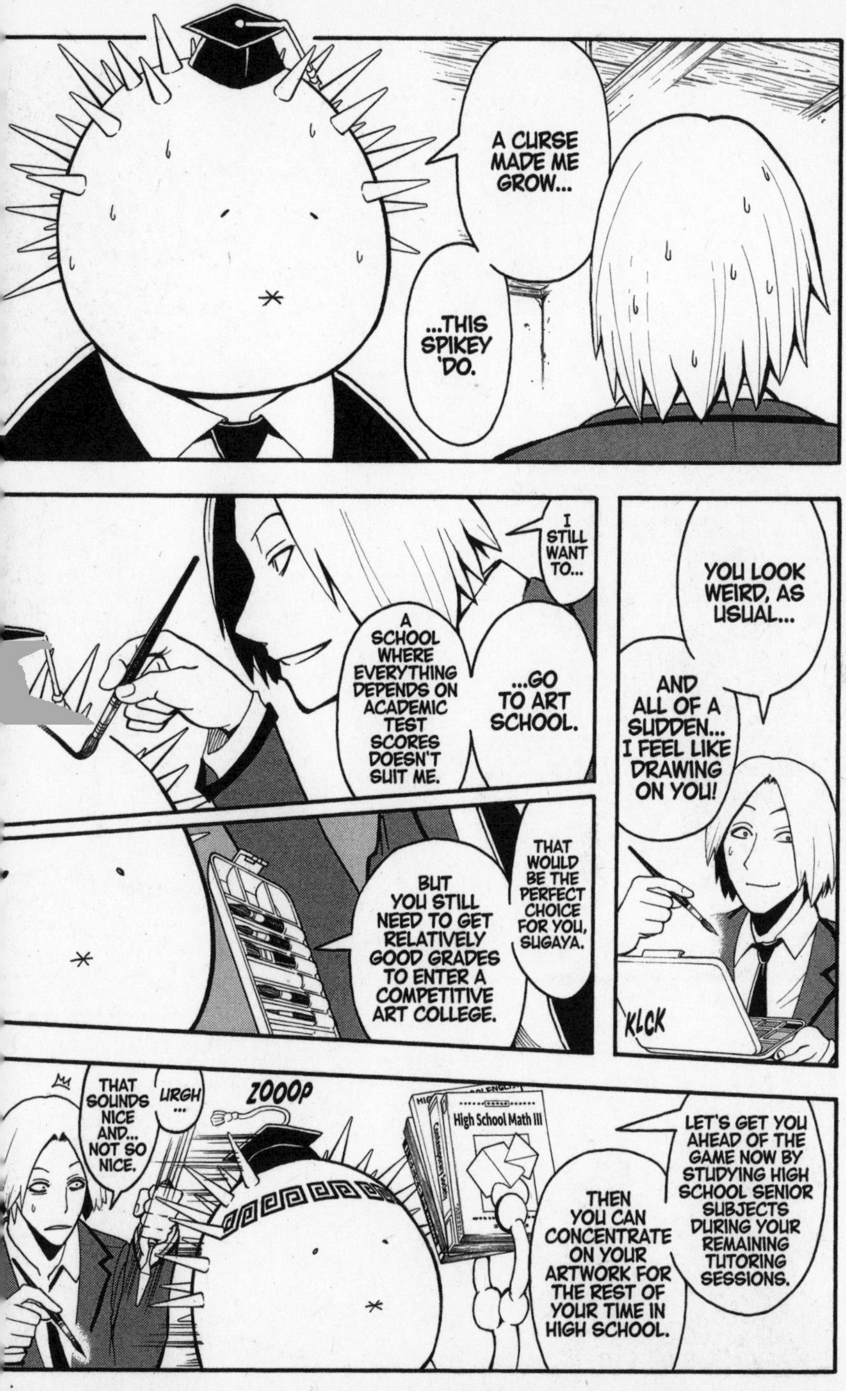
A CURSE MADE ME GROW...
...THIS SPIKEY 'DO.
YOU LOOK WEIRD, AS USUAL...
AND ALL OF A SUDDEN... I FEEL LIKE DRAWING ON YOU!
KLCK
I STILL WANT TO...
...GO TO ART SCHOOL.
A SCHOOL WHERE EVERYTHING DEPENDS ON ACADEMIC TEST SCORES DOESN'T SUIT ME.
THAT WOULD BE THE PERFECT CHOICE FOR YOU, SUGAYA.
BUT YOU STILL NEED TO GET RELATIVELY GOOD GRADES TO ENTER A COMPETITIVE ART COLLEGE.
LET'S GET YOU AHEAD OF THE GAME NOW BY STUDYING HIGH SCHOOL SENIOR SUBJECTS DURING YOUR REMAINING TUTORING SESSIONS.
THEN YOU CAN CONCENTRATE ON YOUR ARTWORK FOR THE REST OF YOUR TIME IN HIGH SCHOOL.
High School Math III
ZOOOP
URGH...
THAT SOUNDS NICE AND... NOT SO NICE.

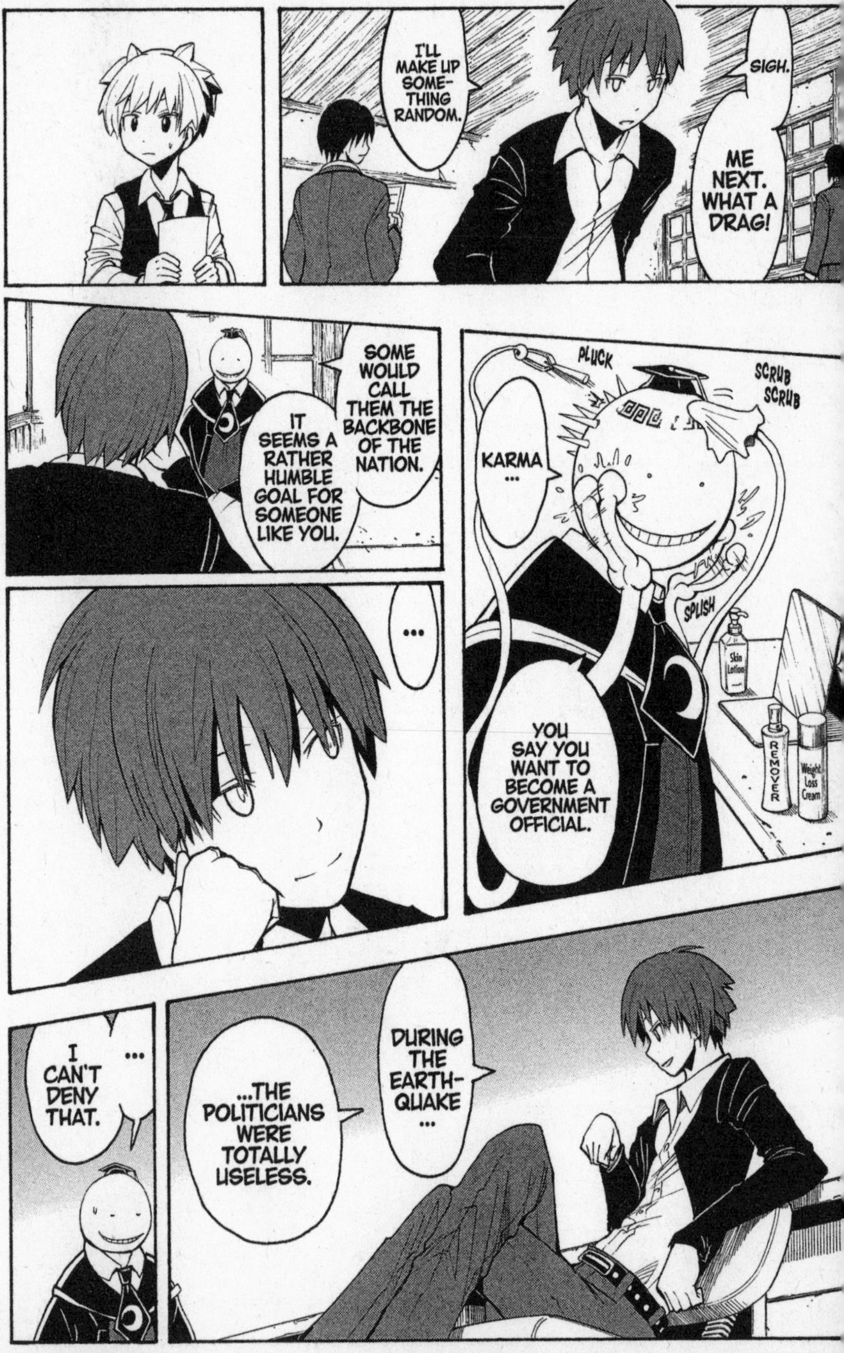
SIGH.
ME NEXT. WHAT A DRAG!
I'LL MAKE UP SOMETHING RANDOM.
PLUCK
SCRUB SCRUB
KARMA...
SPLISH
Skin Lotion
REMOVER
Weight Loss Cream
YOU SAY YOU WANT TO BECOME A GOVERNMENT OFFICIAL.
SOME WOULD CALL THEM THE BACKBONE OF THE NATION.
IT SEEMS A RATHER HUMBLE GOAL FOR SOMEONE LIKE YOU.
...
DURING THE EARTHQUAKE...
...THE POLITICIANS WERE TOTALLY USELESS.
I... CAN'T DENY THAT.

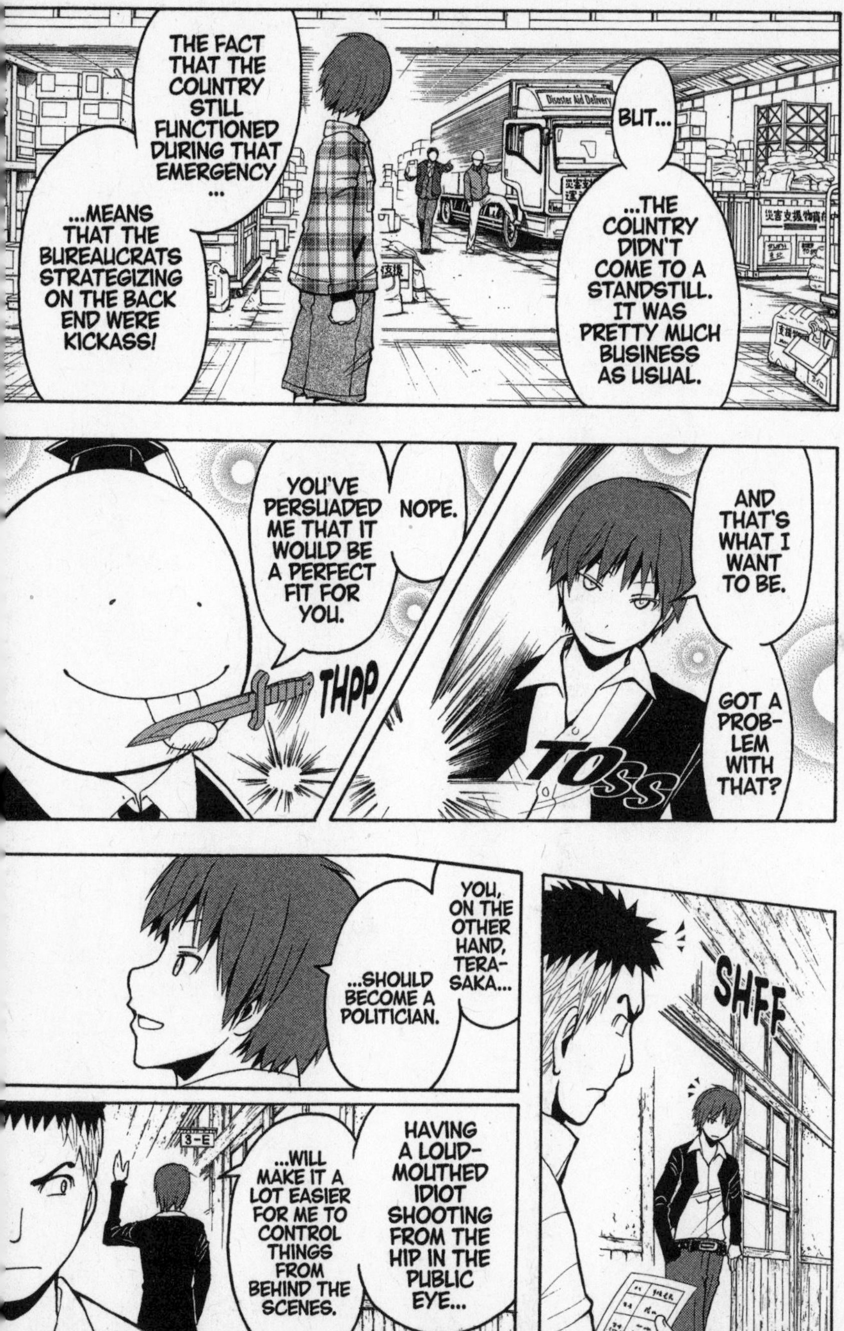
Disaster Aid Delivery
BUT...
...THE COUNTRY DIDN'T COME TO A STANDSTILL. IT WAS PRETTY MUCH BUSINESS AS USUAL.
THE FACT THAT THE COUNTRY STILL FUNCTIONED DURING THAT EMERGENCY...
...MEANS THAT THE BUREAUCRATS STRATEGIZING ON THE BACK END WERE KICKASS!
AND THAT'S WHAT I WANT TO BE.
GOT A PROBLEM WITH THAT?
TOSS
NOPE.
YOU'VE PERSUADED ME THAT IT WOULD BE A PERFECT FIT FOR YOU.
THPP
SHFF
YOU, ON THE OTHER HAND, TERA-SAKA...
...SHOULD BECOME A POLITICIAN.
HAVING A LOUD-MOUTHED IDIOT SHOOTING FROM THE HIP IN THE PUBLIC EYE...
...WILL MAKE IT A LOT EASIER FOR ME TO CONTROL THINGS FROM BEHIND THE SCENES.
3-E

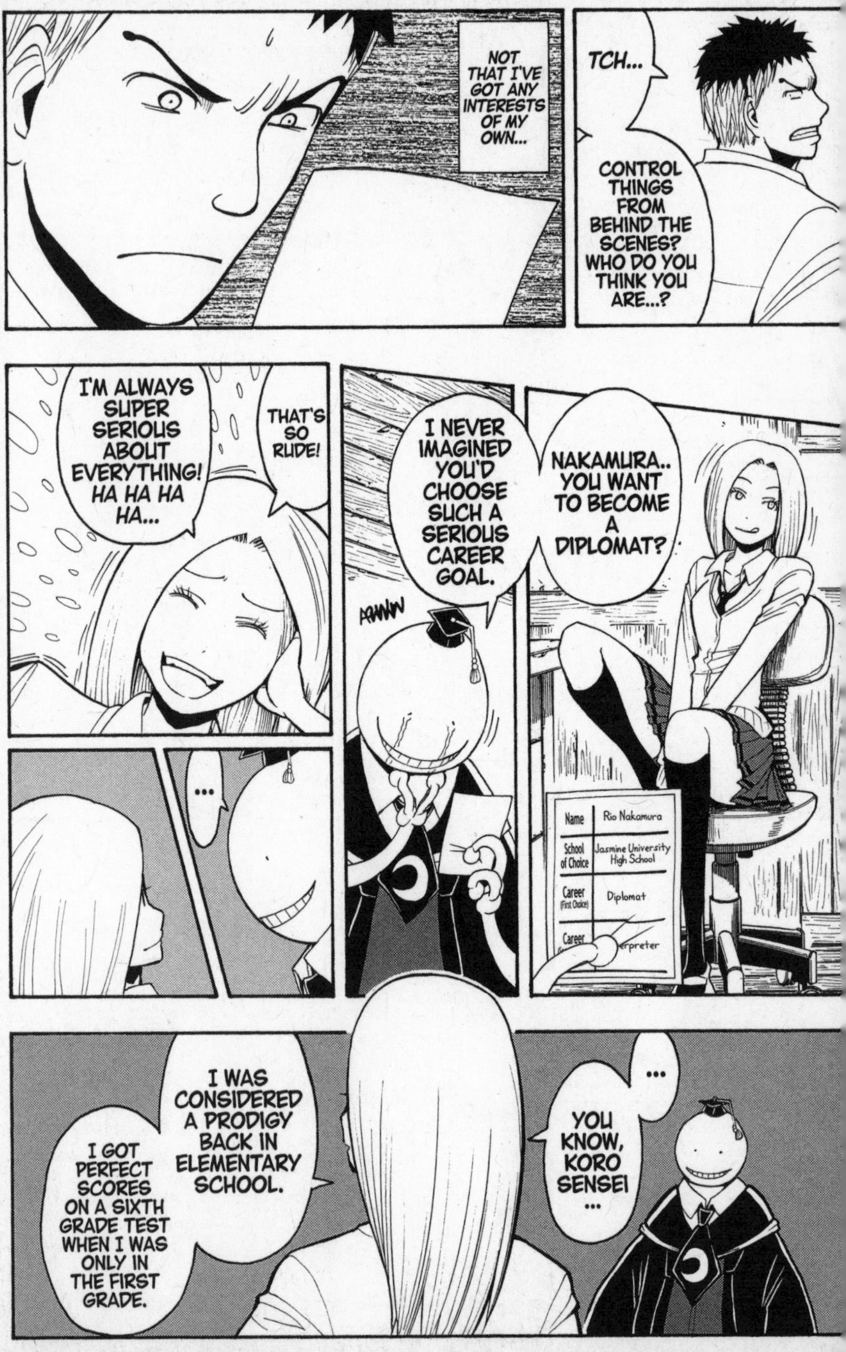
TCH...
CONTROL THINGS FROM BEHIND THE SCENES? WHO DO YOU THINK YOU ARE...?
NOT THAT I'VE GOT ANY INTERESTS OF MY OWN...
NAKAMURA.. YOU WANT TO BECOME A DIPLOMAT?
Name Rio Nakamura
School of Choice Jasmine University High School
Career (First Choice) Diplomat
Career
I NEVER IMAGINED YOU'D CHOOSE SUCH A SERIOUS CAREER GOAL.
THAT'S SO RUDE!
I'M ALWAYS SUPER SERIOUS ABOUT EVERYTHING! HA HA HA HA...
...
...
YOU KNOW, KORO SENSEI ...
I WAS CONSIDERED A PRODIGY BACK IN ELEMENTARY SCHOOL.
I GOT PERFECT SCORES ON A SIXTH GRADE TEST WHEN I WAS ONLY IN THE FIRST GRADE.

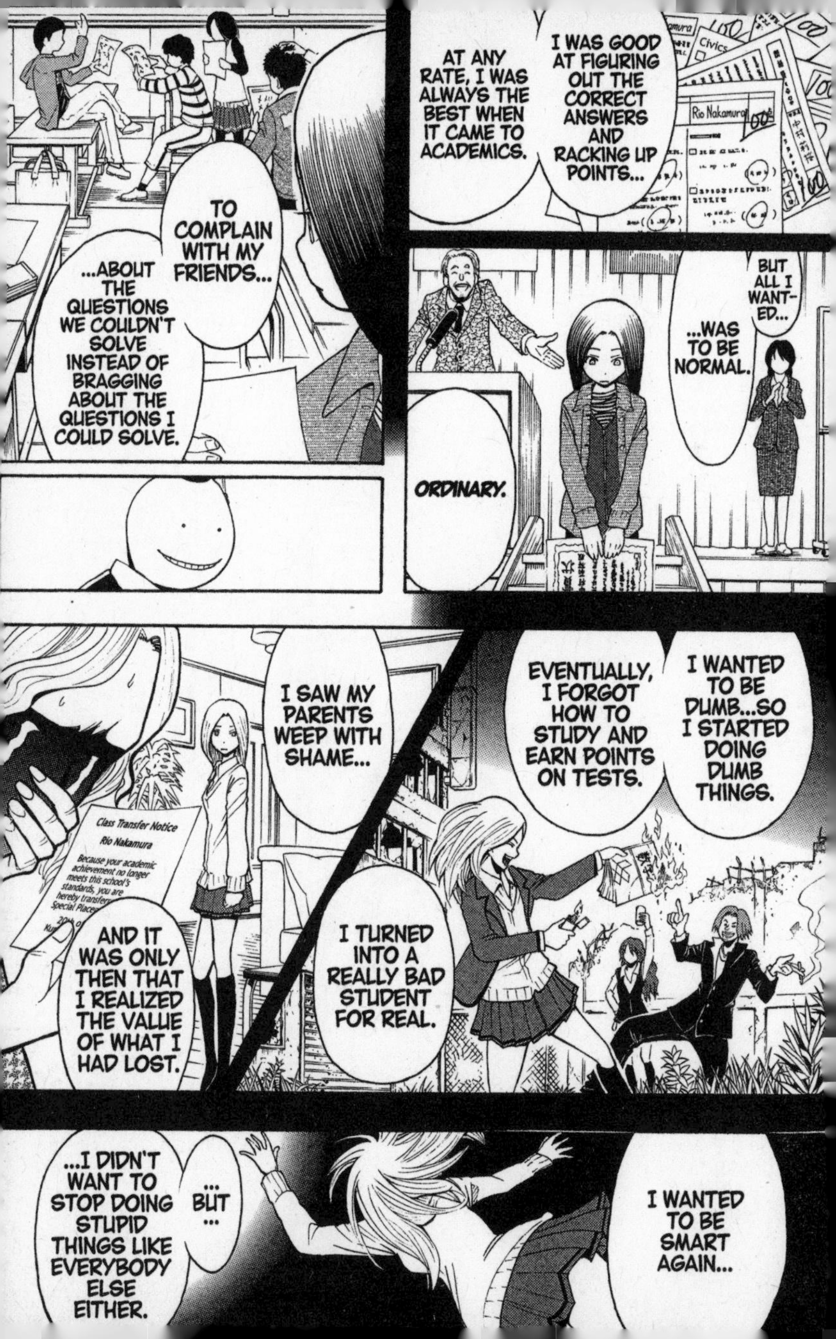
I WAS GOOD AT FIGURING OUT THE CORRECT ANSWERS AND RACKING UP POINTS...
AT ANY RATE, I WAS ALWAYS THE BEST WHEN IT CAME TO ACADEMICS.
Civics
Rio Nakamura
BUT ALL I WANT-ED...
...WAS TO BE NORMAL.
ORDINARY.
TO COMPLAIN WITH MY FRIENDS...
...ABOUT THE QUESTIONS WE COULDN'T SOLVE INSTEAD OF BRAGGING ABOUT THE QUESTIONS I COULD SOLVE.
I WANTED TO BE DUMB...SO I STARTED DOING DUMB THINGS.
EVENTUALLY, I FORGOT HOW TO STUDY AND EARN POINTS ON TESTS.
I TURNED INTO A REALLY BAD STUDENT FOR REAL.
I SAW MY PARENTS WEEP WITH SHAME...
Class Transfer Notice
Rio Nakamura
AND IT WAS ONLY THEN THAT I REALIZED THE VALUE OF WHAT I HAD LOST.
I WANTED TO BE SMART AGAIN...
...BUT...
...I DIDN'T WANT TO STOP DOING STUPID THINGS LIKE EVERYBODY ELSE EITHER.

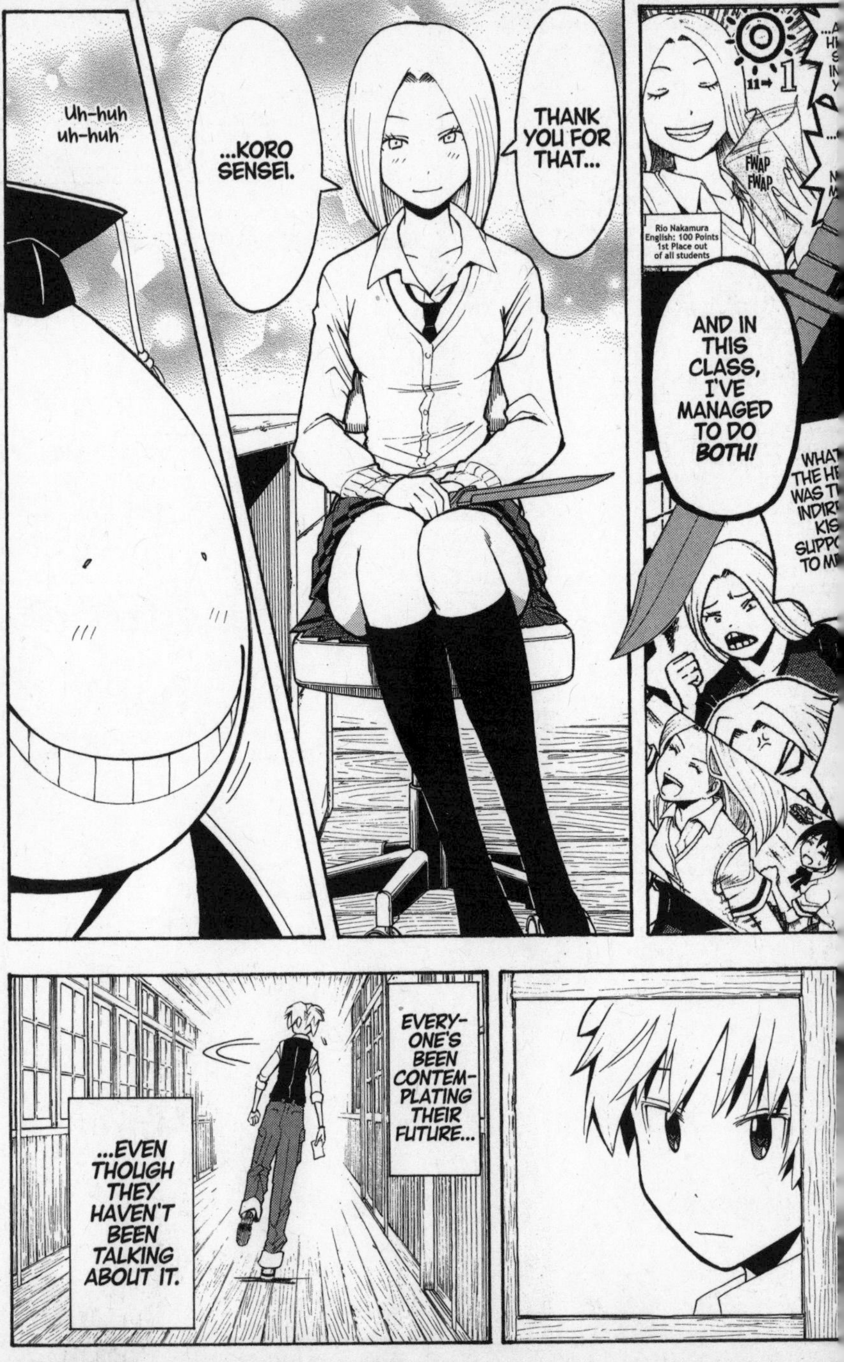
11→1
FWAP FWAP
Rio Nakamura English: 100 Points 1st Place out of all students
AND IN THIS CLASS, I'VE MANAGED TO DO BOTH!
THANK YOU FOR THAT...
...KORO SENSEI.
Uh-huh uh-huh
EVERY-ONE'S BEEN CONTEM-PLATING THEIR FUTURE...
...EVEN THOUGH THEY HAVEN'T BEEN TALKING ABOUT IT.

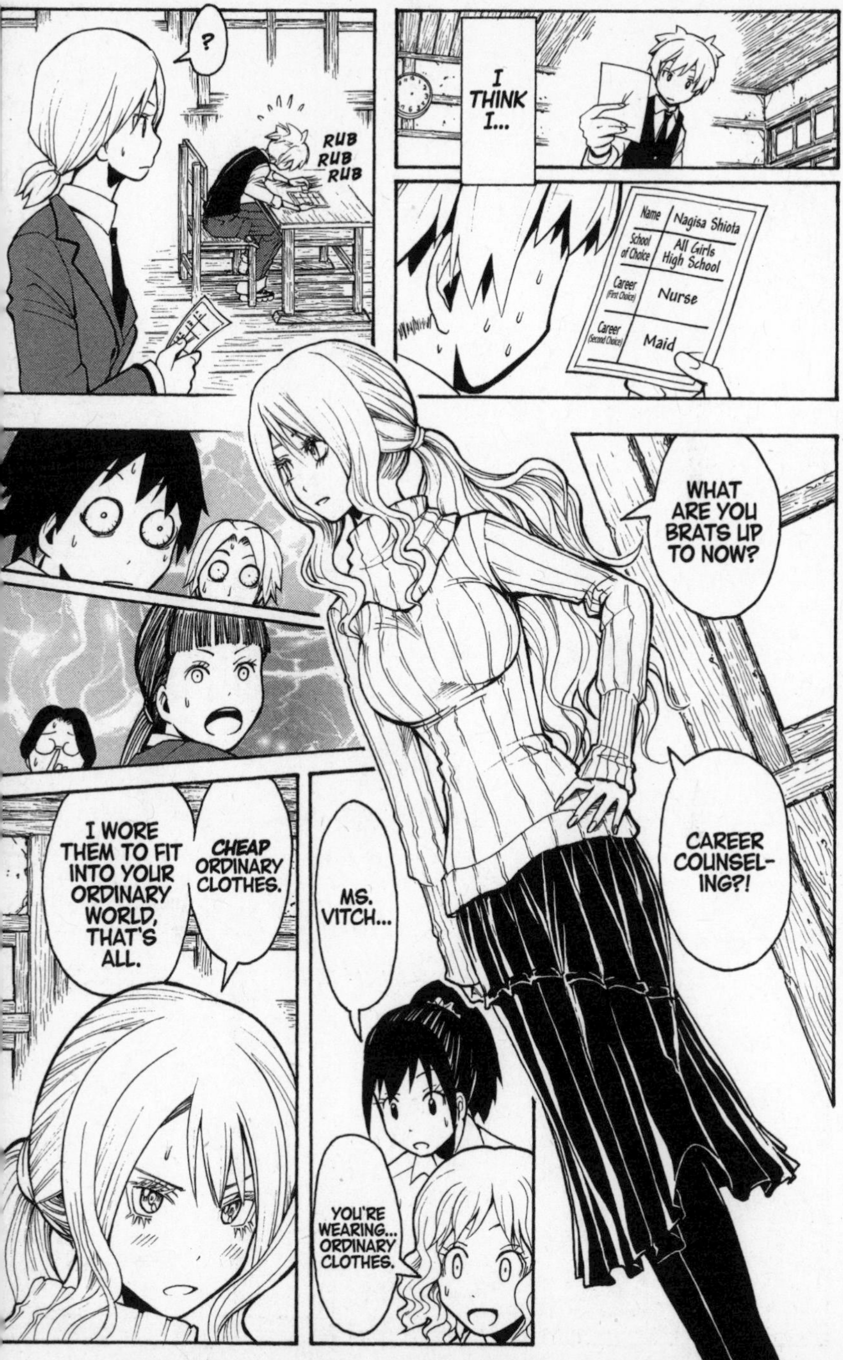
I THINK I...
Name
Nagisa Shiota
School of Choice
All Girls High School
Career (First Choice)
Nurse
Career (Second Choice)
Maid
?
RUB RUB RUB
WHAT ARE YOU BRATS UP TO NOW?
CAREER COUNSEL-ING?!
MS. VITCH...
YOU'RE WEARING... ORDINARY CLOTHES.
CHEAP ORDINARY CLOTHES.
I WORE THEM TO FIT INTO YOUR ORDINARY WORLD, THAT'S ALL.

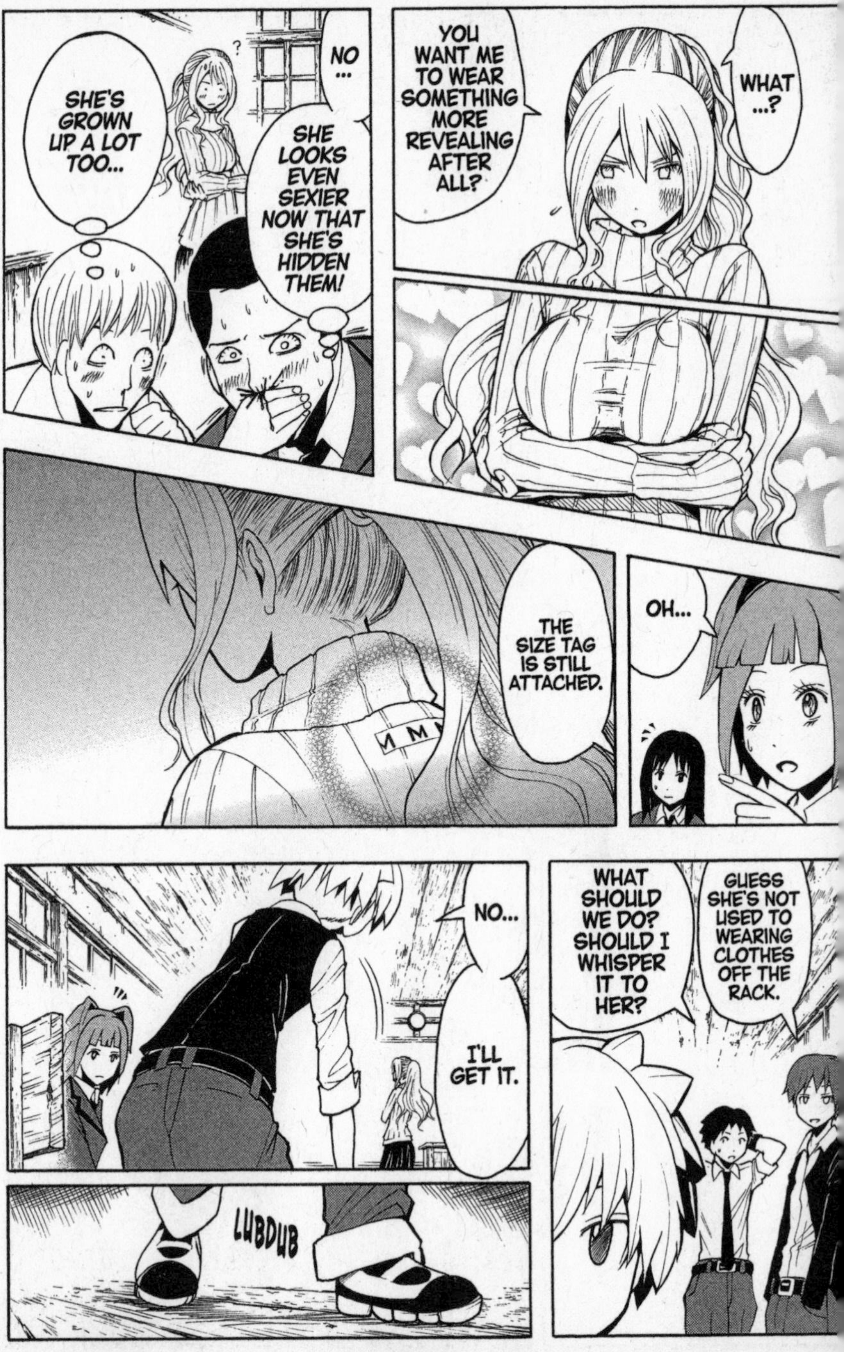
WHAT ...?
YOU WANT ME TO WEAR SOMETHING MORE REVEALING AFTER ALL?
NO ...
SHE LOOKS EVEN SEXIER NOW THAT SHE'S HIDDEN THEM!
SHE'S GROWN UP A LOT TOO...
OH...
THE SIZE TAG IS STILL ATTACHED.
GUESS SHE'S NOT USED TO WEARING CLOTHES OFF THE RACK.
WHAT SHOULD WE DO? SHOULD I WHISPER IT TO HER?
NO...
I'LL GET IT.
LUBDUB

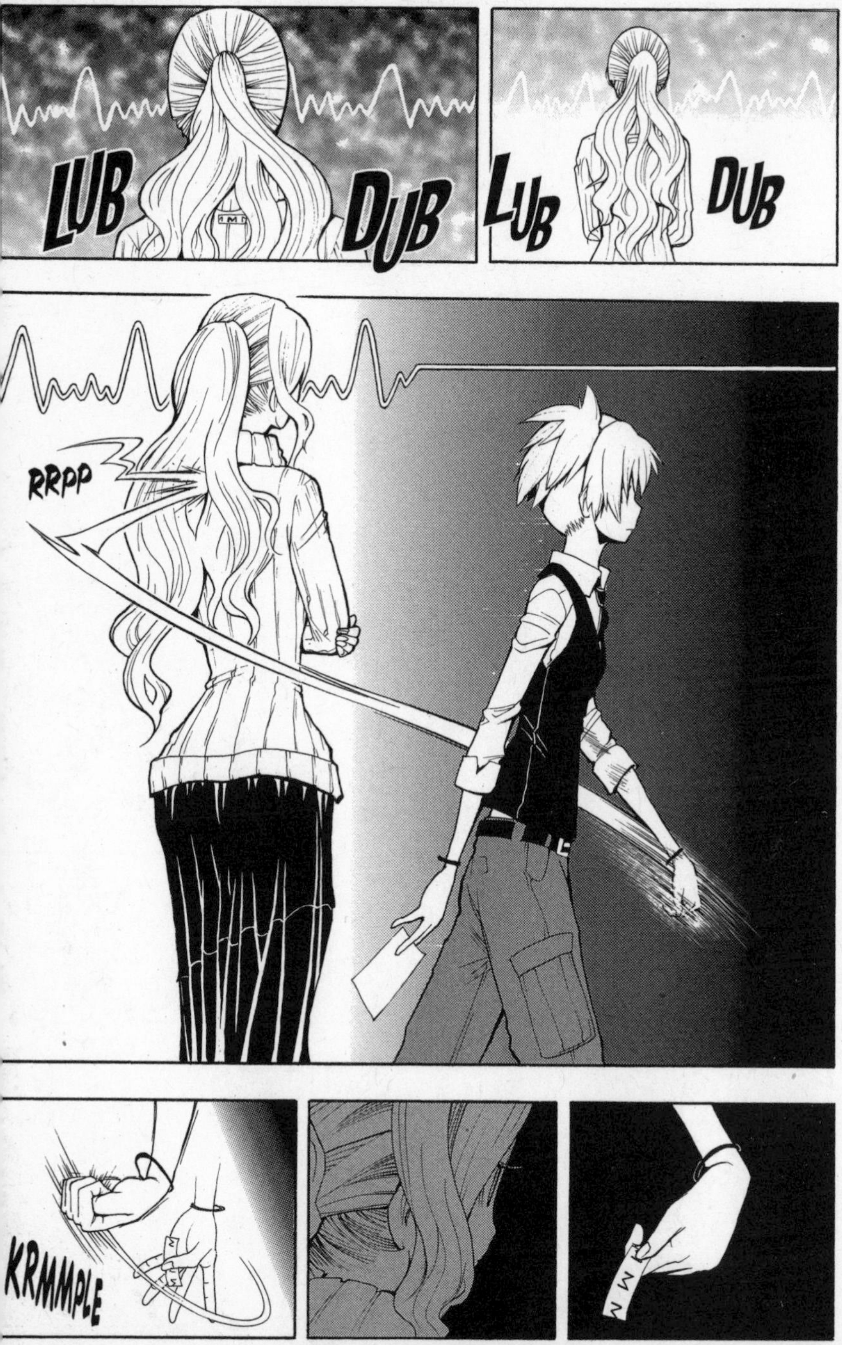
LUB
DUB
LUB
DUB
RRPP
KRMMPLE

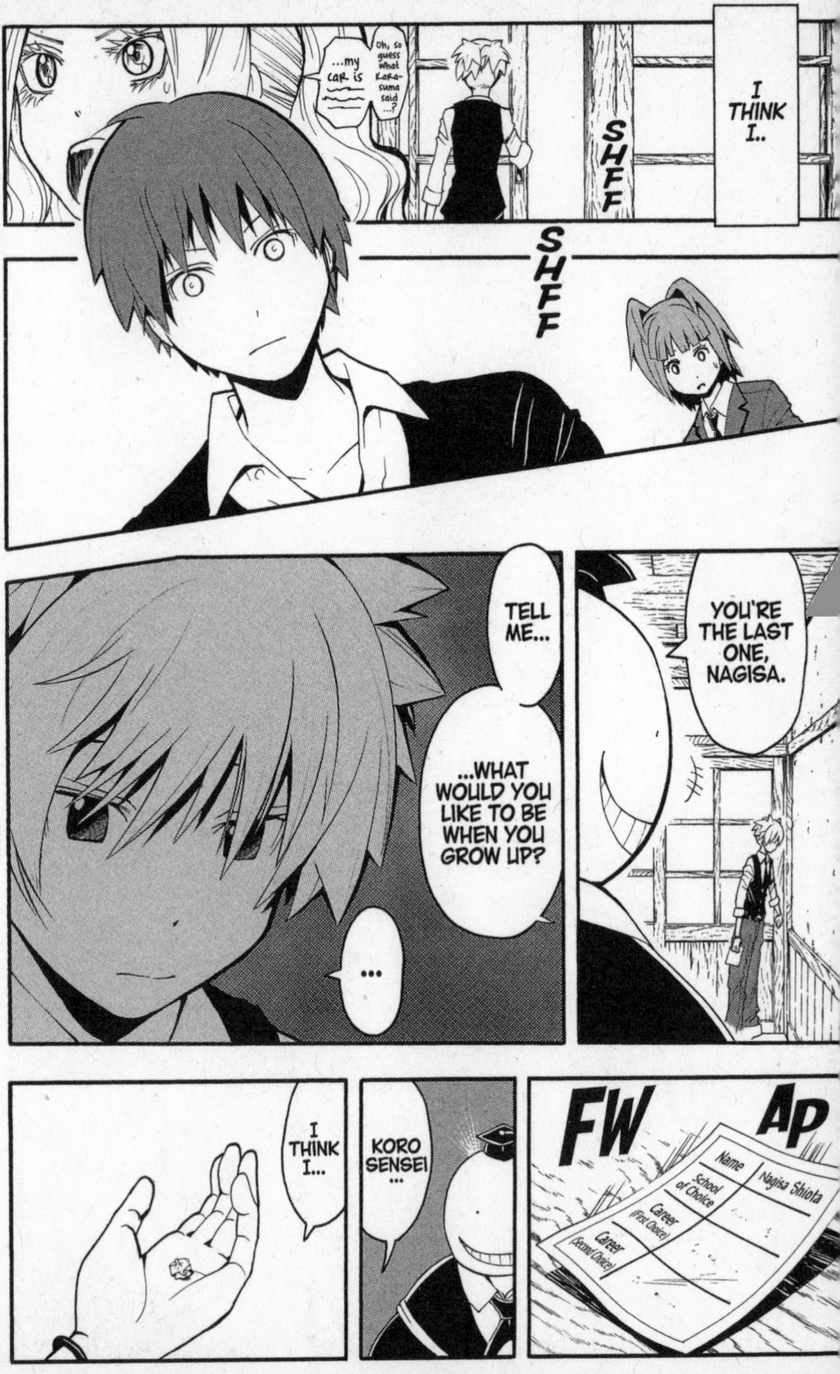
I THINK I..
SHFF
Oh, so guess what Karasuma said...?
...my car is
SHFF
YOU'RE THE LAST ONE, NAGISA.
TELL ME...
...WHAT WOULD YOU LIKE TO BE WHEN YOU GROW UP?
...
FWAP
Name
Nagisa Shiota
School of Choice
Career (First Choice)
Career (Second Choice)
KORO SENSEI...
I THINK I...

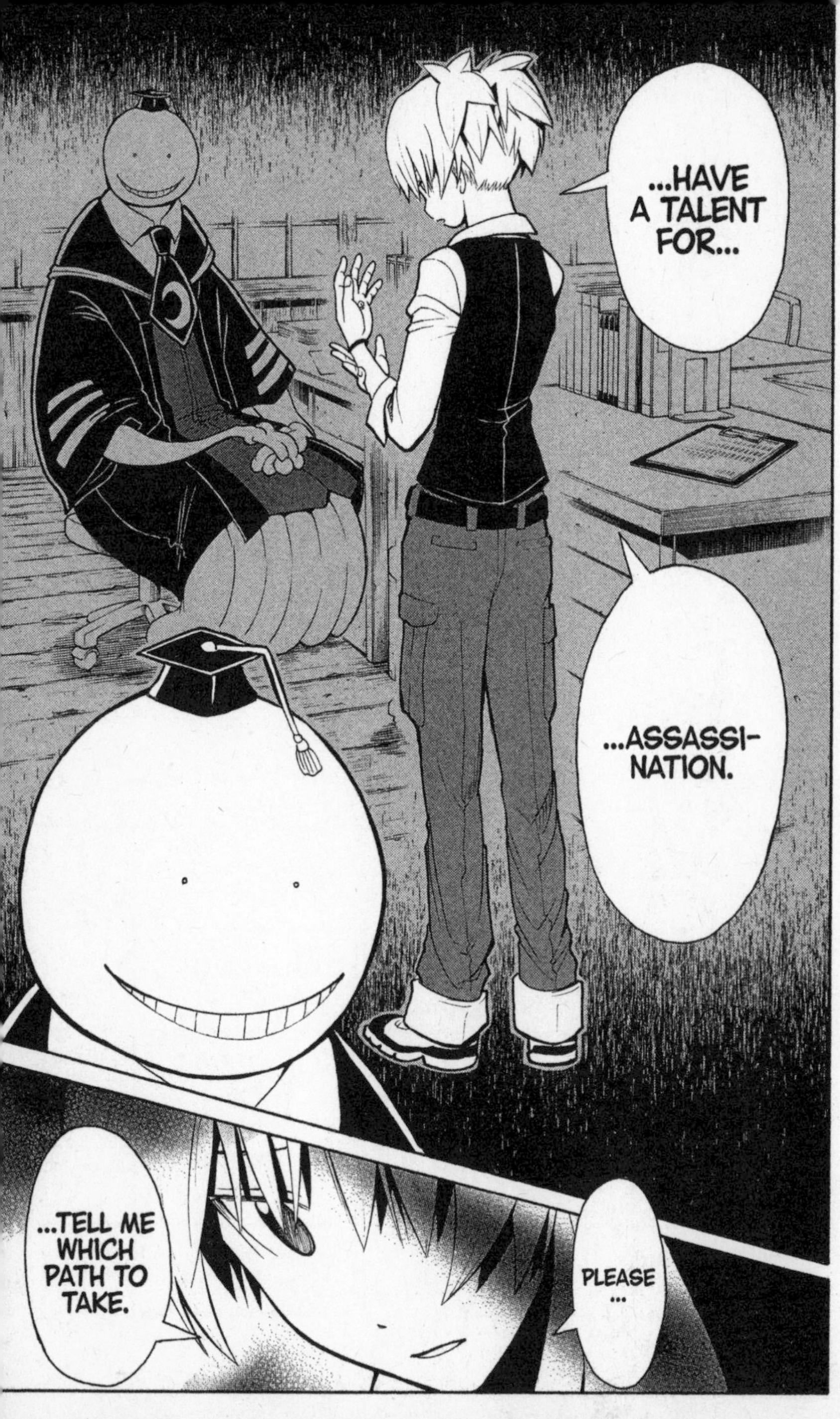
...HAVE A TALENT FOR...
...ASSASSI-NATION.
PLEASE...
...TELL ME WHICH PATH TO TAKE.

Dreams gradually shift toward reality.

Taiga Okajima	Meg Kataoka	Ryunosuke Chiba	
Dream: King of the World	Dream: Knight in Shining Armor	Dream: Mechanical designer for a sci-fi TV series.	Elementary School Freshman
Dream: Great Leader of the North	Dream: Firefighter	Dream: Carpenter	Elementary School Senior
Dream: Porn Actor	Dream: Flight Attendant	Dream: Carpenter	Junior High Freshman
Dream: Photographer	Dream: I'm not sure...	Dream: Architect	Current

CLASS 112 TIME FOR THE NEW GAME PLUS MODE

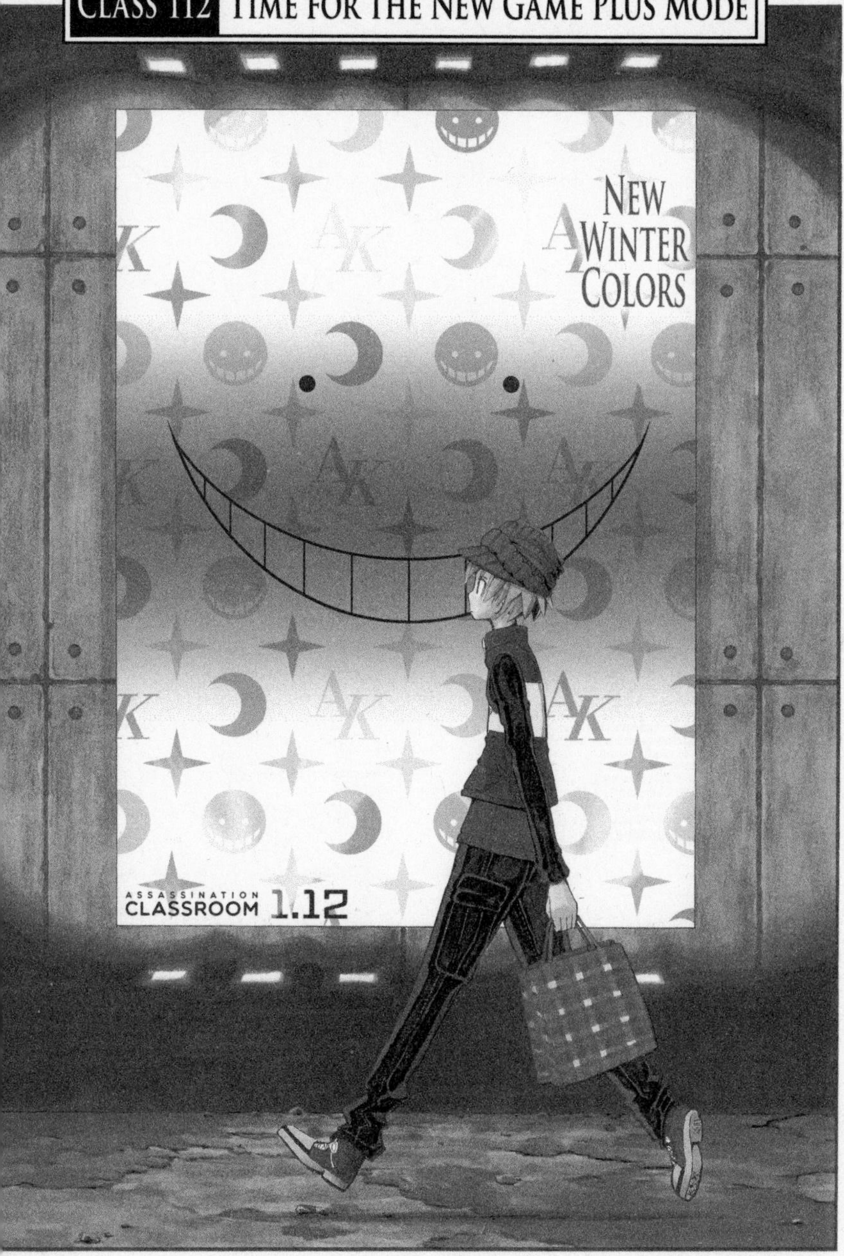
NEW WINTER COLORS
ASSASSINATION CLASSROOM 1.12

E-18 KIRARA HAZAMA

- 😊 BIRTHDAY: MAY 6
- 😊 HEIGHT: 5' 2"
- 😊 WEIGHT: 88 LBS.
- 😊 FAVORITE SUBJECT: JAPANESE
- 😊 LEAST FAVORITE SUBJECT: PHYSICAL EDUCATION
- 😊 HOBBY/SKILL: CURSES, BREEDING SPIDERS
- 😊 FUTURE GOAL: LIBRARIAN
- 😊 FAVORITE FOOD: HUMAN DARKNESS
- 😊 WHAT IF SHE SPENDS A LOT OF TIME WITH KURAHASHI? HER DARKNESS WILL DISSIPATE AND SHE'LL LOSE EVEN MORE WEIGHT.

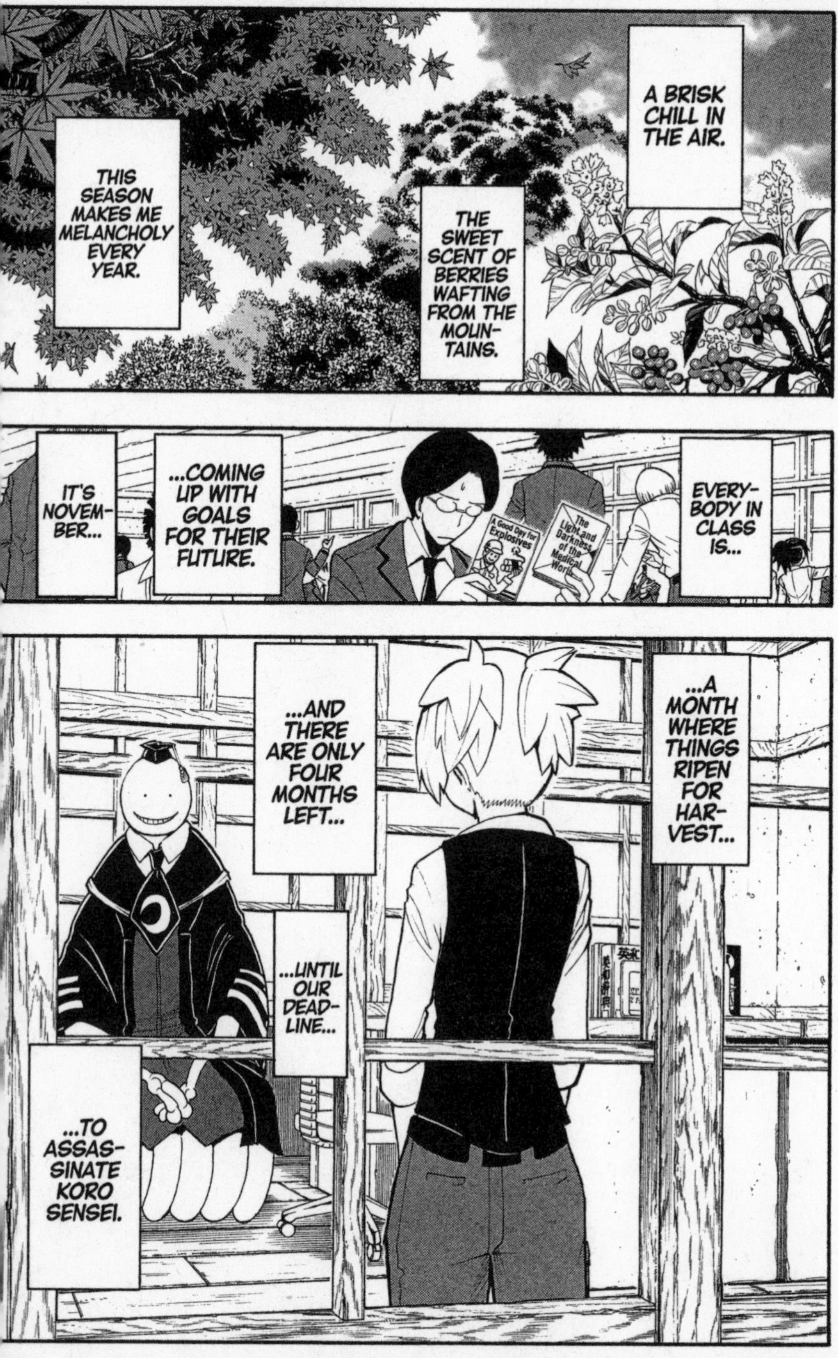
A BRISK CHILL IN THE AIR.
THE SWEET SCENT OF BERRIES WAFTING FROM THE MOUNTAINS.
THIS SEASON MAKES ME MELANCHOLY EVERY YEAR.
EVERYBODY IN CLASS IS...
The Light and Darkness of the Medical World
A Good Day for Explosives
...COMING UP WITH GOALS FOR THEIR FUTURE.
IT'S NOVEMBER...
...A MONTH WHERE THINGS RIPEN FOR HARVEST...
...AND THERE ARE ONLY FOUR MONTHS LEFT...
...UNTIL OUR DEADLINE...
...TO ASSASSINATE KORO SENSEI.

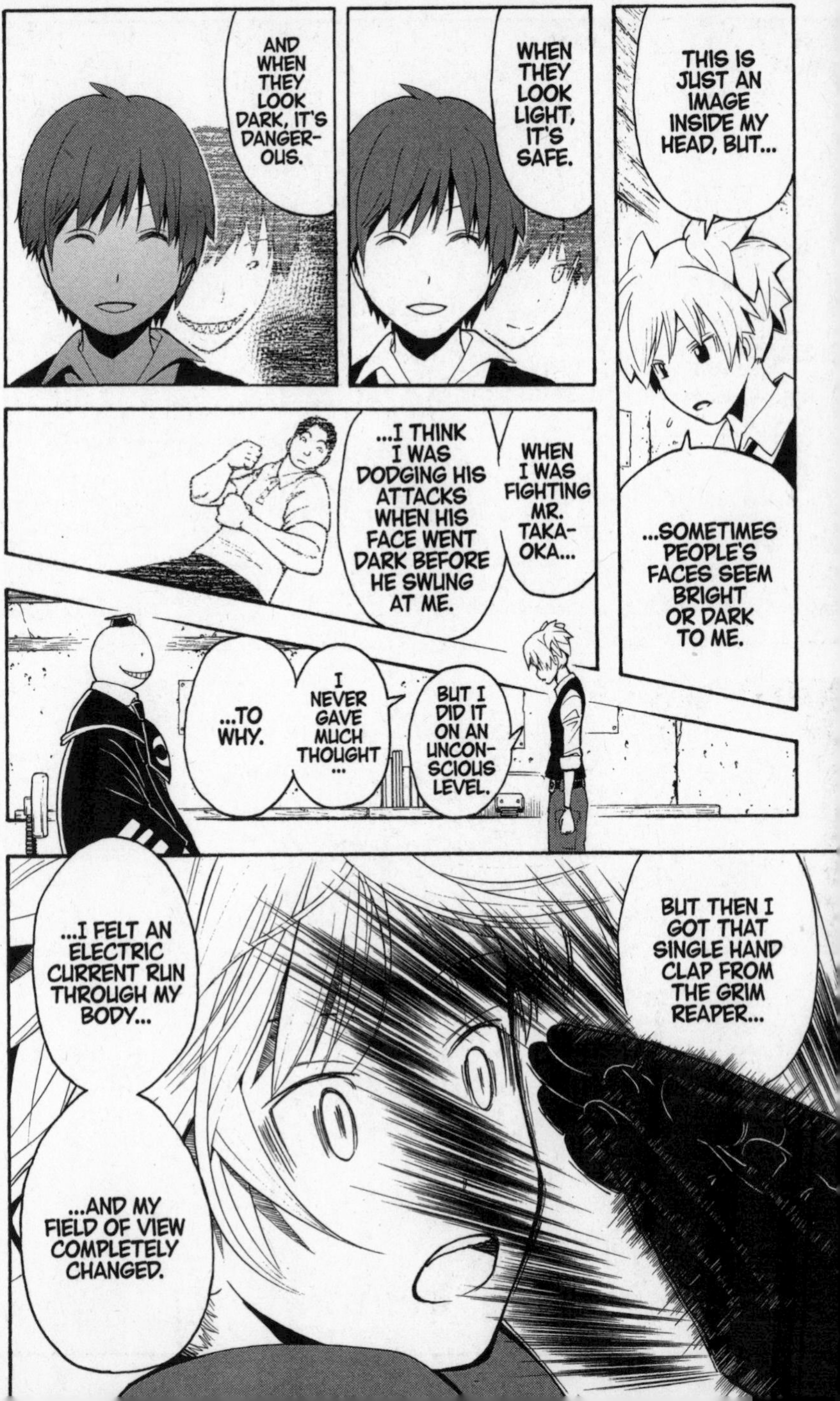
THIS IS JUST AN IMAGE INSIDE MY HEAD, BUT...
...SOMETIMES PEOPLE'S FACES SEEM BRIGHT OR DARK TO ME.
WHEN THEY LOOK LIGHT, IT'S SAFE.
AND WHEN THEY LOOK DARK, IT'S DANGEROUS.
WHEN I WAS FIGHTING MR. TAKAOKA...
...I THINK I WAS DODGING HIS ATTACKS WHEN HIS FACE WENT DARK BEFORE HE SWUNG AT ME.
BUT I DID IT ON AN UNCONSCIOUS LEVEL.
I NEVER GAVE MUCH THOUGHT...
...TO WHY.
BUT THEN I GOT THAT SINGLE HAND CLAP FROM THE GRIM REAPER...
...I FELT AN ELECTRIC CURRENT RUN THROUGH MY BODY...
...AND MY FIELD OF VIEW COMPLETELY CHANGED.

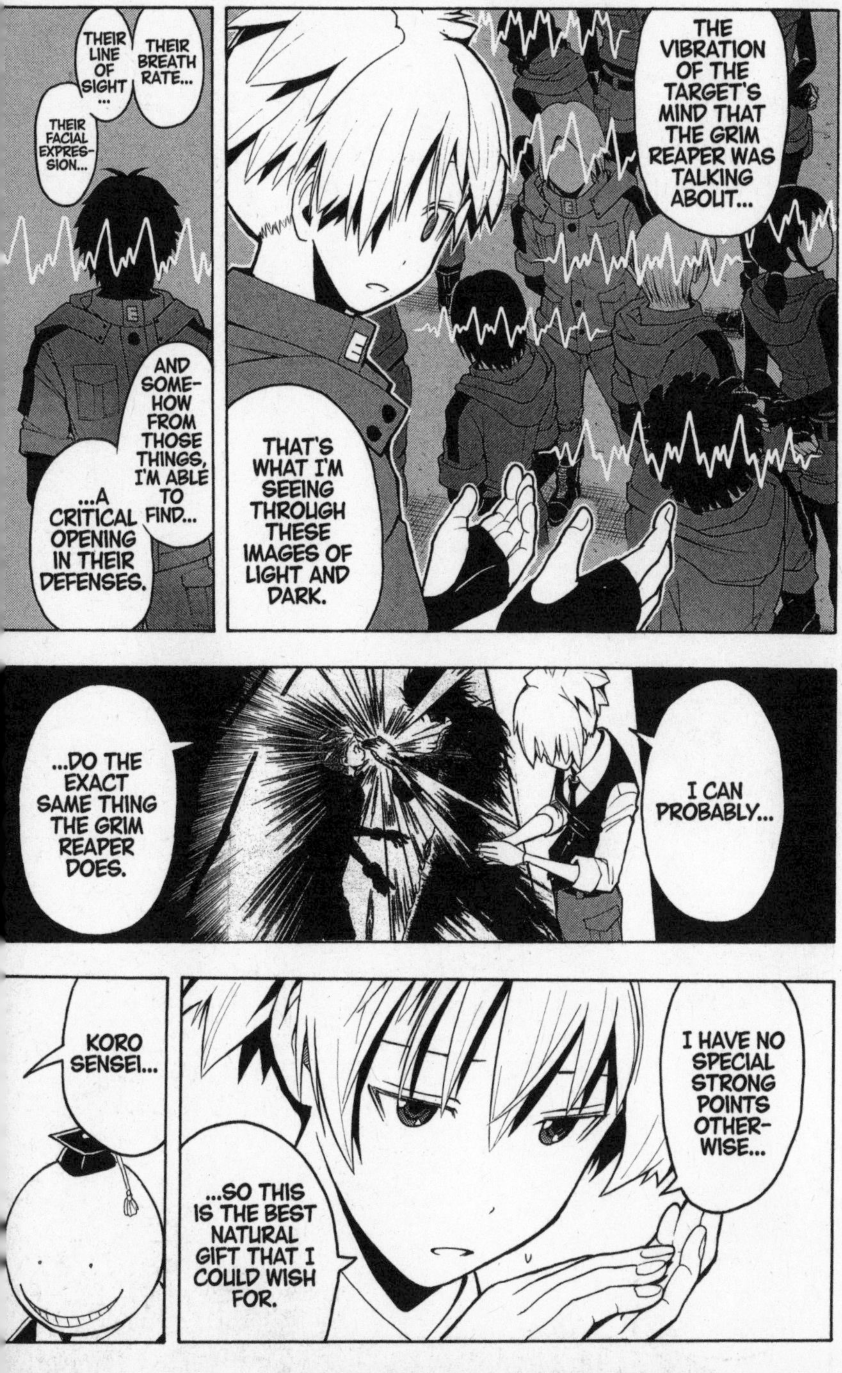
THE VIBRATION OF THE TARGET'S MIND THAT THE GRIM REAPER WAS TALKING ABOUT...
THAT'S WHAT I'M SEEING THROUGH THESE IMAGES OF LIGHT AND DARK.
THEIR BREATH RATE...
THEIR LINE OF SIGHT...
THEIR FACIAL EXPRES-SION...
AND SOME-HOW FROM THOSE THINGS, I'M ABLE TO FIND...
...A CRITICAL OPENING IN THEIR DEFENSES.
I CAN PROBABLY...
...DO THE EXACT SAME THING THE GRIM REAPER DOES.
I HAVE NO SPECIAL STRONG POINTS OTHER-WISE...
...SO THIS IS THE BEST NATURAL GIFT THAT I COULD WISH FOR.
KORO SENSEI...

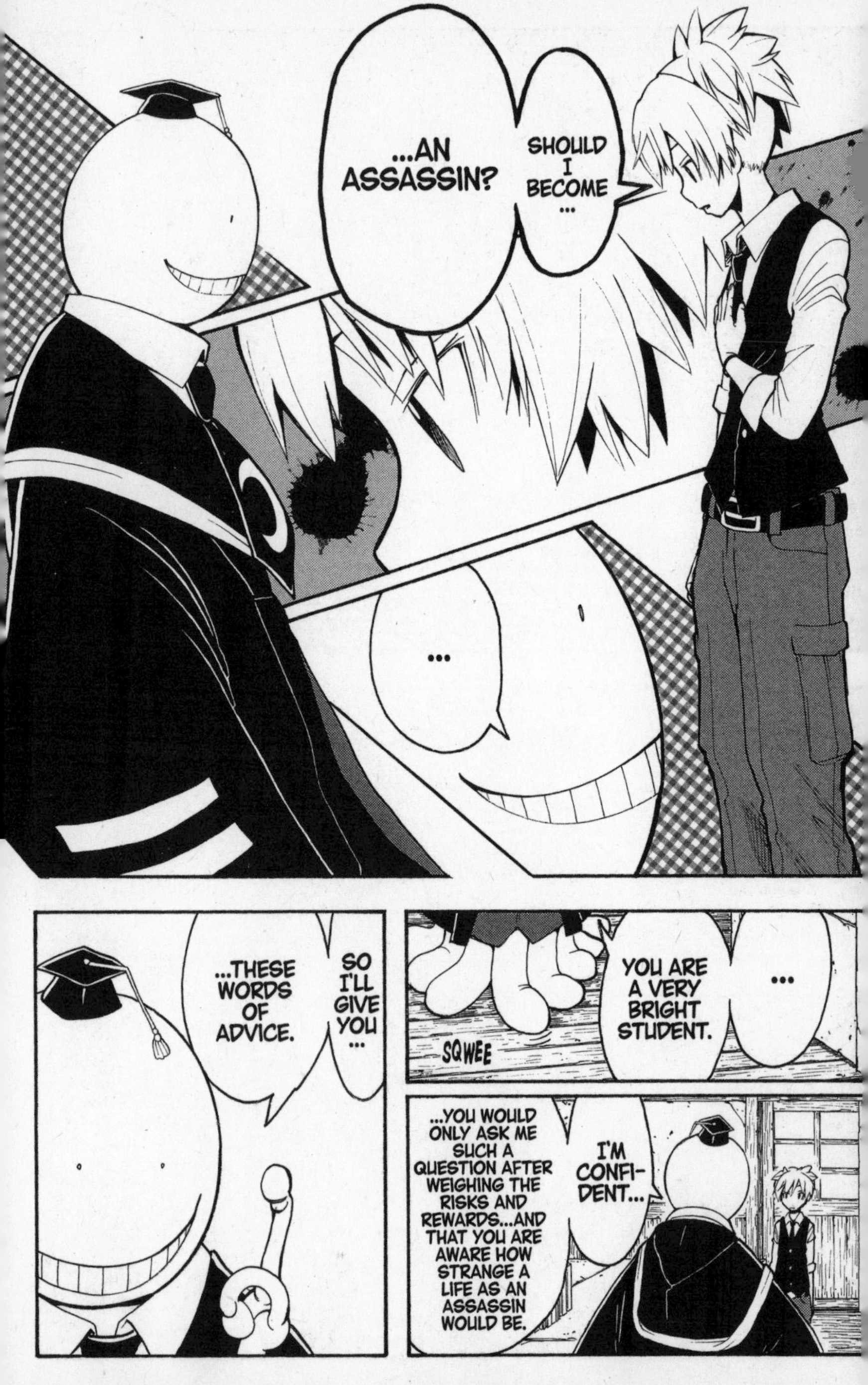
SHOULD I BECOME ...
...AN ASSASSIN?
...
...
YOU ARE A VERY BRIGHT STUDENT.
SQWEE
I'M CONFIDENT...
...YOU WOULD ONLY ASK ME SUCH A QUESTION AFTER WEIGHING THE RISKS AND REWARDS...AND THAT YOU ARE AWARE HOW STRANGE A LIFE AS AN ASSASSIN WOULD BE.
SO I'LL GIVE YOU ...
...THESE WORDS OF ADVICE.

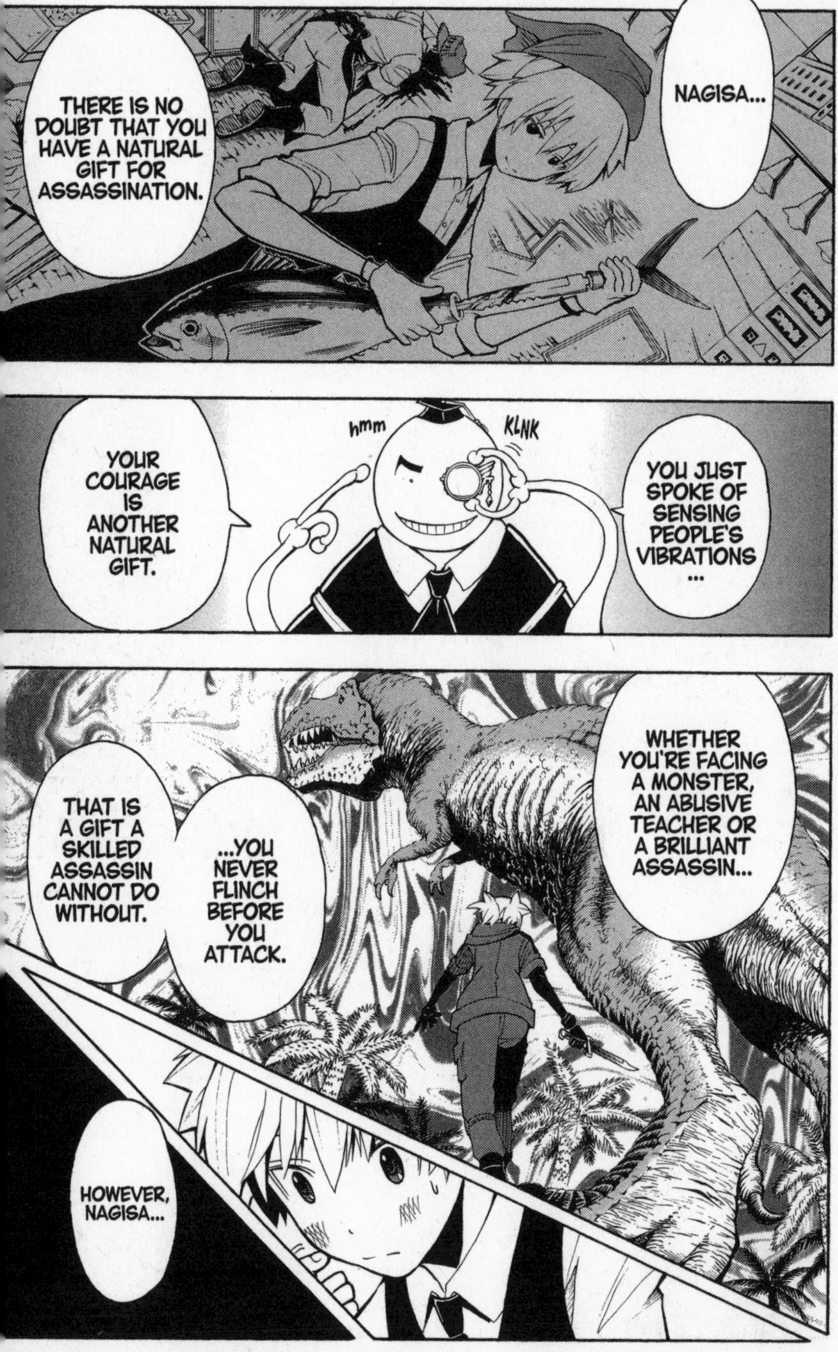
NAGISA...
THERE IS NO DOUBT THAT YOU HAVE A NATURAL GIFT FOR ASSASSINATION.
YOU JUST SPOKE OF SENSING PEOPLE'S VIBRATIONS ...
KLNK
hmm
YOUR COURAGE IS ANOTHER NATURAL GIFT.
WHETHER YOU'RE FACING A MONSTER, AN ABUSIVE TEACHER OR A BRILLIANT ASSASSIN...
...YOU NEVER FLINCH BEFORE YOU ATTACK.
THAT IS A GIFT A SKILLED ASSASSIN CANNOT DO WITHOUT.
HOWEVER, NAGISA...

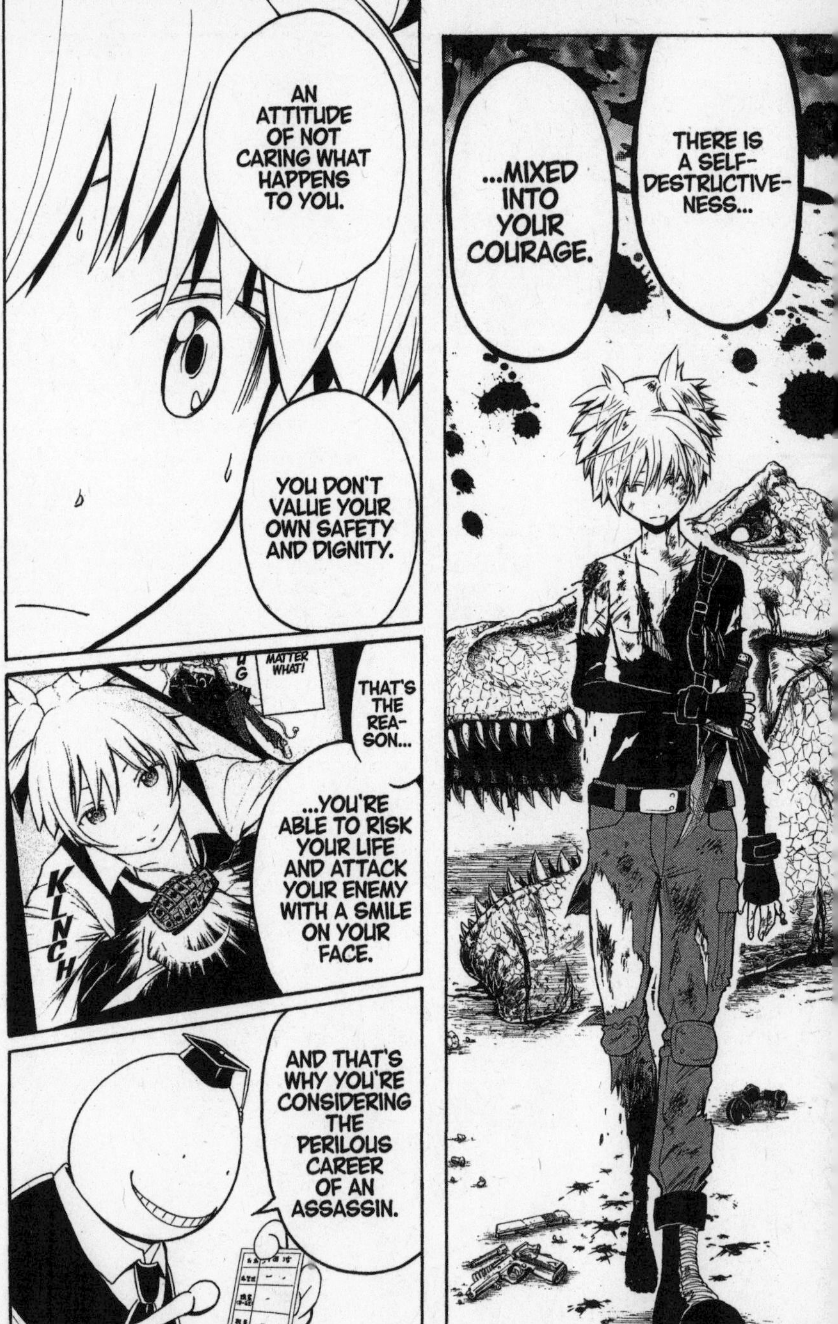
THERE IS A SELF-DESTRUCTIVENESS...
...MIXED INTO YOUR COURAGE.
AN ATTITUDE OF NOT CARING WHAT HAPPENS TO YOU.
YOU DON'T VALUE YOUR OWN SAFETY AND DIGNITY.
THAT'S THE REASON...
...YOU'RE ABLE TO RISK YOUR LIFE AND ATTACK YOUR ENEMY WITH A SMILE ON YOUR FACE.
MATTER WHAT!
KLNCH
AND THAT'S WHY YOU'RE CONSIDERING THE PERILOUS CAREER OF AN ASSASSIN.

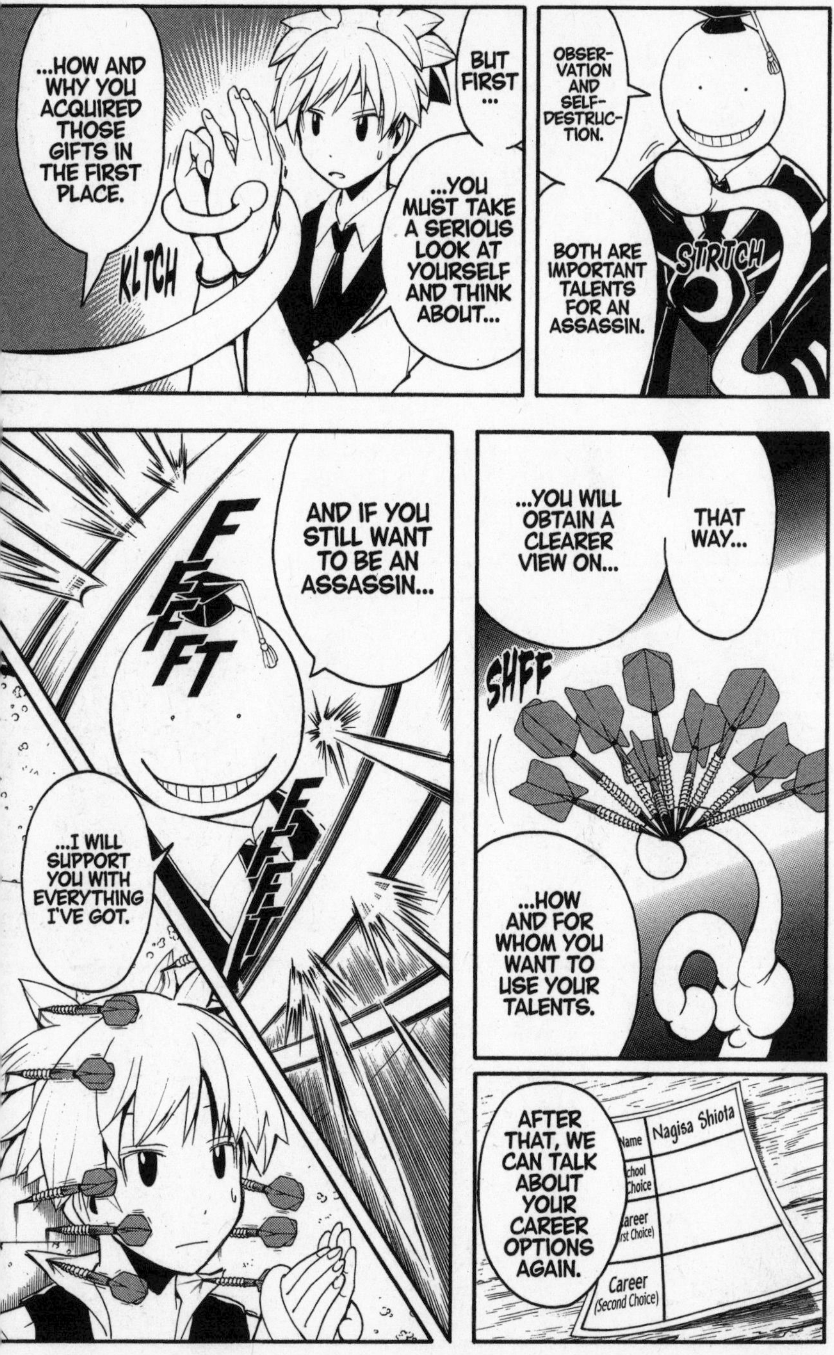
OBSERVATION AND SELF-DESTRUCTION.
BOTH ARE IMPORTANT TALENTS FOR AN ASSASSIN.
STRTCH
BUT FIRST...
...YOU MUST TAKE A SERIOUS LOOK AT YOURSELF AND THINK ABOUT...
...HOW AND WHY YOU ACQUIRED THOSE GIFTS IN THE FIRST PLACE.
KLTCH
THAT WAY...
...YOU WILL OBTAIN A CLEARER VIEW ON...
SHFF
...HOW AND FOR WHOM YOU WANT TO USE YOUR TALENTS.
AFTER THAT, WE CAN TALK ABOUT YOUR CAREER OPTIONS AGAIN.
Name
Nagisa Shiota
Career
(Second Choice)
AND IF YOU STILL WANT TO BE AN ASSASSIN...
FFFFT
FFFFT
...I WILL SUPPORT YOU WITH EVERYTHING I'VE GOT.

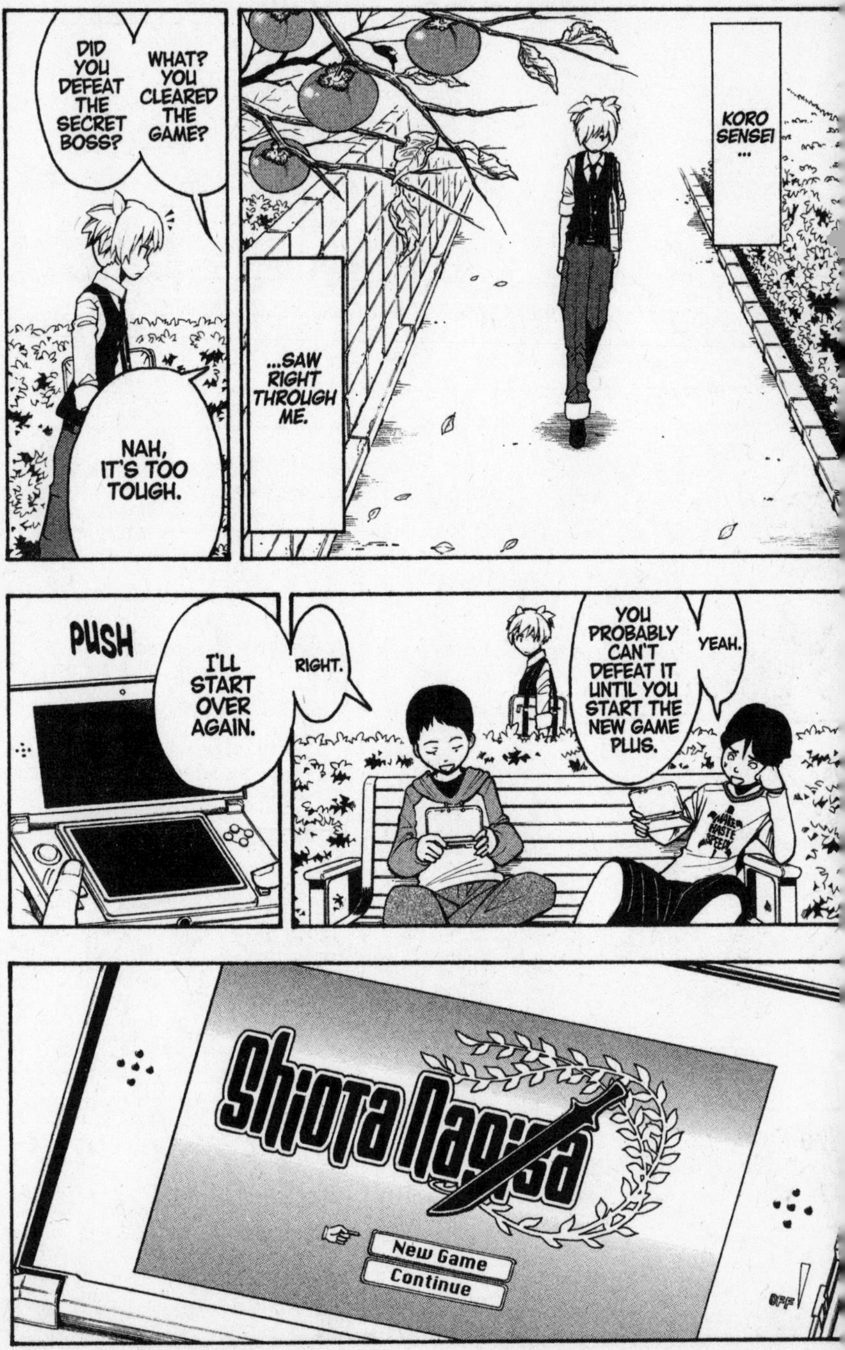
KORO SENSEI ...
...SAW RIGHT THROUGH ME.
WHAT? YOU CLEARED THE GAME?
DID YOU DEFEAT THE SECRET BOSS?
NAH, IT'S TOO TOUGH.
YEAH.
YOU PROBABLY CAN'T DEFEAT IT UNTIL YOU START THE NEW GAME PLUS.
RIGHT.
I'LL START OVER AGAIN.
PUSH
Shiota Nagisa
New Game
Continue
OFF

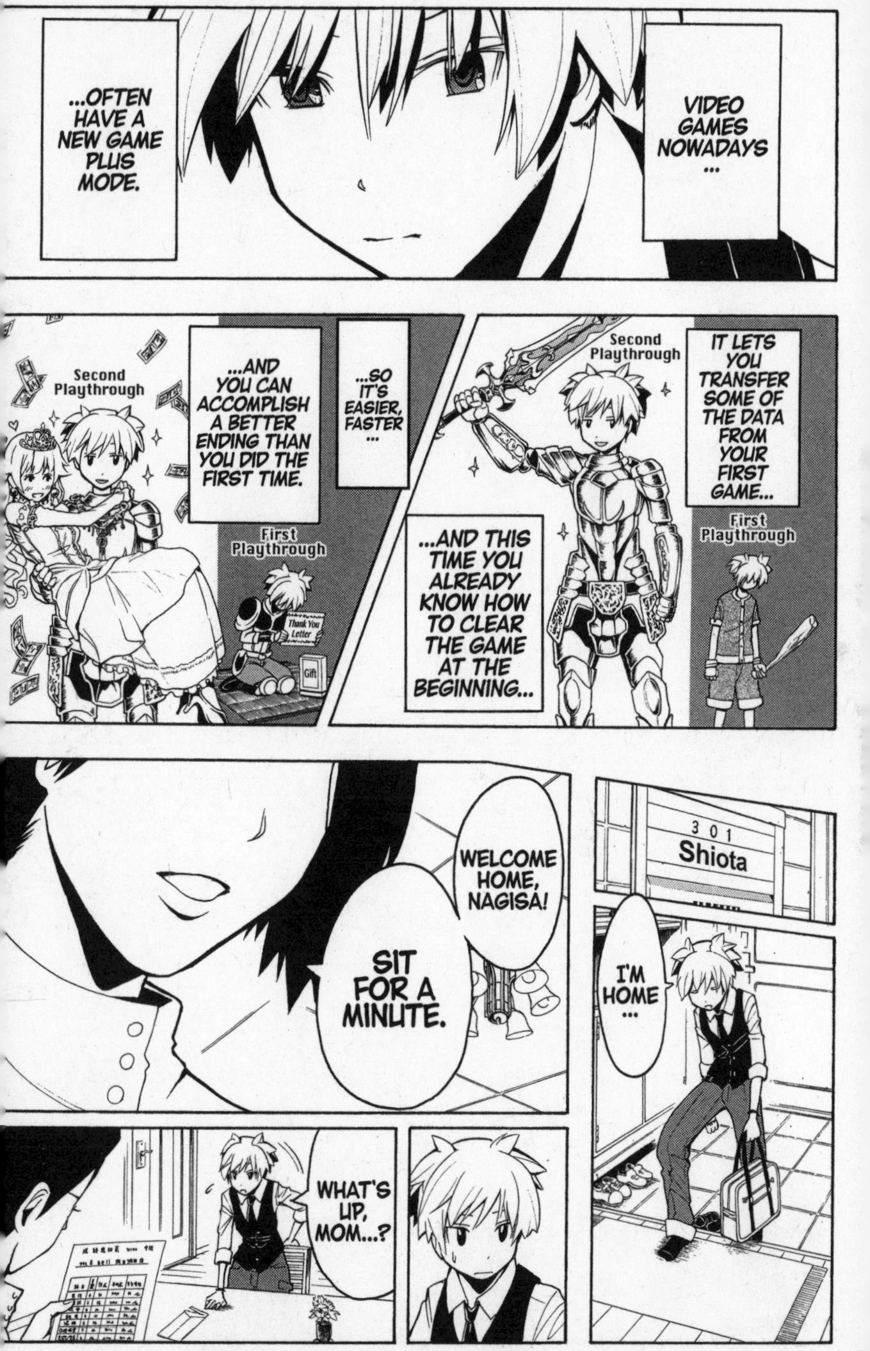
VIDEO GAMES NOWADAYS...
...OFTEN HAVE A NEW GAME PLUS MODE.
IT LETS YOU TRANSFER SOME OF THE DATA FROM YOUR FIRST GAME...
Second Playthrough
First Playthrough
...AND THIS TIME YOU ALREADY KNOW HOW TO CLEAR THE GAME AT THE BEGINNING...
...SO IT'S EASIER, FASTER...
...AND YOU CAN ACCOMPLISH A BETTER ENDING THAN YOU DID THE FIRST TIME.
Second Playthrough
First Playthrough
Thank You Letter
Gift
301
Shiota
I'M HOME...
WELCOME HOME, NAGISA!
SIT FOR A MINUTE.
WHAT'S UP, MOM...?

YOU NEED TO RANK AT LEAST 50TH TO GET BACK INTO THE MAIN SCHOOL BUILDING.

YOU RANKED 54TH ON YOUR MIDTERM EXAM...

I WAS VERY DISAPPOINTED, BUT I FOUND OUT THAT...

Report Card
3rd Year Students Midterm

Shiota Nagisa

Subject	Score	Average Score	Rank in Grade Level
English	77	62	37
Math	57		48
Civics	66		65
Science	78	79	72
Health			55
Phys Ed			
Art/Music			
Home Ec			
Average			54

...RETURN TO THE MAIN SCHOOL BUILDING THREE YEARS AGO—EVEN THOUGH HE WAS RANKED NUMBER 60!

...WAS PERMITTED TO...

...TANAKA'S OLDER BROTHER...

60

Nagisa's Mother
Hiromi Nagisa

I HAVE TO PULL YOU OUT OF...

HIS FAMILY MADE A DONATION TO THE SCHOOL AND BEGGED THE TEACHER AND ADMINISTRATION TO MAKE AN EXCEPTION FOR HIM.

SO I'M GOING TO DO THE SAME FOR YOU.

...CLASS E AS SOON AS I CAN!

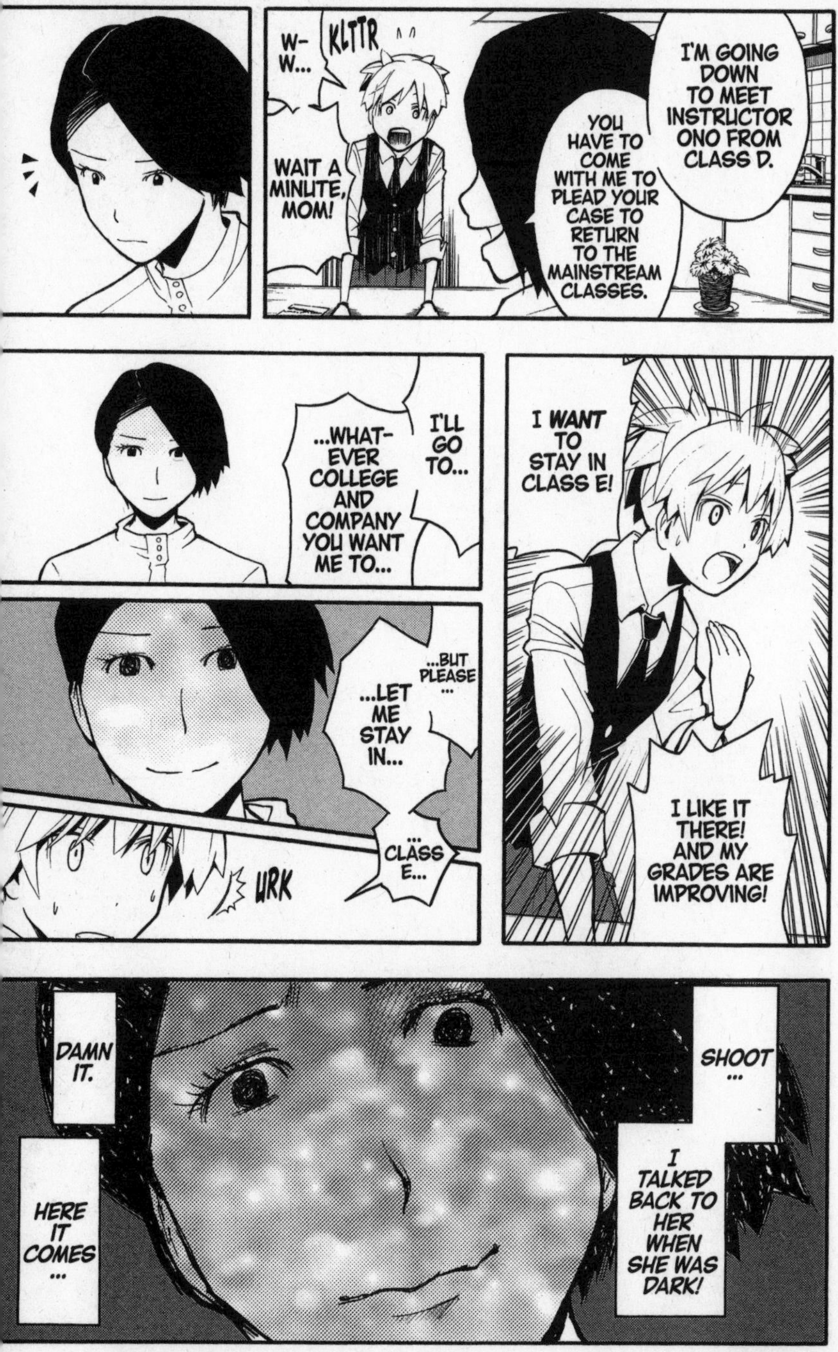
I'M GOING DOWN TO MEET INSTRUCTOR ONO FROM CLASS D.
YOU HAVE TO COME WITH ME TO PLEAD YOUR CASE TO RETURN TO THE MAINSTREAM CLASSES.
KLTTR
W-W...
WAIT A MINUTE, MOM!
I WANT TO STAY IN CLASS E!
I LIKE IT THERE! AND MY GRADES ARE IMPROVING!
I'LL GO TO...
...WHAT-EVER COLLEGE AND COMPANY YOU WANT ME TO...
...BUT PLEASE...
...LET ME STAY IN...
...CLASS E...
URK
SHOOT...
I TALKED BACK TO HER WHEN SHE WAS DARK!
DAMN IT.
HERE IT COMES...

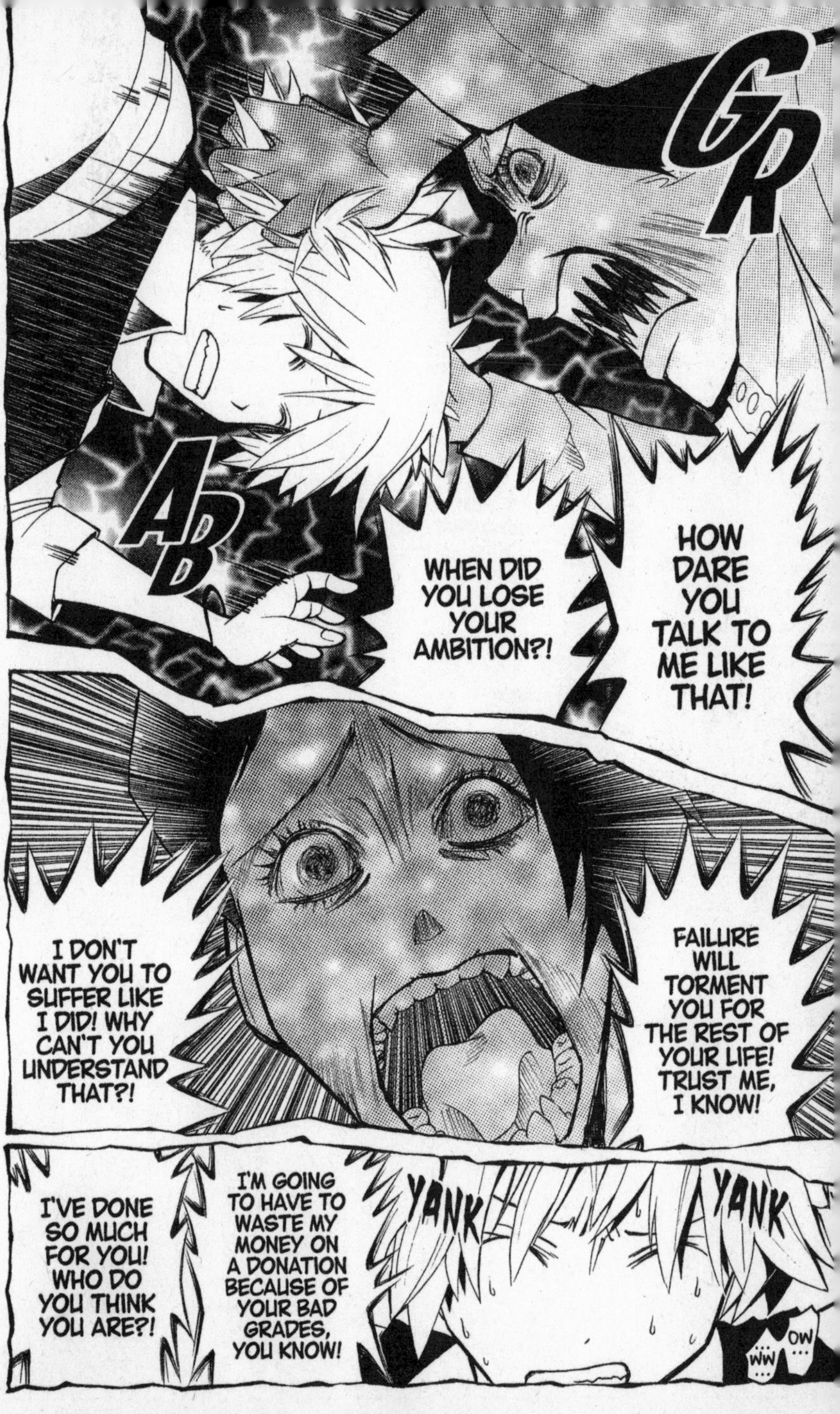
GR
AB
HOW DARE YOU TALK TO ME LIKE THAT!
WHEN DID YOU LOSE YOUR AMBITION?!
FAILURE WILL TORMENT YOU FOR THE REST OF YOUR LIFE! TRUST ME, I KNOW!
I DON'T WANT YOU TO SUFFER LIKE I DID! WHY CAN'T YOU UNDERSTAND THAT?!
YANK
YANK
OW... ...WW...
I'M GOING TO HAVE TO WASTE MY MONEY ON A DONATION BECAUSE OF YOUR BAD GRADES, YOU KNOW!
I'VE DONE SO MUCH FOR YOU! WHO DO YOU THINK YOU ARE?!

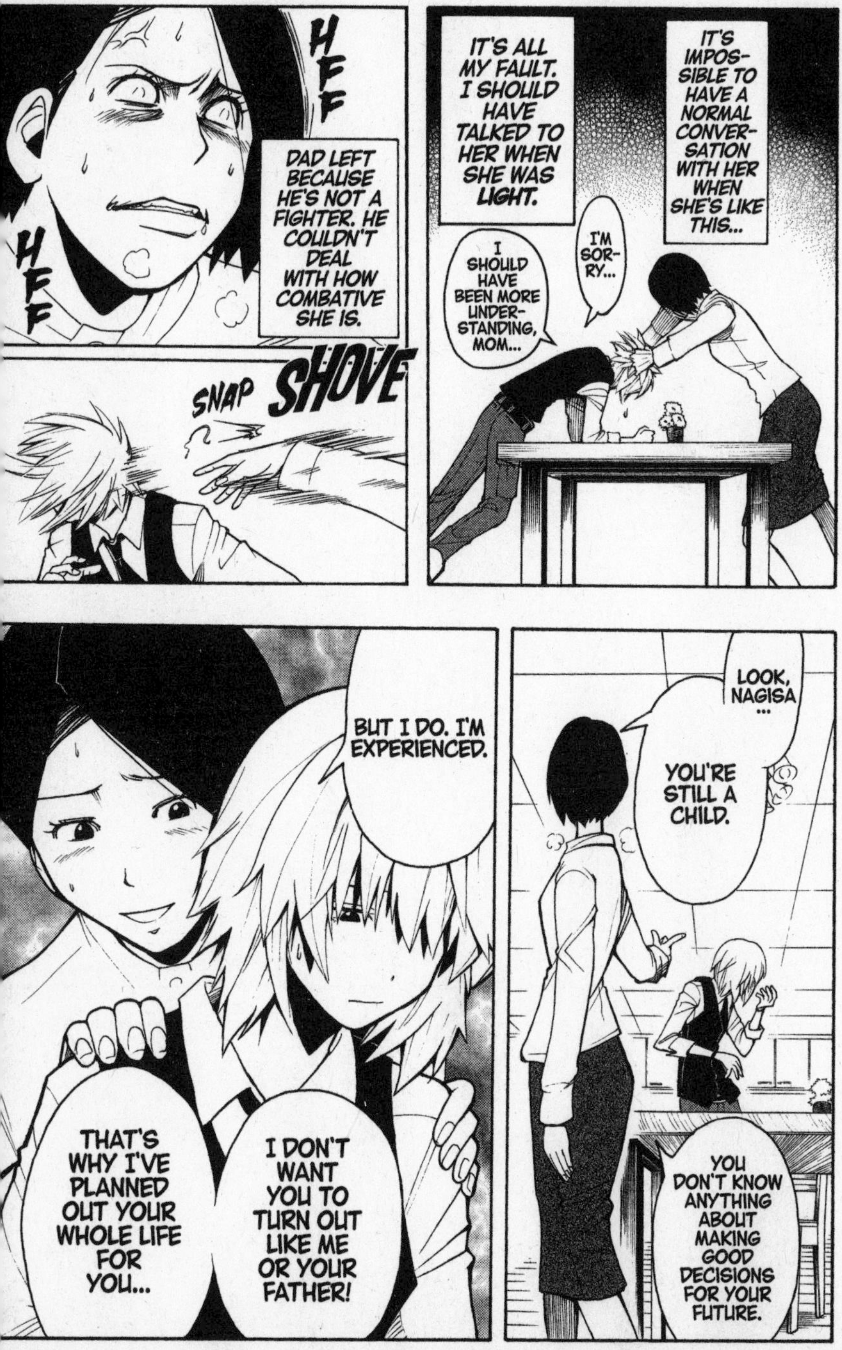
IT'S IMPOSSIBLE TO HAVE A NORMAL CONVERSATION WITH HER WHEN SHE'S LIKE THIS...
IT'S ALL MY FAULT. I SHOULD HAVE TALKED TO HER WHEN SHE WAS LIGHT.
I'M SORRY...
I SHOULD HAVE BEEN MORE UNDERSTANDING, MOM...
HFF
DAD LEFT BECAUSE HE'S NOT A FIGHTER. HE COULDN'T DEAL WITH HOW COMBATIVE SHE IS.
HFF
SHOVE
SNAP
LOOK, NAGISA...
YOU'RE STILL A CHILD.
YOU DON'T KNOW ANYTHING ABOUT MAKING GOOD DECISIONS FOR YOUR FUTURE.
BUT I DO. I'M EXPERIENCED.
I DON'T WANT YOU TO TURN OUT LIKE ME OR YOUR FATHER!
THAT'S WHY I'VE PLANNED OUT YOUR WHOLE LIFE FOR YOU...

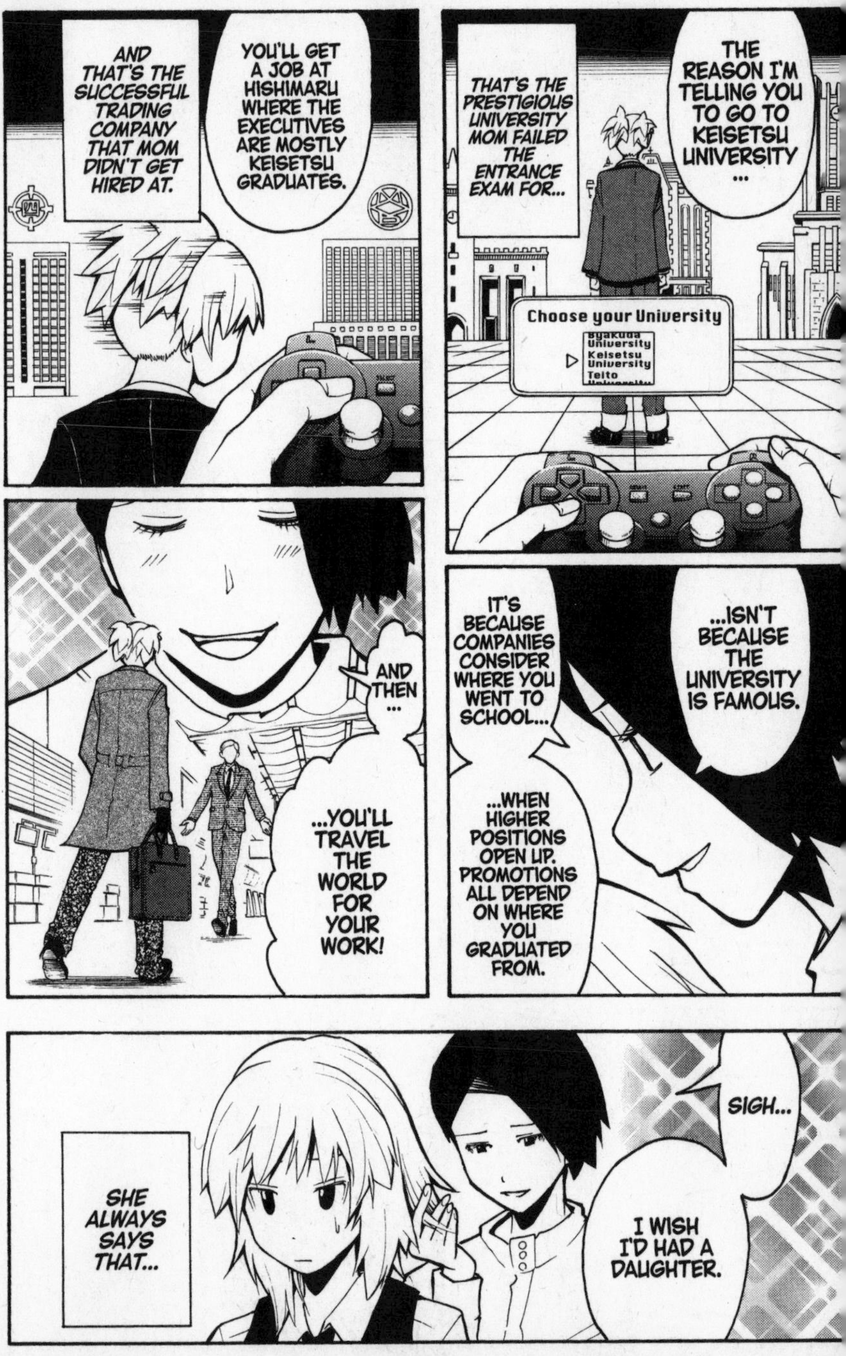
THE REASON I'M TELLING YOU TO GO TO KEISETSU UNIVERSITY...
THAT'S THE PRESTIGIOUS UNIVERSITY MOM FAILED THE ENTRANCE EXAM FOR...
Choose your University
Byakuda University
Keisetsu University
Teito
YOU'LL GET A JOB AT HISHIMARU WHERE THE EXECUTIVES ARE MOSTLY KEISETSU GRADUATES.
AND THAT'S THE SUCCESSFUL TRADING COMPANY THAT MOM DIDN'T GET HIRED AT.
...ISN'T BECAUSE THE UNIVERSITY IS FAMOUS.
IT'S BECAUSE COMPANIES CONSIDER WHERE YOU WENT TO SCHOOL...
...WHEN HIGHER POSITIONS OPEN UP. PROMOTIONS ALL DEPEND ON WHERE YOU GRADUATED FROM.
AND THEN...
...YOU'LL TRAVEL THE WORLD FOR YOUR WORK!
SIGH...
I WISH I'D HAD A DAUGHTER.
SHE ALWAYS SAYS THAT...

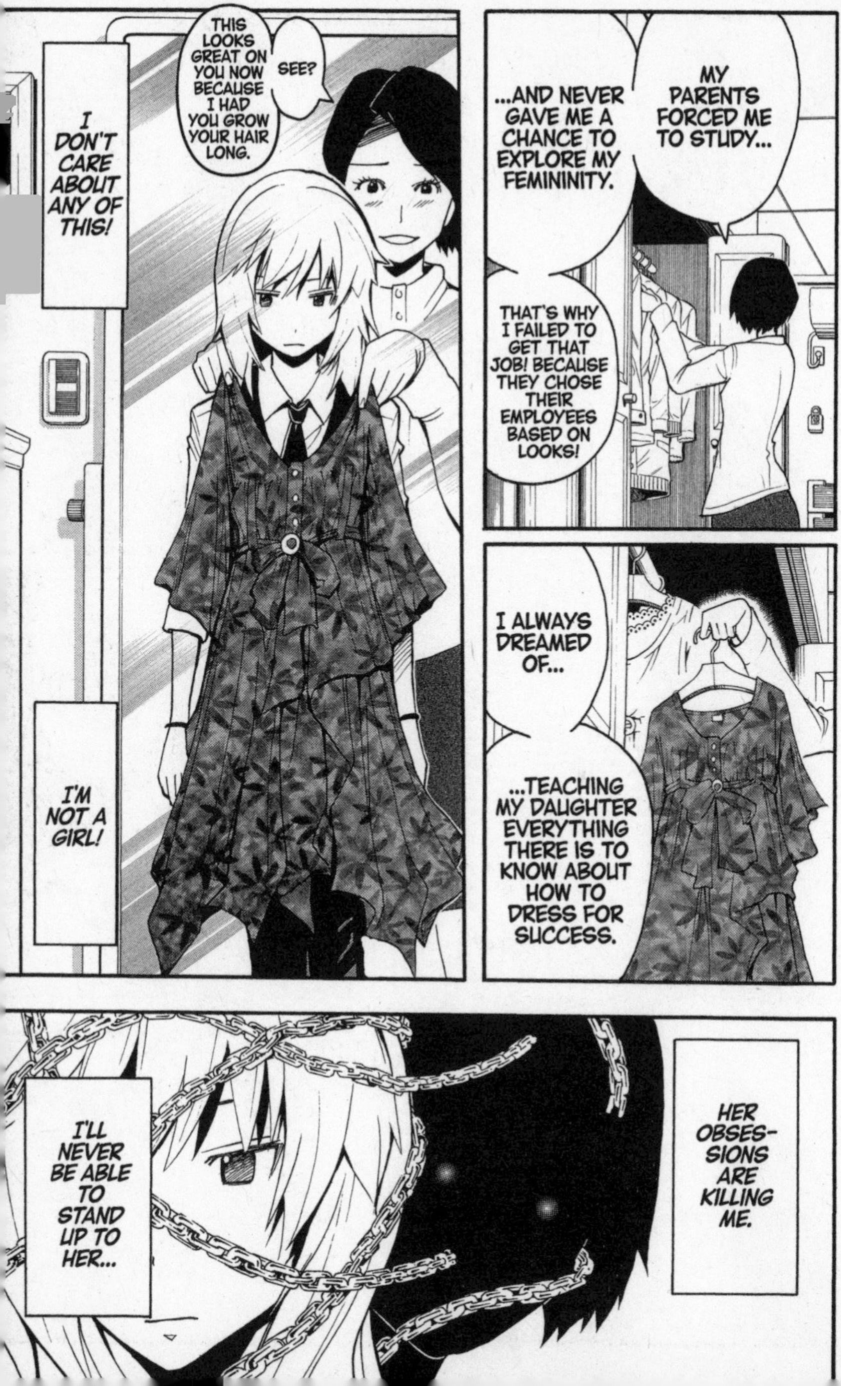
MY PARENTS FORCED ME TO STUDY...
...AND NEVER GAVE ME A CHANCE TO EXPLORE MY FEMININITY.
THAT'S WHY I FAILED TO GET THAT JOB! BECAUSE THEY CHOSE THEIR EMPLOYEES BASED ON LOOKS!
I ALWAYS DREAMED OF...
...TEACHING MY DAUGHTER EVERYTHING THERE IS TO KNOW ABOUT HOW TO DRESS FOR SUCCESS.
SEE?
THIS LOOKS GREAT ON YOU NOW BECAUSE I HAD YOU GROW YOUR HAIR LONG.
I DON'T CARE ABOUT ANY OF THIS!
I'M NOT A GIRL!
HER OBSES-SIONS ARE KILLING ME.
I'LL NEVER BE ABLE TO STAND UP TO HER...

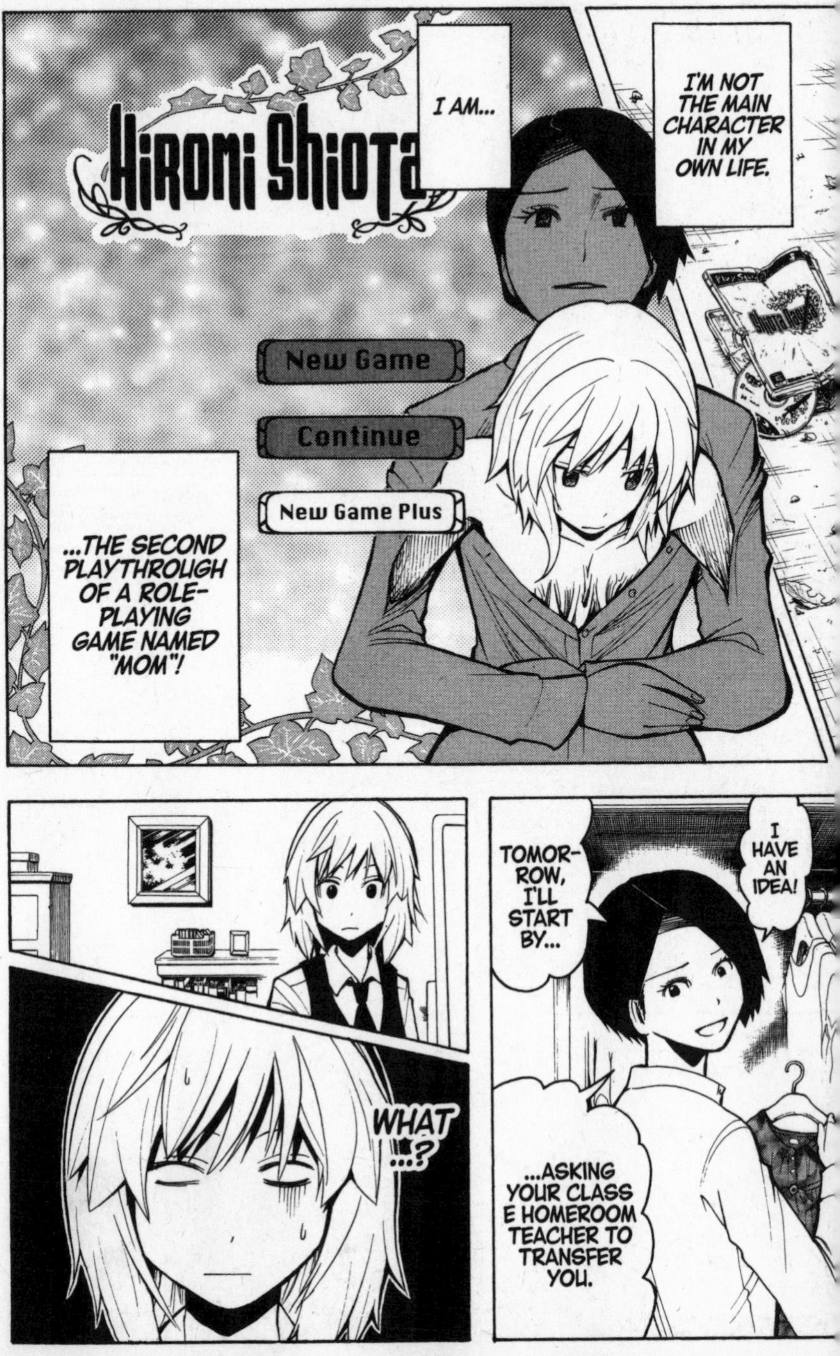
I'M NOT THE MAIN CHARACTER IN MY OWN LIFE.
I AM...
Hiromi Shiota
New Game
Continue
New Game Plus
...THE SECOND PLAYTHROUGH OF A ROLE-PLAYING GAME NAMED "MOM"!
I HAVE AN IDEA!
TOMORROW, I'LL START BY...
...ASKING YOUR CLASS E HOMEROOM TEACHER TO TRANSFER YOU.
WHAT ...?

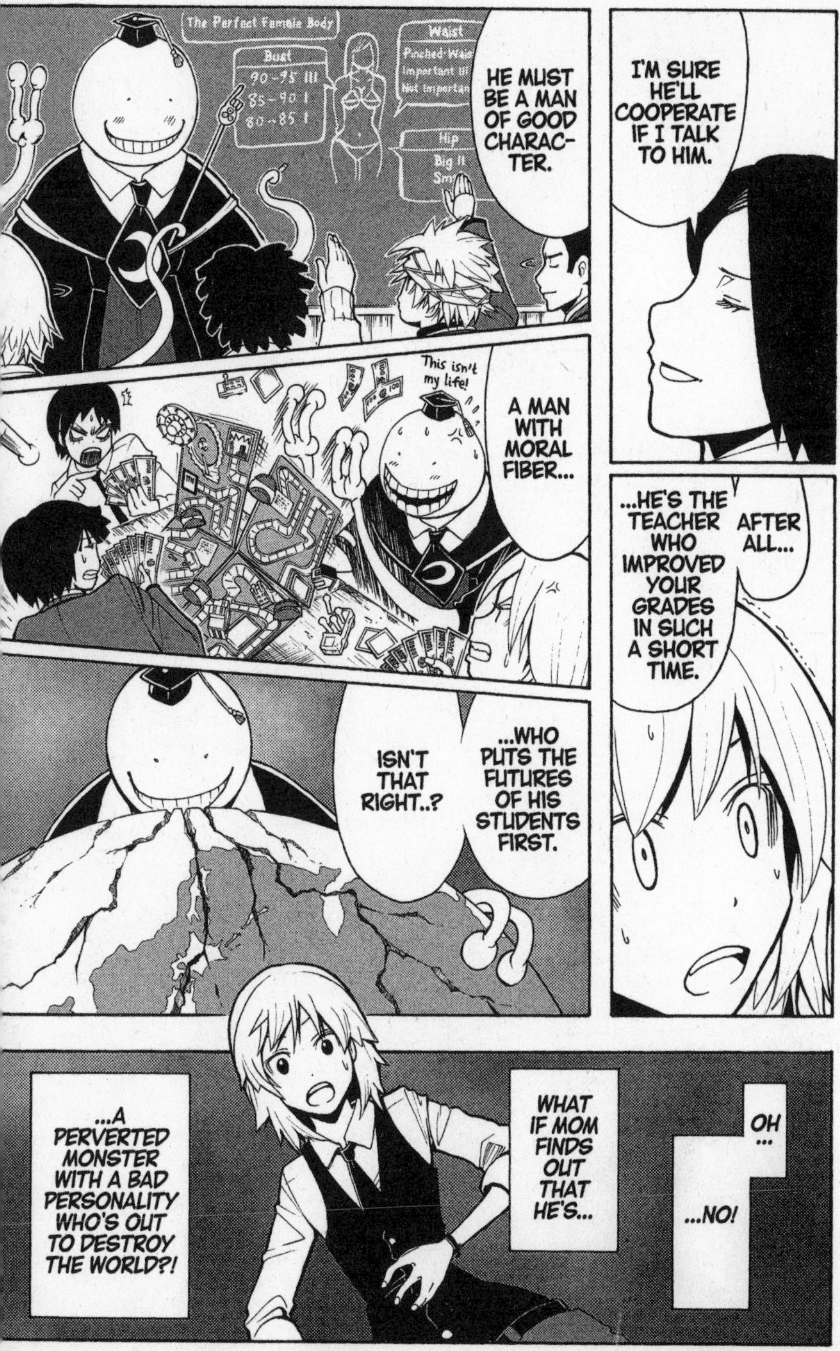
I'M SURE HE'LL COOPERATE IF I TALK TO HIM.
HE MUST BE A MAN OF GOOD CHARACTER.
The Perfect Female Body
Bust
90~95 III
85~90 I
80~85 I
Waist
Hip
A MAN WITH MORAL FIBER...
This isn't my life!
...HE'S THE TEACHER WHO IMPROVED YOUR GRADES IN SUCH A SHORT TIME.
AFTER ALL...
...WHO PUTS THE FUTURES OF HIS STUDENTS FIRST.
ISN'T THAT RIGHT..?
OH...
...NO!
WHAT IF MOM FINDS OUT THAT HE'S...
...A PERVERTED MONSTER WITH A BAD PERSONALITY WHO'S OUT TO DESTROY THE WORLD?!

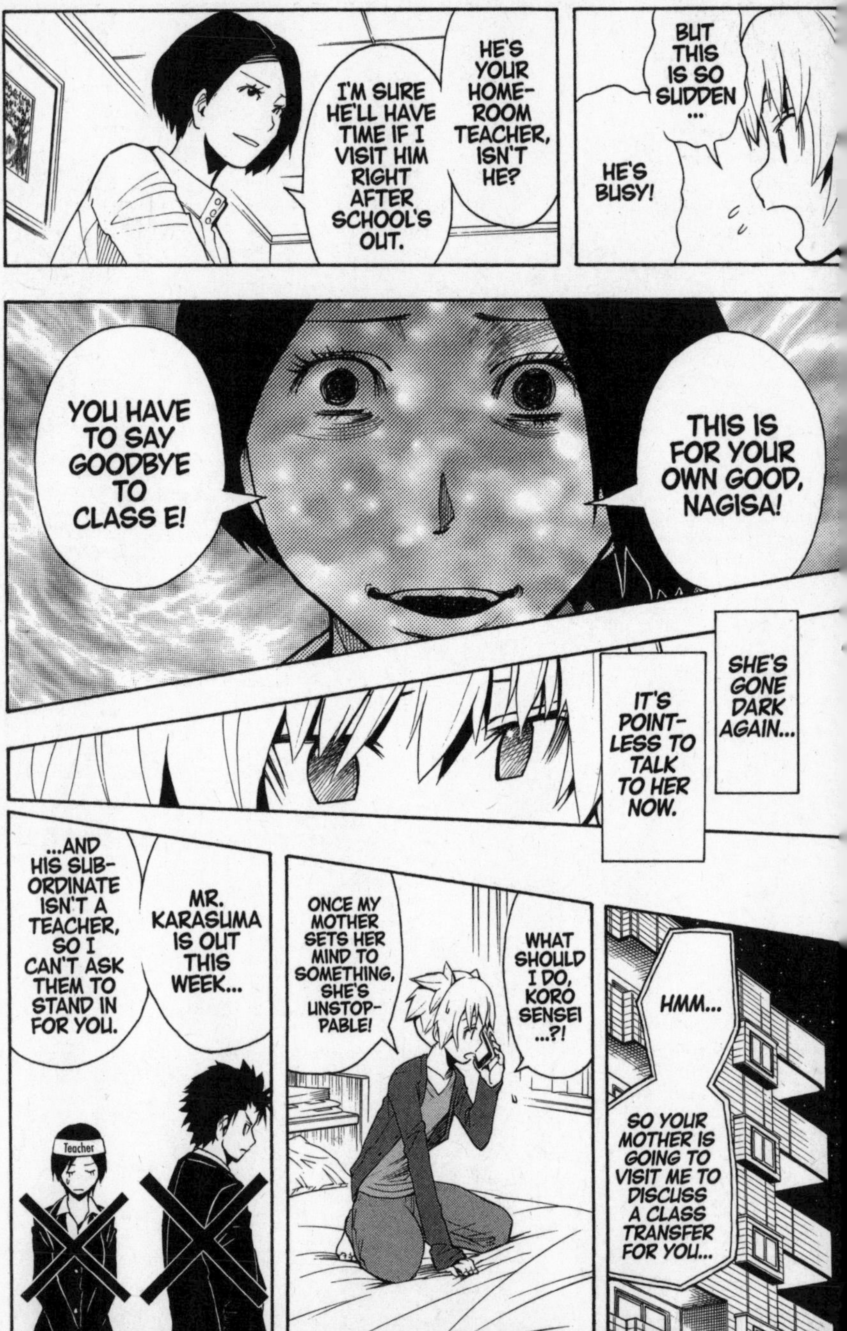
BUT THIS IS SO SUDDEN...
HE'S BUSY!
HE'S YOUR HOME-ROOM TEACHER, ISN'T HE?
I'M SURE HE'LL HAVE TIME IF I VISIT HIM RIGHT AFTER SCHOOL'S OUT.
THIS IS FOR YOUR OWN GOOD, NAGISA!
YOU HAVE TO SAY GOODBYE TO CLASS E!
SHE'S GONE DARK AGAIN...
IT'S POINT-LESS TO TALK TO HER NOW.
HMM...
SO YOUR MOTHER IS GOING TO VISIT ME TO DISCUSS A CLASS TRANSFER FOR YOU...
WHAT SHOULD I DO, KORO SENSEI...?!
ONCE MY MOTHER SETS HER MIND TO SOMETHING, SHE'S UNSTOP-PABLE!
MR. KARASUMA IS OUT THIS WEEK...
...AND HIS SUB-ORDINATE ISN'T A TEACHER, SO I CAN'T ASK THEM TO STAND IN FOR YOU.
Teacher

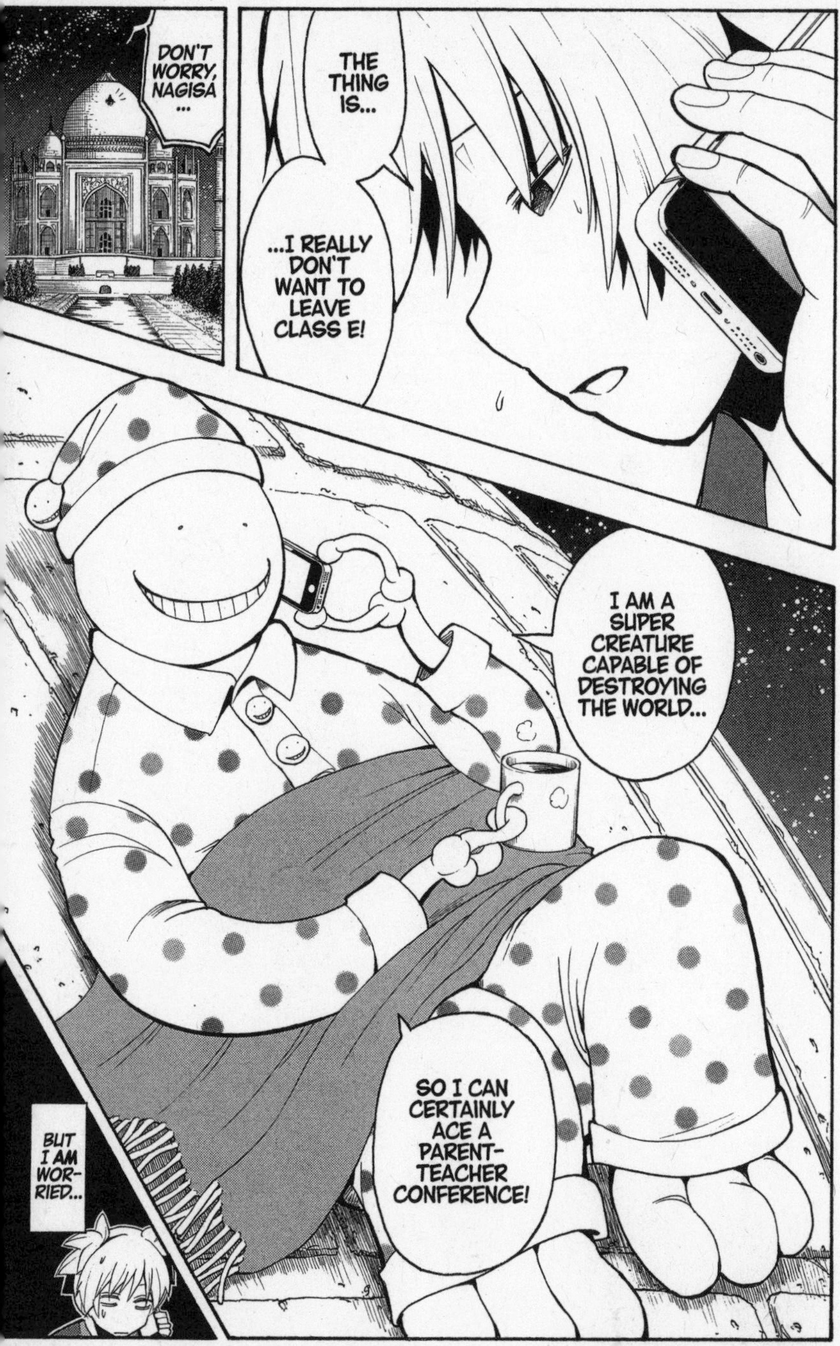
THE THING IS...
...I REALLY DON'T WANT TO LEAVE CLASS E!
DON'T WORRY, NAGISA...
I AM A SUPER CREATURE CAPABLE OF DESTROYING THE WORLD...
SO I CAN CERTAINLY ACE A PARENT-TEACHER CONFERENCE!
BUT I AM WOR-RIED...

Kunugigaoka Junior High Bulletin Board

Kunugigaoka Junior High
Special Placement Class Policies

Amendment

- The regular semester exams will be used to measure the academic performance of Class 3-E students.
- A student who ranks among the top fifty scores for their year will be recognized as a high achiever and earn the right to be reinstated in the main school building.
- A student who just barely missed entering the top fifty will still be recognized as a high achiever if they display another exceptional quality, such as school spirit.

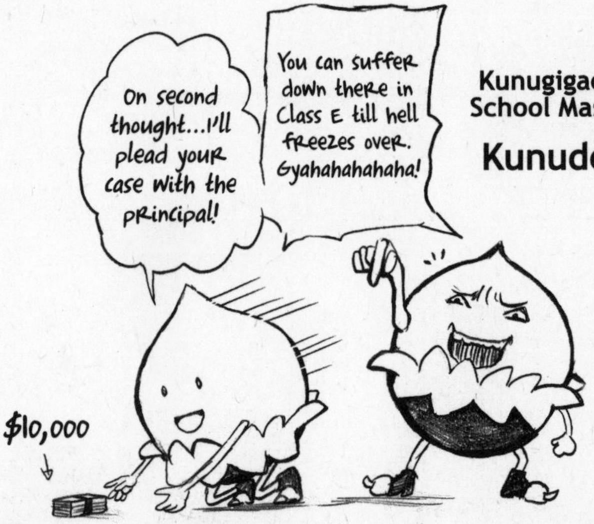
You can suffer down there in Class E till hell freezes over. Gyahahahahaha!
On second thought...I'll plead your case with the principal!
$10,000

Kunugigaoka School Mascot

Kunudon

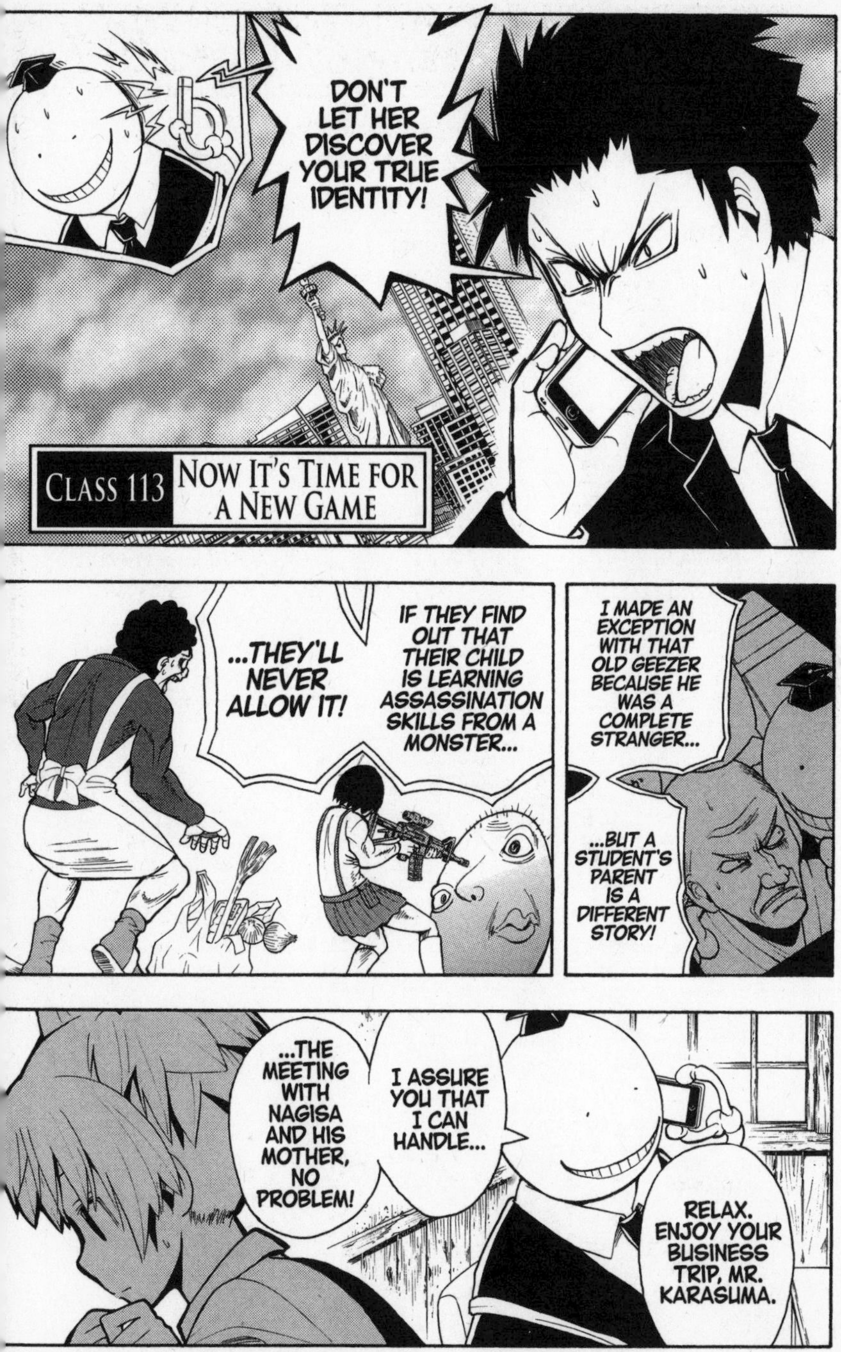
DON'T LET HER DISCOVER YOUR TRUE IDENTITY!
CLASS 113 NOW IT'S TIME FOR A NEW GAME
I MADE AN EXCEPTION WITH THAT OLD GEEZER BECAUSE HE WAS A COMPLETE STRANGER...
...BUT A STUDENT'S PARENT IS A DIFFERENT STORY!
IF THEY FIND OUT THAT THEIR CHILD IS LEARNING ASSASSINATION SKILLS FROM A MONSTER...
...THEY'LL NEVER ALLOW IT!
I ASSURE YOU THAT I CAN HANDLE...
...THE MEETING WITH NAGISA AND HIS MOTHER, NO PROBLEM!
RELAX. ENJOY YOUR BUSINESS TRIP, MR. KARASUMA.

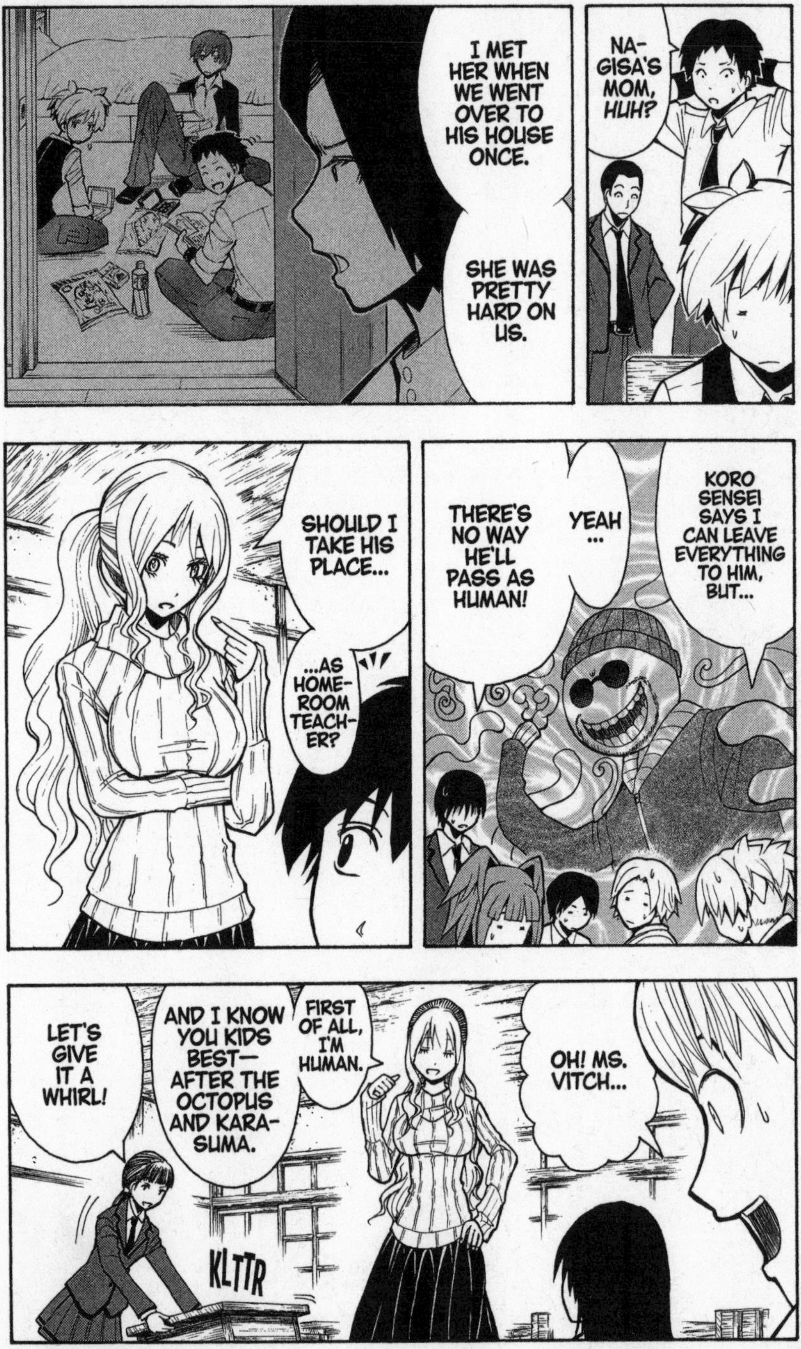
NA-GISA'S MOM, HUH?
I MET HER WHEN WE WENT OVER TO HIS HOUSE ONCE.
SHE WAS PRETTY HARD ON US.
KORO SENSEI SAYS I CAN LEAVE EVERYTHING TO HIM, BUT...
YEAH ...
THERE'S NO WAY HE'LL PASS AS HUMAN!
SHOULD I TAKE HIS PLACE...
...AS HOME-ROOM TEACH-ER?
OH! MS. VITCH...
FIRST OF ALL, I'M HUMAN.
AND I KNOW YOU KIDS BEST—AFTER THE OCTOPUS AND KARA-SUMA.
LET'S GIVE IT A WHIRL!
KLTTR

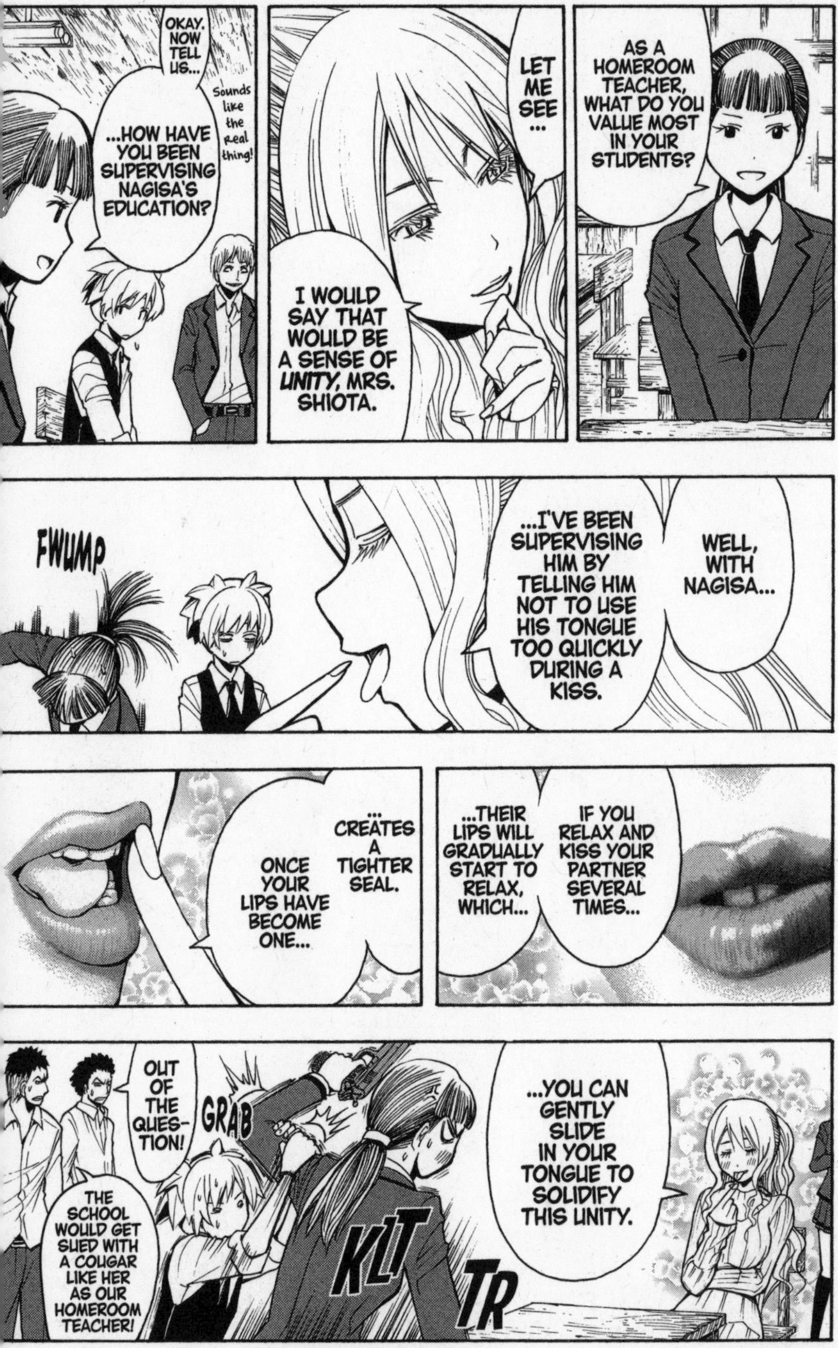
AS A HOMEROOM TEACHER, WHAT DO YOU VALUE MOST IN YOUR STUDENTS?
LET ME SEE...
I WOULD SAY THAT WOULD BE A SENSE OF *UNITY*, MRS. SHIOTA.
OKAY. NOW TELL US...
Sounds like the real thing!
...HOW HAVE YOU BEEN SUPERVISING NAGISA'S EDUCATION?
WELL, WITH NAGISA...
...I'VE BEEN SUPERVISING HIM BY TELLING HIM NOT TO USE HIS TONGUE TOO QUICKLY DURING A KISS.
FWUMP
IF YOU RELAX AND KISS YOUR PARTNER SEVERAL TIMES...
...THEIR LIPS WILL GRADUALLY START TO RELAX, WHICH...
...CREATES A TIGHTER SEAL.
ONCE YOUR LIPS HAVE BECOME ONE...
...YOU CAN GENTLY SLIDE IN YOUR TONGUE TO SOLIDIFY THIS UNITY.
TR
KLIT
GRAB
OUT OF THE QUES-TION!
THE SCHOOL WOULD GET SUED WITH A COUGAR LIKE HER AS OUR HOMEROOM TEACHER!

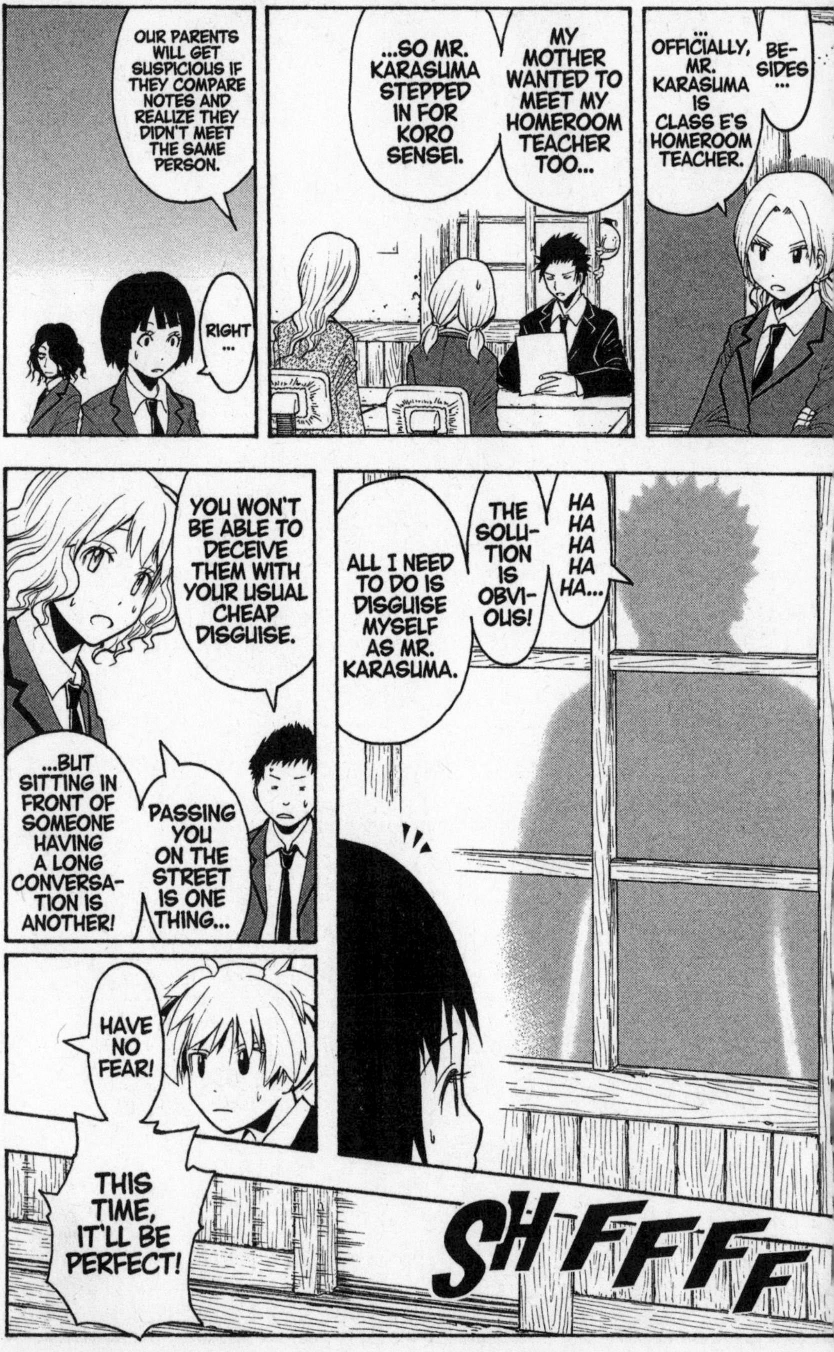
BESIDES...
...OFFICIALLY, MR. KARASUMA IS CLASS E'S HOMEROOM TEACHER.
MY MOTHER WANTED TO MEET MY HOMEROOM TEACHER TOO...
...SO MR. KARASUMA STEPPED IN FOR KORO SENSEI.
OUR PARENTS WILL GET SUSPICIOUS IF THEY COMPARE NOTES AND REALIZE THEY DIDN'T MEET THE SAME PERSON.
RIGHT...
HA HA HA HA HA...
THE SOLUTION IS OBVIOUS!
ALL I NEED TO DO IS DISGUISE MYSELF AS MR. KARASUMA.
YOU WON'T BE ABLE TO DECEIVE THEM WITH YOUR USUAL CHEAP DISGUISE.
PASSING YOU ON THE STREET IS ONE THING...
...BUT SITTING IN FRONT OF SOMEONE HAVING A LONG CONVERSATION IS ANOTHER!
HAVE NO FEAR!
SHFFFF
THIS TIME, IT'LL BE PERFECT!

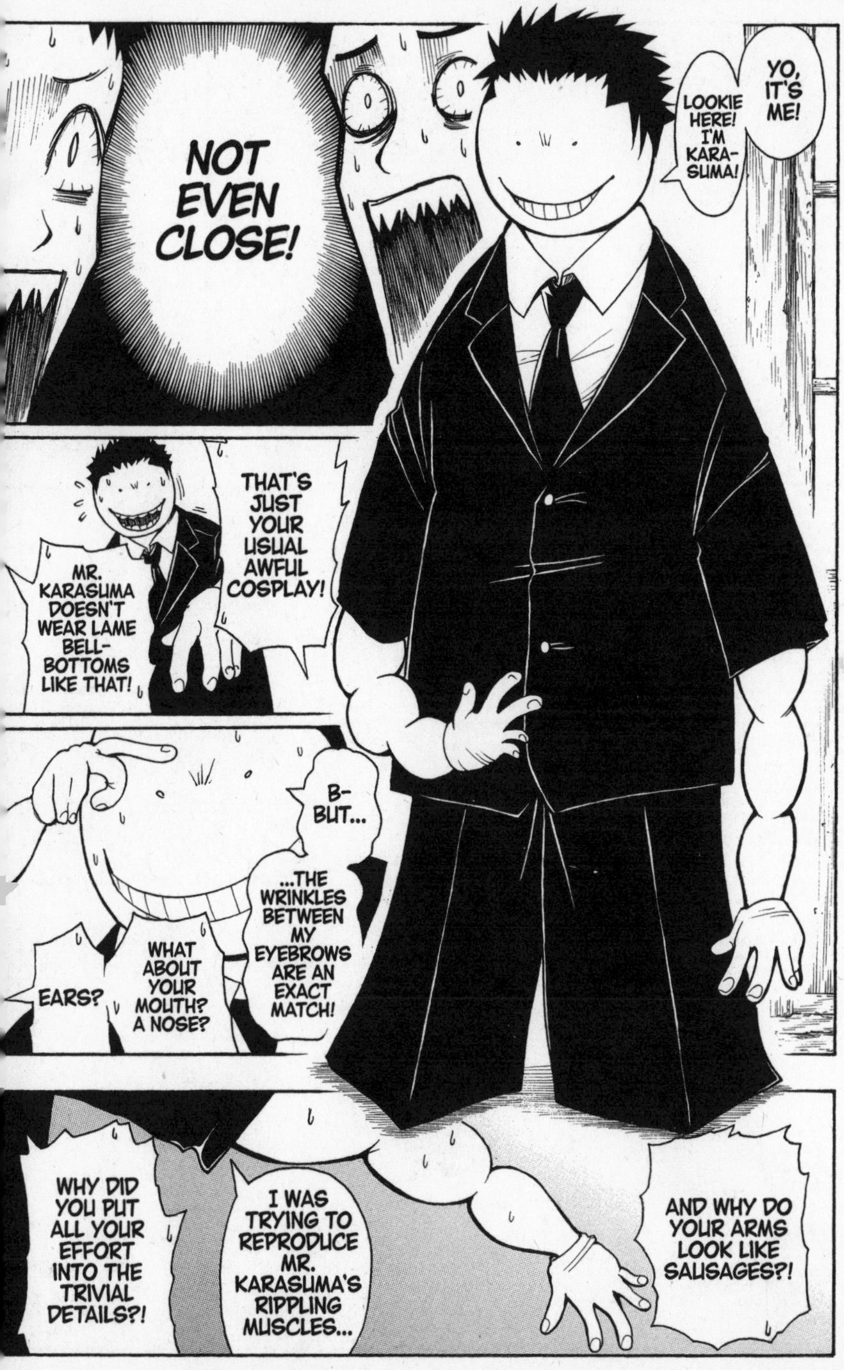
YO, IT'S ME!
LOOKIE HERE! I'M KARASUMA!
NOT EVEN CLOSE!
THAT'S JUST YOUR USUAL AWFUL COSPLAY!
MR. KARASUMA DOESN'T WEAR LAME BELL-BOTTOMS LIKE THAT!
B-BUT...
...THE WRINKLES BETWEEN MY EYEBROWS ARE AN EXACT MATCH!
WHAT ABOUT YOUR MOUTH? A NOSE?
EARS?
AND WHY DO YOUR ARMS LOOK LIKE SAUSAGES?!
I WAS TRYING TO REPRODUCE MR. KARASUMA'S RIPPLING MUSCLES...
WHY DID YOU PUT ALL YOUR EFFORT INTO THE TRIVIAL DETAILS?!

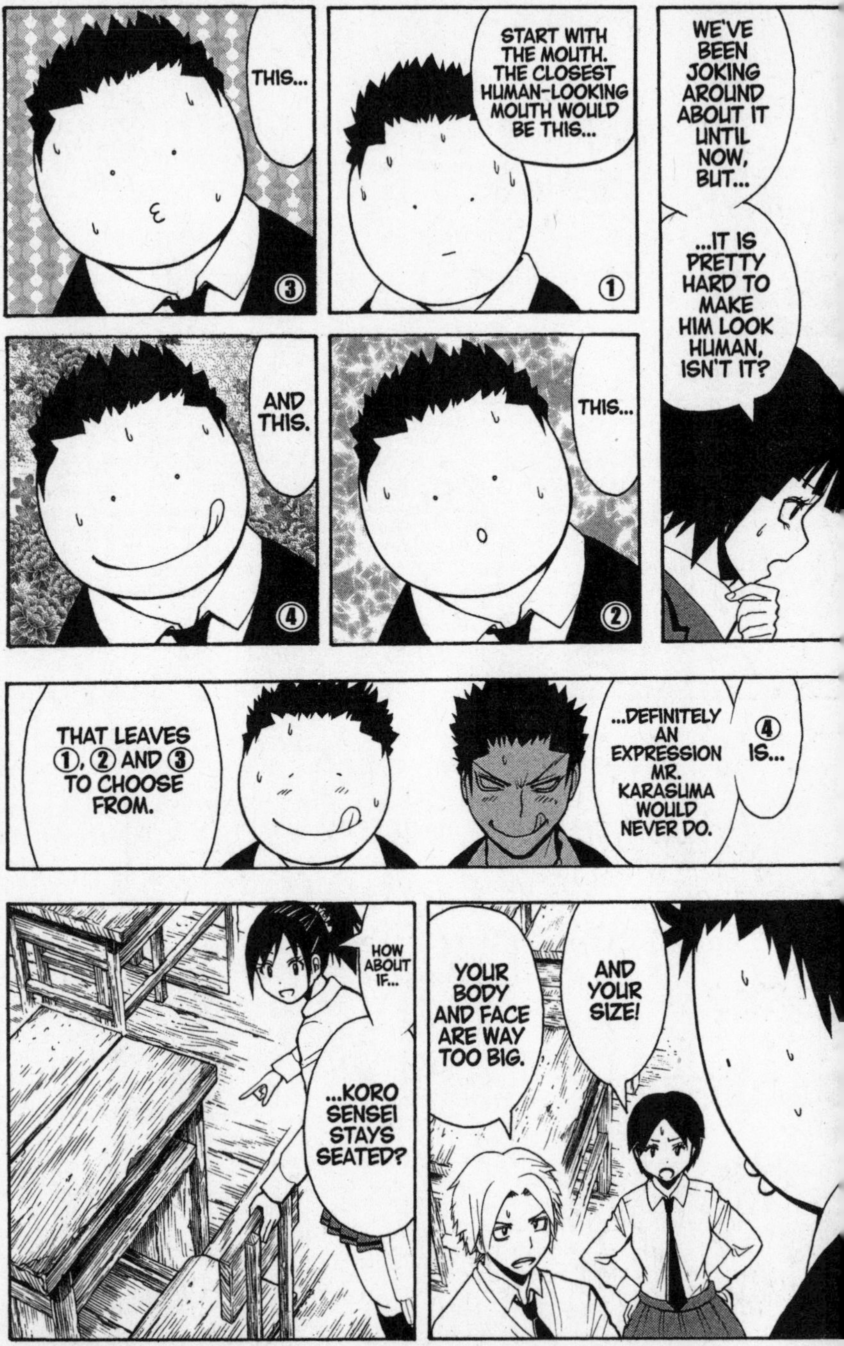
WE'VE BEEN JOKING AROUND ABOUT IT UNTIL NOW, BUT...
...IT IS PRETTY HARD TO MAKE HIM LOOK HUMAN, ISN'T IT?
START WITH THE MOUTH. THE CLOSEST HUMAN-LOOKING MOUTH WOULD BE THIS...
①
THIS...
③
THIS...
②
AND THIS.
④
④ IS...
...DEFINITELY AN EXPRESSION MR. KARASUMA WOULD NEVER DO.
THAT LEAVES ①, ② AND ③ TO CHOOSE FROM.
AND YOUR SIZE!
YOUR BODY AND FACE ARE WAY TOO BIG.
HOW ABOUT IF...
...KORO SENSEI STAYS SEATED?

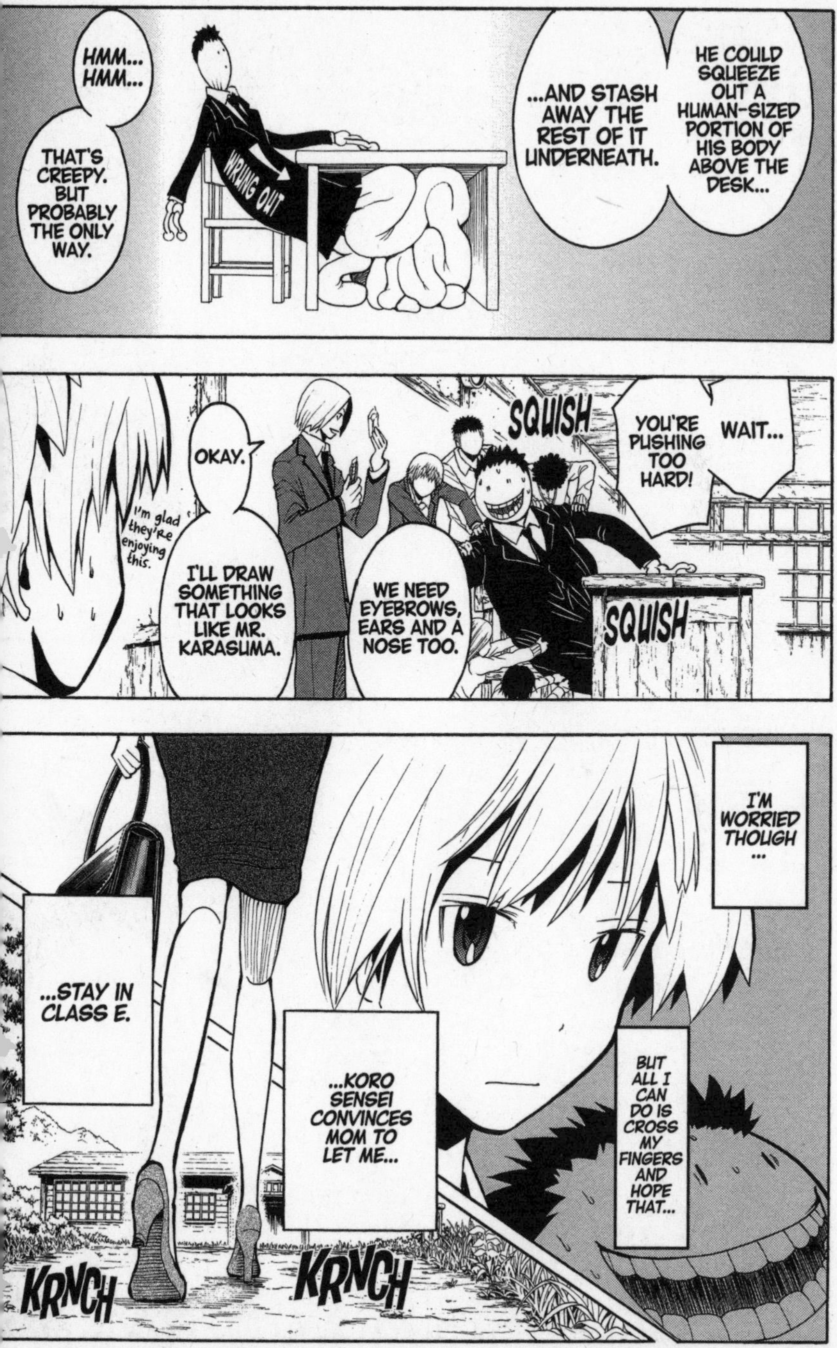
HE COULD SQUEEZE OUT A HUMAN-SIZED PORTION OF HIS BODY ABOVE THE DESK...
...AND STASH AWAY THE REST OF IT UNDERNEATH.
WRUNG OUT
HMM... HMM...
THAT'S CREEPY. BUT PROBABLY THE ONLY WAY.
WAIT...
YOU'RE PUSHING TOO HARD!
SQUISH
SQUISH
WE NEED EYEBROWS, EARS AND A NOSE TOO.
OKAY.
I'LL DRAW SOMETHING THAT LOOKS LIKE MR. KARASUMA.
I'm glad they're enjoying this.
I'M WORRIED THOUGH...
BUT ALL I CAN DO IS CROSS MY FINGERS AND HOPE THAT...
...KORO SENSEI CONVINCES MOM TO LET ME...
...STAY IN CLASS E.
KRNCH
KRNCH

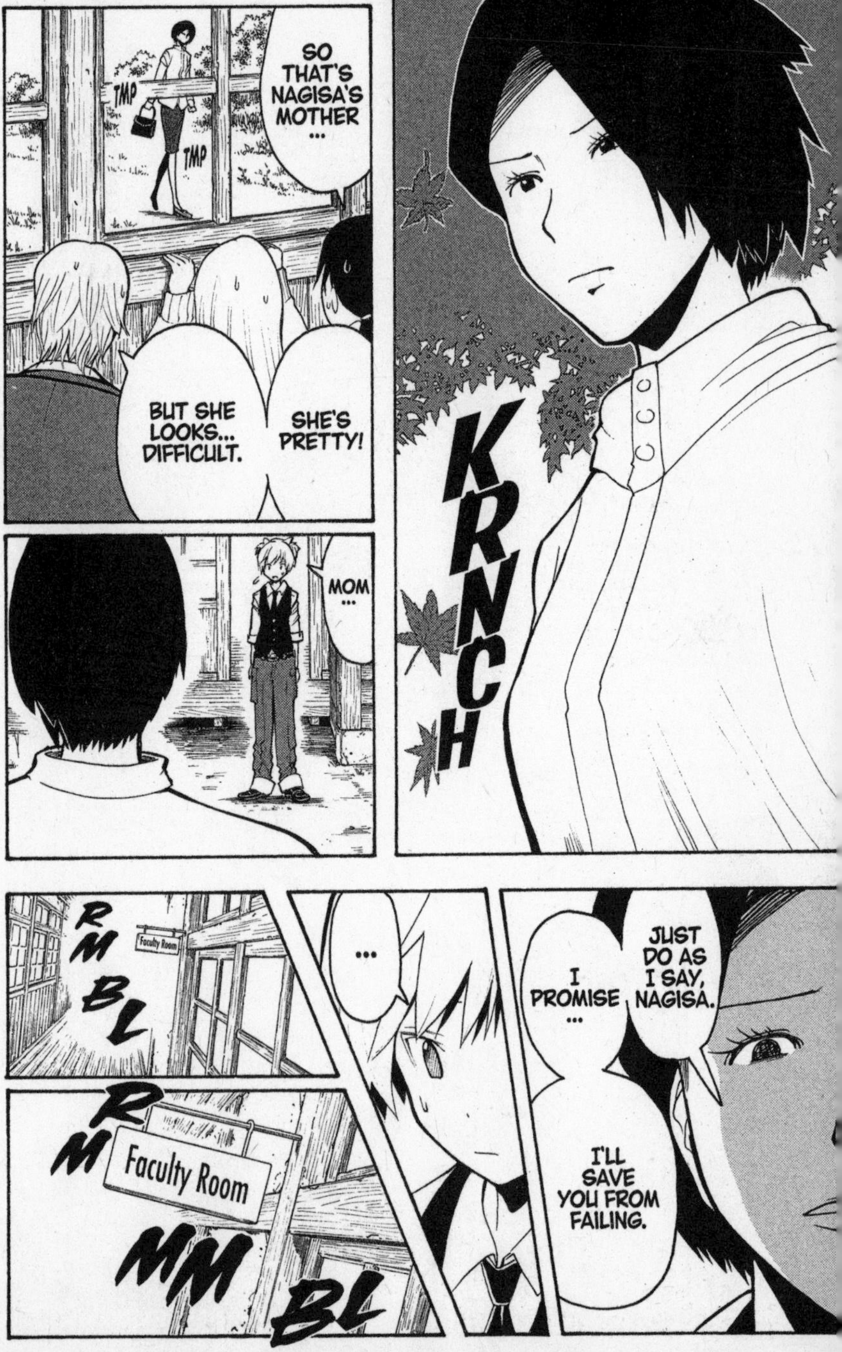
KRNCH
SO THAT'S NAGISA'S MOTHER ...
SHE'S PRETTY!
BUT SHE LOOKS... DIFFICULT.
TMP
TMP
MOM ...
JUST DO AS I SAY, NAGISA.
I PROMISE ...
I'LL SAVE YOU FROM FAILING.
...
RMBL
Faculty Room
RMMMBL
Faculty Room

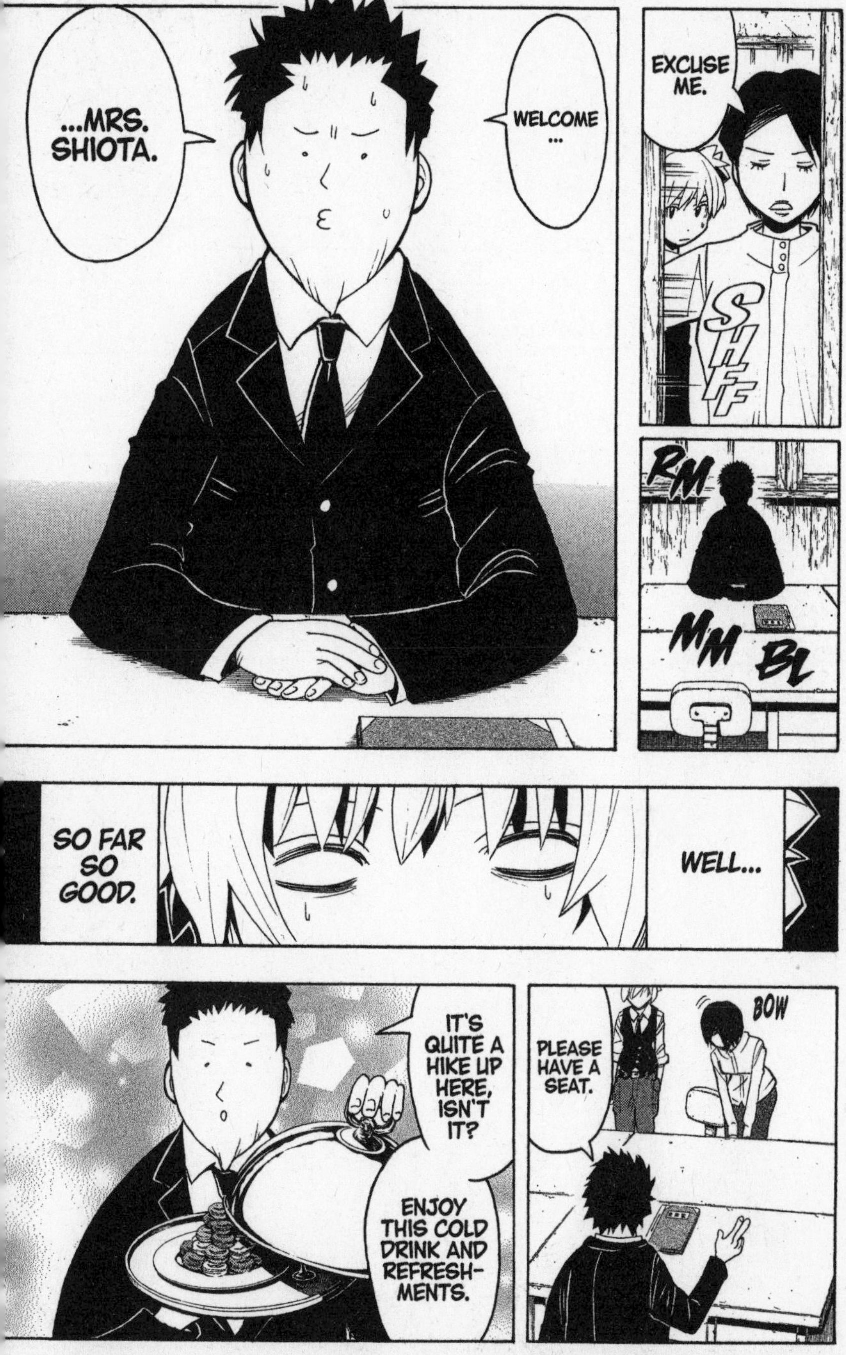
EXCUSE ME.
SHFF
RM
MM
BL
WELCOME...
...MRS. SHIOTA.
WELL...
SO FAR SO GOOD.
BOW
PLEASE HAVE A SEAT.
IT'S QUITE A HIKE UP HERE, ISN'T IT?
ENJOY THIS COLD DRINK AND REFRESH-MENTS.

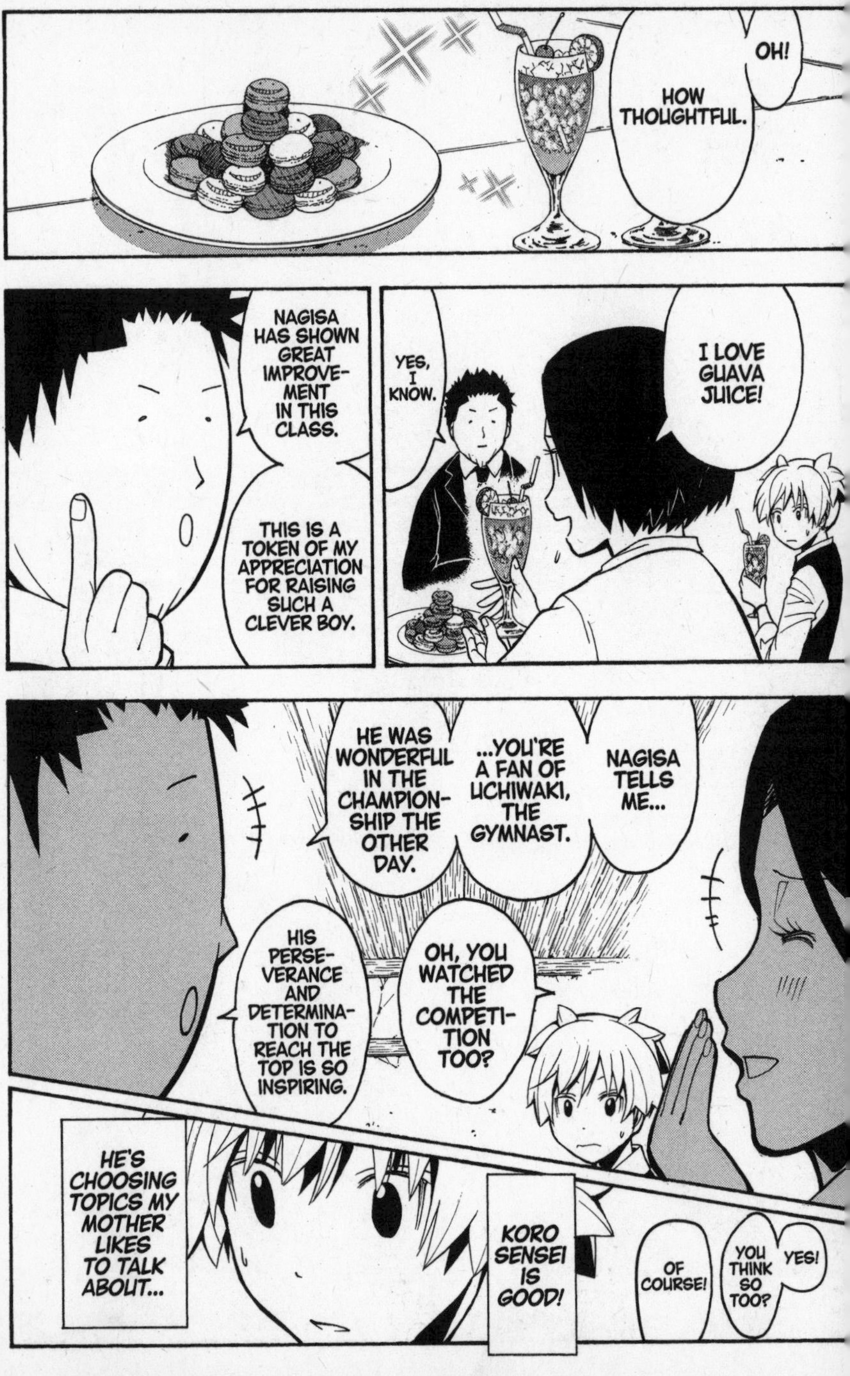
OH!
HOW THOUGHTFUL.
I LOVE GUAVA JUICE!
YES, I KNOW.
NAGISA HAS SHOWN GREAT IMPROVE-MENT IN THIS CLASS.
THIS IS A TOKEN OF MY APPRECIATION FOR RAISING SUCH A CLEVER BOY.
NAGISA TELLS ME...
...YOU'RE A FAN OF UCHIWAKI, THE GYMNAST.
HE WAS WONDERFUL IN THE CHAMPION-SHIP THE OTHER DAY.
OH, YOU WATCHED THE COMPETI-TION TOO?
HIS PERSE-VERANCE AND DETERMINA-TION TO REACH THE TOP IS SO INSPIRING.
YES!
YOU THINK SO TOO?
OF COURSE!
KORO SENSEI IS GOOD!
HE'S CHOOSING TOPICS MY MOTHER LIKES TO TALK ABOUT...

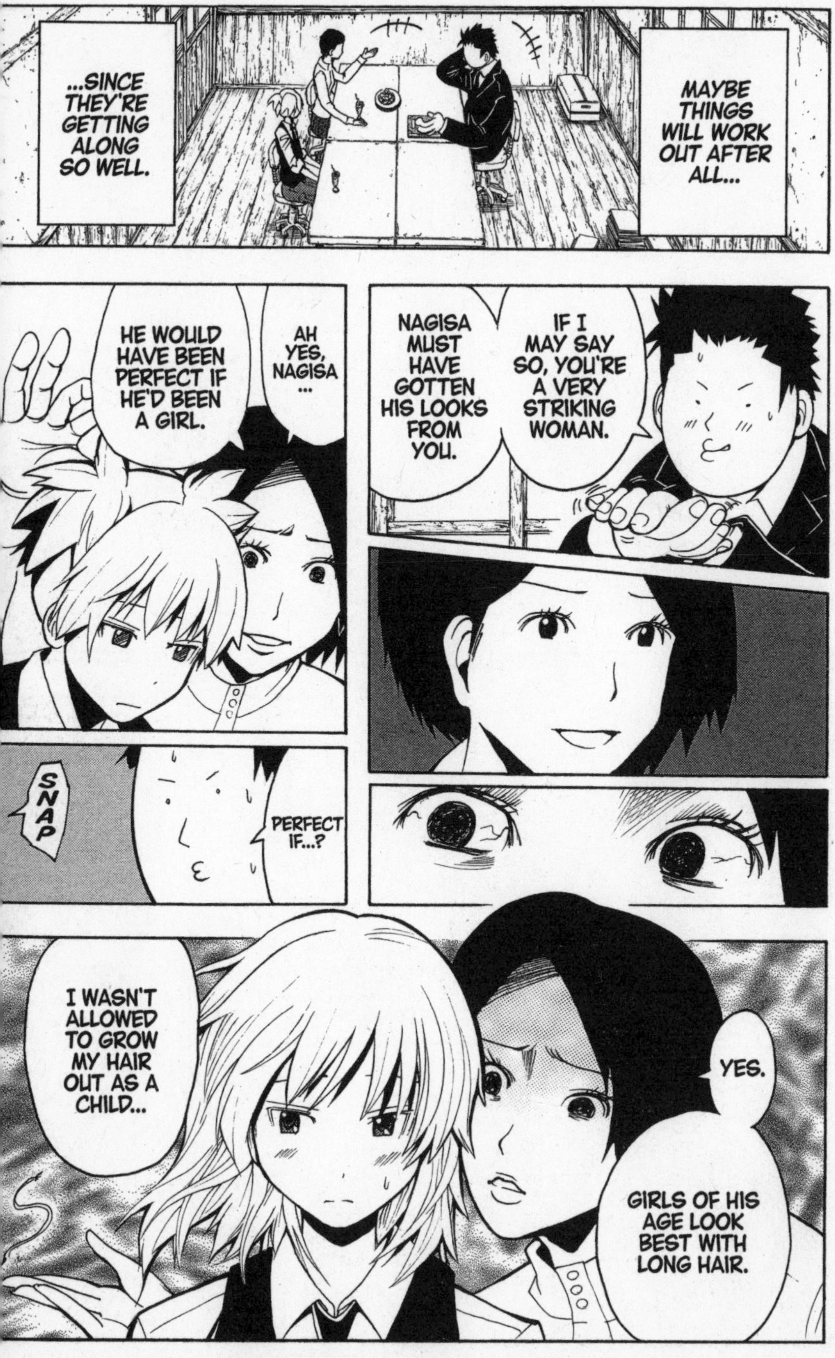
MAYBE THINGS WILL WORK OUT AFTER ALL...
...SINCE THEY'RE GETTING ALONG SO WELL.
IF I MAY SAY SO, YOU'RE A VERY STRIKING WOMAN.
NAGISA MUST HAVE GOTTEN HIS LOOKS FROM YOU.
AH YES, NAGISA...
HE WOULD HAVE BEEN PERFECT IF HE'D BEEN A GIRL.
PERFECT IF...?
SNAP
YES.
GIRLS OF HIS AGE LOOK BEST WITH LONG HAIR.
I WASN'T ALLOWED TO GROW MY HAIR OUT AS A CHILD...

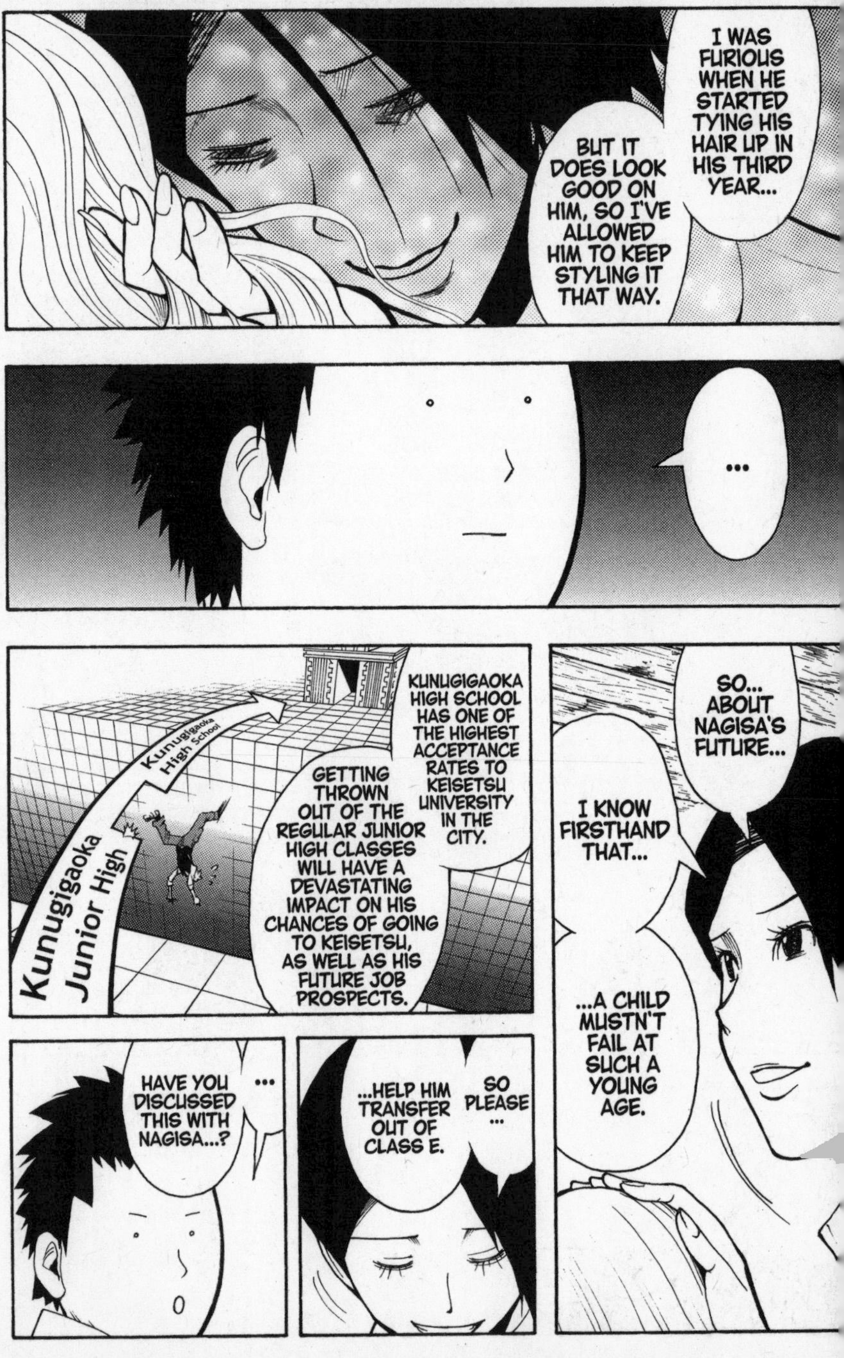
I WAS FURIOUS WHEN HE STARTED TYING HIS HAIR UP IN HIS THIRD YEAR...
BUT IT DOES LOOK GOOD ON HIM, SO I'VE ALLOWED HIM TO KEEP STYLING IT THAT WAY.
...
SO... ABOUT NAGISA'S FUTURE...
I KNOW FIRSTHAND THAT...
...A CHILD MUSTN'T FAIL AT SUCH A YOUNG AGE.
KUNUGIGAOKA HIGH SCHOOL HAS ONE OF THE HIGHEST ACCEPTANCE RATES TO KEISETSU UNIVERSITY IN THE CITY.
GETTING THROWN OUT OF THE REGULAR JUNIOR HIGH CLASSES WILL HAVE A DEVASTATING IMPACT ON HIS CHANCES OF GOING TO KEISETSU, AS WELL AS HIS FUTURE JOB PROSPECTS.
Kunugigaoka High School
Kunugigaoka Junior High
SO PLEASE...
...HELP HIM TRANSFER OUT OF CLASS E.
...
HAVE YOU DISCUSSED THIS WITH NAGISA...?

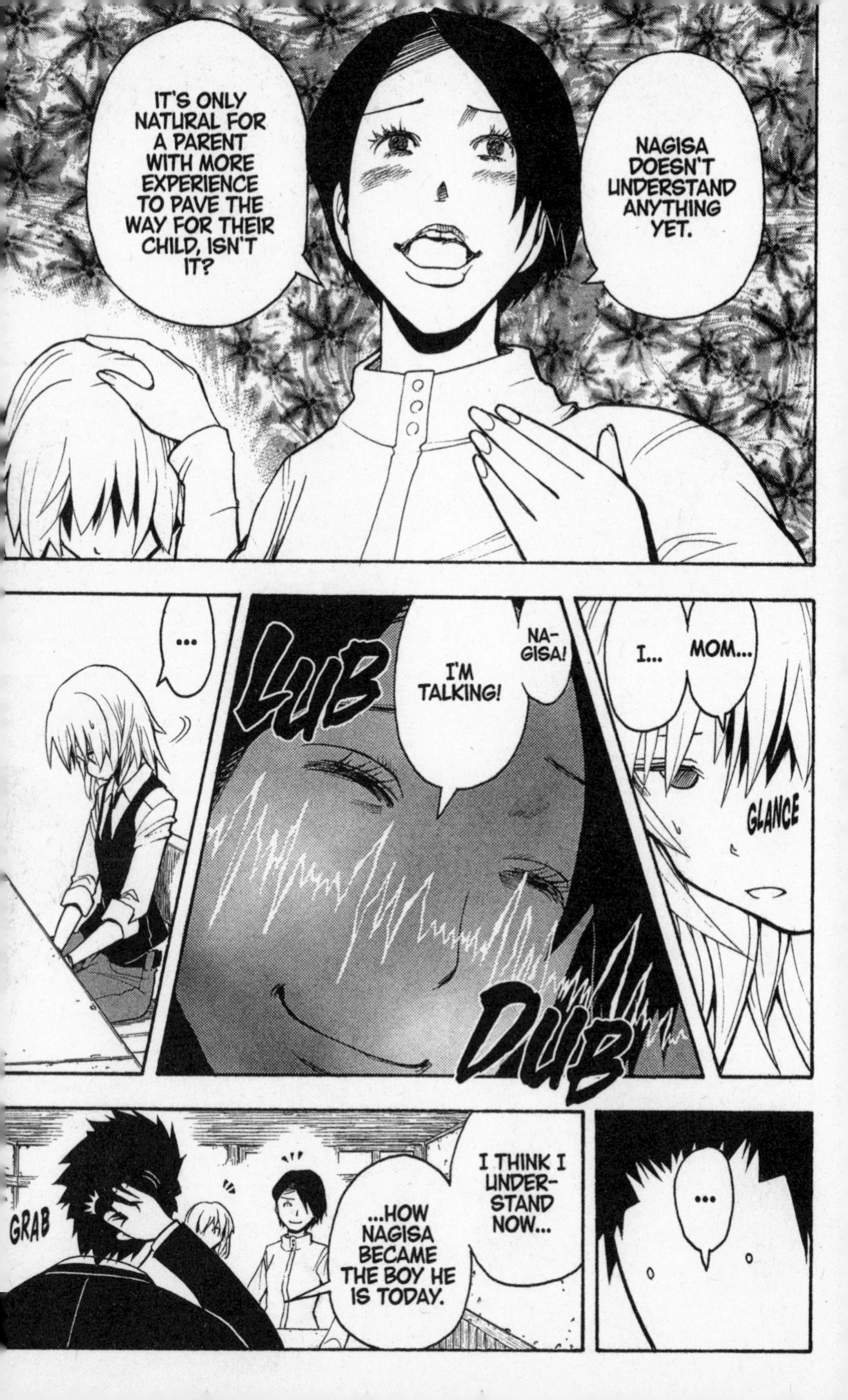
NAGISA DOESN'T UNDERSTAND ANYTHING YET.
IT'S ONLY NATURAL FOR A PARENT WITH MORE EXPERIENCE TO PAVE THE WAY FOR THEIR CHILD, ISN'T IT?
MOM...
I...
GLANCE
NA-GISA!
I'M TALKING!
LUB
DUB
...
...
I THINK I UNDER-STAND NOW...
...HOW NAGISA BECAME THE BOY HE IS TODAY.
GRAB

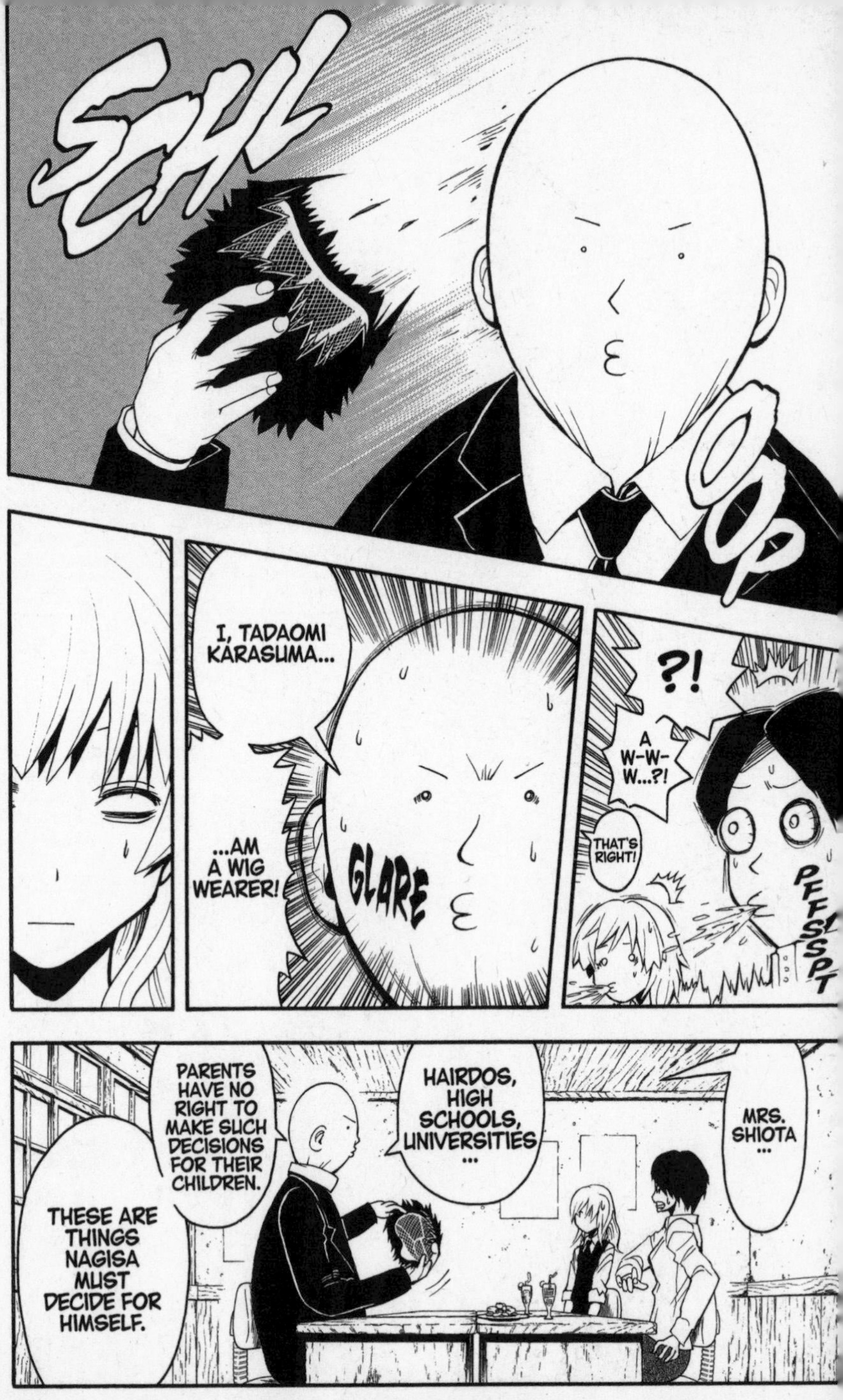
SCHL
OOP
?!
A W-W-W...?!
THAT'S RIGHT!
PFFSSPT
I, TADAOMI KARASUMA...
...AM A WIG WEARER!
GLARE
MRS. SHIOTA...
HAIRDOS, HIGH SCHOOLS, UNIVERSITIES...
PARENTS HAVE NO RIGHT TO MAKE SUCH DECISIONS FOR THEIR CHILDREN.
THESE ARE THINGS NAGISA MUST DECIDE FOR HIMSELF.

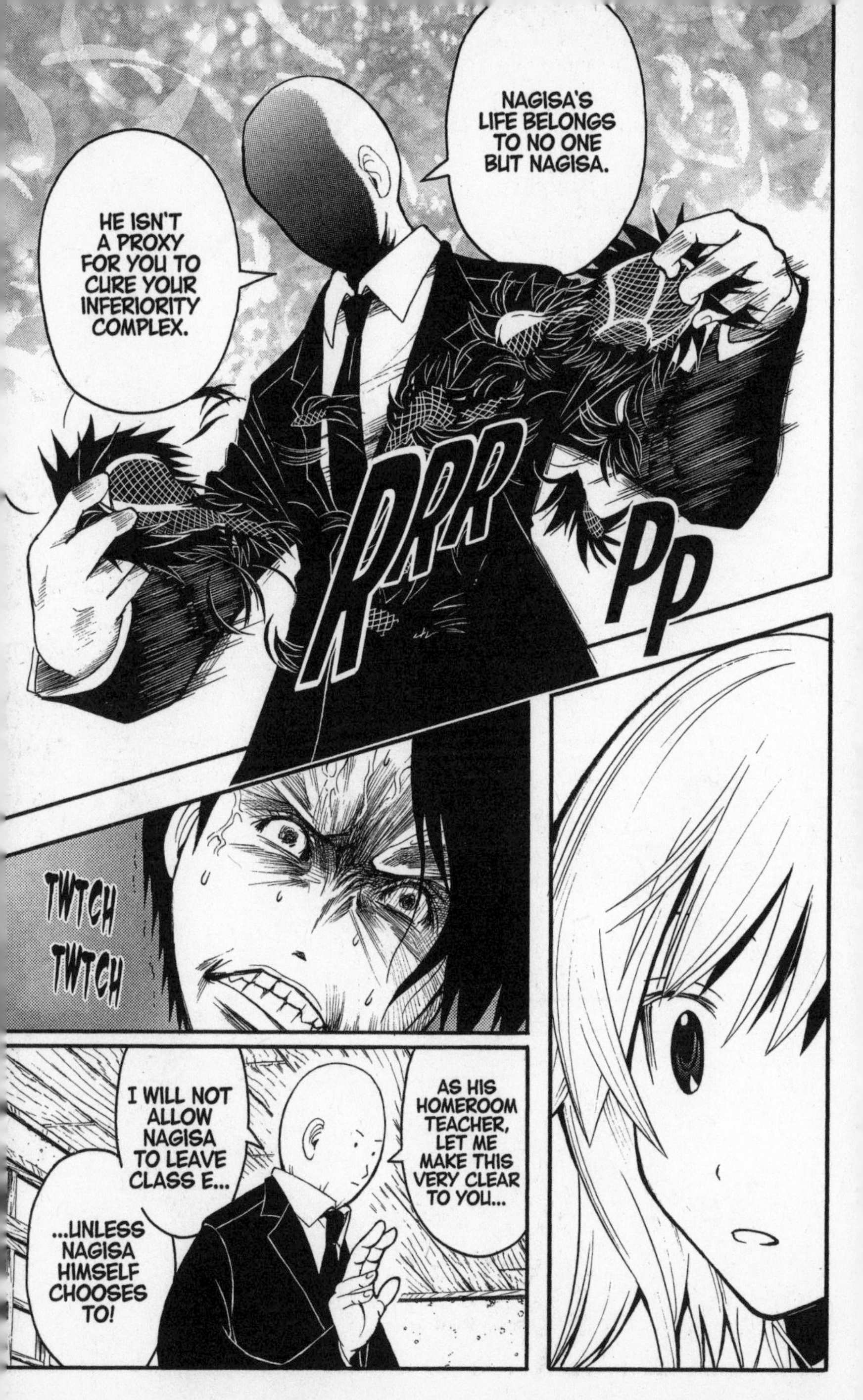
NAGISA'S LIFE BELONGS TO NO ONE BUT NAGISA.
HE ISN'T A PROXY FOR YOU TO CURE YOUR INFERIORITY COMPLEX.
RRRR
PP
TWTCH TWTCH
AS HIS HOMEROOM TEACHER, LET ME MAKE THIS VERY CLEAR TO YOU...
I WILL NOT ALLOW NAGISA TO LEAVE CLASS E...
...UNLESS NAGISA HIMSELF CHOOSES TO!

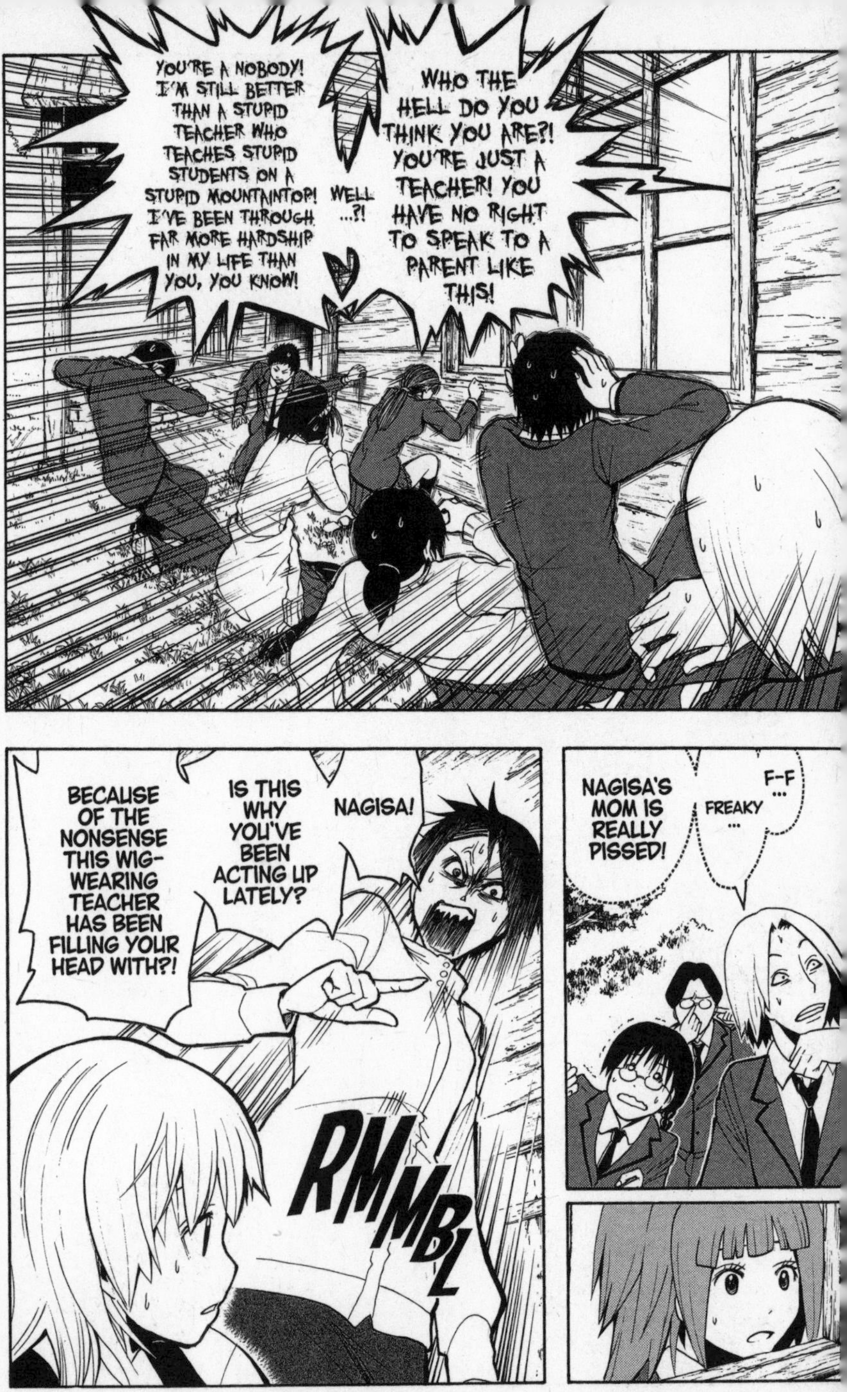
WHO THE HELL DO YOU THINK YOU ARE?! YOU'RE JUST A TEACHER! YOU HAVE NO RIGHT TO SPEAK TO A PARENT LIKE THIS!
WELL ...?!
YOU'RE A NOBODY! I'M STILL BETTER THAN A STUPID TEACHER WHO TEACHES STUPID STUDENTS ON A STUPID MOUNTAINTOP! I'VE BEEN THROUGH FAR MORE HARDSHIP IN MY LIFE THAN YOU, YOU KNOW!
F-F ... FREAKY ...
NAGISA'S MOM IS REALLY PISSED!
NAGISA!
IS THIS WHY YOU'VE BEEN ACTING UP LATELY?
BECAUSE OF THE NONSENSE THIS WIG-WEARING TEACHER HAS BEEN FILLING YOUR HEAD WITH?!
RMMBL

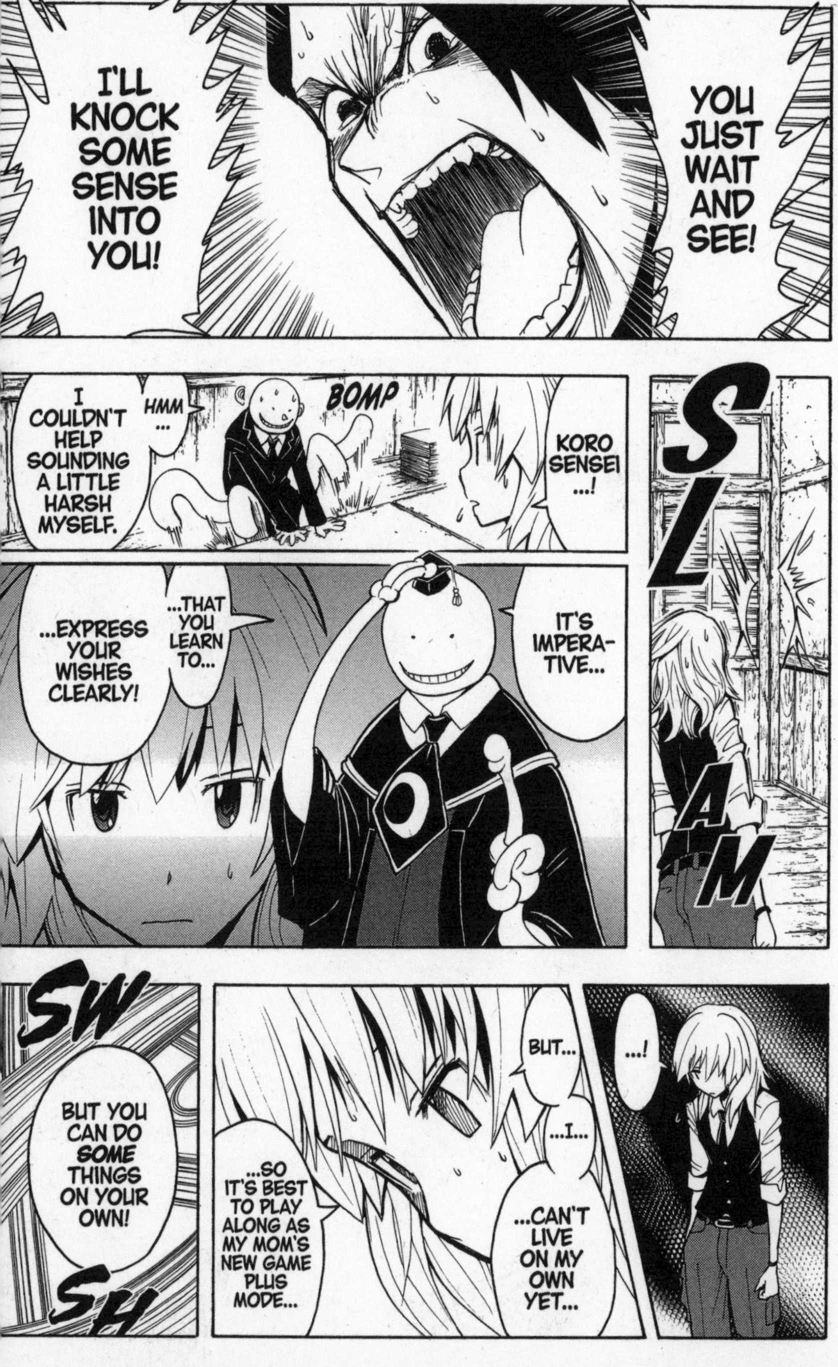
YOU JUST WAIT AND SEE!
I'LL KNOCK SOME SENSE INTO YOU!
SLAM
KORO SENSEI ...!
BOMP
HMM ...
I COULDN'T HELP SOUNDING A LITTLE HARSH MYSELF.
IT'S IMPERA-TIVE...
...THAT YOU LEARN TO...
...EXPRESS YOUR WISHES CLEARLY!
...!
BUT...
...I...
...CAN'T LIVE ON MY OWN YET...
...SO IT'S BEST TO PLAY ALONG AS MY MOM'S NEW GAME PLUS MODE...
SWSH
BUT YOU CAN DO SOME THINGS ON YOUR OWN!

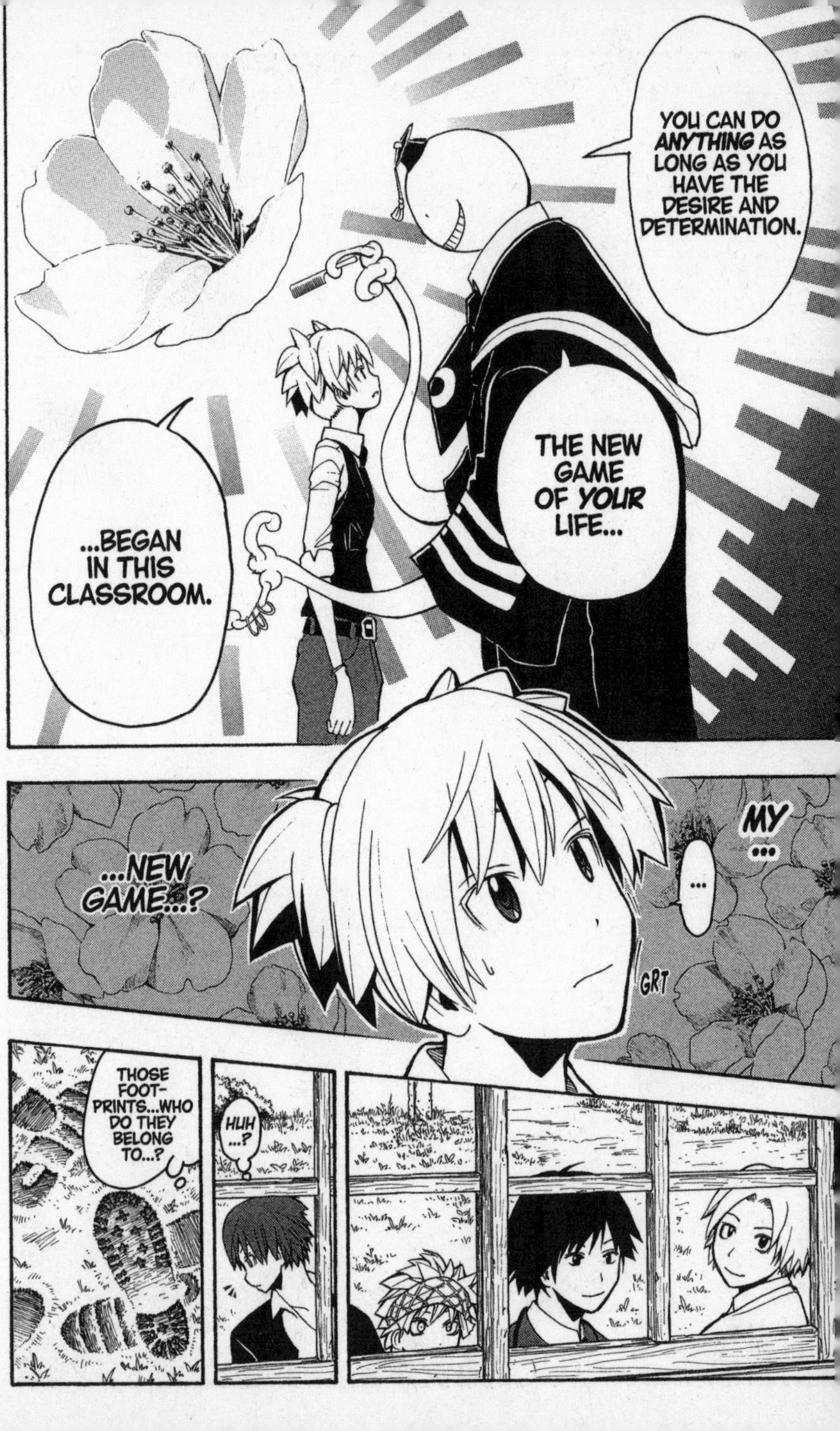
YOU CAN DO ANYTHING AS LONG AS YOU HAVE THE DESIRE AND DETERMINATION.
THE NEW GAME OF YOUR LIFE...
...BEGAN IN THIS CLASSROOM.
MY...
...
GRT
...NEW GAME...?
HUH...?
THOSE FOOT-PRINTS...WHO DO THEY BELONG TO...?

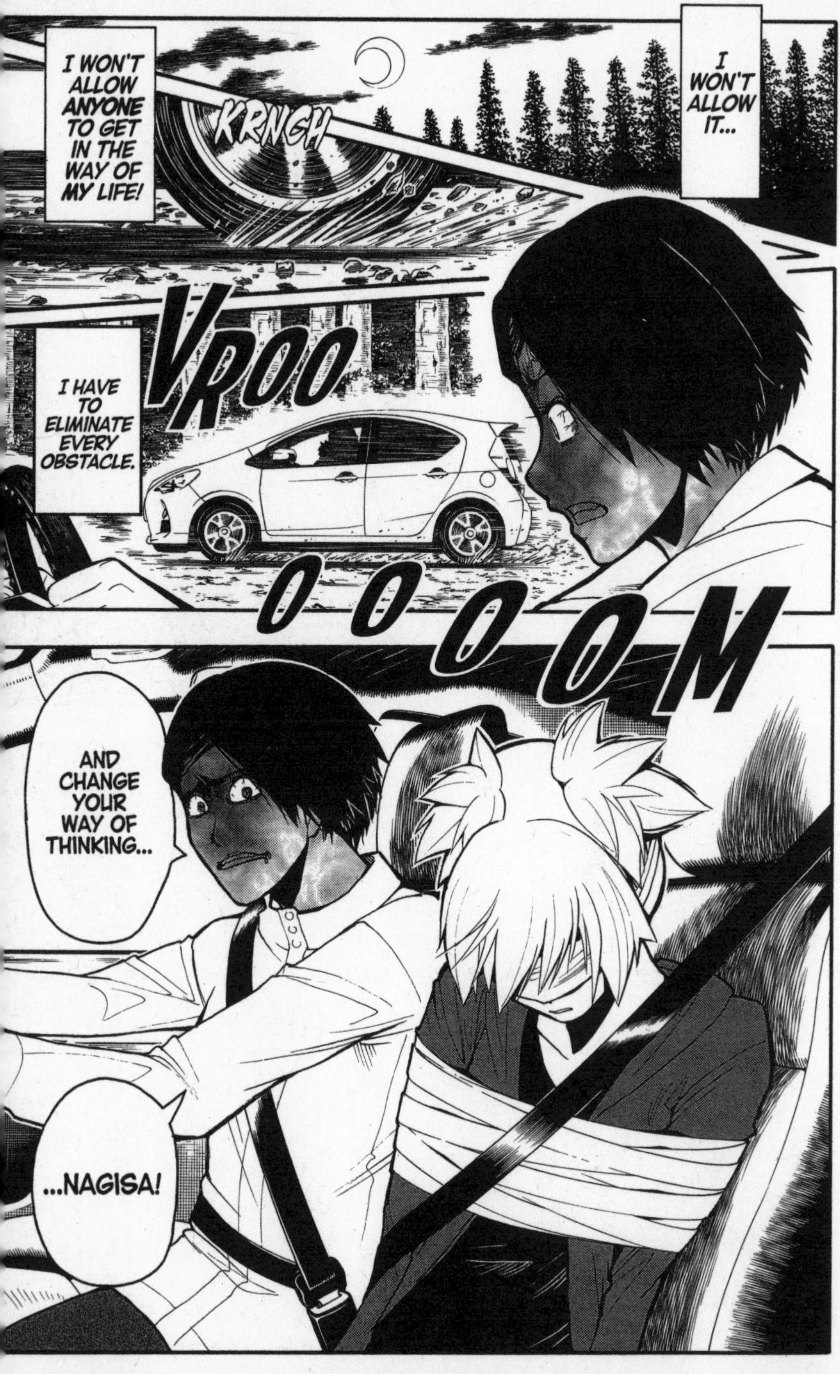
I WON'T ALLOW IT...
I WON'T ALLOW ANYONE TO GET IN THE WAY OF MY LIFE!
KRNGH
I HAVE TO ELIMINATE EVERY OBSTACLE.
VROOOOOOOM
AND CHANGE YOUR WAY OF THINKING...
...NAGISA!

The Collaboration of a Lifetime

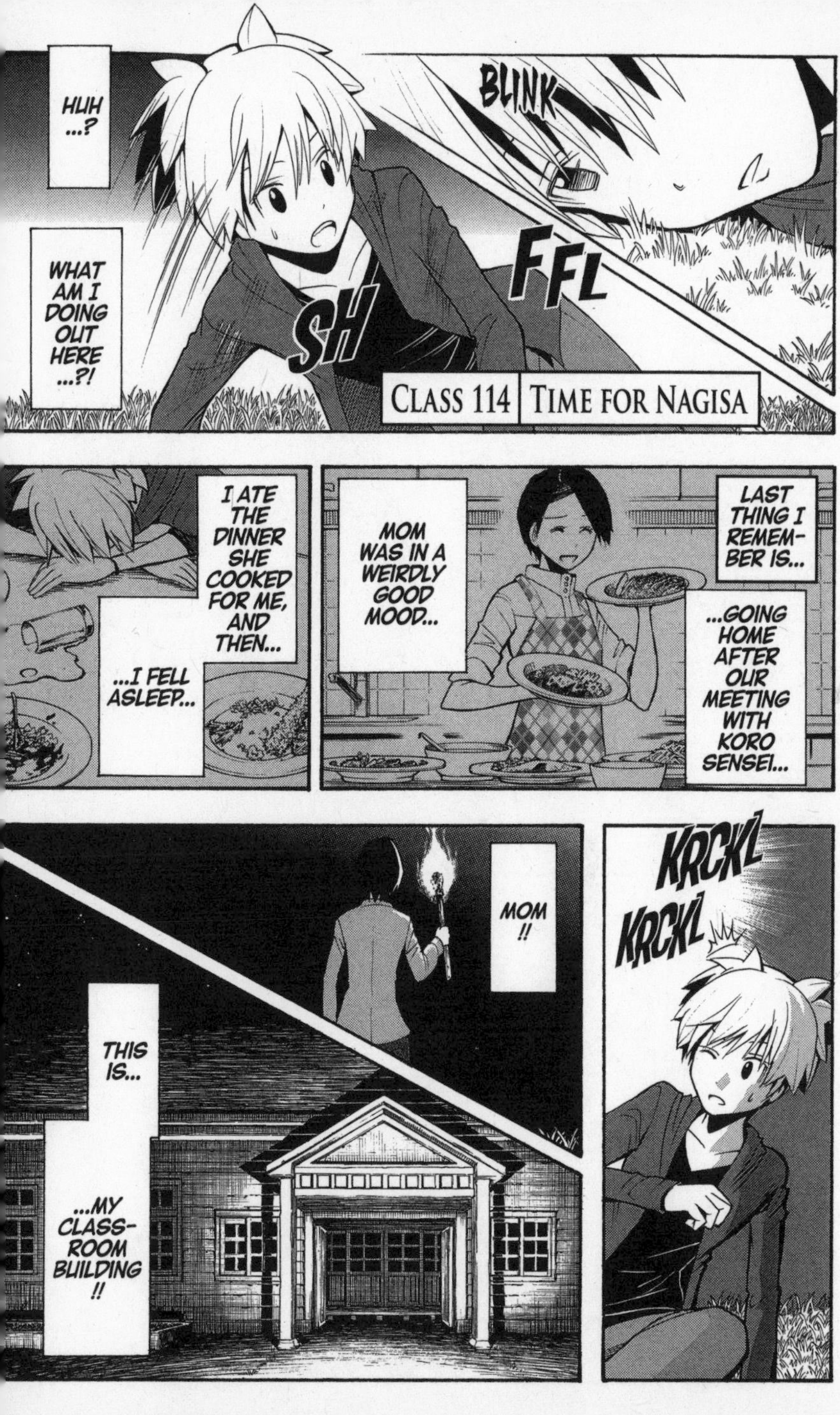
BLINK
FFL
SH
HUH...?
WHAT AM I DOING OUT HERE...?!
CLASS 114 TIME FOR NAGISA
LAST THING I REMEMBER IS...
...GOING HOME AFTER OUR MEETING WITH KORO SENSEI...
MOM WAS IN A WEIRDLY GOOD MOOD...
I ATE THE DINNER SHE COOKED FOR ME, AND THEN...
...I FELL ASLEEP...
KRCKL
KRCKL
MOM!!
THIS IS...
...MY CLASSROOM BUILDING!!

Class 114 Time for Nagisa

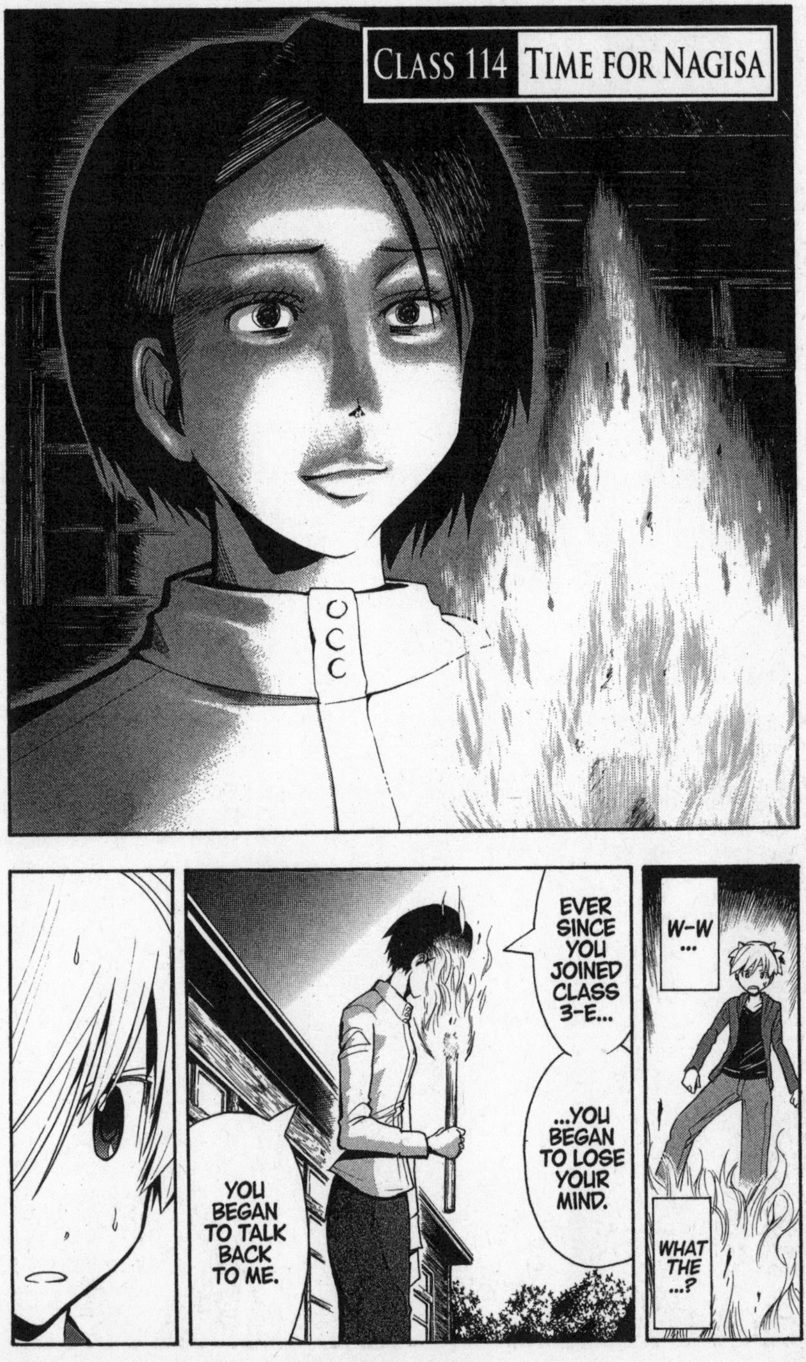
W-W ...
WHAT THE ...?
EVER SINCE YOU JOINED CLASS 3-E...
...YOU BEGAN TO LOSE YOUR MIND.
YOU BEGAN TO TALK BACK TO ME.

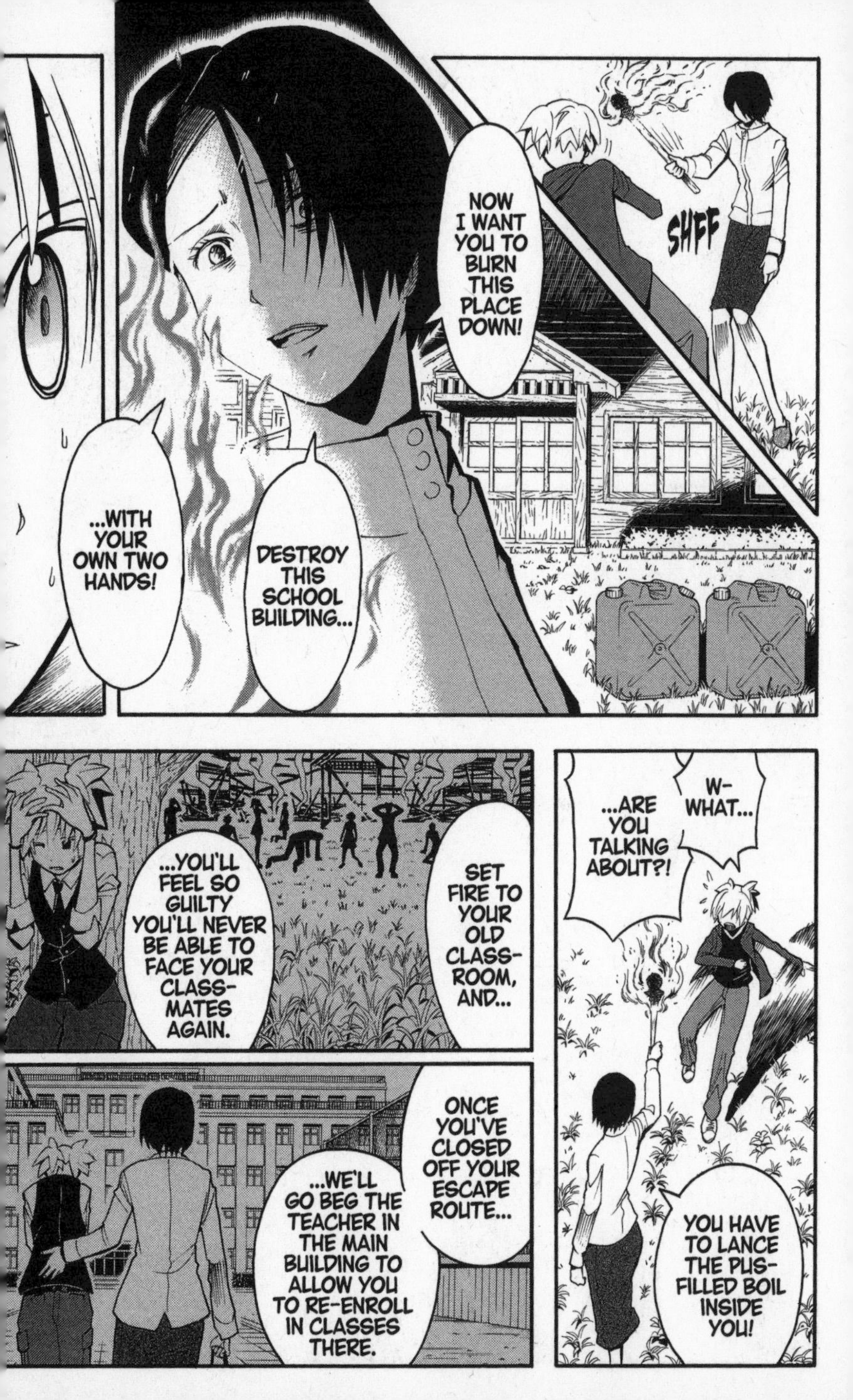
NOW I WANT YOU TO BURN THIS PLACE DOWN!
SHFF
DESTROY THIS SCHOOL BUILDING...
...WITH YOUR OWN TWO HANDS!
W-WHAT...
...ARE YOU TALKING ABOUT?!
YOU HAVE TO LANCE THE PUS-FILLED BOIL INSIDE YOU!
SET FIRE TO YOUR OLD CLASS-ROOM, AND...
...YOU'LL FEEL SO GUILTY YOU'LL NEVER BE ABLE TO FACE YOUR CLASS-MATES AGAIN.
ONCE YOU'VE CLOSED OFF YOUR ESCAPE ROUTE...
...WE'LL GO BEG THE TEACHER IN THE MAIN BUILDING TO ALLOW YOU TO RE-ENROLL IN CLASSES THERE.

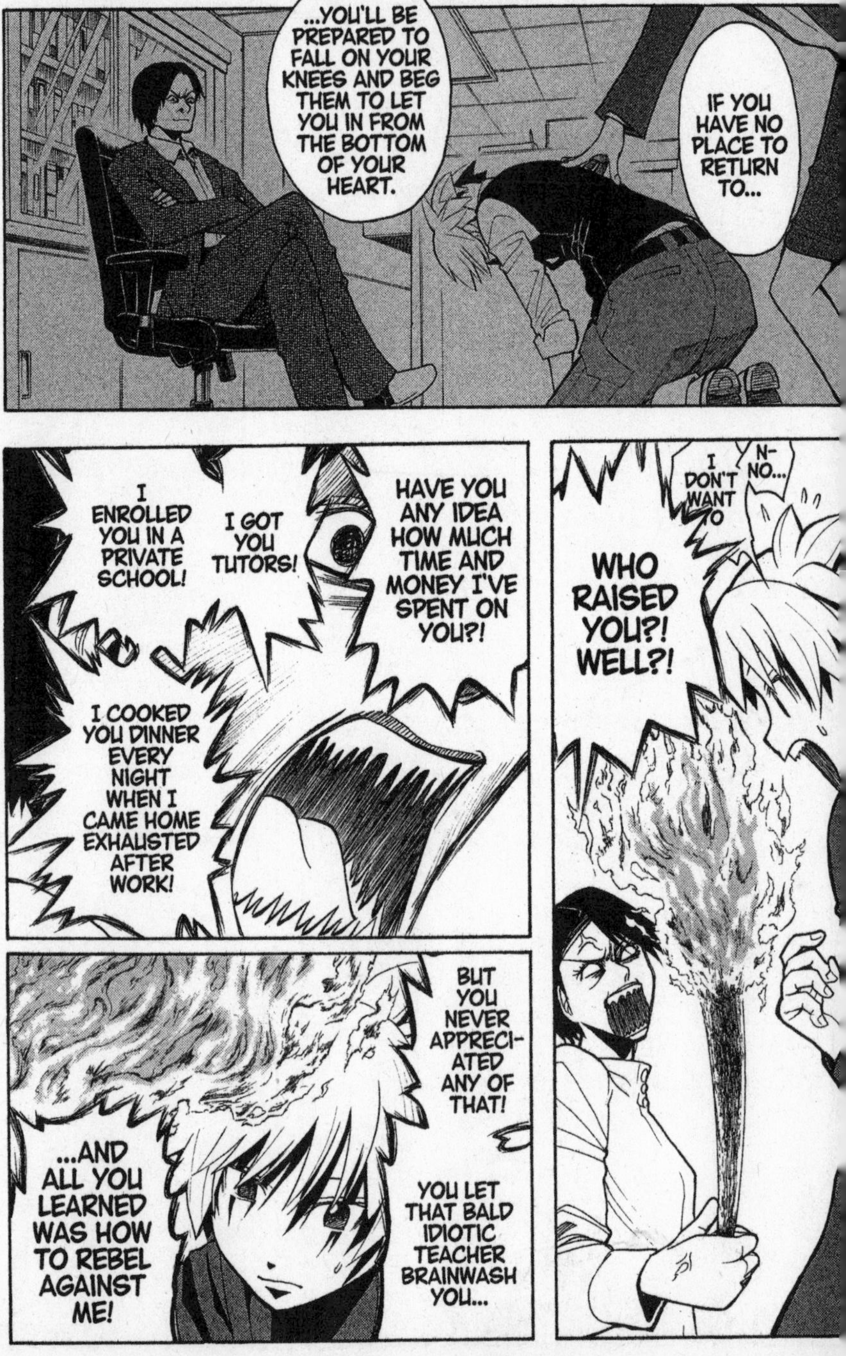
IF YOU HAVE NO PLACE TO RETURN TO...
...YOU'LL BE PREPARED TO FALL ON YOUR KNEES AND BEG THEM TO LET YOU IN FROM THE BOTTOM OF YOUR HEART.
N-NO...
I DON'T WANT TO
WHO RAISED YOU?! WELL?!
HAVE YOU ANY IDEA HOW MUCH TIME AND MONEY I'VE SPENT ON YOU?!
I GOT YOU TUTORS!
I ENROLLED YOU IN A PRIVATE SCHOOL!
I COOKED YOU DINNER EVERY NIGHT WHEN I CAME HOME EXHAUSTED AFTER WORK!
BUT YOU NEVER APPRECIATED ANY OF THAT!
YOU LET THAT BALD IDIOTIC TEACHER BRAINWASH YOU...
...AND ALL YOU LEARNED WAS HOW TO REBEL AGAINST ME!

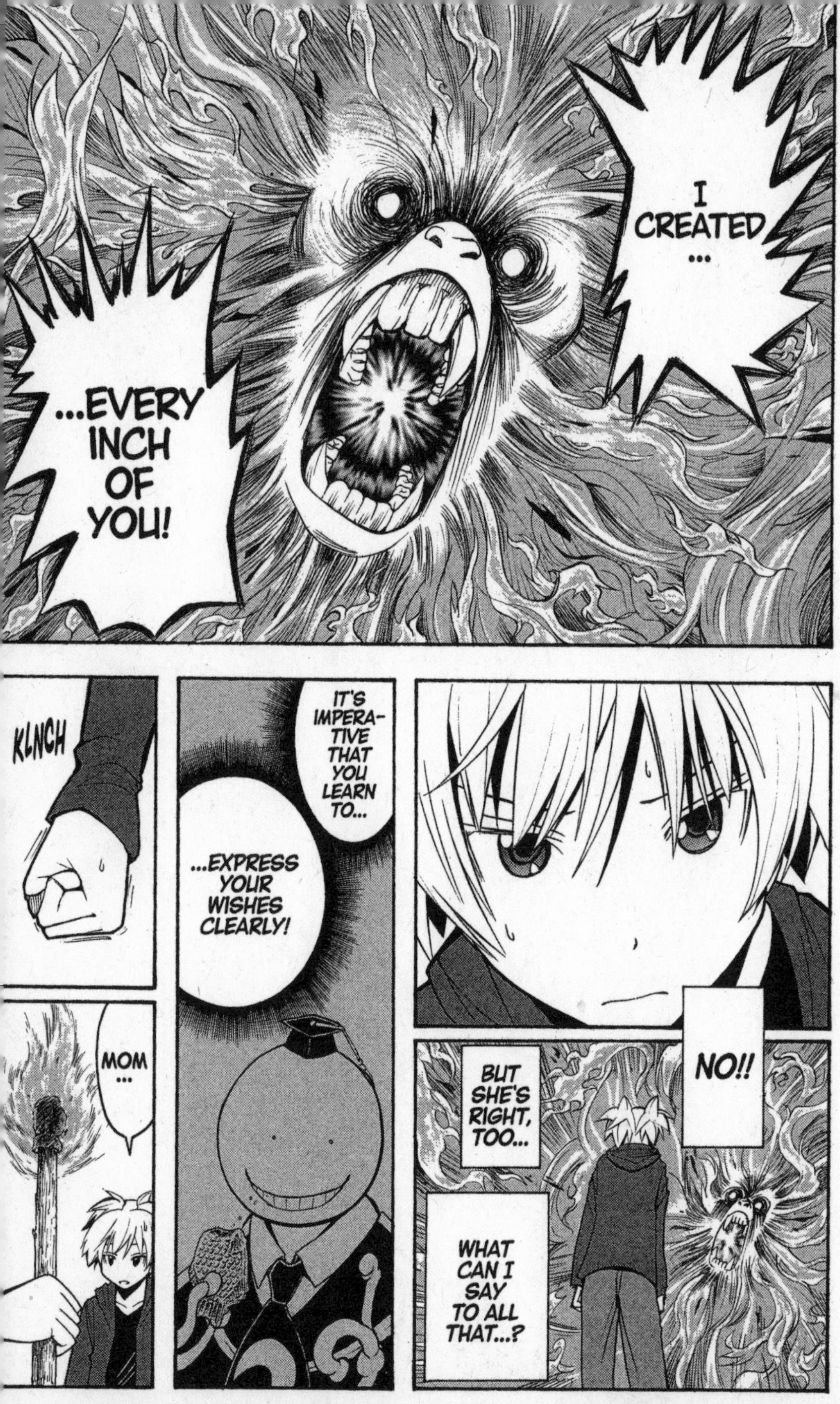
I CREATED...
...EVERY INCH OF YOU!
NO!!
BUT SHE'S RIGHT, TOO...
WHAT CAN I SAY TO ALL THAT...?
IT'S IMPERA-TIVE THAT YOU LEARN TO...
...EXPRESS YOUR WISHES CLEARLY!
KLNCH
MOM...

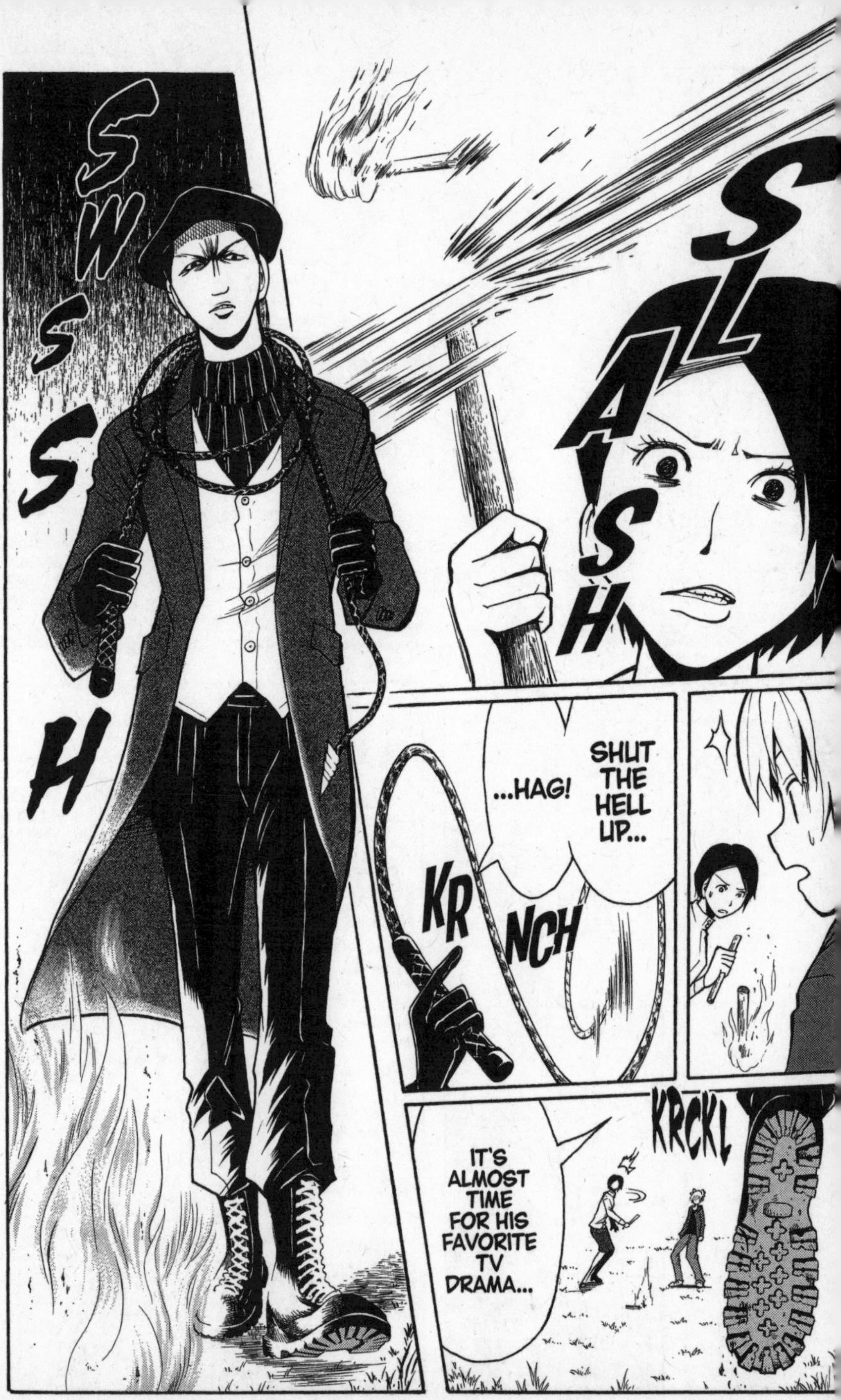
SLASH
SHUT THE HELL UP...
...HAG!
KRNCH
KRCKL
IT'S ALMOST TIME FOR HIS FAVORITE TV DRAMA...
SWSSSH

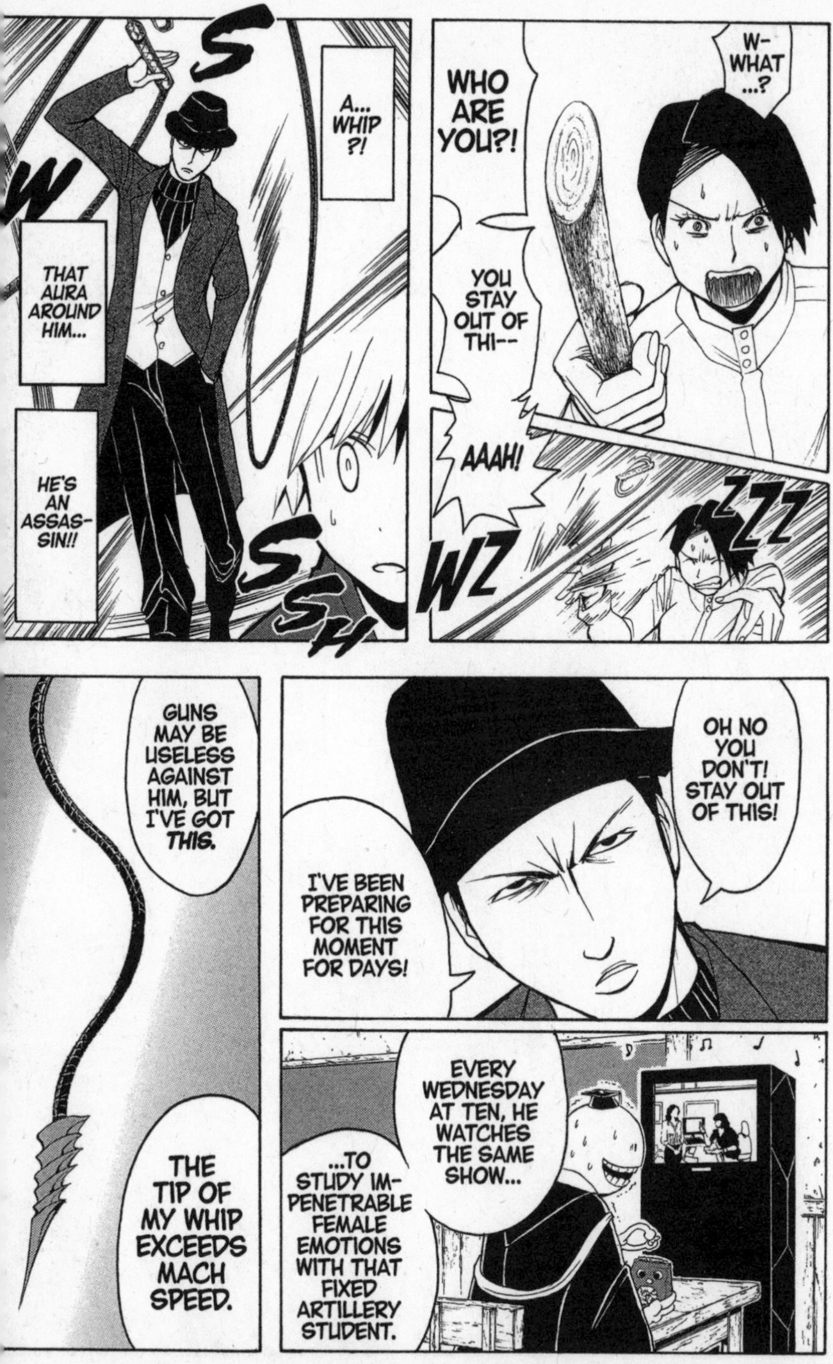
W- WHAT ...?
WHO ARE YOU?!
YOU STAY OUT OF THI--
AAAH!
ZZZ
WZ
S
A... WHIP ?!
W
THAT AURA AROUND HIM...
HE'S AN ASSAS-SIN!!
SSH
OH NO YOU DON'T! STAY OUT OF THIS!
I'VE BEEN PREPARING FOR THIS MOMENT FOR DAYS!
EVERY WEDNESDAY AT TEN, HE WATCHES THE SAME SHOW...
...TO STUDY IM-PENETRABLE FEMALE EMOTIONS WITH THAT FIXED ARTILLERY STUDENT.
GUNS MAY BE USELESS AGAINST HIM, BUT I'VE GOT *THIS*.
THE TIP OF MY WHIP EXCEEDS MACH SPEED.

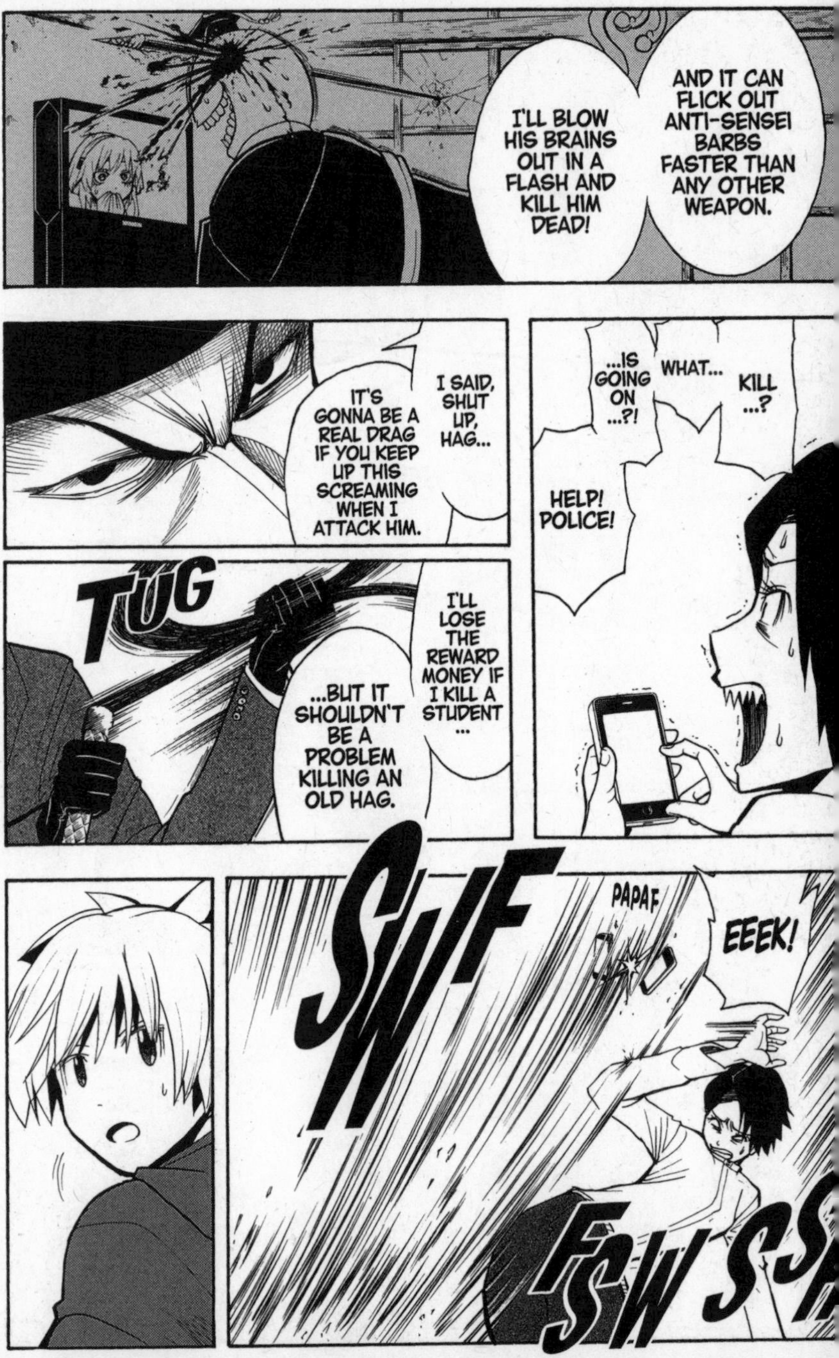
AND IT CAN FLICK OUT ANTI-SENSEI BARBS FASTER THAN ANY OTHER WEAPON.
I'LL BLOW HIS BRAINS OUT IN A FLASH AND KILL HIM DEAD!
KILL ...?
WHAT...
...IS GOING ON ...?!
HELP! POLICE!
I SAID, SHUT UP, HAG...
IT'S GONNA BE A REAL DRAG IF YOU KEEP UP THIS SCREAMING WHEN I ATTACK HIM.
TUG
I'LL LOSE THE REWARD MONEY IF I KILL A STUDENT ...
...BUT IT SHOULDN'T BE A PROBLEM KILLING AN OLD HAG.
EEEK!
PAPAF
SWF
FSW SS

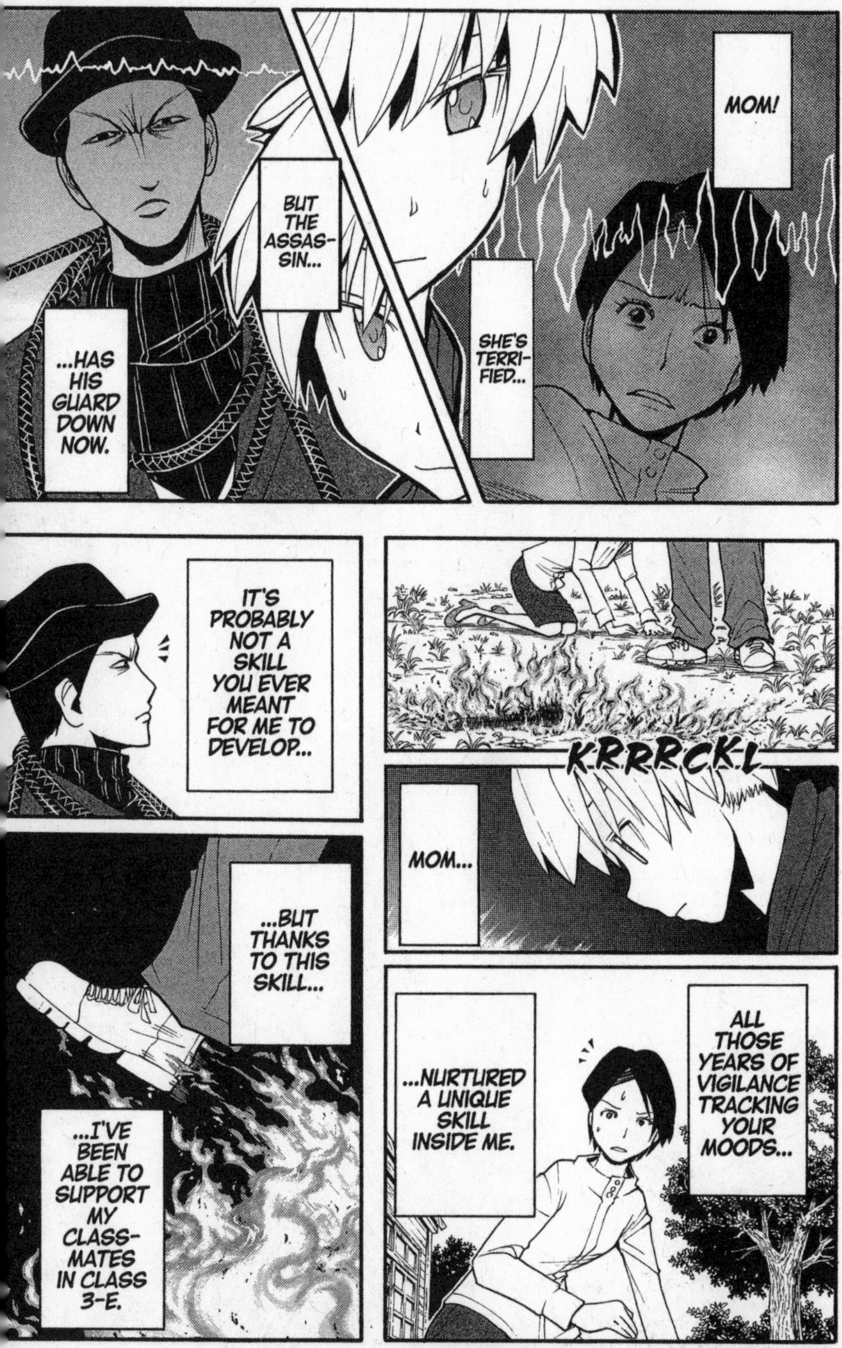
MOM!
SHE'S TERRIFIED...
BUT THE ASSASSIN...
...HAS HIS GUARD DOWN NOW.
KRRRCKL
MOM...
ALL THOSE YEARS OF VIGILANCE TRACKING YOUR MOODS...
...NURTURED A UNIQUE SKILL INSIDE ME.
IT'S PROBABLY NOT A SKILL YOU EVER MEANT FOR ME TO DEVELOP...
...BUT THANKS TO THIS SKILL...
...I'VE BEEN ABLE TO SUPPORT MY CLASSMATES IN CLASS 3-E.

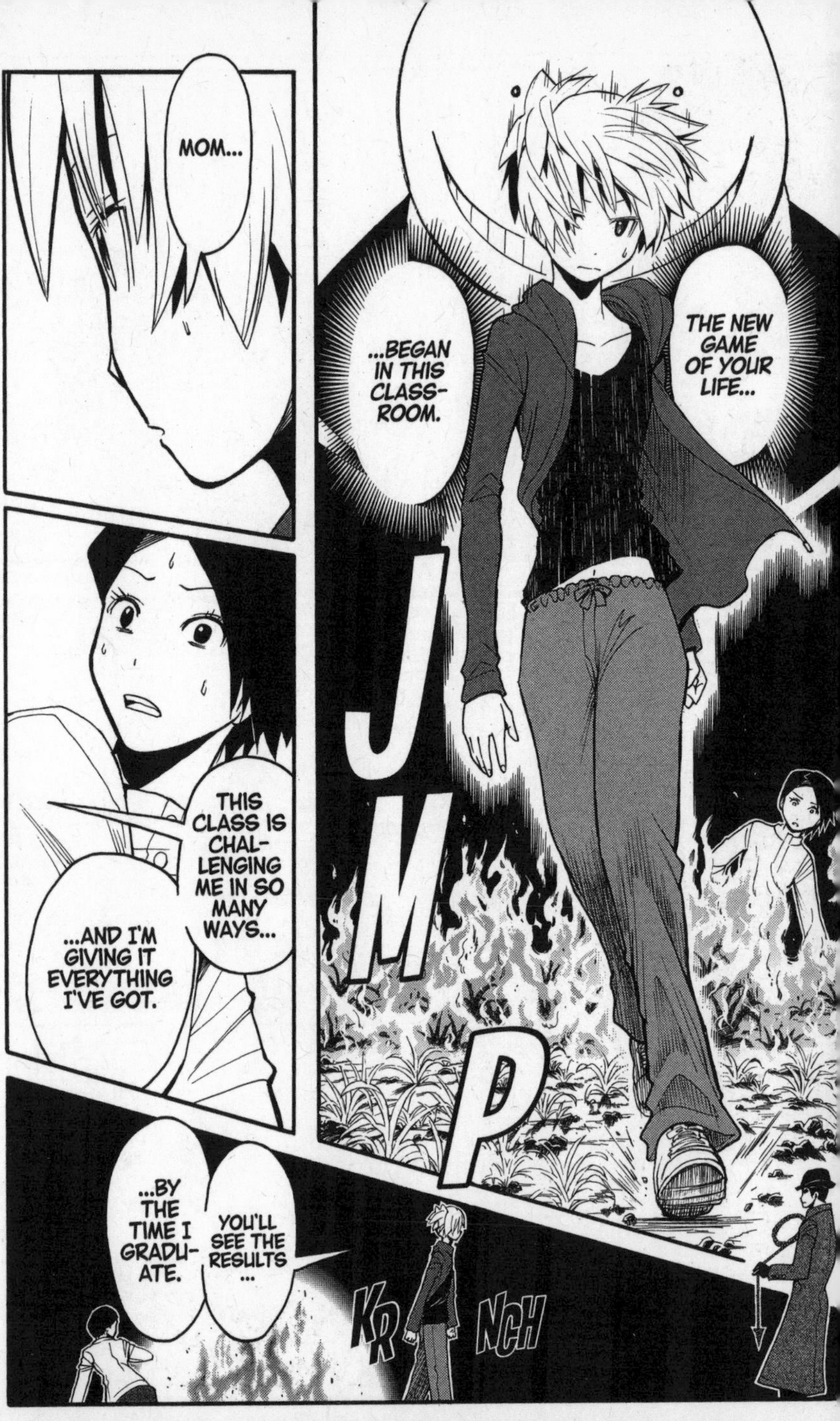
THE NEW GAME OF YOUR LIFE...
...BEGAN IN THIS CLASS-ROOM.
JUMP
MOM...
THIS CLASS IS CHAL-LENGING ME IN SO MANY WAYS...
...AND I'M GIVING IT EVERYTHING I'VE GOT.
YOU'LL SEE THE RESULTS...
...BY THE TIME I GRADU-ATE.
KRNCH

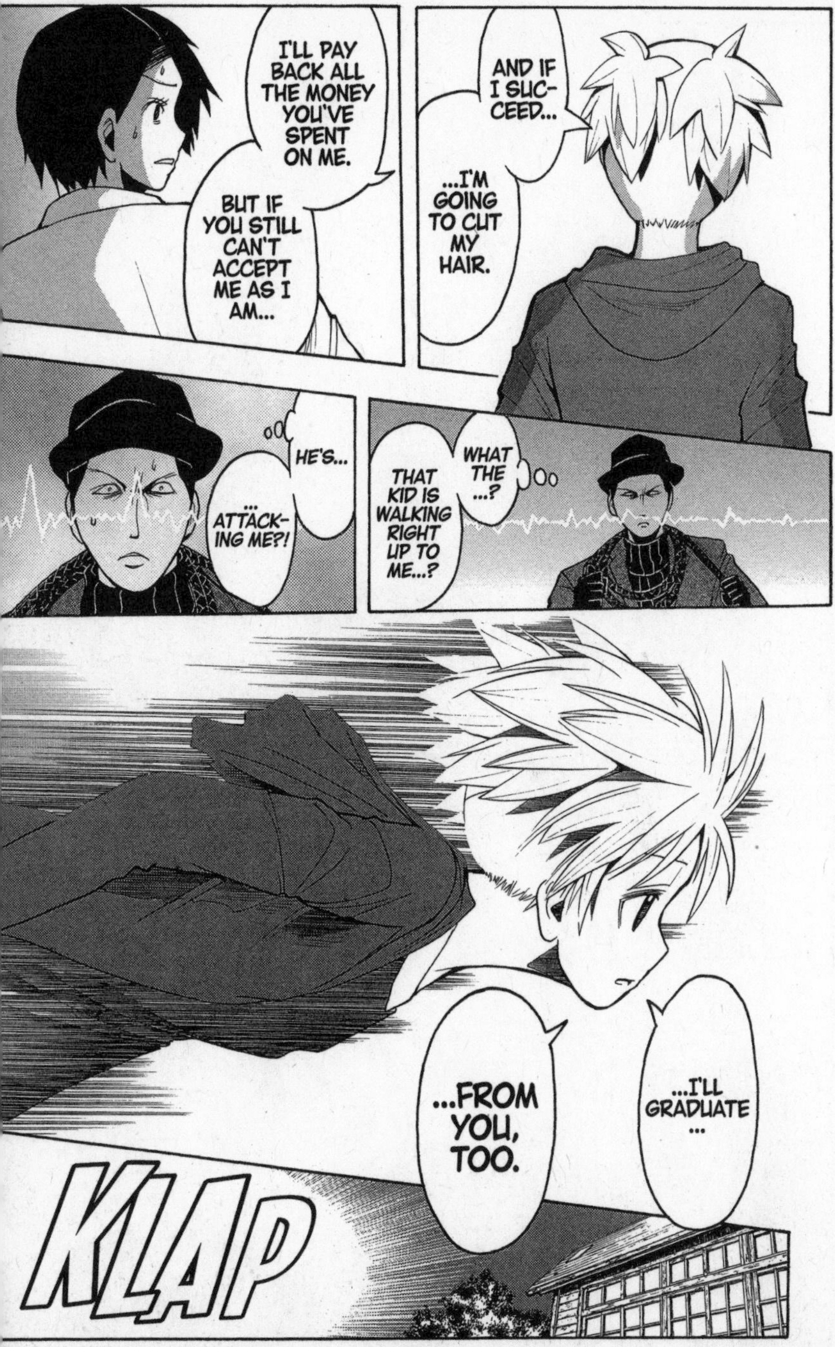
AND IF I SUC-CEED...
...I'M GOING TO CUT MY HAIR.
I'LL PAY BACK ALL THE MONEY YOU'VE SPENT ON ME.
BUT IF YOU STILL CAN'T ACCEPT ME AS I AM...
WHAT THE ...?
THAT KID IS WALKING RIGHT UP TO ME...?
HE'S...
...ATTACK-ING ME?!
...I'LL GRADUATE ...
...FROM YOU, TOO.
KLAP

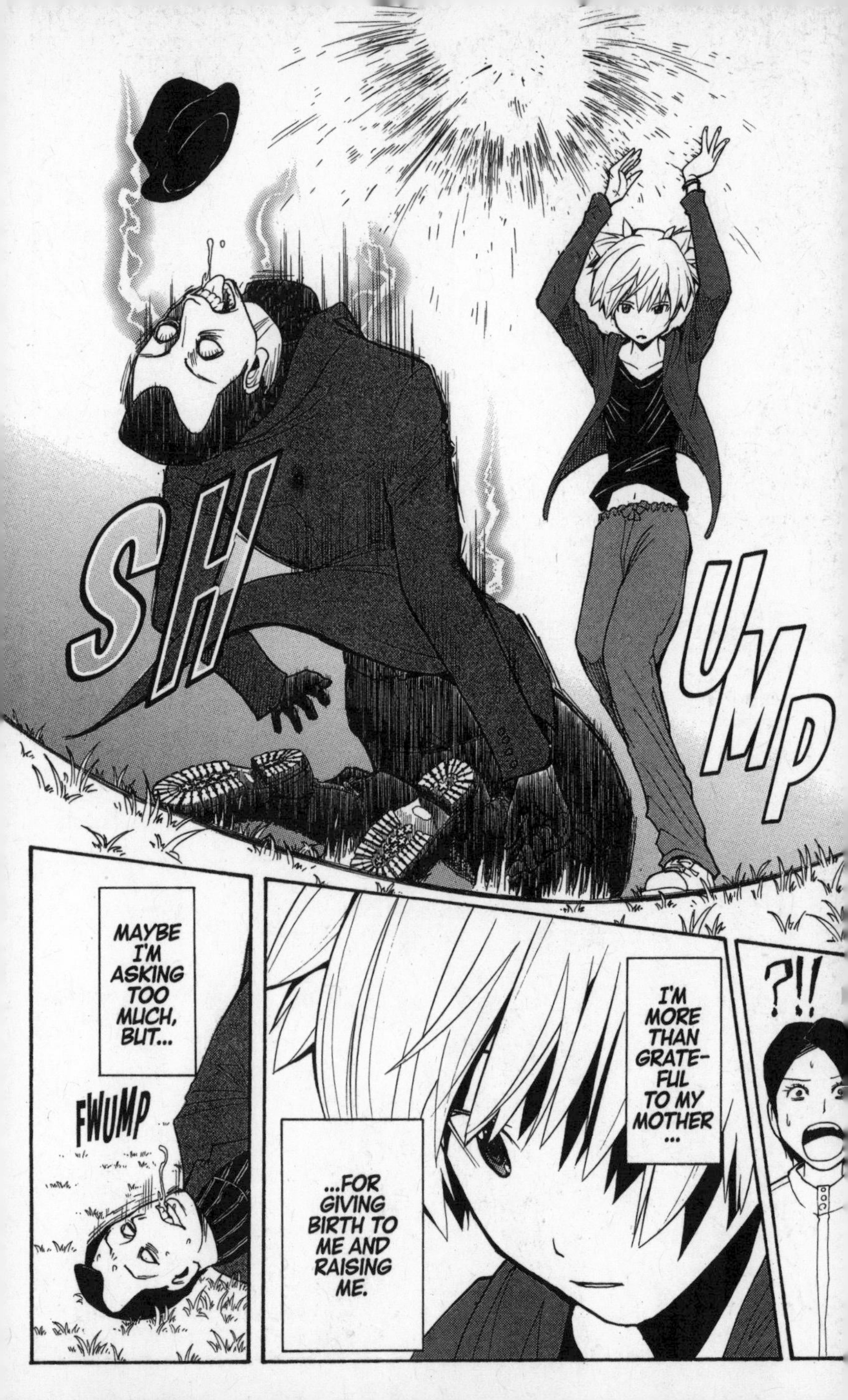
SHUMP
?!!
I'M MORE THAN GRATE-FUL TO MY MOTHER...
...FOR GIVING BIRTH TO ME AND RAISING ME.
MAYBE I'M ASKING TOO MUCH, BUT...
FWUMP

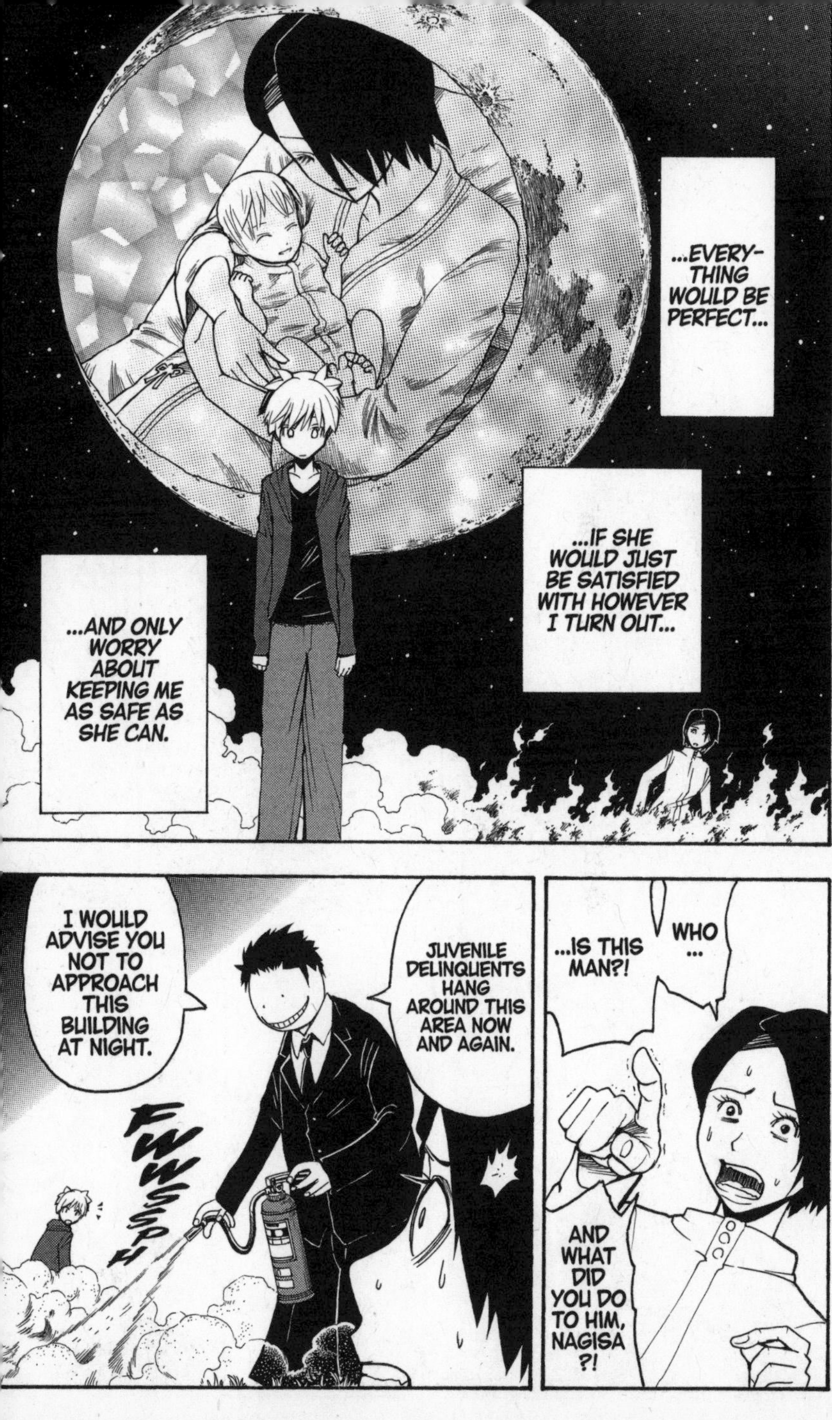
...EVERY-THING WOULD BE PERFECT...
...IF SHE WOULD JUST BE SATISFIED WITH HOWEVER I TURN OUT...
...AND ONLY WORRY ABOUT KEEPING ME AS SAFE AS SHE CAN.
WHO ...
...IS THIS MAN?!
AND WHAT DID YOU DO TO HIM, NAGISA ?!
JUVENILE DELINQUENTS HANG AROUND THIS AREA NOW AND AGAIN.
I WOULD ADVISE YOU NOT TO APPROACH THIS BUILDING AT NIGHT.
FWWSSPH

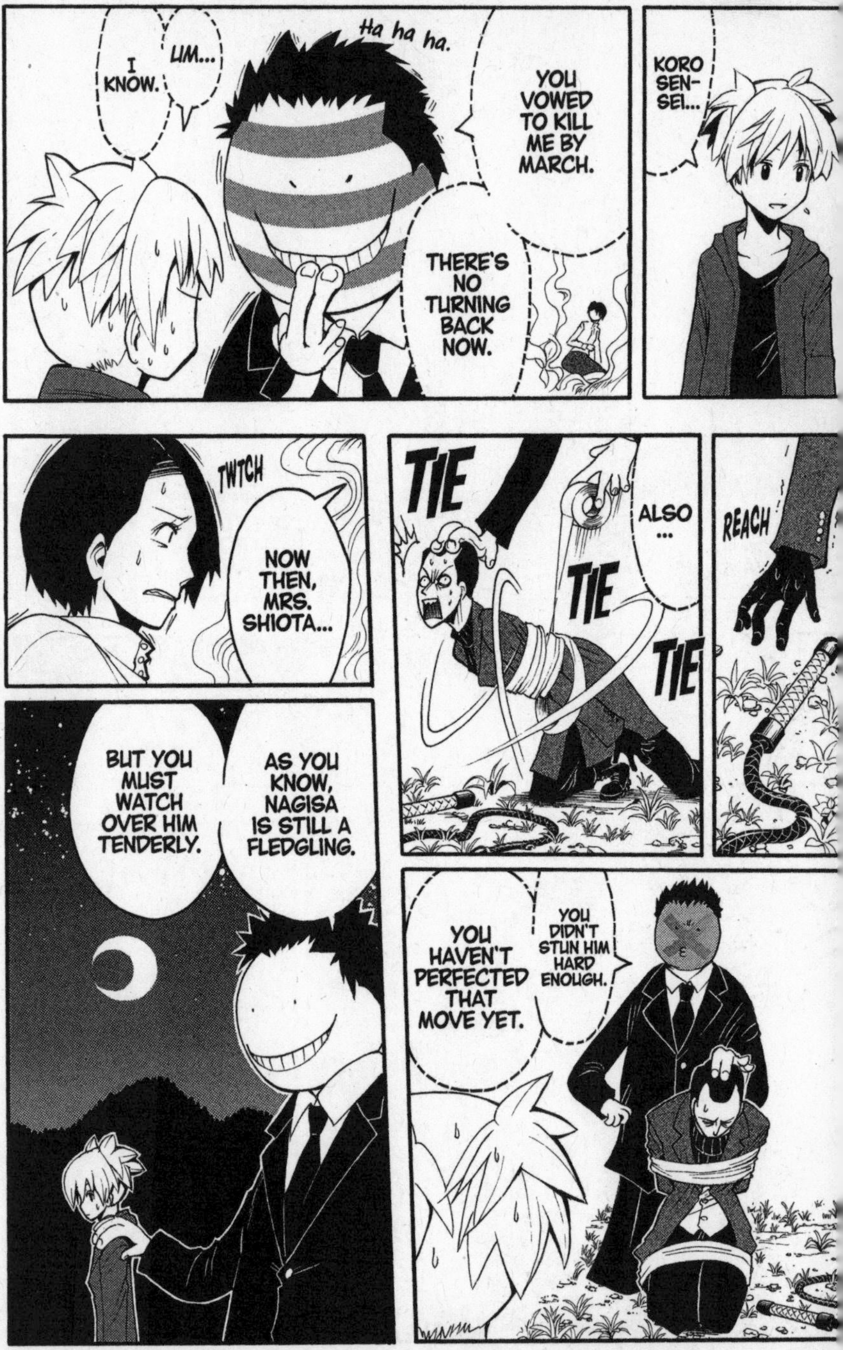
KORO SEN-SEI...
YOU VOWED TO KILL ME BY MARCH.
Ha ha ha.
THERE'S NO TURNING BACK NOW.
UM...
I KNOW.
REACH
ALSO ...
TIE
TIE
TIE
TWTCH
NOW THEN, MRS. SHIOTA...
YOU DIDN'T STUN HIM HARD ENOUGH.
YOU HAVEN'T PERFECTED THAT MOVE YET.
AS YOU KNOW, NAGISA IS STILL A FLEDGLING.
BUT YOU MUST WATCH OVER HIM TENDERLY.

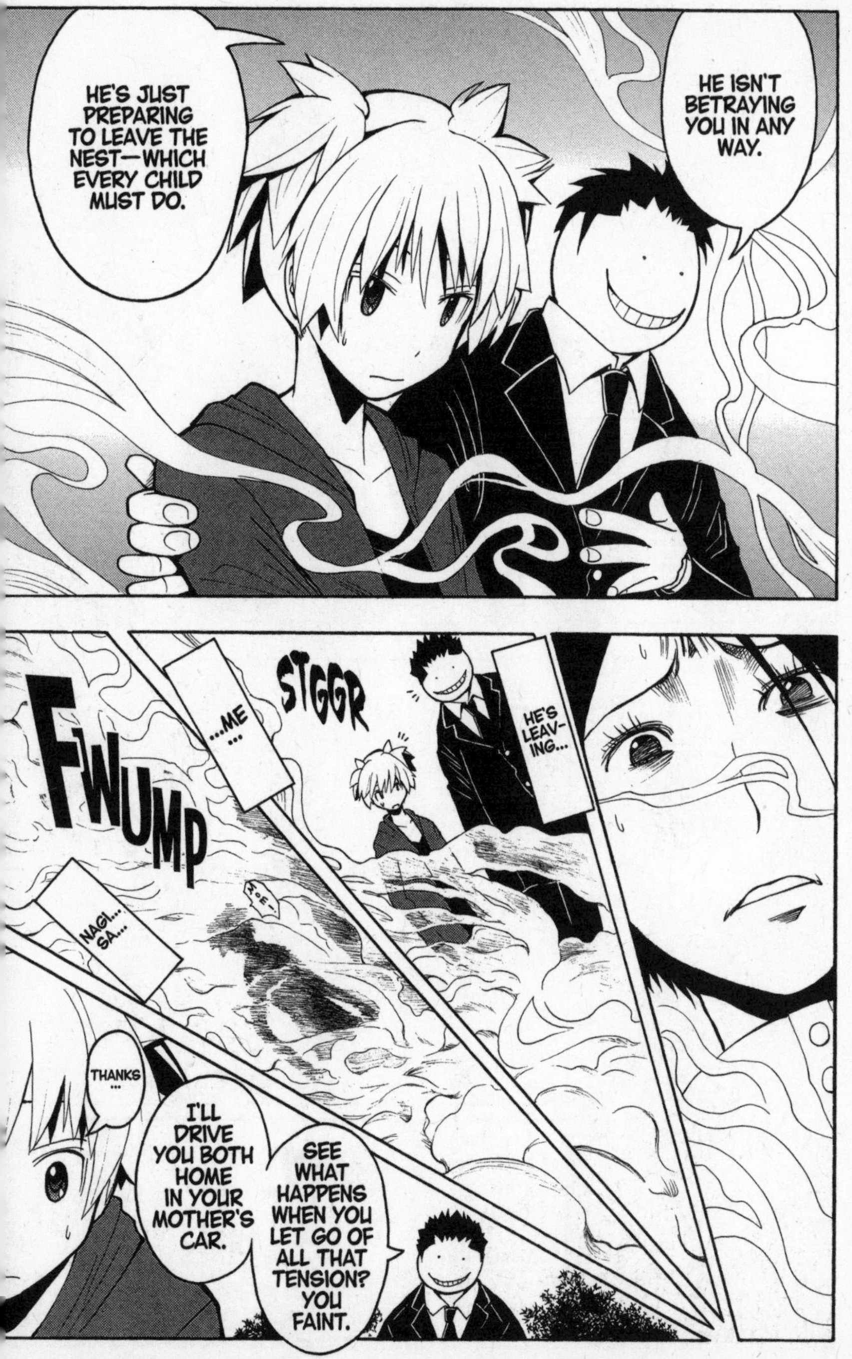
HE ISN'T BETRAYING YOU IN ANY WAY.
HE'S JUST PREPARING TO LEAVE THE NEST—WHICH EVERY CHILD MUST DO.
HE'S LEAVING...
STGGR
...ME ...
FWUMP
MOE-!
NAGI... SA...
SEE WHAT HAPPENS WHEN YOU LET GO OF ALL THAT TENSION? YOU FAINT.
I'LL DRIVE YOU BOTH HOME IN YOUR MOTHER'S CAR.
THANKS ...

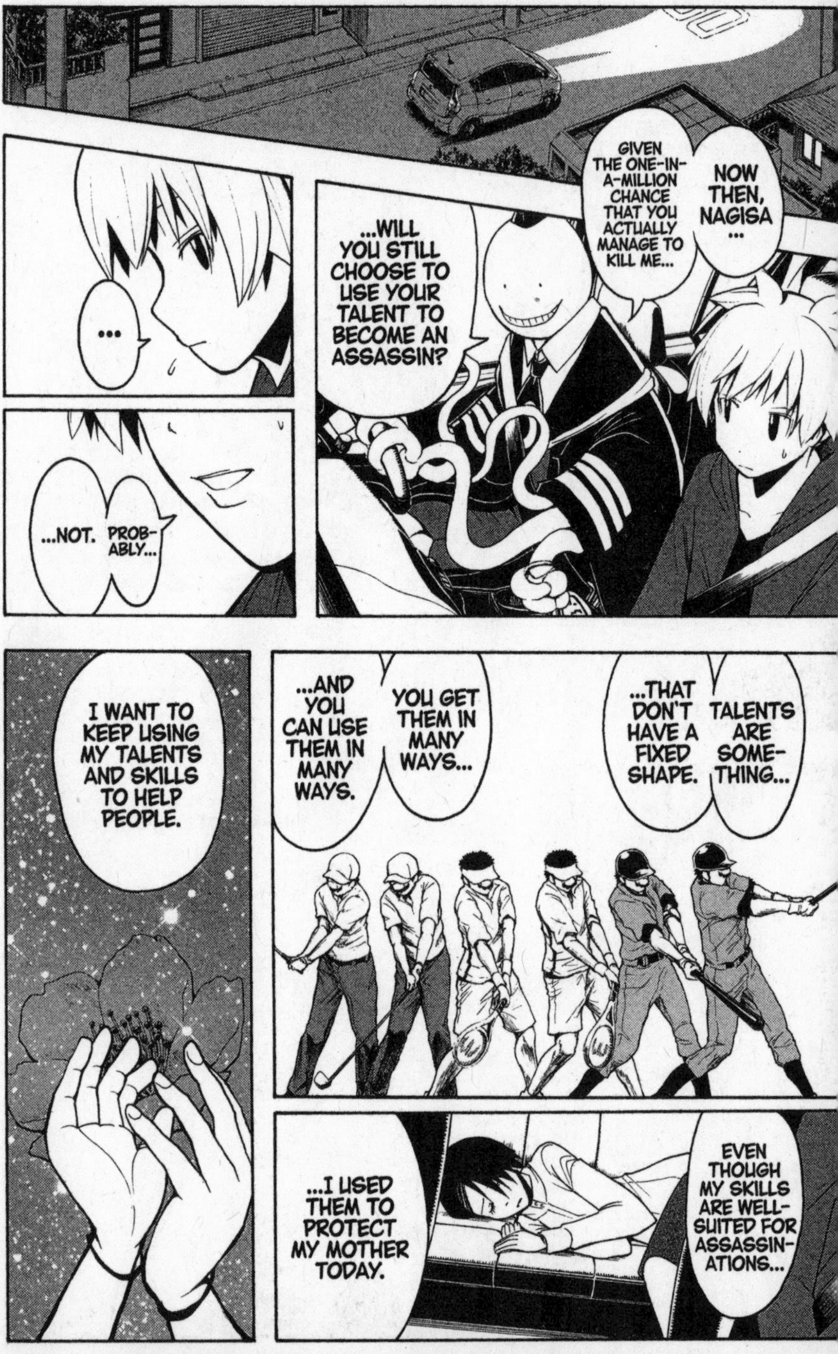
NOW THEN, NAGISA...
GIVEN THE ONE-IN-A-MILLION CHANCE THAT YOU ACTUALLY MANAGE TO KILL ME...
...WILL YOU STILL CHOOSE TO USE YOUR TALENT TO BECOME AN ASSASSIN?
...
PROBABLY...
...NOT.
TALENTS ARE SOMETHING...
...THAT DON'T HAVE A FIXED SHAPE.
YOU GET THEM IN MANY WAYS...
...AND YOU CAN USE THEM IN MANY WAYS.
EVEN THOUGH MY SKILLS ARE WELL-SUITED FOR ASSASSINATIONS...
...I USED THEM TO PROTECT MY MOTHER TODAY.
I WANT TO KEEP USING MY TALENTS AND SKILLS TO HELP PEOPLE.

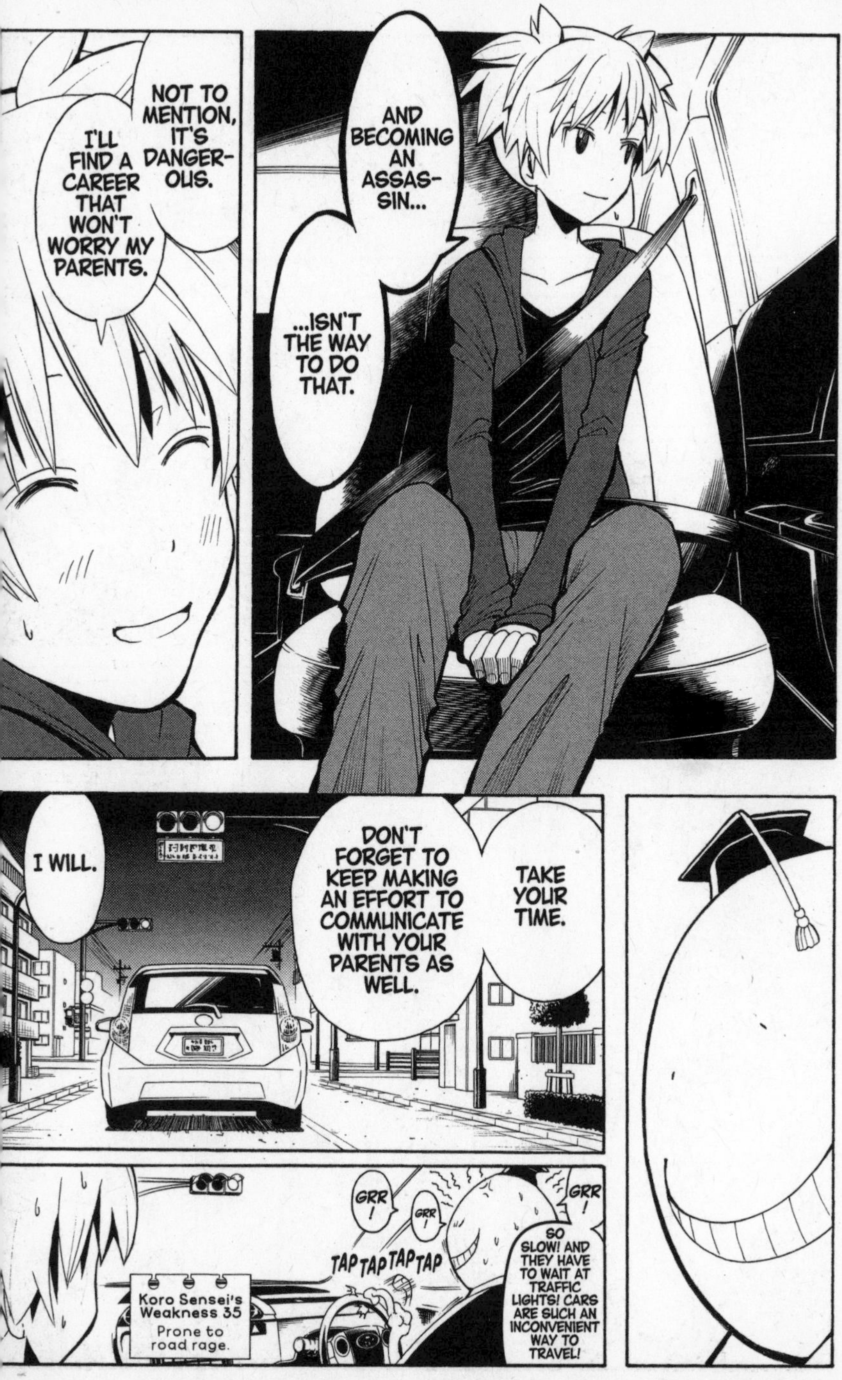
AND BECOMING AN ASSASSIN...
...ISN'T THE WAY TO DO THAT.
NOT TO MENTION, IT'S DANGEROUS.
I'LL FIND A CAREER THAT WON'T WORRY MY PARENTS.
TAKE YOUR TIME.
DON'T FORGET TO KEEP MAKING AN EFFORT TO COMMUNICATE WITH YOUR PARENTS AS WELL.
I WILL.
GRR!
SO SLOW! AND THEY HAVE TO WAIT AT TRAFFIC LIGHTS! CARS ARE SUCH AN INCONVENIENT WAY TO TRAVEL!
GRR!
GRR!
TAP TAP TAP TAP
Koro Sensei's Weakness 35
Prone to road rage.

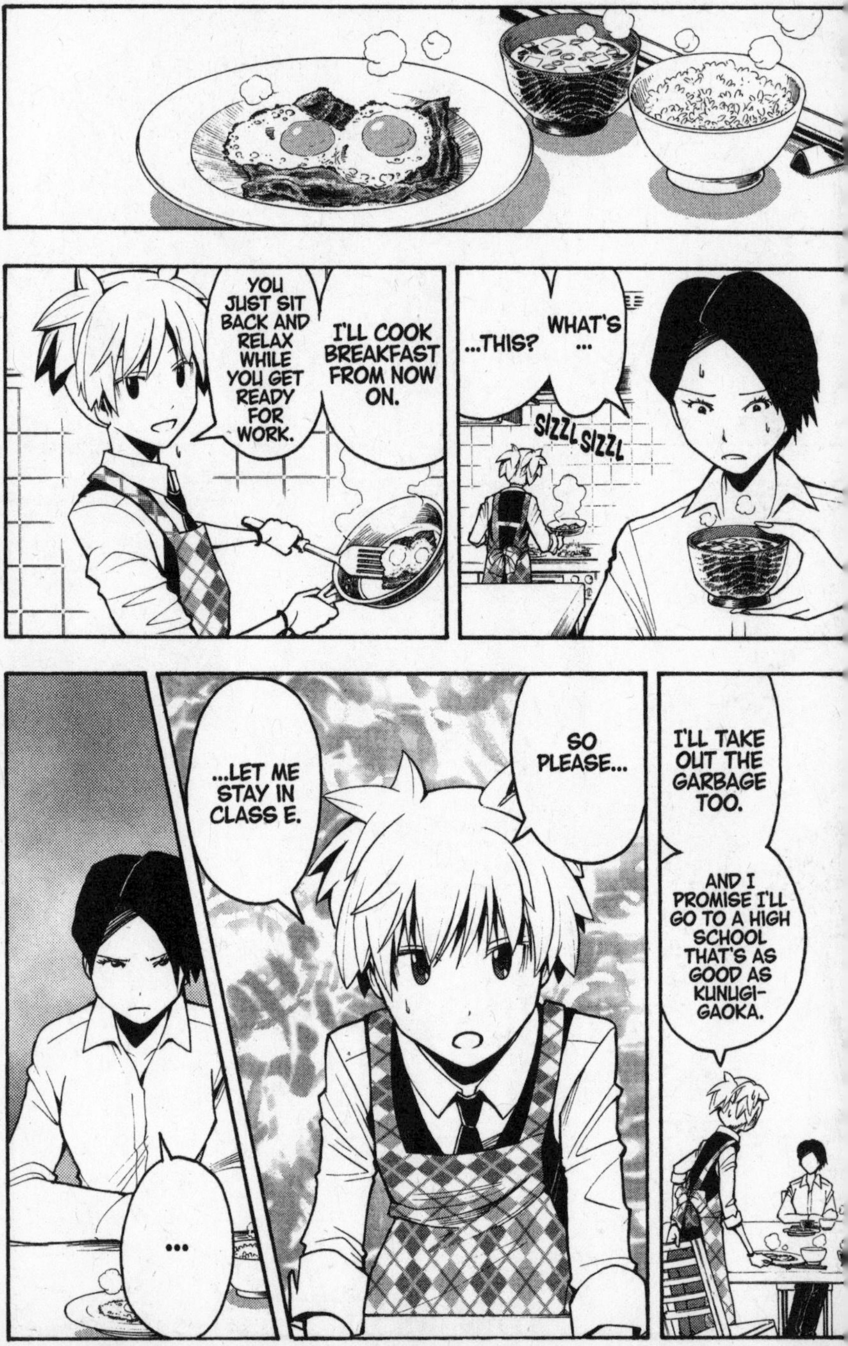
WHAT'S ...
...THIS?
SIZZL SIZZL
I'LL COOK BREAKFAST FROM NOW ON.
YOU JUST SIT BACK AND RELAX WHILE YOU GET READY FOR WORK.
I'LL TAKE OUT THE GARBAGE TOO.
AND I PROMISE I'LL GO TO A HIGH SCHOOL THAT'S AS GOOD AS KUNUGI-GAOKA.
SO PLEASE...
...LET ME STAY IN CLASS E.
...

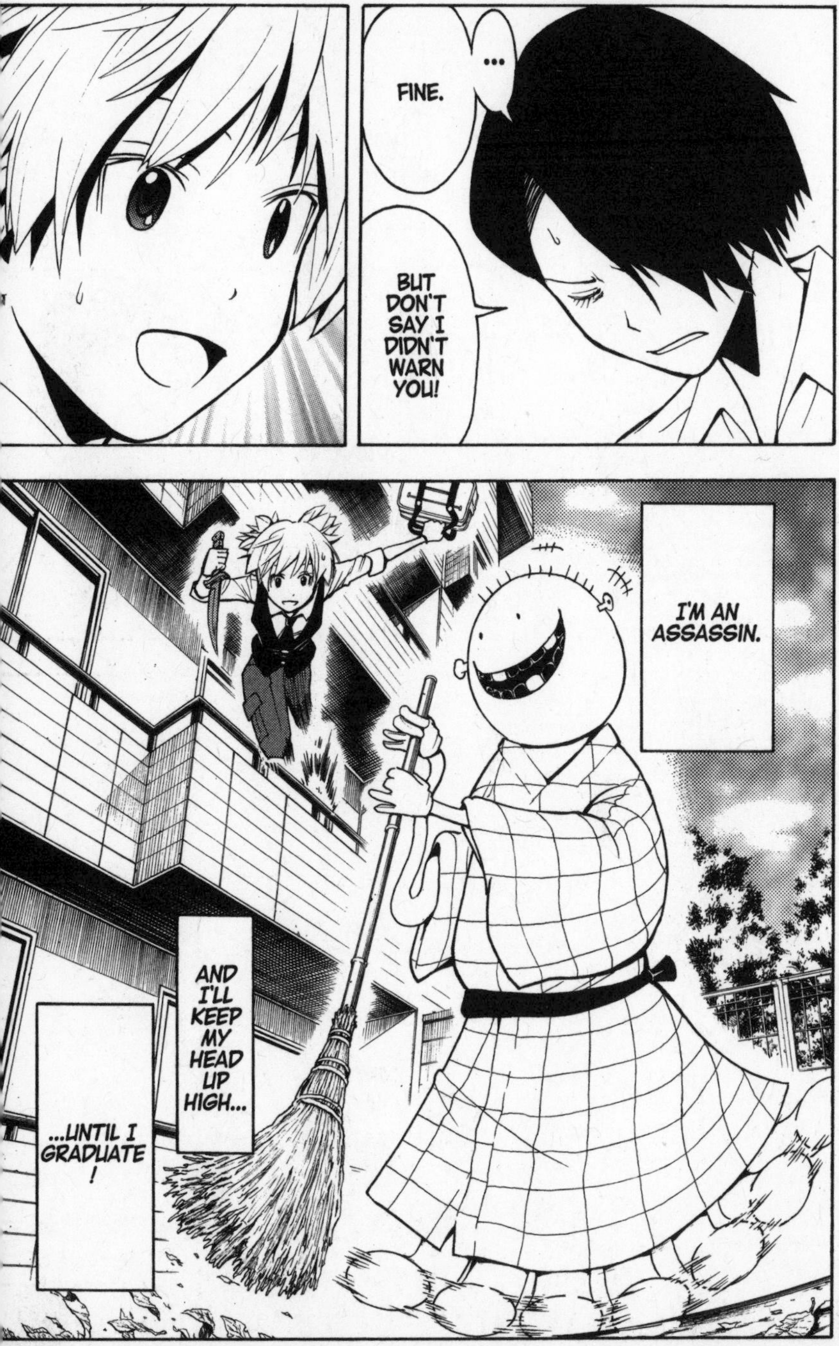
...
FINE.
BUT DON'T SAY I DIDN'T WARN YOU!
I'M AN ASSASSIN.
AND I'LL KEEP MY HEAD UP HIGH...
...UNTIL I GRADUATE!

Moving on!

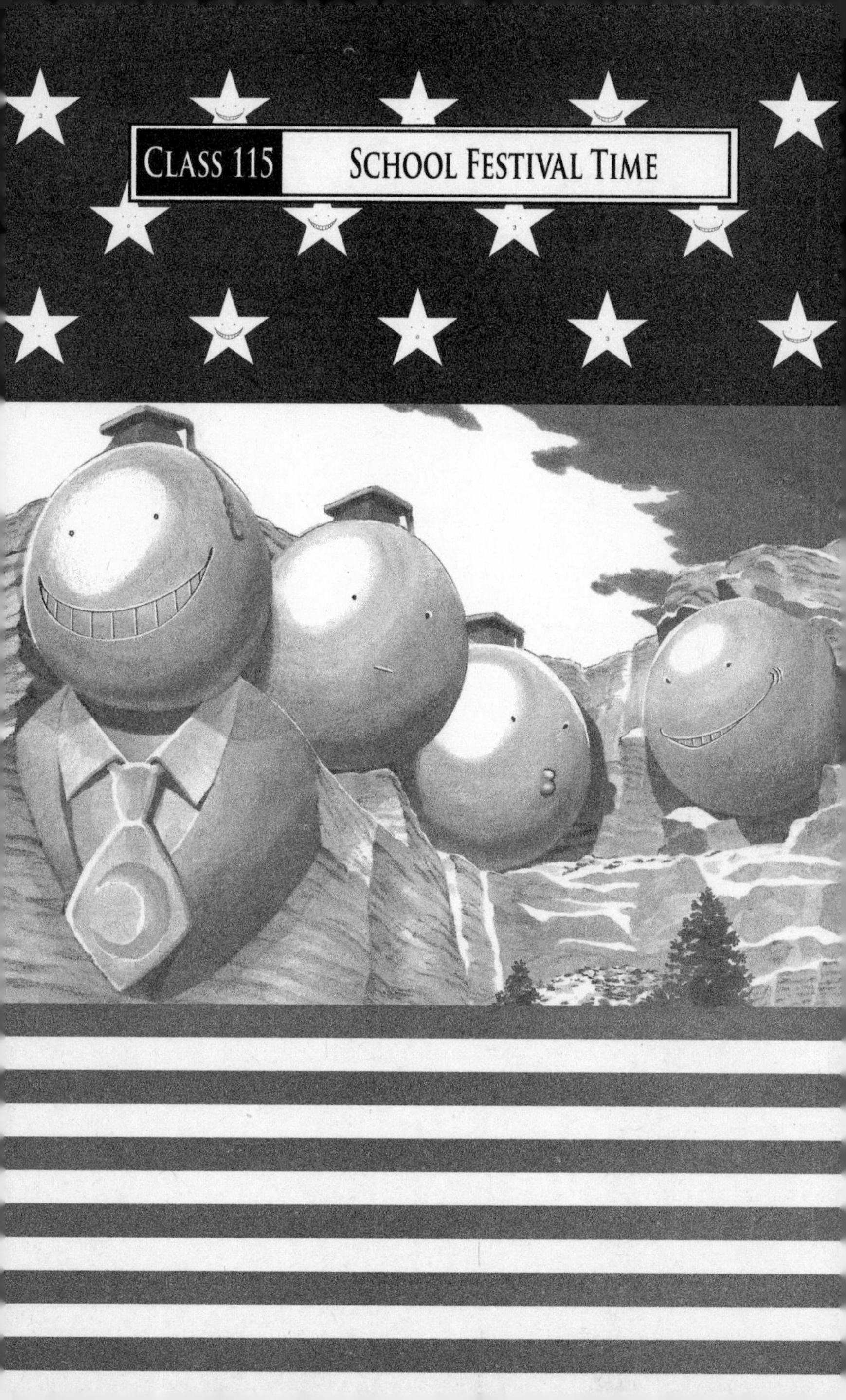
CLASS 115
SCHOOL FESTIVAL TIME

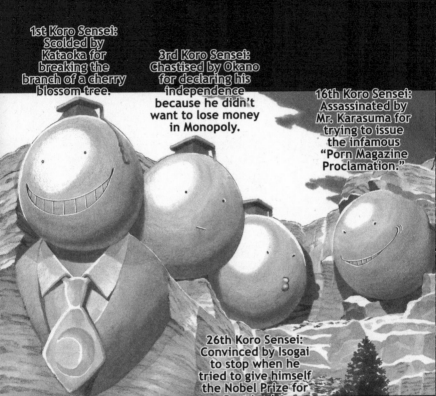

16th Koro Sensei: Assassinated by Mr. Karasuma for trying to issue the infamous "Porn Magazine Proclamation."
3rd Koro Sensei: Chastised by Okano for declaring his independence because he didn't want to lose money in Monopoly.
1st Koro Sensei: Scolded by Kataoka for breaking the branch of a cherry blossom tree.
26th Koro Sensei: Convinced by Isogai to stop when he tried to give himself the Nobel Prize for Best Looks.

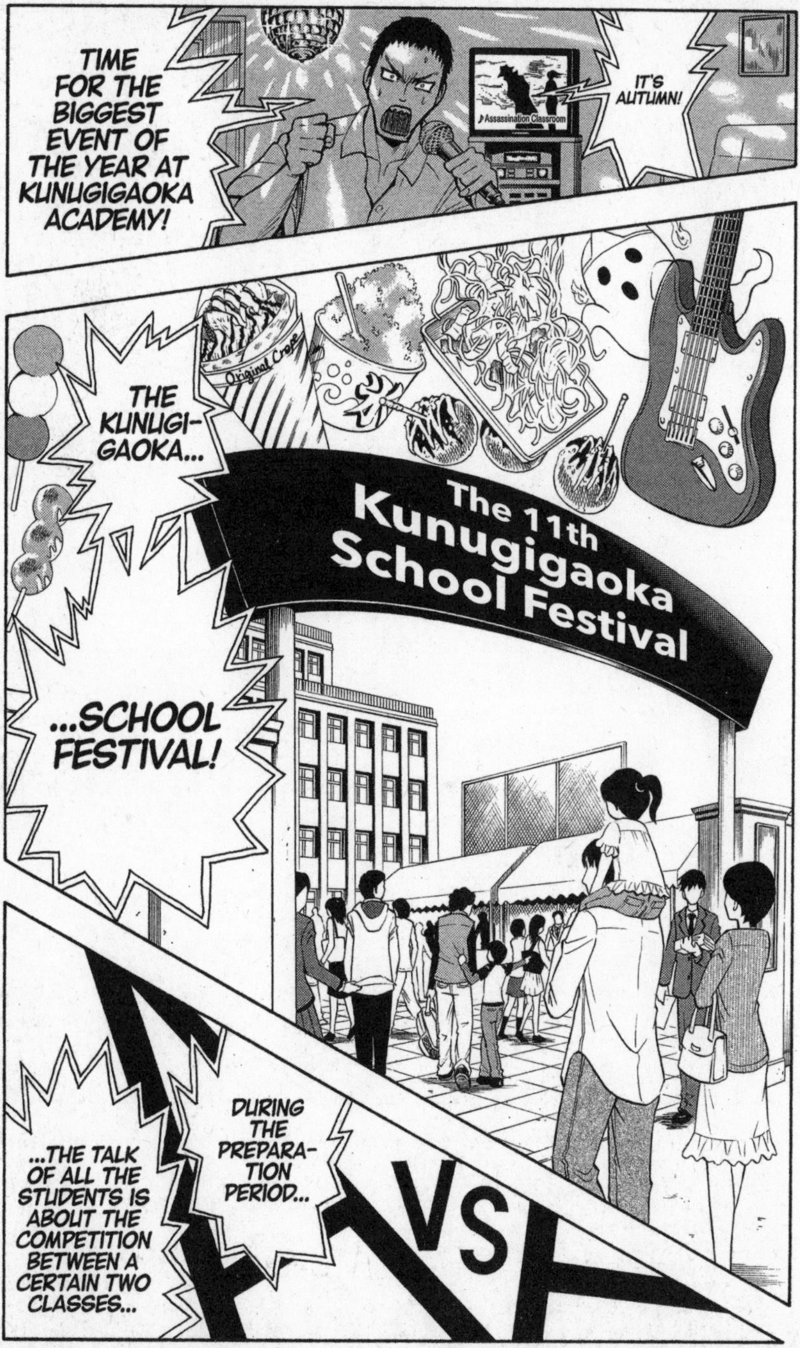
♪Assassination Classroom
IT'S AUTUMN!
TIME FOR THE BIGGEST EVENT OF THE YEAR AT KUNUGIGAOKA ACADEMY!
Original Crepe
The 11th Kunugigaoka School Festival
THE KUNUGI-GAOKA...
...SCHOOL FESTIVAL!
DURING THE PREPARA-TION PERIOD...
...THE TALK OF ALL THE STUDENTS IS ABOUT THE COMPETITION BETWEEN A CERTAIN TWO CLASSES...
VS

EVERYONE IN THE MAIN SCHOOL BUILDING LOOKS SO SERIOUS...

I HAD NO IDEA THE SCHOOL FESTIVAL WAS SUCH A BIG DEAL!

RKKKT

TNK TNK

Thanks. I'll get it.

TNK TNK

OUR SCHOOL FESTIVAL IS FAMOUS AS A REAL BUSINESS COMPETITION.

1	HS 3-A	Samurai House of Terror
2	HS 3-C	Natural Shaved Ice
3	HS 2-A	Domestic Berkshire Pork Pot Dumplings
4		herry Crepes
		tal Costumes oto Session
		ool Festival
		cots vs. Kunudon

WE DONATE ALL THE MONEY WE MAKE, BUT...

...THE AMOUNT EACH CLASS EARNS WILL BE POSTED FOR EVERYONE TO SEE.

...CAN PUT IT ON THEIR RESUMES AS A BUSINESS ACHIEVEMENT.

THE CLASS THAT WINS FIRST PLACE...

THERE WILL BE A LOT OF STANDS THAT LOOK ALMOST PROFESSIONAL.

THAT'S WHY EVERYONE PUTS SO MUCH EFFORT INTO THIS PROJECT.

menu
Meat Sauce
Carbonara
Pescatore
Bolognaise
Spicy and Spicy Cod Roe

PASTA

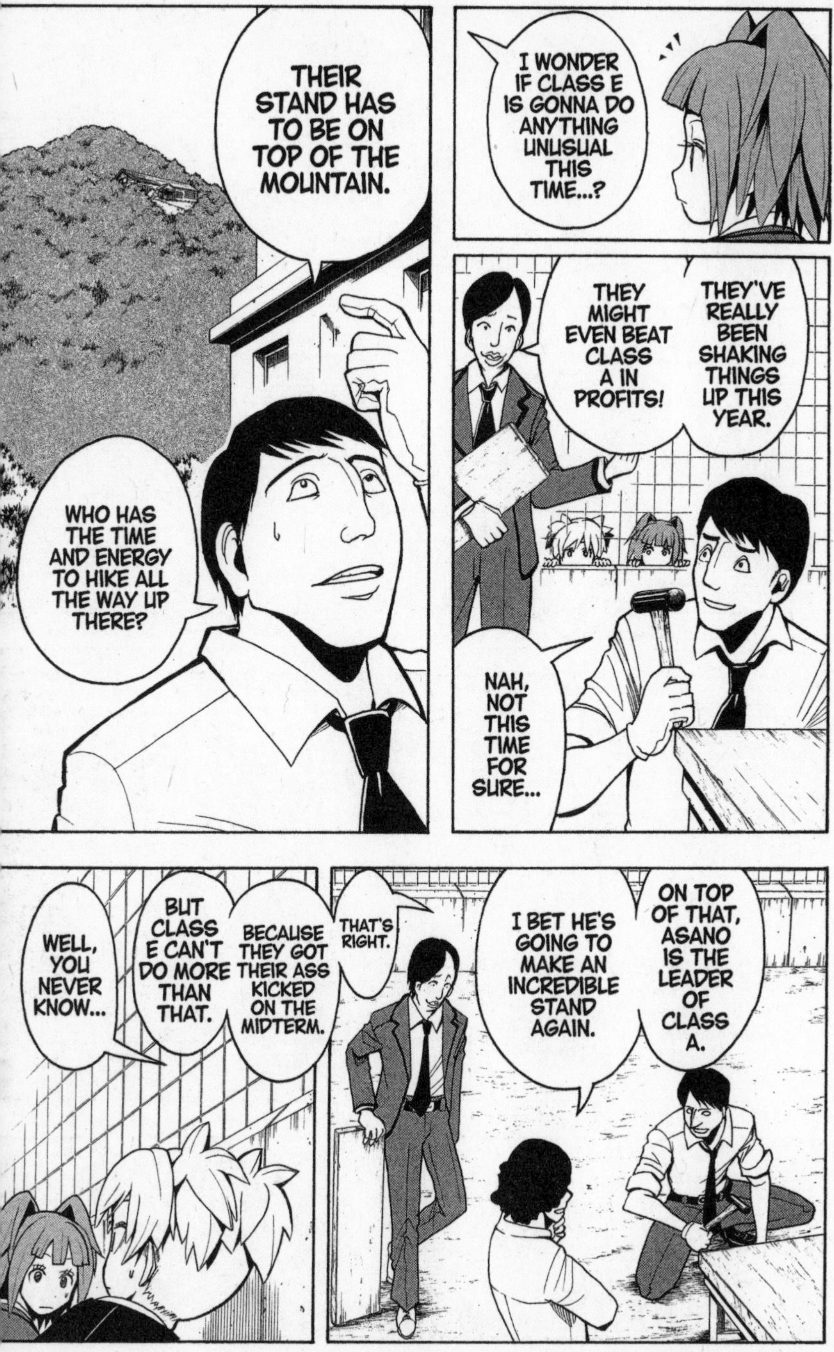
I WONDER IF CLASS E IS GONNA DO ANYTHING UNUSUAL THIS TIME...?
THEY'VE REALLY BEEN SHAKING THINGS UP THIS YEAR.
THEY MIGHT EVEN BEAT CLASS A IN PROFITS!
NAH, NOT THIS TIME FOR SURE...
THEIR STAND HAS TO BE ON TOP OF THE MOUNTAIN.
WHO HAS THE TIME AND ENERGY TO HIKE ALL THE WAY UP THERE?
ON TOP OF THAT, ASANO IS THE LEADER OF CLASS A.
I BET HE'S GOING TO MAKE AN INCREDIBLE STAND AGAIN.
THAT'S RIGHT.
BECAUSE THEY GOT THEIR ASS KICKED ON THE MIDTERM.
BUT CLASS E CAN'T DO MORE THAN THAT.
WELL, YOU NEVER KNOW...

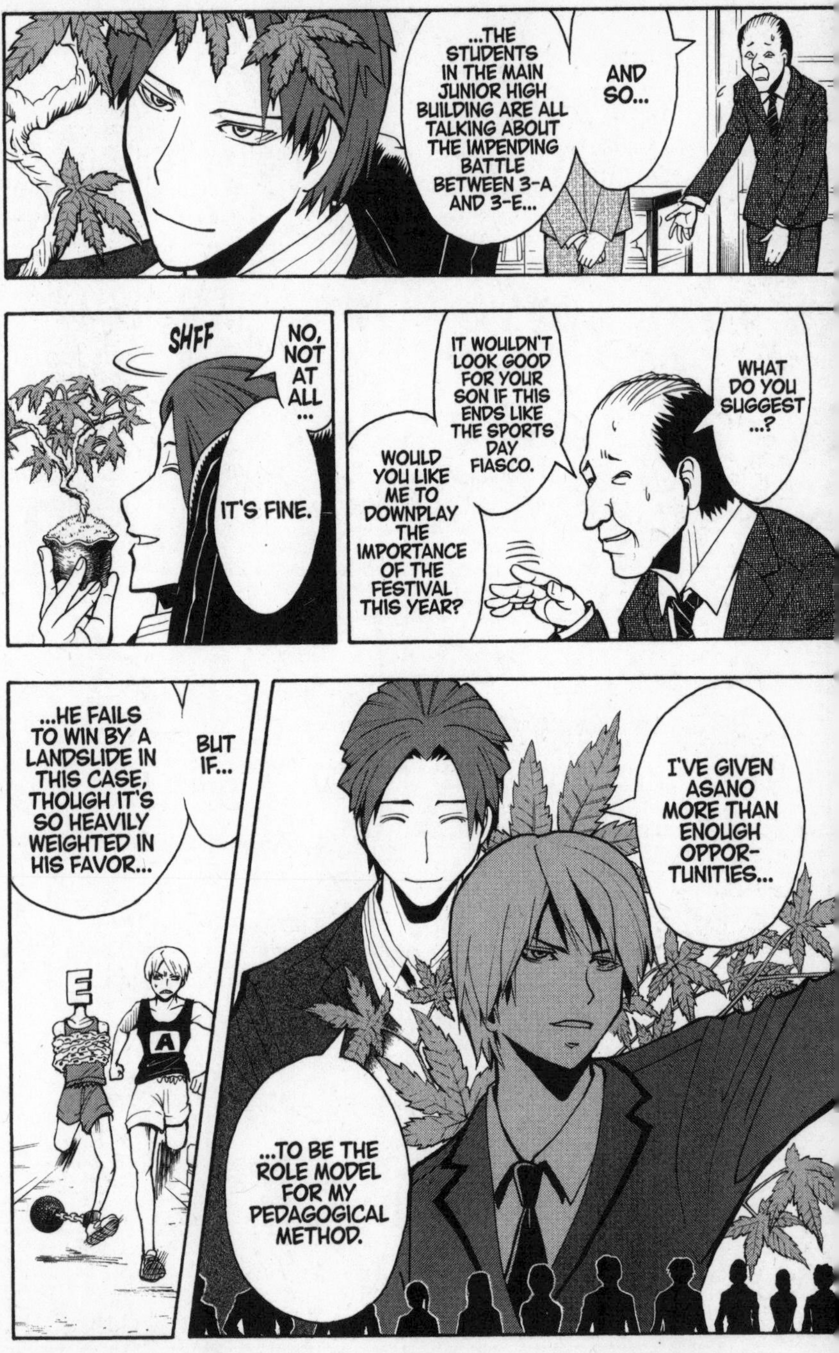
AND SO...
...THE STUDENTS IN THE MAIN JUNIOR HIGH BUILDING ARE ALL TALKING ABOUT THE IMPENDING BATTLE BETWEEN 3-A AND 3-E...
WHAT DO YOU SUGGEST ...?
IT WOULDN'T LOOK GOOD FOR YOUR SON IF THIS ENDS LIKE THE SPORTS DAY FIASCO.
WOULD YOU LIKE ME TO DOWNPLAY THE IMPORTANCE OF THE FESTIVAL THIS YEAR?
SHFF
NO, NOT AT ALL ...
IT'S FINE.
I'VE GIVEN ASANO MORE THAN ENOUGH OPPOR-TUNITIES...
...TO BE THE ROLE MODEL FOR MY PEDAGOGICAL METHOD.
BUT IF...
...HE FAILS TO WIN BY A LANDSLIDE IN THIS CASE, THOUGH IT'S SO HEAVILY WEIGHTED IN HIS FAVOR...
E
A

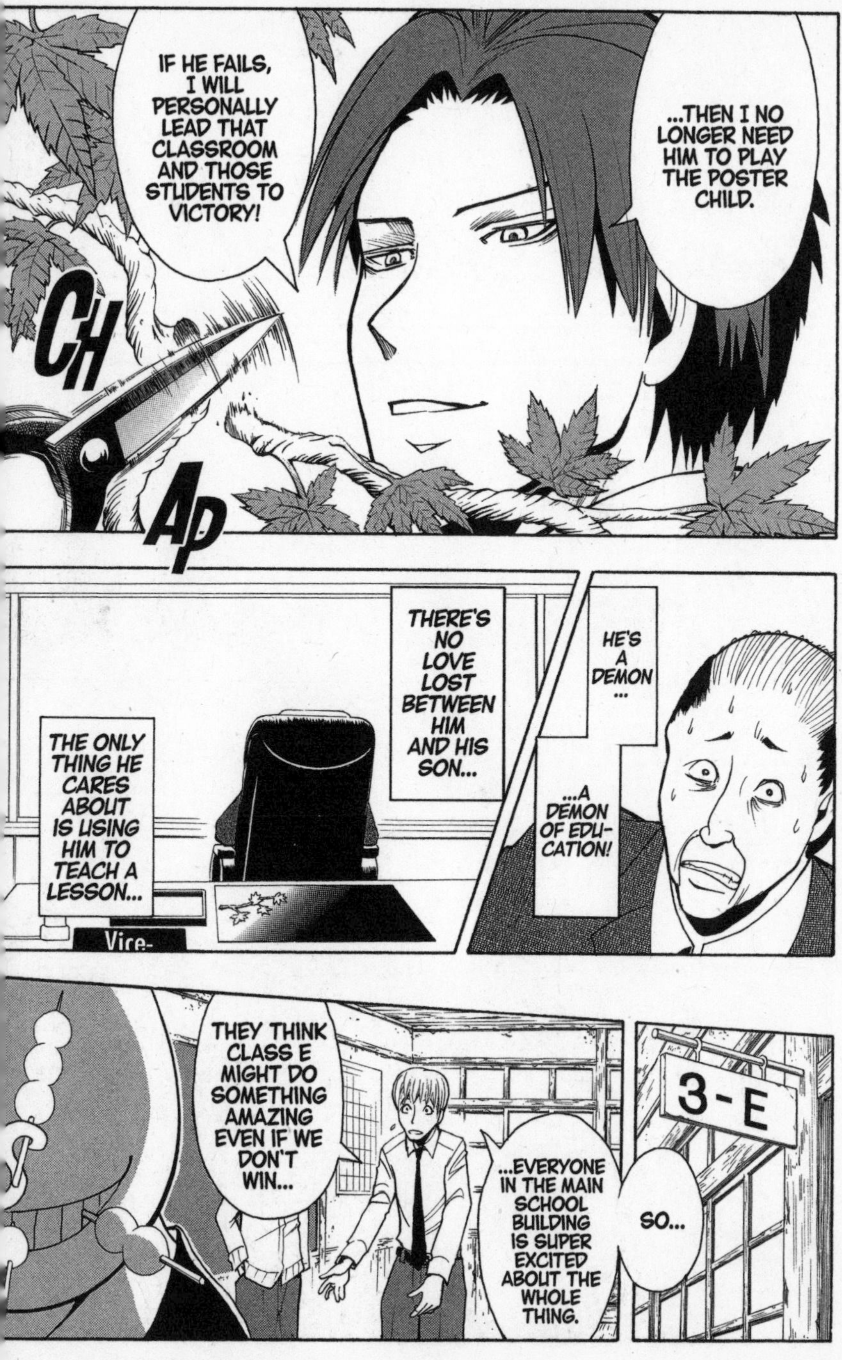
...THEN I NO LONGER NEED HIM TO PLAY THE POSTER CHILD.
IF HE FAILS, I WILL PERSONALLY LEAD THAT CLASSROOM AND THOSE STUDENTS TO VICTORY!
CHAP
HE'S A DEMON...
...A DEMON OF EDUCATION!
THERE'S NO LOVE LOST BETWEEN HIM AND HIS SON...
THE ONLY THING HE CARES ABOUT IS USING HIM TO TEACH A LESSON...
Vice-
3-E
SO...
...EVERYONE IN THE MAIN SCHOOL BUILDING IS SUPER EXCITED ABOUT THE WHOLE THING.
THEY THINK CLASS E MIGHT DO SOMETHING AMAZING EVEN IF WE DON'T WIN...

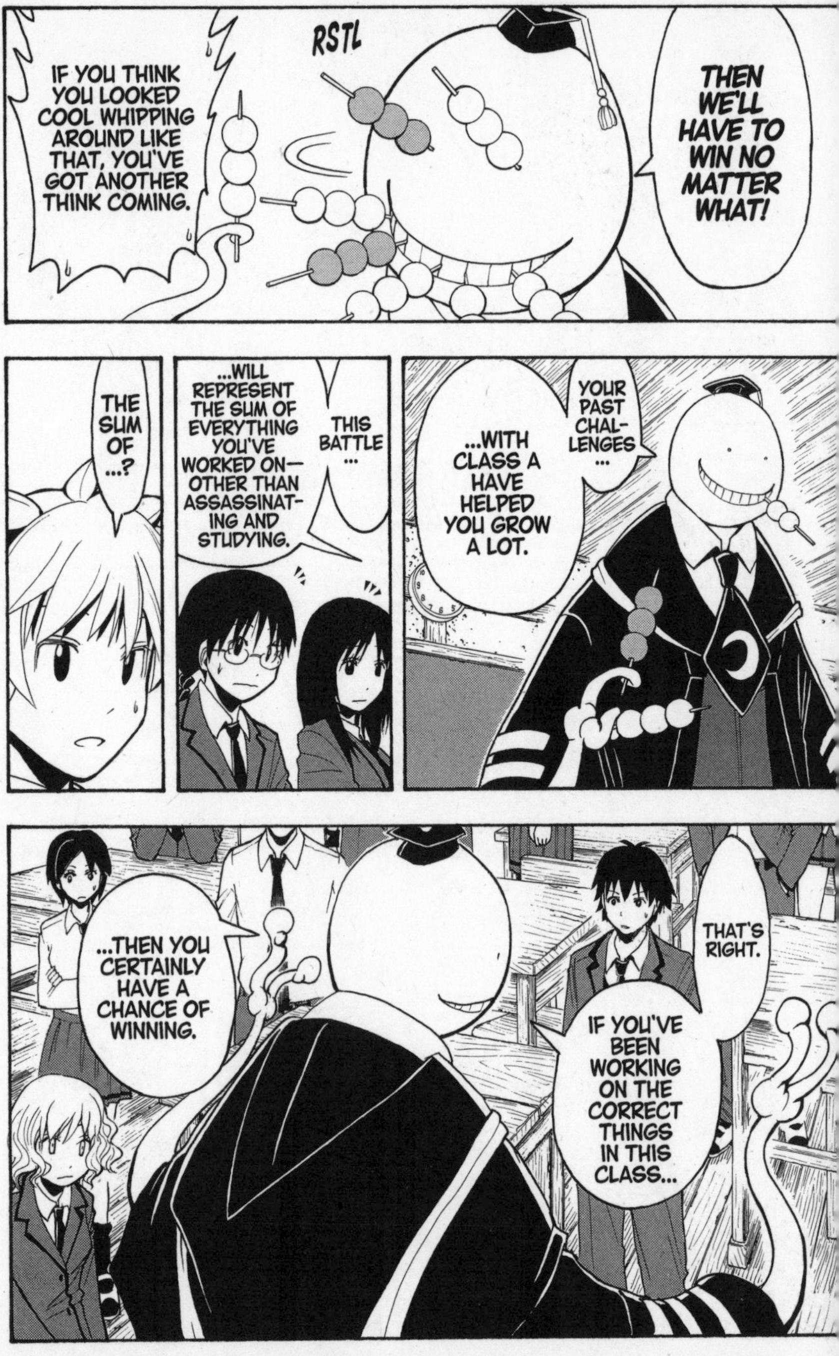
THEN WE'LL HAVE TO WIN NO MATTER WHAT!
RSTL
IF YOU THINK YOU LOOKED COOL WHIPPING AROUND LIKE THAT, YOU'VE GOT ANOTHER THINK COMING.
YOUR PAST CHAL-LENGES...
...WITH CLASS A HAVE HELPED YOU GROW A LOT.
THIS BATTLE...
...WILL REPRESENT THE SUM OF EVERYTHING YOU'VE WORKED ON—OTHER THAN ASSASSINAT-ING AND STUDYING.
THE SUM OF...?
THAT'S RIGHT.
IF YOU'VE BEEN WORKING ON THE CORRECT THINGS IN THIS CLASS...
...THEN YOU CERTAINLY HAVE A CHANCE OF WINNING.

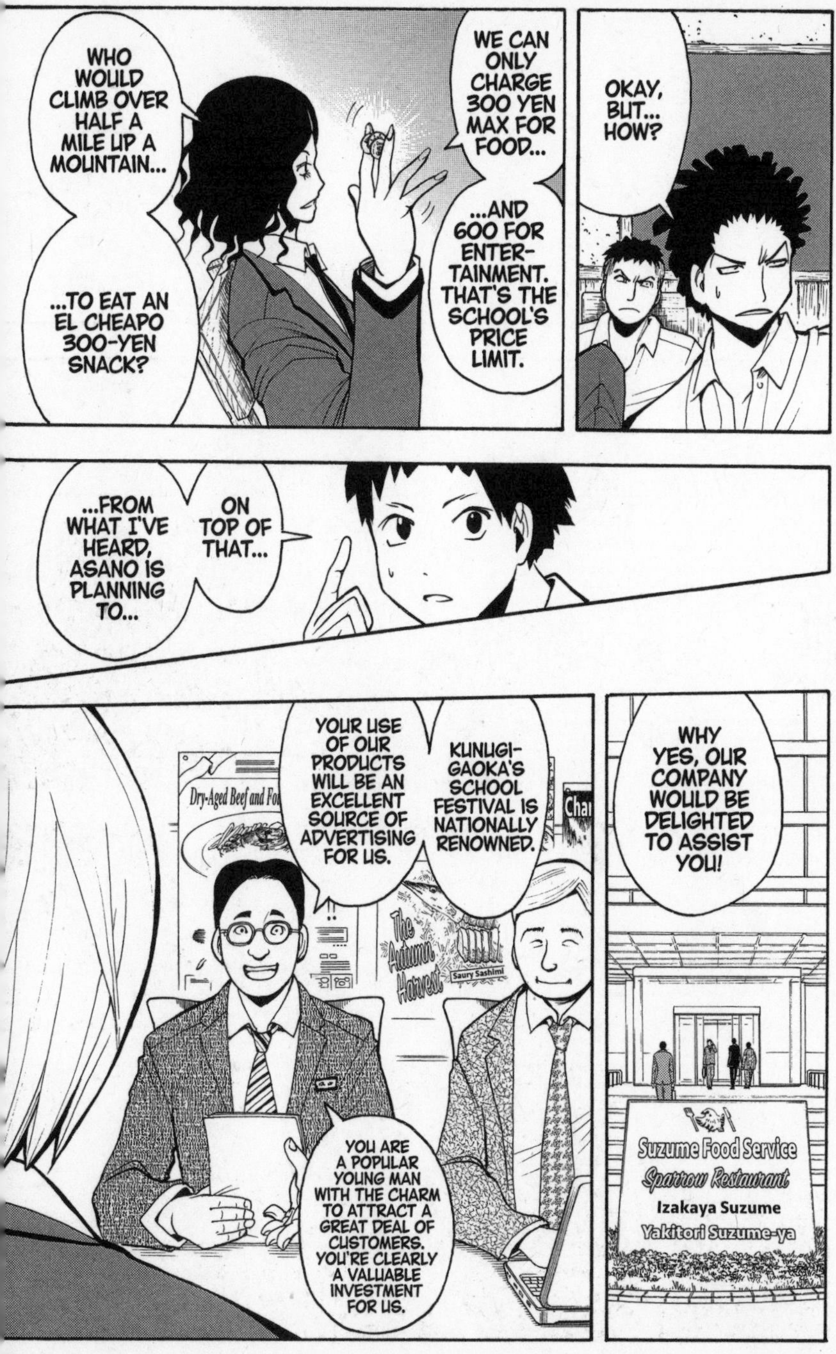
OKAY, BUT... HOW?
WE CAN ONLY CHARGE 300 YEN MAX FOR FOOD...
...AND 600 FOR ENTERTAINMENT. THAT'S THE SCHOOL'S PRICE LIMIT.
WHO WOULD CLIMB OVER HALF A MILE UP A MOUNTAIN...
...TO EAT AN EL CHEAPO 300-YEN SNACK?
ON TOP OF THAT...
...FROM WHAT I'VE HEARD, ASANO IS PLANNING TO...
WHY YES, OUR COMPANY WOULD BE DELIGHTED TO ASSIST YOU!
Suzume Food Service
Sparrow Restaurant
Izakaya Suzume
Yakitori Suzume-ya
KUNUGIGAOKA'S SCHOOL FESTIVAL IS NATIONALLY RENOWNED.
YOUR USE OF OUR PRODUCTS WILL BE AN EXCELLENT SOURCE OF ADVERTISING FOR US.
Dry-Aged Beef and Fo
The Autumn Harvest
Saury Sashimi
YOU ARE A POPULAR YOUNG MAN WITH THE CHARM TO ATTRACT A GREAT DEAL OF CUSTOMERS. YOU'RE CLEARLY A VALUABLE INVESTMENT FOR US.

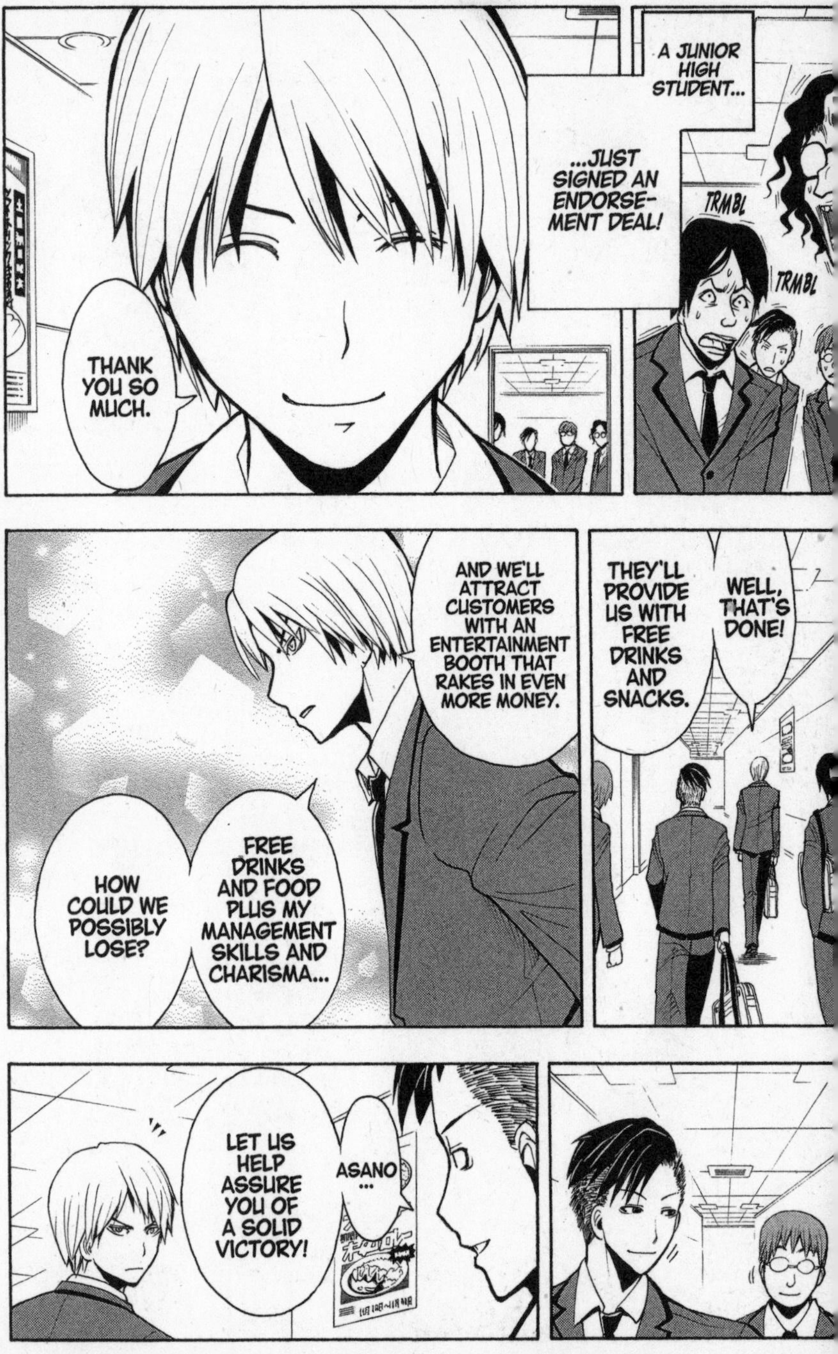
A JUNIOR HIGH STUDENT...
...JUST SIGNED AN ENDORSEMENT DEAL!
TRMBL
TRMBL
THANK YOU SO MUCH.
WELL, THAT'S DONE!
THEY'LL PROVIDE US WITH FREE DRINKS AND SNACKS.
AND WE'LL ATTRACT CUSTOMERS WITH AN ENTERTAINMENT BOOTH THAT RAKES IN EVEN MORE MONEY.
FREE DRINKS AND FOOD PLUS MY MANAGEMENT SKILLS AND CHARISMA...
HOW COULD WE POSSIBLY LOSE?
ASANO...
LET US HELP ASSURE YOU OF A SOLID VICTORY!

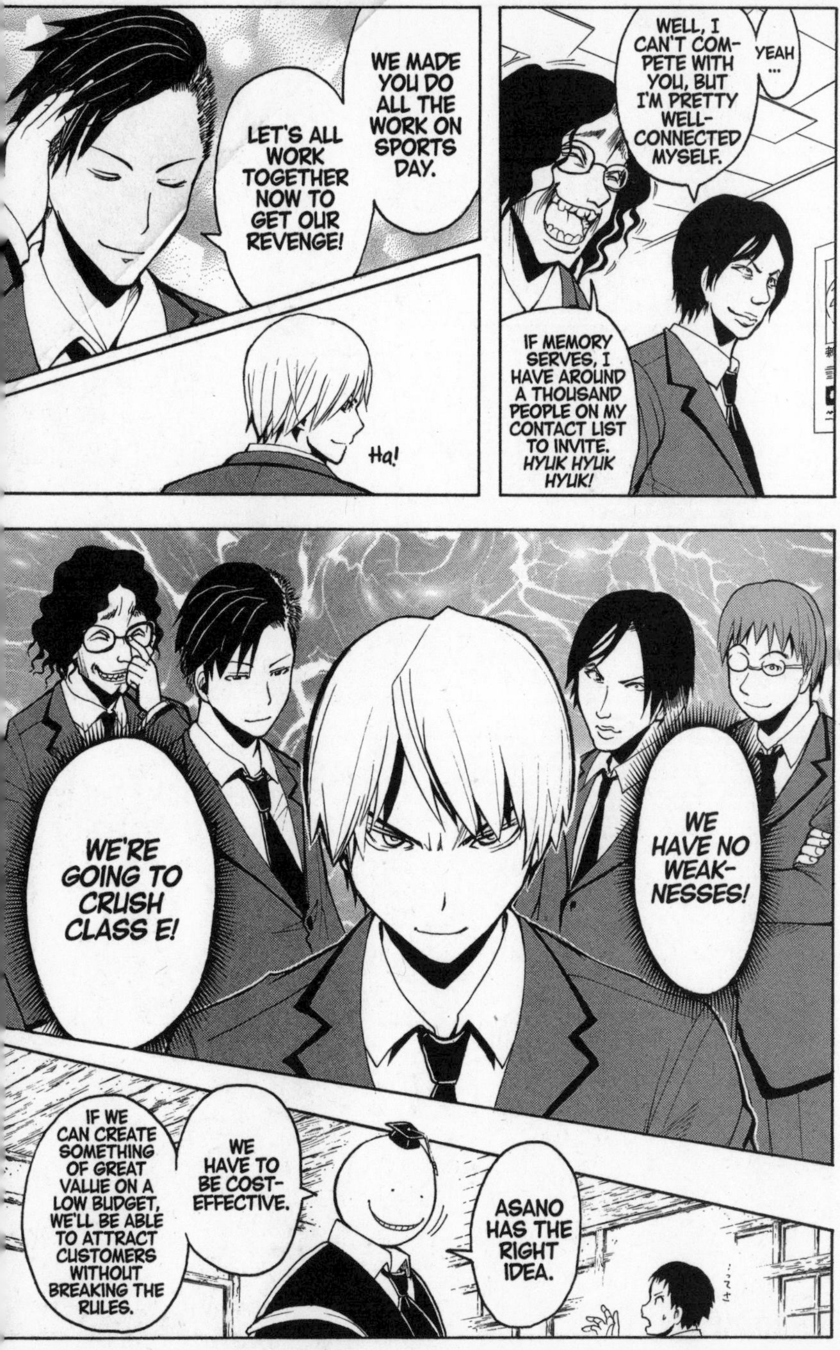
YEAH ...
WELL, I CAN'T COMPETE WITH YOU, BUT I'M PRETTY WELL-CONNECTED MYSELF.
IF MEMORY SERVES, I HAVE AROUND A THOUSAND PEOPLE ON MY CONTACT LIST TO INVITE. HYUK HYUK HYUK!
WE MADE YOU DO ALL THE WORK ON SPORTS DAY.
LET'S ALL WORK TOGETHER NOW TO GET OUR REVENGE!
Ha!
WE HAVE NO WEAKNESSES!
WE'RE GOING TO CRUSH CLASS E!
ASANO HAS THE RIGHT IDEA.
WE HAVE TO BE COST-EFFECTIVE.
IF WE CAN CREATE SOMETHING OF GREAT VALUE ON A LOW BUDGET, WE'LL BE ABLE TO ATTRACT CUSTOMERS WITHOUT BREAKING THE RULES.

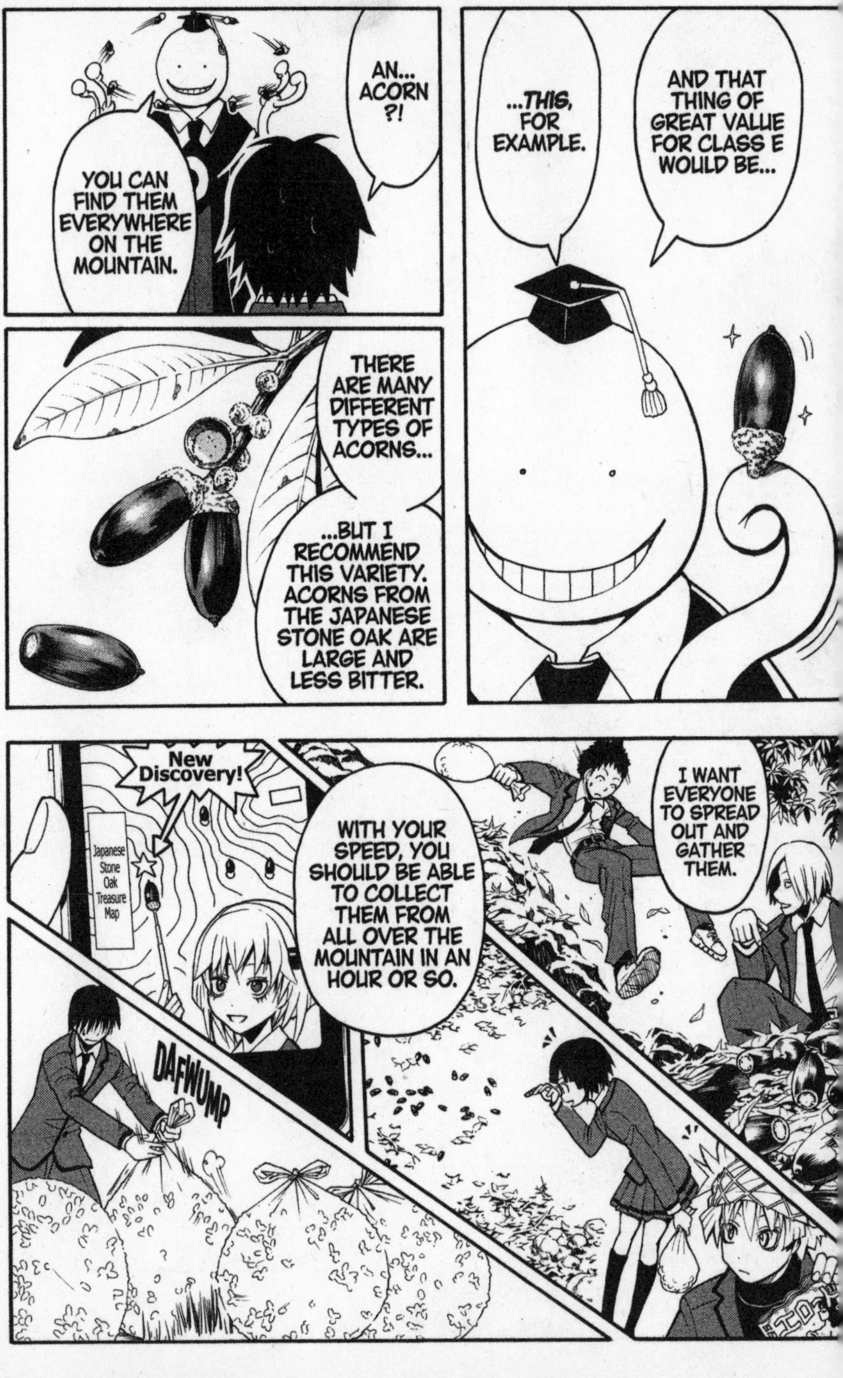
AND THAT THING OF GREAT VALUE FOR CLASS E WOULD BE...
...THIS, FOR EXAMPLE.
AN... ACORN ?!
YOU CAN FIND THEM EVERYWHERE ON THE MOUNTAIN.
THERE ARE MANY DIFFERENT TYPES OF ACORNS...
...BUT I RECOMMEND THIS VARIETY. ACORNS FROM THE JAPANESE STONE OAK ARE LARGE AND LESS BITTER.
I WANT EVERYONE TO SPREAD OUT AND GATHER THEM.
WITH YOUR SPEED, YOU SHOULD BE ABLE TO COLLECT THEM FROM ALL OVER THE MOUNTAIN IN AN HOUR OR SO.
New Discovery!
Japanese Stone Oak Treasure Map
DAFWUMP

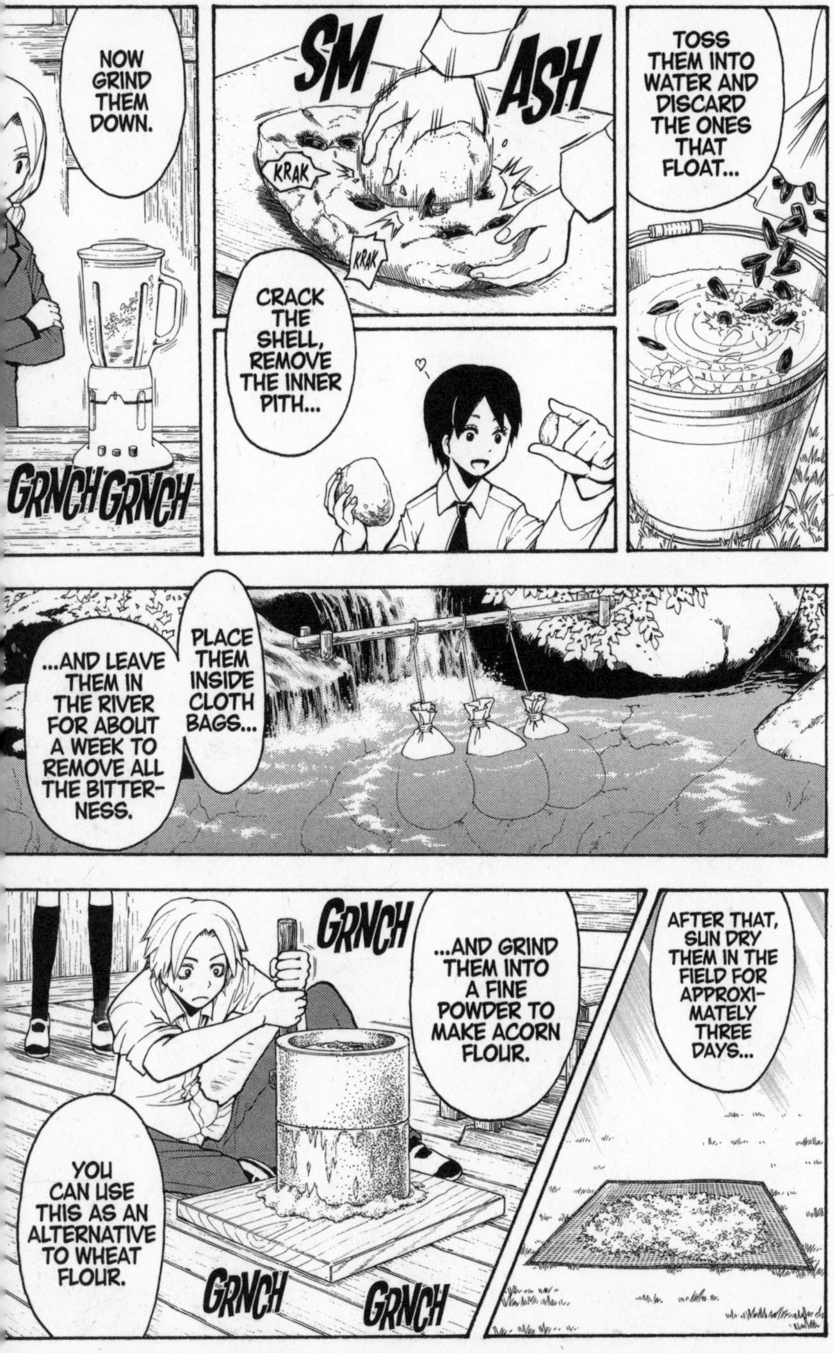
TOSS THEM INTO WATER AND DISCARD THE ONES THAT FLOAT...
SM ASH
KRAK
KRAK
CRACK THE SHELL, REMOVE THE INNER PITH...
NOW GRIND THEM DOWN.
GRNCH GRNCH
PLACE THEM INSIDE CLOTH BAGS...
...AND LEAVE THEM IN THE RIVER FOR ABOUT A WEEK TO REMOVE ALL THE BITTER-NESS.
AFTER THAT, SUN DRY THEM IN THE FIELD FOR APPROXI-MATELY THREE DAYS...
GRNCH
...AND GRIND THEM INTO A FINE POWDER TO MAKE ACORN FLOUR.
YOU CAN USE THIS AS AN ALTERNATIVE TO WHEAT FLOUR.
GRNCH
GRNCH

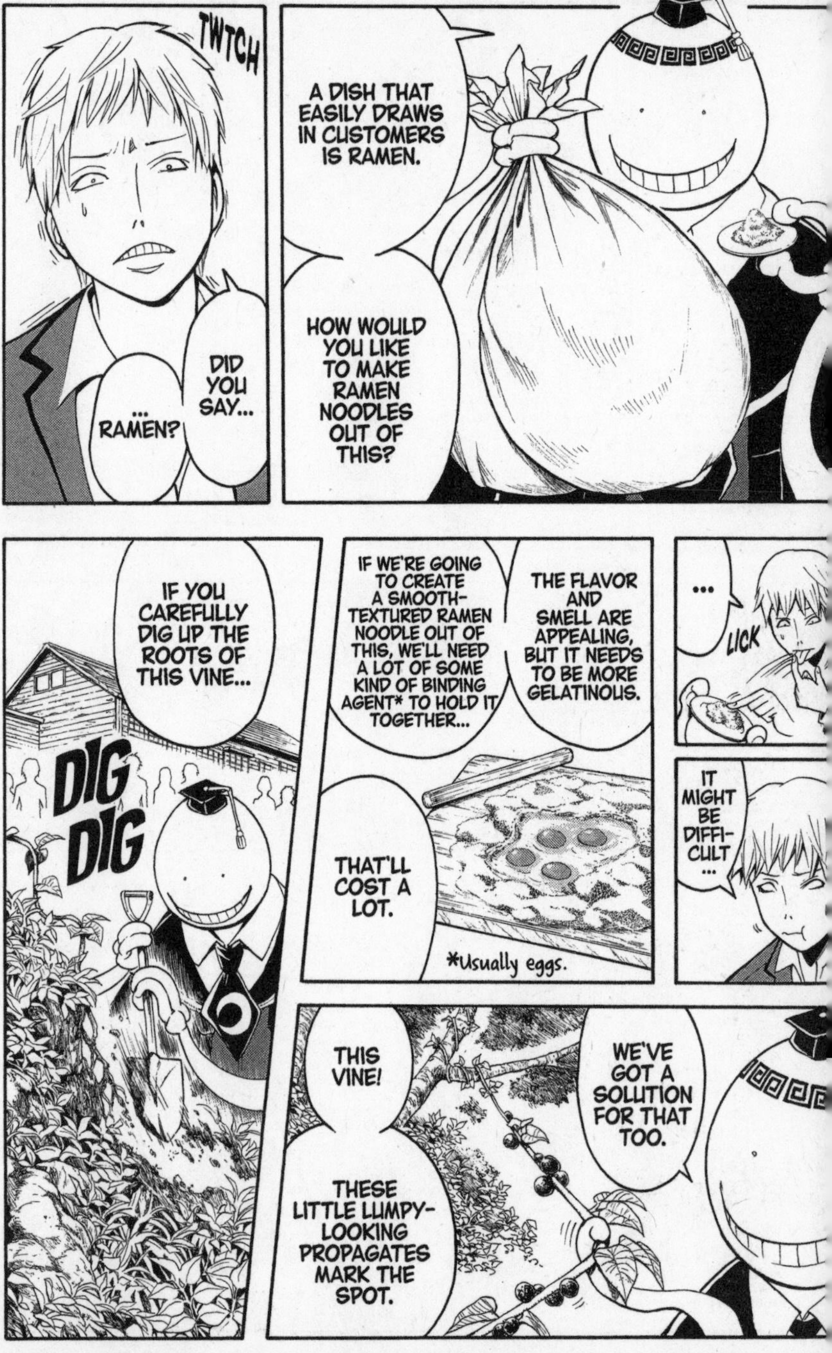
A DISH THAT EASILY DRAWS IN CUSTOMERS IS RAMEN.
HOW WOULD YOU LIKE TO MAKE RAMEN NOODLES OUT OF THIS?
TWTCH
DID YOU SAY...
...RAMEN?
...
LICK
IT MIGHT BE DIFFI-CULT...
THE FLAVOR AND SMELL ARE APPEALING, BUT IT NEEDS TO BE MORE GELATINOUS.
IF WE'RE GOING TO CREATE A SMOOTH-TEXTURED RAMEN NOODLE OUT OF THIS, WE'LL NEED A LOT OF SOME KIND OF BINDING AGENT* TO HOLD IT TOGETHER...
THAT'LL COST A LOT.
*Usually eggs.
WE'VE GOT A SOLUTION FOR THAT TOO.
THIS VINE!
THESE LITTLE LUMPY-LOOKING PROPAGATES MARK THE SPOT.
IF YOU CAREFULLY DIG UP THE ROOTS OF THIS VINE...
DIG DIG

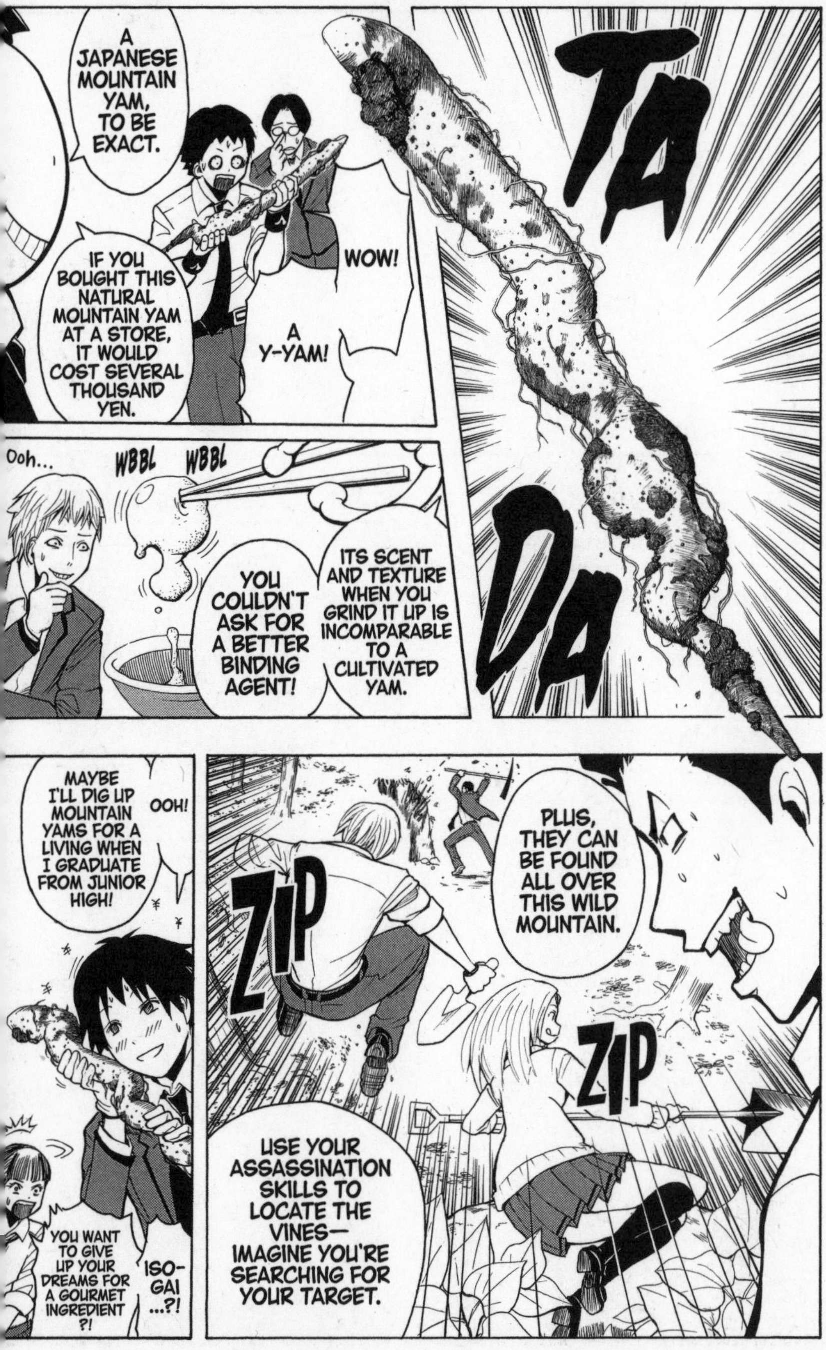
TA
DA
WOW!
A Y-YAM!
A JAPANESE MOUNTAIN YAM, TO BE EXACT.
IF YOU BOUGHT THIS NATURAL MOUNTAIN YAM AT A STORE, IT WOULD COST SEVERAL THOUSAND YEN.
WBBL WBBL
ITS SCENT AND TEXTURE WHEN YOU GRIND IT UP IS INCOMPARABLE TO A CULTIVATED YAM.
YOU COULDN'T ASK FOR A BETTER BINDING AGENT!
Ooh...
PLUS, THEY CAN BE FOUND ALL OVER THIS WILD MOUNTAIN.
ZIP
ZIP
USE YOUR ASSASSINATION SKILLS TO LOCATE THE VINES—IMAGINE YOU'RE SEARCHING FOR YOUR TARGET.
OOH!
MAYBE I'LL DIG UP MOUNTAIN YAMS FOR A LIVING WHEN I GRADUATE FROM JUNIOR HIGH!
ISO-GAI...?!
YOU WANT TO GIVE UP YOUR DREAMS FOR A GOURMET INGREDIENT?!

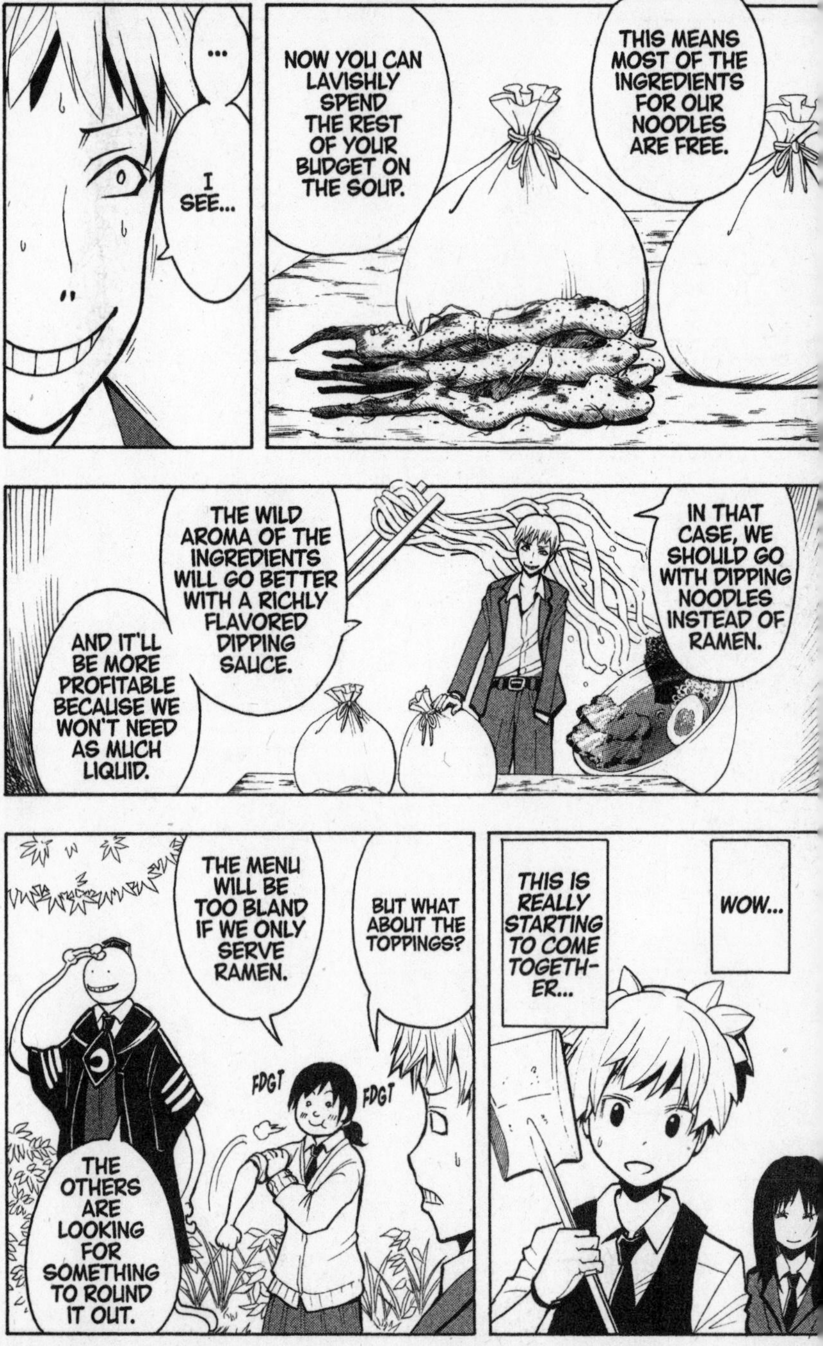
THIS MEANS MOST OF THE INGREDIENTS FOR OUR NOODLES ARE FREE.
NOW YOU CAN LAVISHLY SPEND THE REST OF YOUR BUDGET ON THE SOUP.
...
I SEE...
IN THAT CASE, WE SHOULD GO WITH DIPPING NOODLES INSTEAD OF RAMEN.
THE WILD AROMA OF THE INGREDIENTS WILL GO BETTER WITH A RICHLY FLAVORED DIPPING SAUCE.
AND IT'LL BE MORE PROFITABLE BECAUSE WE WON'T NEED AS MUCH LIQUID.
WOW...
THIS IS REALLY STARTING TO COME TOGETH-ER...
BUT WHAT ABOUT THE TOPPINGS?
THE MENU WILL BE TOO BLAND IF WE ONLY SERVE RAMEN.
FDGT
FDGT
THE OTHERS ARE LOOKING FOR SOMETHING TO ROUND IT OUT.

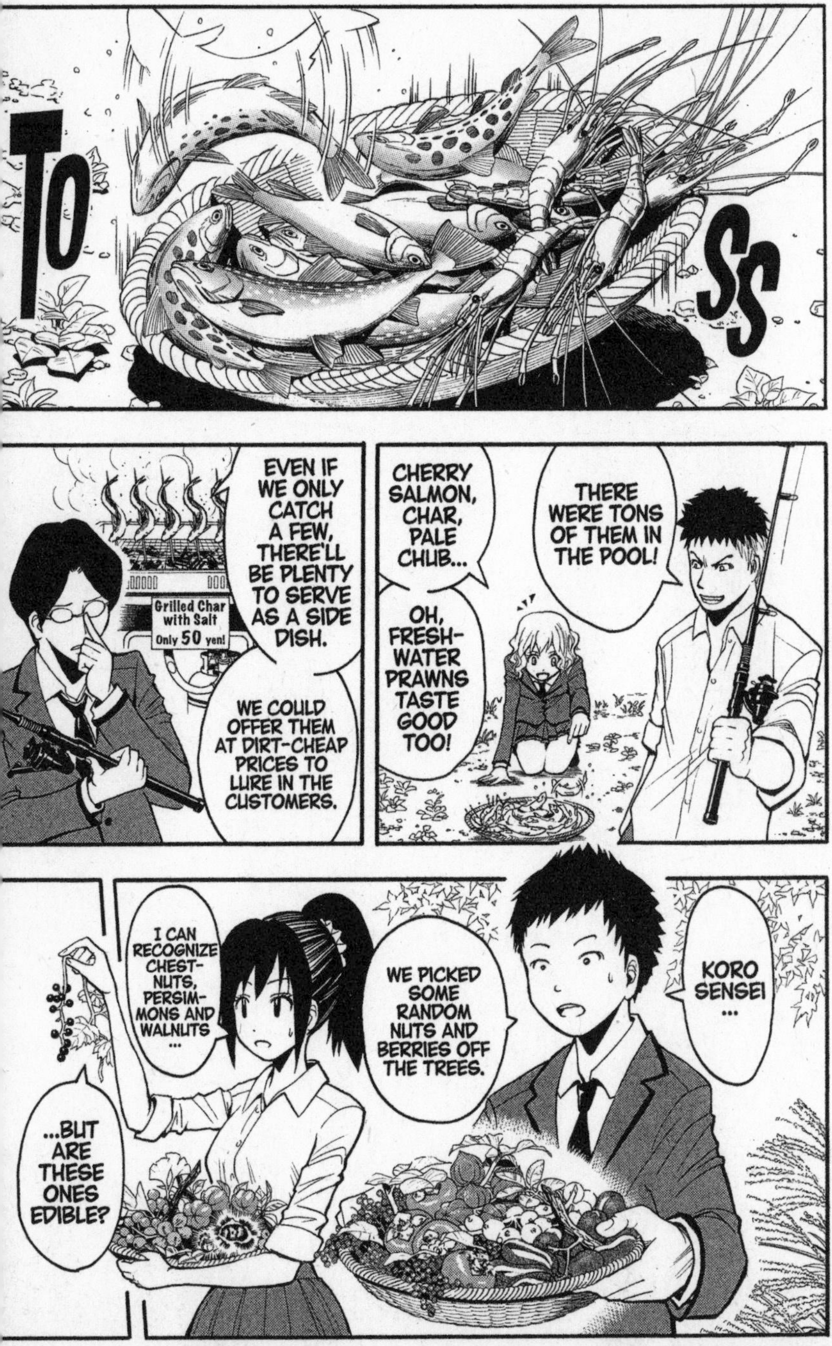
TOSS
THERE WERE TONS OF THEM IN THE POOL!
CHERRY SALMON, CHAR, PALE CHUB...
OH, FRESH-WATER PRAWNS TASTE GOOD TOO!
EVEN IF WE ONLY CATCH A FEW, THERE'LL BE PLENTY TO SERVE AS A SIDE DISH.
Grilled Char with Salt Only 50 yen!
WE COULD OFFER THEM AT DIRT-CHEAP PRICES TO LURE IN THE CUSTOMERS.
KORO SENSEI...
WE PICKED SOME RANDOM NUTS AND BERRIES OFF THE TREES.
I CAN RECOGNIZE CHESTNUTS, PERSIMMONS AND WALNUTS...
...BUT ARE THESE ONES EDIBLE?

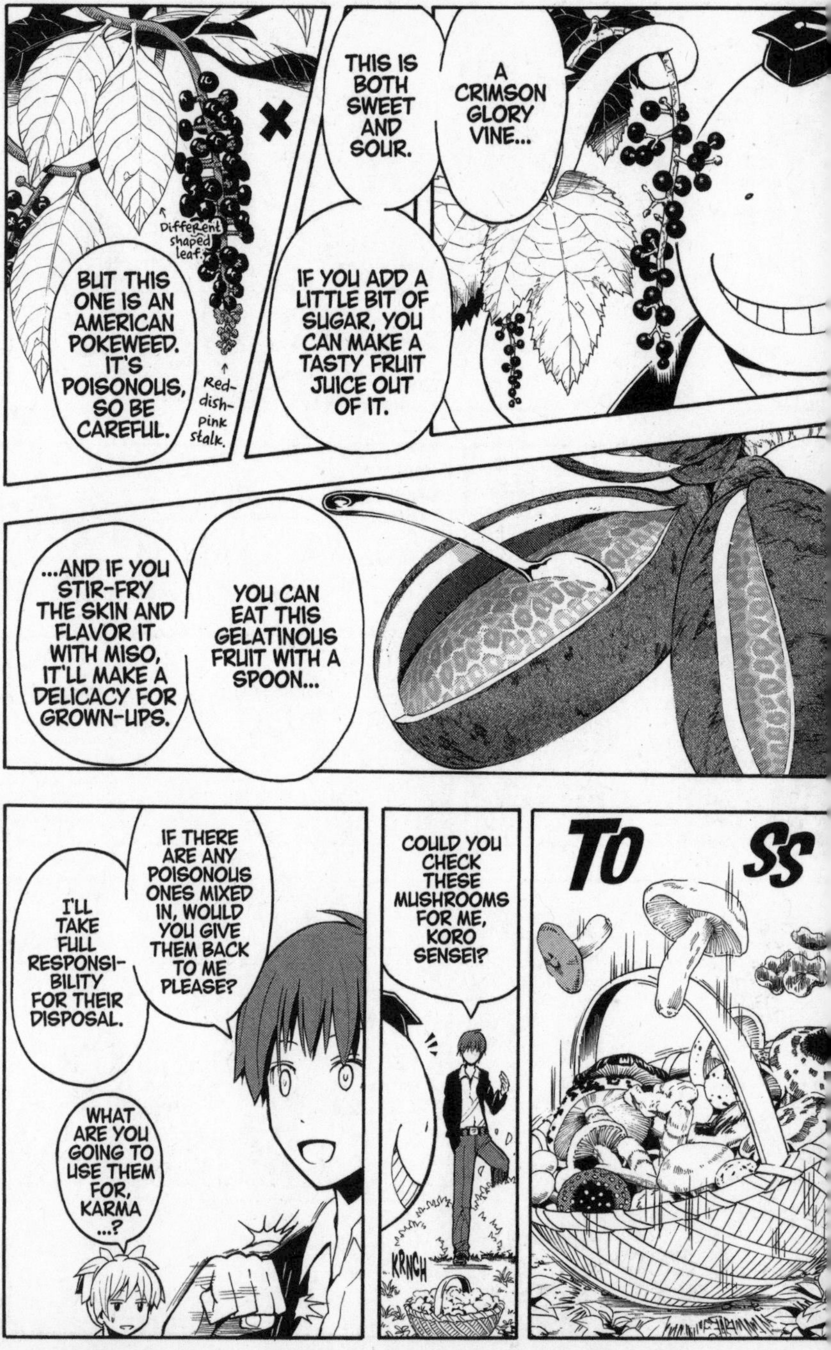
A CRIMSON GLORY VINE...
THIS IS BOTH SWEET AND SOUR.
IF YOU ADD A LITTLE BIT OF SUGAR, YOU CAN MAKE A TASTY FRUIT JUICE OUT OF IT.
Different shaped leaf.
BUT THIS ONE IS AN AMERICAN POKEWEED. IT'S POISONOUS, SO BE CAREFUL.
Reddish-pink stalk.
YOU CAN EAT THIS GELATINOUS FRUIT WITH A SPOON...
...AND IF YOU STIR-FRY THE SKIN AND FLAVOR IT WITH MISO, IT'LL MAKE A DELICACY FOR GROWN-UPS.
TOSS
COULD YOU CHECK THESE MUSHROOMS FOR ME, KORO SENSEI?
KRNCH
IF THERE ARE ANY POISONOUS ONES MIXED IN, WOULD YOU GIVE THEM BACK TO ME PLEASE?
I'LL TAKE FULL RESPONSI-BILITY FOR THEIR DISPOSAL.
WHAT ARE YOU GOING TO USE THEM FOR, KARMA ...?

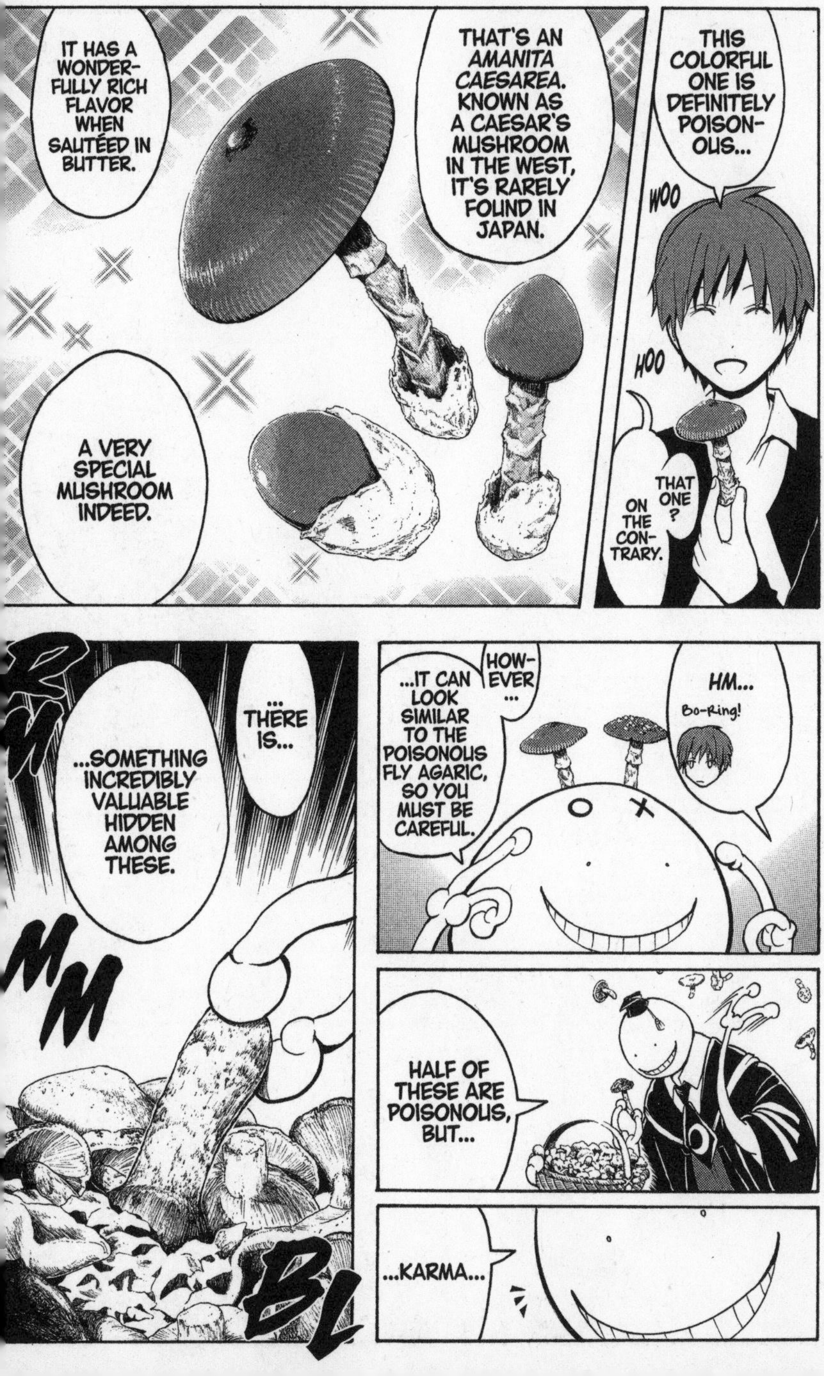
THIS COLORFUL ONE IS DEFINITELY POISON-OUS...
WOO
HOO
THAT ONE?
ON THE CON-TRARY.
THAT'S AN *AMANITA CAESAREA.* KNOWN AS A CAESAR'S MUSHROOM IN THE WEST, IT'S RARELY FOUND IN JAPAN.
IT HAS A WONDER-FULLY RICH FLAVOR WHEN SAUTÉED IN BUTTER.
A VERY SPECIAL MUSHROOM INDEED.
HM...
Bo-Ring!
HOW-EVER...
...IT CAN LOOK SIMILAR TO THE POISONOUS FLY AGARIC, SO YOU MUST BE CAREFUL.
HALF OF THESE ARE POISONOUS, BUT...
...KARMA...
... THERE IS...
...SOMETHING INCREDIBLY VALUABLE HIDDEN AMONG THESE.

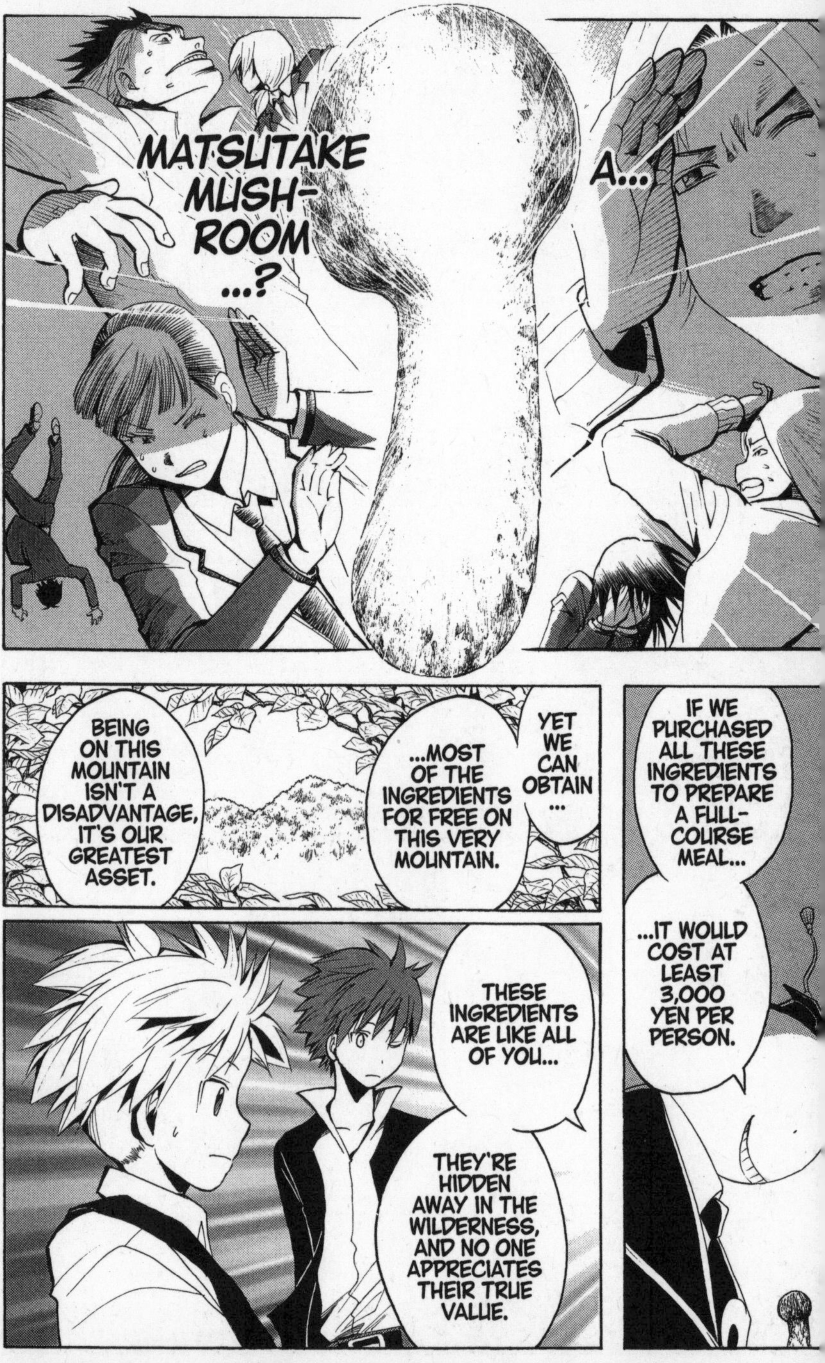
A...
MATSUTAKE MUSH-ROOM ...?
IF WE PURCHASED ALL THESE INGREDIENTS TO PREPARE A FULL-COURSE MEAL...
...IT WOULD COST AT LEAST 3,000 YEN PER PERSON.
YET WE CAN OBTAIN ...
...MOST OF THE INGREDIENTS FOR FREE ON THIS VERY MOUNTAIN.
BEING ON THIS MOUNTAIN ISN'T A DISADVANTAGE, IT'S OUR GREATEST ASSET.
THESE INGREDIENTS ARE LIKE ALL OF YOU...
THEY'RE HIDDEN AWAY IN THE WILDERNESS, AND NO ONE APPRECIATES THEIR TRUE VALUE.

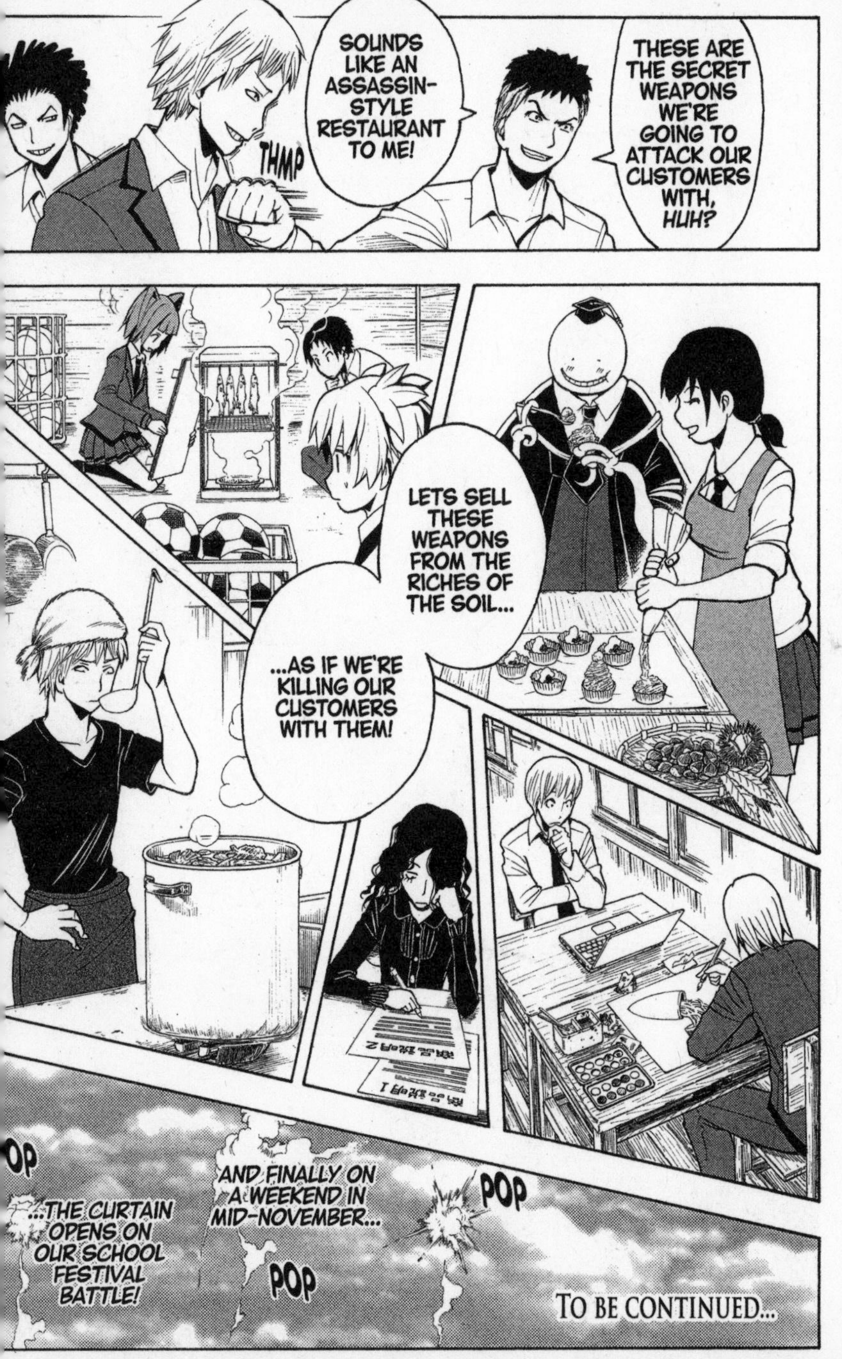
THESE ARE THE SECRET WEAPONS WE'RE GOING TO ATTACK OUR CUSTOMERS WITH, HUH?
SOUNDS LIKE AN ASSASSIN-STYLE RESTAURANT TO ME!
THMP
LETS SELL THESE WEAPONS FROM THE RICHES OF THE SOIL...
...AS IF WE'RE KILLING OUR CUSTOMERS WITH THEM!
POP
AND FINALLY ON A WEEKEND IN MID-NOVEMBER...
POP
OP
...THE CURTAIN OPENS ON OUR SCHOOL FESTIVAL BATTLE!
TO BE CONTINUED...

Valentine's
Day